BY JOHN K. WINKLER

WILLIAM RANDOLPH HEARST

William Randolph Hearst

A NEW APPRAISAL

BY

JOHN K. WINKLER

HASTINGS HOUSE · PUBLISHERS · NEW YORK

ACKNOWLEDGEMENTS

Acknowledgements are due to Simon & Schuster, The Viking
Press and Appleton-Century-Crofts for quotations from previous
biographies of W. R. Hearst. Specific credits are given to these
and other sources in the text. The author's indebtedness to Edmond D. Coblentz for quotations from his authoritative *William
Randolph Hearst: A Portrait In His Own Words* is particularly
great and is expressed here as well as in the text with thanks.
Thanks are also due to W. R. Hearst, Jr. and the Hearst Trustees
and officers of the Hearst Corporation for their co-operation in
making personal and confidential files available without restriction. Many others were helpful with first hand information about
W. R. Hearst and individuals associated with him; the endeavor
has been made to mention all of them in the text.

The Blondie comic strip by Chic Young, and cartoons by
James Swinnerton, T. A. "Tad" Dorgan, George Herriman, Fred
Lasswell, Robert L. Ripley, E. C. Segar, Frederick Burr Opper
are copyrighted by King Features Syndicate, Inc. and are reproduced by special permission. Other cartoons are from *Puck,* the
New York *American,* New York *Journal,* New York *Mirror,* San
Francisco *Examiner,* Chicago *American.* The photographs are
from the Hearst family files, Charles Rounds, Detroit Institute
of Fine Arts, International News Photos.

Illustrations selected and annotated and the footnotes prepared
by Clark Kinnaird. Jacket design and picture insert layout by
John Wolter.

To my wife

W. R. Hearst in 1896, facing a remarkable future. He had taken possession of the New York *Journal* a few months before, at the age of 32, and
he anticipated the coming titanic journalistic struggle to conquer New York
with gaiety and zest. The sketch was made by a young artist, whom Hearst
discovered in San Francisco—Homer Davenport.

Contents

WILLIAM RANDOLPH HEARST

Does This Explain
William Randolph Hearst?

> Money as such bores him . . . He is a builder.
> He wants to build buildings, newspapers, mag-
> azines, hotels, ranches. His idea is to build, build,
> build all the time . . . In his makeup there is
> just a blank space in relation to money.
>
> JOHN FRANCIS NEYLAN

1

AT RARE INTERVALS, in human experience, arises an individual of such towering ability and diversified talents as to assume not only
leadership but domination of his chosen field.

Such an individual was William Randolph Hearst.

This phenomenal American placed his stamp upon world journalism
as has no other, before or since. William Randolph Hearst evolved new
techniques in newspaper making, strikingly synchronizing his type, his
text and his illustrations. An artist to his finger tips, he succeeded in challenging and arresting the attention of the eye and of the mind, achieving
effects hitherto unattempted. His methods have been so widely imitated
and so universally adopted that the originator has been all but lost sight of.

Hearst's active career spanned two-thirds of a century, his life one-half
that of his country. It was typical of him that he should have died in harness,
a pad and pencil at his bedside.

For, in all the triumphs and defeats and backwashes and vicissitudes of
the crowded decades, Mr. Hearst took the fiercest pride in calling himself
a working newspaper man. "If I had my life to live over again," he once
remarked, "I would be a newspaper man, and merely try to be a better
one." It is as a matchless journalist that posterity will best remember him.

1

Entering journalism as a callow youth of twenty-three, young Will Hearst mastered every branch of his craft so thoroughly and so brilliantly that eventually he owned and operated the largest publishing business on earth. No comparable chain of newspapers and magazines has ever appeared under a single ownership. Also, he organized and brought to profitable fruition syndicates and news services that became the principal suppliers of news, features and pictures to newspapers all over the world.

Hearst mass produced newspapers as Henry Ford did motorcars or the A & P stores groceries, but his task was infinitely more difficult, his success the more unique. A newspaper is perhaps the most volatile and delicate instrument in human relations man has yet devised. Hearst truly transformed journalism into Big Business, yet his papers, with their enormous circulations, managed to retain the intimate personal touch of the country weekly or the small city daily. This was the man's most astounding and resounding triumph.

With vision, imagination, infinite industry and resourcefulness, and incredible audacity, Hearst revolutionized the manners and methods, indeed the very appearance, of the American press. So distinctive were his innovations, so striking the presentation of his news and features and illustrations that for two generations his name has been applied to his inimitable publishing techniques.

Hearst Journalism was colorful, exciting, flamboyant; vigorous in its advocacy of God and country; virile in its exposés of political opponents and in its public-service crusades; merciless in its lampooning, chockablock with broad humor. It was frankly aimed at reaching and winning the masses, not alone the native born but the immigrant struggling painfully to master a strange tongue and a bewildering new way of life in the Land of Promise.

The toilers and the workers, the plain people of America, yearned for a spokesman and a champion. Hearst came forward at precisely the right moment. He was welcomed with fervor and emotion. Indeed, so overwhelming was the response that Hearst's personal reward, save for circumstances and for certain traits of his own character and temperament, might well have been election to the Presidency of the United States.

At the time, nearing the turn of the century, America was at once the beneficiary and the victim of the unprecedented growth of corporate industrialism which had followed the Civil War. Rockefeller, Morgan, Harriman, Huntington and other titans were welding great aggregations of capital into monopolistic control of oil, steel, railroads, shipping. Monopoly fathered greed. Gas, oil, water, street-railway and other combinations entered boldly into the business of controlling legislation, the courts, administrative offices in towns, cities, counties, states, nation. Such of the press as was not purchasable was lying down on its job.

2

In this huge, tangled skein of corruption, Hearst saw his opportunity. "Pirate privilege" was the dragon, and the American people eagerly awaited the coming of a St. George. Hearst constituted himself a St. George, thundering against "amalgamated greed." The young editor hurled his journalistic bolts as they had not been hurled since the antislavery crusade of Horace Greeley and the New York *Tribune*. Hearst's barbed harpoons landed often and effectively in the quivering hide of the "highwaymen of high finance"—and Hearst won gold, glory and circulation. In the process, he put on the most spectacular one-man show since the Romans and almost turned the United States topsy-turvy.

Hearst operated on a scale comparable to that of his Big Business opponents and, like them, did not permit himself to be hampered by conventional ethics or too strict interpretation of generally accepted moral codes. He was always more interested in ends than in means. "I determined to restore democracy in the United States," he said later of those hot, crusading years. "My program was conservative, almost reactionary. I merely purposed to go back to what was originally intended by Jefferson and Jackson and Lincoln. 'Jeffersonian democracy' was never an empty phrase with me. I had studied Jefferson and Jackson and Lincoln. I had carefully examined the history of this country until I believed I knew what it meant to say 'equal rights for all and privileges for none.' I believed I knew what this meant in words and what those words meant as to consequences."

At his crest, Hearst spoke to the greatest audience ever reached by a single medium; and in many a golden year his two-score newspapers and magazines returned him a net profit roughly estimated as high as $30,-000,000. Parenthetically, because of his passion for opulent living and for collecting art on a scale seldom, if ever, equaled by a private citizen, Hearst's expenditures almost invariably exceeded even this enormous income.

One reason young Will Hearst caught the heart of America so unerringly was that he and his young country were so much alike. Both were brash, adventurous, imaginative, bursting at the seams with energy and enthusiasm, insatiably curious, dauntlessly self-confident. Nothing was beyond us, we thought, and we set out to prove it, with high hearts and sometimes, it must be confessed, with high hands. We were both doers and dreamers, chauvinistic, flag-waving, boastful, chivalrous in a rough, frontier sense, not overscrupulous in our passionate pursuit of the dollar, yet warmhearted, generous, courageous, quick to resent and to avenge injustice. Unjaundiced foreign observers thought our very immaturity added to our attractiveness as a people.

Hearst himself lived and died an eternal juvenile, never losing his capacity for wide-eyed wonderment and enthusiasm. He was generous to a fault, never forgot a favor, and possessed a streak of sentimentality a yard wide.

3

He never asked, yet often gave quarter. Still there was something in his nature—perhaps a deep-seated psychical drawback—that prevented him from giving himself completely to anyone. He always seemed to hold something in reserve. Many knew a part or a phase of him but no one, not even those in closest contact, ever felt that he had penetrated completely the inner core of his strange, enigmatic personality. He reminded one of a small boy closing off a secret citadel even from adoring and baffled parents. Little wonder that the boy who became the man, over the decades, dazzled, infuriated and perplexed his fellow citizens, in almost equal measure, and managed to keep them in constant ferment.

Hearst's public position on matters political and economic gradually shifted from radicalism to extreme conservatism. To him, most issues were all black or all white, without shading, whereas, as most of us have found, life is not quite so simple. So positive, so didactic were his pronouncements that he seemed to many like a deaf man hearing only his own voice. He had no apologies for these frequent shifts in position. "I always feel that it is not as important to be consistent as it is to be correct," he said. "A man who is completely consistent never learns anything. Conditions change, and he does not."

So far as the public could judge, Hearst never permitted himself to doubt his own infallibility. While manipulating the herd, bending it to his will, he himself remained aloof on his own Olympian hill, seemingly recognizing no greater law than his own will and desires. His attributes were those of a genius—or an anarchist. Truly a Shakespearian character—perverse, brilliant, nihilistic.

Hearst's romance with journalism began young. On his first trip abroad, at ten, he became fascinated in Germany with the gay comic picture books which the Germans called *Bilder Bücher* and collected hundreds of them. More than twenty years later, Hearst and one of his pioneer comic artists, Rudolph Dirks, used this collection to create the famous "Katzenjammer Kids," the oldest American comic strip in point of continuity.

During a second European tour with his mother, when he was seventeen, Hearst read and compared the leading newspapers and popular periodicals in England and on the Continent. Later, during a brief stay at St. Paul's School in New Hampshire, he subscribed to the *Times* of London and introduced it into the reading room of his form.

At Harvard, he voluntarily assumed the business management of the *Lampoon* and pulled it out of the red by tapping new sources of advertising revenue.

At Harvard, also, despite some raffish exploits that finally resulted in his expulsion, young Hearst found time to pursue his journalistic excursions. Obtaining an introduction to Charles H. Taylor, distinguished proprietor

4

"The young editor hurled his journalistic bolts as they had not been hurled since the antislavery crusade of Horace Greeley and the *New York Tribune*. Hearst's barbed harpoons landed often and effectively in the quivering hide of the 'highwaymen of high finance'—and Hearst won gold, glory and circulation"—*page 3*. Frederick Burr Opper synchronized cartoon shafts like this with Hearst editorials against financial manipulators till the reforms for which Hearst crusaded were effected.

5

of the Boston *Globe,* the tall, pale, lymphatic-looking youth soon became a familiar figure in the editorial and press rooms of this paper. Everything connected with the making of a newspaper fascinated him: how the news was gathered, why certain stories were considered more important than others, what constituted a good page layout. He delved into financial and circulation problems. He was enthralled with the basic mechanics of publishing and the improvements being made in them.

The *Globe* and other large papers used sheet-fed, belt-driven cylinder presses. Hearst stood for hours watching the paper being fed from rolls into the presses and passing between cylinders upon which were clamped stereotyped plates. Printed on both sides, the paper was cut and delivered in folded sheets. The web press, printing at high speed from rolls of paper, was an innovation.

Photoengraving also was in its infancy. There were no half tones; no photographs were to be reproduced upon newsprint paper for more than a decade. The method of photographing pen-and-ink pictures through a dotted cross-line screen and transferring the negatives to zinc plates, etched with acid, had just been devised by Frederic E. Ives.

It was after one of his nocturnal excursions to the *Globe* office that young Hearst extracted one newspaper from a mound and drawled to a bevy of cronies, gathered as was their wont, in his beautifully paneled rooms in Matthews Hall: "Say, fellows, do you know who's running the best paper in the country? It's a man named Pulitzer down in New York. I have been studying his methods and I think I have caught on to what he is trying to do. My pop has a paper on the Coast, the San Francisco *Examiner*. Maybe I'll take it over and give you all jobs."

The idea of taking over the stumbling little *Examiner* matured and, in 1885, the young man wrote to his father asking boldly that the paper be made over to him, "with enough money to carry out my schemes." He confessed that he was "possessed of the weakness, which at some time or other of their lives, pervades most men; I am convinced that I could run a newspaper successfully."

He explained that he would widen the columns, space the type more, go in for stimulating illustrations, hire a staff of energetic young men, advertise the paper "from Oregon to New Mexico." The "new" *Examiner* would be modeled upon the New York *World,* "which depends for its success upon enterprise, energy and a certain startling originality and not upon the wisdom of its political opinions or the lofty style of its editorials." It was his hope to purchase some telegraphic news from the *World,* whose net profit, he set forth in awe, was more than $1,000 a day. "Just think, over one thousand dollars a day and four years ago it belonged to Jay Gould and was losing money rapidly."

The sanguine publisher-in-embryo announced that all of his proposed innovations would be made in one swoop "so that the improvement will be very marked and noticeable and will attract universal attention and comment." *

Hard-bitten George Hearst thought his only son's ambition chimerical in the extreme when there were mining and ranching and banking to choose from. The bluff, bearded old Argonaut dangled before his son's eyes the management and eventual control of his million-acre ranch in Chihuahua, Mexico; Anaconda, the silver mine that turned out to be the world's richest copper lode; even the fabulous Homestake gold mine in South Dakota. Young Hearst could not be tempted. "Dodgasted," his father snorted, "when Billy Buster wants something, he just keeps on wanting it until he gets it."

During the tug of wills, Hearst went to New York and worked for a few months on the *World* under that paper's brilliant editor, Ballard Smith. At the end of his brief novitiate Smith told him that in his opinion Hearst was fully qualified to edit a newspaper of the type of the *Examiner*. Ballard Smith, who invariably managed to liven up his front page with a dramatic human interest story, long remained Hearst's beau ideal as a newspaper executive. However, Hearst was never able to lure him into his service.

After his father capitulated, Hearst dashed off another exuberant letter in which he outlined the sort of newspaper he intended to establish and the policy he would follow. The paper would be honest, independent, fearless; also, "alarmingly enterprising and startlingly original." He ventured to add a prophecy: "In a year we will have increased at least ten thousand in circulation. In two years we will be paying. And in five years we will be the biggest paper on the Pacific slope. We won't be paying for two years because up to that time I propose turning back into the improvement of the paper every cent that comes in." This prediction proved all too modest.

The name of "W. R. Hearst, Proprietor" went up on the editorial masthead of the little San Francisco *Examiner* on the morning of March 4, 1887. The tall, slim stripling with low-pitched voice and shy, almost diffident manner, walked home on air. "Nothing will ever again seem quite so important to me," he said many years later.

Moving with sure touch, Hearst improved the *Examiner's* plant, installing new presses and acquiring every modern mechanical device as soon as it was perfected. Later he was to go beyond this and do a little inventing and improving on his own hook. He enlarged his staff of reporters and editors, enlisting, as he had jokingly promised, some of his former buddies at Harvard, and worked in the office day and night. Ideas flew from his facile brain like sparks from an anvil. The office became a place of excitement and fun. A genius was at work in his laboratory.

* The complete text is in *A Treasury of the World's Great Letters*, edited by M. Lincoln Schuster, Simon & Schuster, 1940.

A dizzy series of crusades, campaigns and spectacular exploits were launched. Hearst attacked abuses wherever he found them, proclaimed radical democracy, introduced striking typographical effects into the make-up and smashed all journalistic traditions. In getting the news and in *making* the news nothing daunted the *Examiner*—distance, cost, labor. Public response was gratifying.

In a community of 300,000, the *Examiner's* circulation boomed in steady, ladderlike rises to 80,000. Within two years, the sleazy little sheet had been transformed into the foremost feature newspaper in the West—and within five or six years the paper had become by far the biggest money-maker on the Coast. Crackerjack reporters, editors, cartoonists, feature writers flocked to Hearst's service. Hearst favored men who shared his passion for Charles Dickens and who were able to introduce into their work some of the magic of the great English humanist.

The young editor corralled most of his headliners himself. One of his personal recruits, Ambrose Bierce, who wrote a brilliant column for the *Examiner* for many years, gives us a delicious account of his first meeting with Hearst:—

> I heard a gentle tapping at my apartment door. I opened, and I found a young man, the youngest young man, it seems to me, that I had ever confronted. His appearance, his attitude, his entire personality suggested extreme diffidence. I did not ask him to come in, install him in my better chair (I had two) and inquire how we could serve each other. If my memory is not at fault, I merely said, "Well?" and waited results. "I am from the San Francisco *Examiner*," he exclaimed in a voice like the fragrance of violets made audible, and backed away a little. "Oh," I said, "you come from Mr. Hearst." Then that unearthly child lifted his blue eyes and cooed, "I am Mr. Hearst."

The *Examiner* began to be watched and quoted all over the country. Before his father died in 1891, Billy Buster was able to show him a substantial money-maker. The time soon came for expansion.

In 1895, Hearst purchased the New York *Morning Journal* and went gaily into battle with the Jupiters of Eastern journalism, headed by the redoubtable Joseph Pulitzer. The young man from California was backed by the ample millions of his mother, whom Hearst senior had cautiously left in sole control of the family purse strings.

In New York, Billy Buster introduced his formula of pyrotechnic journalism upon a scale never before attempted and, after epic warfare with paper and ink, won enormous success and wide influence.

The *Journal* was bright, enterprising, full of clever sketches and striking cartoons. And it dramatized stories as the news had never been played up

"Hearst's importance in the picture of American journalism is inescapably great. He has always been among the first to seize upon new inventions in printing and publishing industries and demonstrate their possibilities and value."—*History of Journalism in the United States,* by Robert W. Jones (E. P. Dutton & Co., New York, 1947). This story in the New York *Journal* in October, 1896, records Hearst's pioneer use of an Edison invention in picture transmission.

9

before. In addition to a staff of noted male writers, Hearst opened his columns to many able women, including Ella Wheeler Wilcox, Dorothy Dix, Winifred Black, Gertrude Atherton and Susan B. Anthony. The latter became a "Special Commissioner" proselyting for woman suffrage. Hearst was the first prominent publicist to come out for votes for women. With his sensitive, almost androgynous nature, Hearst always knew instinctively how to interest women readers.

Pulitzer's *World* remained willing and able to do battle with the upstart from the West, and it, too, came up with some popular innovations. It got the jump on Hearst bringing out a Sunday section printed upon a four-color press. Morrill Goddard, one of Pulitzer's bright young men, thought of putting colored cartoons into the section. Sparked by Goddard, an artist named Richard Outcault, who had come to the Sunday *World* from the *Electrical World* to do drawings for feature stories, got up a series of cartoons depicting events in a fictitious "Hogan's Alley." The series had one continuing character, a nameless, hairless and wistful gamin clad in a floursack, who attracted the sympathetic attention of readers. The child's single garment had various hues before it settled down to one and identified the first famous newspaper comic character—the Yellow Kid.

Hearst rushed to get a color press for the *Journal* and outdo the *World*. He hired Outcault away from Pulitzer and launched other series by Rudolph Dirks, Jimmy Swinnerton and his pick of the artists of the humorous weeklies and monthlies. The *Journal* was the first newspaper to print a complete section of comics in colors—"eight pages of iridescent polychromous effulgence that make the rainbow look like a lead pipe," its advertisements boasted.

The *World* followed suit with a color comic section, including a "Yellow Kid" carried on by George Luks, and tried to keep pace with Hearst in flamboyancy in promotion and treatment of news and features. An editor of James Gordon Bennett's New York *Herald,* smarting under loss of circulation to its younger rivals, readily seized upon the phrase "yellow journalism" * to describe the tactics of Hearst and Pulitzer. This was echoed by foes of crusading newspapers until it was an accepted synonym for any sensational publication. Meanwhile, the *Herald,* which had been the first big sensational newspaper in the country, hired Outcault to draw a colored comic page for its own Sunday edition.**

Yellow Journalism has been analyzed and dissected by many students of our social mores. There is no doubt that its methods were often dema-

---

* The phrase was not original. The publication of sensational stories in inexpensive form, often in yellow covers, had been described by Poe and other writers as "yellow-backed pamphleteering" from 1846 on.

** Outcault produced a greater success than the short-lived "Yellow Kid." It was Buster Brown (see appendix).

"The High Priests of the Sacred Flame," a cartoon attack by Joseph Keppler on W. R. Hearst and Joseph Pulitzer in *Puck*. In the original, printed in full color, the words "Freedom of the Press" appeared in the flame in pink and the two editors were robed in yellow. The epithet "yellow journal" was first flung at Pulitzer's New York *World*.

gogic, disgusting, degrading. Pulitzer and Hearst fought for circulation like shoeshine boys, with no holds barred. Both raked the dregs of human experience for their sensations. Looking back today over the heavy black headlines and the riot of color, one wonders that these men found a clientele so naive as to buy their papers by the millions. Yellow Journalism is an episode in American life best forgotten. Yet there was a solid core of principle beneath the blackguardism; and great segments of the populace hailed Hearst in particular as a veritable paladin of the people.

When the young crusader settled down for the long haul and began to extend his unique brand of journalism into Chicago, Los Angeles, Boston and other large cities, it became abundantly clear that he was not in business merely to shock and to amuse. He enunciated and practiced his own code of rampant and challenging Americanism, fashioning his social and political philosophy in the interests of the underdog. With Hearst in mind, Finley Peter Dunne's immortal Mr. Dooley tickled the risibilities of the country with his observation that a modern newspaper's mission seemed to be "to comfort the afflicted and to afflict the comfortable." W. R. Hearst, however, cut much deeper than that. Opponents of the cool young editor, no matter how powerful, discovered to their chagrin and puzzled amazement that Hearst actually could not be bluffed, bossed or bribed. Even when his voice was a minority of one, he made that voice heard.

This was strikingly illustrated during the first World War which Hearst regarded, as now do some impartial historians, as purely a struggle for economic domination between Germany and the British Empire. While the fratricidal struggle devastated Europe, the Hearst papers sought to keep America's men, munitions and money out of the war. This attitude naturally brought them under the bitter displeasure of those sympathetic to the Anglo-French cause.

The situation was further strained when Hearst succeeded in breaking through the strangulating ring of Allied censorship and bringing his readers some suppressed facts of the war. He had worked out an ingenious code with his correspondents in Europe. A series of stunning news beats was climaxed when the Hearst organs published stories and a photo of the sinking of the British dreadnaught *Audacious* off the Irish coast. Publication of this news naturally enraged British authorities who had denied that the ship had been torpedoed. [The photo is in this book's picture section.]

In early October, 1916, as Hearst stood in the reception hall of his New York home chatting with one of his executives, a cablegram was brought to him from his London manager informing him that the British Government would deny the mails and cables to him unless Hearst would give his personal guarantee that all future despatches would be printed exactly as received after passage through the British censorship. Hearst flushed and trembled with anger. He handed the message to his companion, who in years of association had never before witnessed the faintest flutter in his chief's uncanny control.

"What are you going to do?" asked the executive.

"Do?" exploded Hearst, "I am going to tell them to go to hell!"

The irate publicist did just that and on October 11 the British Government made good its threat. France followed suit. In November, the Canadian Government barred the Hearst papers from Canada, where they had important holdings in paper mills. Hearst backed down not one inch, saying: "When I inscribed the watchword 'An American Paper for the American People' over the titles of my newspapers, I meant just what the motto said. I will just add the verses of 'The Star-Spangled Banner' to my editorial mottoes and, like that free flag, continue to wave."

Hearst continued to get the news through his membership in the Associated Press and through special despatches and comments of such illustrious European writers as Rudyard Kipling, Bernard Shaw, Arnold Bennett, Maurice Maeterlinck, Guglielmo Ferrero and Gabriele d'Annunzio. And he continued to thunder with bitter invective against our increasing involvement with the Allies.

As the U. S. rushed headlong toward war, Hearst became a victim of the very mob spirit he himself had been so often accused of arousing. His papers were boycotted in many places, barred from homes and clubs, and he was burned in effigy. Overheated patriots demanded action against him under the sedition laws. Tight-lipped, he fought back. Although well aware that he was in the toughest spot of his singular career, he gave no outward sign of the strain.

At this juncture, returning to New York from California, Hearst was met in Utah by a messenger bearing a round robin signed by most of his leading executives. They threatened to resign in a body if he did not immediately alter his attitude on the war. "Sorry, I hate to lose good men," remarked the embattled publisher. When Hearst faced them in New York, the rebels, rather shamefacedly, withdrew their ultimatum. Hearst always seemed to exercise peculiar hypnosis over his men, a compound of awed admiration and fear.

In New York, Hearst learned that one of his top men had given out a statement publicly disagreeing with the Hearst stand on the war. Assuming that the individual in question would be discharged at once, the general manager of the organization asked: "Chief, whom shall I get to take Mr. Blank's place?" Hearst's blue eyes reflected surprise. "Why, no one," he said. "Why should I fire an able man just because he can't help being a liar?"

The Chief furnished another example of his oblique moral viewpoint in the case of an employee who had been caught grafting. "We'll just transfer him to another post where we can watch him more carefully," he said.

Hearst celebrated his fifty-sixth birthday on April 29, 1919. He had filled out into a bear of a man, upward of six-feet-two and well over two hundred pounds. He still rode, swam, played tennis with vigor and zest and his capacity for work was seemingly inexhaustible. With advancing years, his rather narrow eyes, set curiously in a high forehead abaft a long, prominent nose, had become more steel-colored than blue, cold sharp, penetrating. The nose struck straight down from the forehead. The hair was blond, sandy in shade, thinning and graying. One would have set down his age as the early forties. There was no outward indication that he was going through a critical period of life. Yet there occurred now events which can only be accounted for on physiological and psychological lines.

These events were to affect profoundly the remainder of Hearst's long life. In April his adored mother, Mrs. Phoebe Apperson Hearst, died. She was perhaps the only individual who could exert compelling influence upon her strong-willed son. Her late husband's mining and ranching fortune, estimated at his death at $17,000,000, had greatly appreciated under her capable management. The bulk of it came outright to her son.

Master now of truly impressive wealth, Hearst began transforming the family ranch at San Simeon in central California into the costliest and most imposing private estate on the North American continent.

This active year also signalized Hearst's renewed interest on a larger scale of motion pictures, into which he had entered back in 1913 through newsreels and the historic serial, *The Perils of Pauline.* During the ensuing fifteen years, the fantastic world of filmed make-believe absorbed so much of his energy and dissipated so many of his millions that one who knew him intimately as any one could remarked sadly to the writer, "The movies damn near ruined the old man."

His motion picture company had acquired a new star. She was a comely blonde miss who had been introduced to Hearst while she was a performer in the Ziegfeld Follies. Her stage name was Marion Davies. She had been born Marion Cecilia Douras, one of four daughters of a lawyer in Brooklyn, N. Y. She had taffy-blonde hair, eyes of pastel blue, and an excited little stammer. She bubbled with fun and animal spirits. Like Hearst himself, she possessed a considerable gift of mimicry. Following her graduation from a convent in Hastings, N. Y., she had modeled dresses for Fifth Avenue firms, then appeared in the chorus of two Broadway musicals, "Chu Chin Chow" and "Oh Boy," before being chosen by Ziegfeld as a Follies showgirl.

Beginning with "Cecilia of the Pink Roses," Marion Davies starred in a dozen lavishly mounted motion pictures that were elaborately exploited and lauded in the Hearst press. Hearst was seen with his star constantly, on and off the set.

Gossip concerning their association swelled and burst into the open in August, 1924, under circumstances detailed in a later chapter of this book.

In consequence, a story circulated for years that Hearst was the father of illegitimate children.

There is no record or recollection of this inflexible man's taking the slightest cognizance of the rumors before he wrote his will. Then he sought to dispose of the canard once and for all by denying categorically that he had fathered any issue other than his five sons and heirs, George, William junior, John, David and Randolph.

Meanwhile, however, Marion Davies was the chatelaine of wondrous San Simeon, with its thirty miles of shore front, its great herds of cattle, its private zoo and airfields, its extravagant swimming pools, its gleaming art-filled alabaster castles and guest houses, and of other Hearst homes in California.

At San Simeon, Hearst reigned in feudal splendor. Here came men and women of prominence from all lands. Most of the guests, however, were Hollywood figures and Hearst's own employees. From his Celestial Suite beneath the carilloned dual towers, the master of San Simeon, with un-flagging zeal, carried on the multifarious and far-flung activities detailed in the pages of this book.

Following a heart seizure, during which he lost consciousness, Hearst closed San Simeon and, in 1947, moved into Marion Davies' palm-ringed mansion in Beverly Hills. Here he adjusted himself to semi-invalidism, yet remained in close touch with his far-flung enterprises and with events. The body, which had served him so well, steadily weakened, but his resolution remained strong.

Even while his candle flickered, he dictated many directives and suggestions to his sons and other executives, beginning with the familiar, "The Chief suggests." Many editorials were composed in painful longhand, criticizing the Truman Administration and the Korean War. With old-time vigor, he flew to the defense of General Douglas MacArthur when the latter was relieved of his command. He denounced as "Made in England" the scheme to ship strategic war supplies to Russia and the Chinese Reds. More than once, when urged to conserve his energy, he quoted a favorite bit of philosophy: "The time to retire is when God retires you, not before."

This complex, little-understood man was still planning for the future when Providence sent him into reluctant retirement in his eighty-ninth year on the morning of August 14, 1951.

Boyhood of a Genius

> It is not enough to be the possessor of genius—
> the time and the man must conjoin. An Alex-
> ander the Great, born into an age of profound
> peace, might scarce have troubled the world—
> a Newton, grown up in a thieves' den, might
> have devised little but a new and ingenious pick-
> lock.
>
> *Diversions of Historical Thought*
> JOHN CLEVELAND COTTON

2

WILLIAM RANDOLPH HEARST sprang of resourceful and tenacious pioneer stock. The family name, which genealogists have traced back to the Lowlands of Scotland in the Middle Ages, has undergone several mutations. Originally, in ancient Anglo-Saxon, it was spelled Hyrst, meaning "a thicket."

In those dim days, when the border peoples were alternately feuding and fraternizing, some members of the family seeped into England, as far south as Salisbury, and there changed the spelling of the name to Hurst. The beautiful old churchyard of Salisbury Cathedral today contains several headstones so marked.

In the 16th century, during the Reformation, the Hursts became Presbyterians and one of them, John Hurst, emigrated to America in 1608, settling in what was to become Isle of Wight County in Virginia. He farmed a modest tract, with the help of several slaves, and sired a large family. Some of the sons moved farther south into the Carolinas where, early in the 18th century, the family surname was changed to Hearst. These Carolina Hearsts were prolific and remained devout Presbyterians—so much so, in fact, that on one occasion three Hearst daughters married three brothers, all of them Presbyterian clergymen.

Like most pioneers, the Hearsts were restless and land hungry. No exception was one William G. Hearst, of Abbeville County, South Carolina. This adventurous young man sensed an opportunity to better himself when Thomas Jefferson, in 1803, purchased from Napoleon the vast territory extending from the Mississippi to the Rocky Mountains and from the Gulf of Mexico to British America, thus at one dramatic stroke doubling the land mass of the United States.

In 1808, William G. Hearst trekked out to Missouri, settling on a hilltop in Franklin County, not far from the farm site where, a century later, a future President of the United States, Harry S. Truman, was to learn, in the words of his mother, to plough "the straightest furrow in the state." So far as known, William Hearst never uttered so proud a boast but in the rich, virgin soil he raised bumper crops of wheat and corn, bred horses and cattle, operated a tiny crossroads store and traded modestly with the growing pioneer city of St. Louis. Nine years after his arrival, the transplanted South Carolinian married Elizabeth Collins, daughter of a neighboring settler from Georgia. She presented him with two children, a boy and a girl. The girl died unmarried. The boy, George, born in 1820, became a Senator of the United States and the father of William Randolph Hearst.

In that sparsely settled, primitive country, it was hard work and little fun for the average farm boy. George Hearst was able to obtain less than two years of formal schooling. Fortunately, intellectual stimulation came to him elsewhere. Lead mines were discovered some fifteen miles from the Hearst homestead and a settlement sprang up around them. The mine superintendent and his men craved fresh meat and the elder Hearst contracted to supply them with pork on the hoof. It was young George's task to drive the hogs to the settlement. He became enthralled with the processes of mining and hung around for hours asking innumerable questions. Although he did not then realize it, an illustrious life career was forming for him.

When the boy was fifteen, a lead mine was found only a mile from his home and he passed every spare moment at the diggings, absorbing all the knowledge that he could and sometimes earning "from four to six bits a day." The boy seemed to divine, through a sort of sixth sense, just where minerals could be located. So uncanny was this intuition that the Indians of the neighborhood called him "Boy-That-Earth-Talked-To."

Boy-That-Earth-Talked-To was twenty-six when his father died in 1846. To show for a life of unremitting toil, farmer William Hearst left three small farms, all mortgaged, four slaves, a country store and several thousand dollars in debts. However, George already held a profitable interest in one of the nearby lead mines and he bent to the task of clearing up his father's obligations. This was accomplished in three years.

Late in 1849 the news of gold discoveries in California worked fiercely in the breasts of the youth of the country and more than two hundred and fifty thousand young men started for the Pacific Coast. George Hearst was drawn from his Missouri farm by the gold lure. On May 12, 1850, in a party of eight men and six women, the stalwart six-footer set off on horseback beside an ox-drawn covered wagon for the two thousand mile trek to the Nevada and California gold fields. The journey required six months and was stippled with adventure. The party fought Indians and cholera and endured hardships about which George Hearst was afterward a little hesitant in speaking. Once, racked by fever, he sank down in the mud and rain near Fort Laramie and actually prayed for death. But the weakness and depression passed. A rugged constitution and natural buoyancy of disposition pulled him through.

Arriving in the fabled new Eldorado, a mature man of thirty, the Missourian found himself in an entirely strange social milieu "governed by the noose, the bowie knife and the pistol." Men lived in tents and hastily constructed lean-tos. The first unpainted shacks were occupied by liquor sellers, gamblers and frowsy "percentage girls" who swarmed in from everywhere. The very names tacked onto the settlements reflected the recklessness and lawless exuberance of the gold hunters: Hell-Out-for-Noon City, Ground Hog Glory, Delirium Tremens, Poverty Flat, Red Dog, Jackass Gulch, Hangtown.

After testing his luck at Hangtown and Jackass Gulch, George Hearst moved on to Grass Valley and Nevada City. Like so many others, he found that placer mining was backbreaking work. Shining nuggets were not to be fished out of every mountain brook. So the newcomer opened a general store in partnership with Hamlet Davis, who later became the first mayor of Nevada City. In their roomy loft, the storekeepers built a rude stage, installed a few rough benches and branched out as theatrical producers, presenting ballad singers, dramatic readers and occasional traveling stock companies, performing tear-jerking melodramas and ten-twenty-thirty shockers.

With capital earned in this venture, Hearst went to Sacramento and opened a general merchandising establishment. However, he was poorly equipped to compete with such shrewd and entrenched merchants as Leland Stanford, Collis P. Huntington, Mark Hopkins and Charles Crocker. Luckily, he had never given up his geological explorations and when just about at the end of his financial tether, located two profitable quartz mines, and formed a company to exploit them. From that time on fortune smiled more often than it frowned on George Hearst. However, it was not until 1859 that he made his first big strike, when he was again living in Nevada City.

One day word reached town that a new gold lode had been uncovered on the slopes of Mount Davidson near the Carson River in Nevada. With two associates, Hearst rode at breakneck speed to the scene and, after a quick survey, paid one Alvah Gould $450 for his share in a mine which experts had pronounced worthless. Gould was so convinced he had put

18

over a slick deal that, legend has it, he went galloping down Gold Canyon, shouting, "I've got away with the Californians!" Recounting the incident in their biography of W.R., *Hearst, Lord of San Simeon,** Oliver Carlson and Ernest Sutherland Bates remark wryly that a few years later Alvah Gould was running a peanut stand and George Hearst was a United States Senator, adding:—

> The mine that Gould so lightly parted with was indeed poor in gold, and what there was could not be got out because of the abundance of a blue-black ore that constantly impeded the miners' operations—but that blue-black ore contained silver, and the mine was a part of the now famous Comstock Lode, the richest silver deposit in the world. By good fortune, Hearst and his partners had also bought for a few hundred dollars a one-sixth interest in the Ophir mine, the most important in the whole lode. During the summer of 1859 they mined forty-five tons of the silver-bearing ore, and in the fall, with a long pack-train of mules, they carried the entire amount over the wretched roads through the mountain passes and down the valleys all the way to San Francisco. Their forty-five tons proved to be worth $2,200 a ton. And there were untold thousands, perhaps millions, of such tons owned by them on the sides of Mount Davidson! The story of their success ran up and down the streets of San Francisco. The gold craze of 1849 was succeeded by the silver craze of 1860.

Although there were to be rocky days ahead—twice great fortunes were swept from his grasp—George Hearst's interest in Ophir mine started him on the road to wealth. As a judge of the value of a mine, the self-taught geologist's reputation grew. Old placer men swore he was the best judge of a mine in the entire country. It was said that a brief trip through the underground workings of any mine was enough. On his return to the surface he was ready to deliver his opinion, to make his offer if he decided to buy into the property, and he was rarely mistaken in his valuation.

Hearst was convivial and gregarious, but could be as reticent as the Sphinx when the occasion demanded. He could empty a bottle as quickly as the next man, bet his whole poke on the turn of a card, yet kept himself free from sordid roistering. Generally speaking, his ethical standards reflected the times. As with the other storied bonanza kings of the pioneer West, he became embroiled in lawsuits, boundary disputes and charges of fraud and violence.

Soon after the outbreak of the Civil War, the Indians in Nevada became restive and began raiding and pillaging the mining settlements. George Hearst decided to suspend operations temporarily and pay a long overdue

* The Viking Press, New York, 1936.

visit to Missouri. He found his sister dead, his mother dying. Although overwhelmingly Southern in sympathy, Missouri had not yet become a hotbed of vendettas and vengeful border raids.

A local hero because he had won fortune in the far places, Hearst lingered on in Franklin County. The reason soon became apparent when he began courting a pretty, vivacious young schoolmarm with a passion for self improvement. Her name was Phoebe Elizabeth Apperson. Her father, Randolph Walker Apperson, was the richest farmer in the county. Randolph Apperson sprang from a long line of land-owning Virginians. His wife's family had resided in South Carolina from colonial days.

Phoebe Apperson was not yet nineteen and the Appersons at first were decidedly cool to the suit of a man in early middle age. However, to the young girl, the bearded man who told such fascinating tales of travel and adventure symbolized romance and opportunity and together they won over her parents. George Hearst and Phoebe Apperson were married at Stedville, Missouri, on June 15, 1862. They left immediately on a wedding trip to New York, whence they sailed to Panama and, after crossing the isthmus, embarked on another boat for San Francisco. It was a thrilling panorama for the young bride who had never been farther from home than St. Louis.

In San Francisco, the couple lived for a time in the ornate new Lick House and then took rooms in the Stevenson House, a quiet family hotel on the southwest corner of California and Montgomery Streets. Here, on April 29, 1863, was born their only child, a son. Combining the given names of his parental and maternal grandfathers, the infant was called William Randolph. Sonny, as he was quickly christened in the family circle, possessed his mother's clear, gray-blue eyes, his father's high, imaginative brow. His lungs were his very own as his matronly Irish nurse, Eliza Pike, could attest.

Receiving word that the Indian outbreaks had been quelled, George Hearst prepared to return to Nevada. Before he left, he ensconced his wife and son in a handsome brick dwelling on fashionable Rincon Hill. There were a charming garden and long French windows opening on a gallery.

The young mother luxuriated in her new surroundings. Although she made friends easily and was soon drawn into a coterie of congenial people, she had little taste for formal social life. Instead, she took up painting and music and renewed a passionate interest in literature and the study of foreign languages. Phoebe Hearst's joy was boundless when her parents yielded to her persuasion, sold their properties in Missouri, and bought a spacious, tree-filled ranch near the old mission town of Santa Clara. This sunny ranch house and its garden, with a riotous profusion of plants and flowers, was to become a second home to Sonny Hearst.

One day, while Mrs. Hearst and her parents were house hunting, Eliza

Pike took it upon herself to solve a problem which had long troubled her devout Roman Catholic soul. In great agitation, the faithful Irish nurse met her young mistress at the door. "Madam," she explained, "I love the baby like my own flesh and blood, and I couldn't sleep nights for thinkin' he might die—there is always maysles and dipthayria, and scarlet fayver—"

"Eliza! Eliza, what's the matter?" cried Mrs. Hearst, her heart in her throat. "Did you let the baby fall?"

"The baby is all right, ma'am, but he might have died. So I took him down to my own church today. Blissed, dear good Fayther baptized him—"

"But, Eliza," protested Mrs. Hearst, "I am a Presbyterian."

"No matter, ma'am, the baby is a Christian!"

The young mother doubled over with laughter and relief.

Meanwhile, the Ophir mine was crunching out its precious tons of gold and silver. In its first four years the lode yielded $15,000,000 worth of ore. In the spirit of the times, Hearst and his associates were ruthless in the acquisition of claims. At one time the mine was involved in no less than thirty-seven lawsuits. Jury fixing, bribery, gun thuggery were openly resorted to. The gigantic William M. Stewart (afterwards to serve with George Hearst in the United States Senate) was attorney for Ophir. Of one of his cases (Ophir vs. McCall) a contemporary commentator remarks with unconscious playfulness that "the only shooting which attended the trial was directed at witnesses on their way to and from the scene."

While these stirring events were occurring in the West, the forces of the North and South were locked in a death struggle in the East. As a Missourian and the son of a South Carolinian, George Hearst had aligned himself with the so-called "Lecompton Democrats," who had favored the secession of California. Immediately after the war, as a delegate to the Democratic state convention, Hearst supported resolutions restoring full political and civil rights to the people of the South. The mere introduction of these resolutions precipitated a riot in which, we are told, "inkstands and cuspidors were hurled, hickory canes were brought into play, chairs were broken and chair-legs used as bludgeons." Nevertheless, the pro-Southern group was defeated by the narrow margin of but three votes and subsequently was strong enough to elect George Hearst and some others to the sixteenth session of the California state legislature. The Hearsts and their two-year-old son, now called Billy Buster by the family, attended this session at Sacramento. Billy Buster didn't like the state capital because dinner at the Brannan House was served late and because he couldn't bring along Prince, his adored Newfoundland playmate of the Apperson ranch. Besides, on the steamer coming home, he wandered away from Eliza Pike and almost fell overboard.

Home for the Hearsts was now an imposing double chalet on Chestnut Street, purchased from its builder, a Frenchman. Its beautifully appointed rooms contained much carved rosewood furniture. From its upper porch and high hanging gardens stretched a dreamlike panorama of San Francisco Bay with its shipping, grim Fort Alcatraz, the Contra Costa hills, and to the north Mount Tamalpais.

Hardly had the family settled in the new house when a turn of the wheel jeopardized George Hearst's hard-won fortune. Output dropped sharply at Ophir. Several other ventures backfired. His cash reserves dwindled. Once more the big grizzled prospector (he was now approaching fifty) took to the trail on horseback, a pack burro at his mount's rump, exploring for minerals in the wilds of Nevada, Wyoming and California. His wife and Billy Buster would not see him for months at a time. Then he would ride in, bedraggled, grimy, his saddlebags filled with specimens, and sometimes with a gleam of triumph in his piercing eyes. A lucky strike or two furnished another stake, to which was added $100,000 profit in a San Francisco real estate deal, and soon the Hearsts were again listed high among those favorites of fortune who dwelt in the aristocratic section just beginning to be called Nob Hill.

Equally significant of his rising status, George Hearst about this time was invited into partnership with two of the most picturesque and successful speculators and all-around capitalistic freebooters of the old West—Lloyd Tevis and James Ben Ali Haggin.

Tevis was a beefy, full-blooded Scot, with thistles and heather in his throat, who concealed a thoroughly unscrupulous nature behind a façade of bluff friendliness. Already (1870) he was deeply involved in deals with the Central Pacific Railroad and its owner-promoters, those brigandish and unsavory former Sacramento merchants, Stanford, Huntington, Hopkins and Crocker.

In striking contrast to Tevis, Ben Ali Haggin was swarthy, suave and soft-spoken, qualities inherited from his mother, a Christian Turk. At absurdly low prices, he was buying up great tracts of government land in the Sacramento, San Joaquin and Kern River valleys, irrigating it cheaply, and reselling it to settlers at enormous profit.

Another associate of Hearst senior in real estate deals was the wealthy William M. Lent, whose son Eugene became a boyhood chum of young Willie Hearst. The friendship was to endure throughout their lives.

From earliest childhood, Billy Buster Hearst enjoyed a very special position in life. Lone child of wealthy and indulgent parents, the boy could scarcely be censured for coming to believe early that other people existed mainly to gratify his own whims and desires. The result was an inevitable narcissism which was evident throughout his life.

In her saccharine and heavily embroidered official biography, *William Randolph Hearst, American,** Cora Baggerly Older unwittingly recounts

---

* D. Appleton-Century Company, New York, 1936.

many instances of overindulgence on the part of the boy's parents. On one occasion, Willie and several other Chestnut Street youngsters were playing on the stairway winding up to the Hearst house. Quoting Mrs. Older:—

> George Hearst appeared in the doorway, tall, erect, with aquiline nose, broad brow and long graying beard. He wore the usual cutaway coat, high top-boots and slouch hat. Would Willie ask his dad for ice cream money? Emphatically Willie would. Anxiously the boys watched George Hearst's hand enter his right pocket. Would Willie get 'two bits' or 'four bits?' Neither. George Hearst gave his son twenty dollars. That glittering coin made history for the Chestnut Street boys. Willie led them to a little shop where they banqueted like young Luculluses on cake and more cake, and ice cream and more ice cream, and watermelon and more watermelon, until the twenty dollars vanished. From that day George Hearst was to the Chestnut Street boys the grandest man in San Francisco.

Phoebe Hearst was equally generous. She designed an elaborate playhouse in the large barn for Willie and his chums and installed the first Punch and Judy show ever seen in San Francisco. She encouraged the boy's passion for animals by buying him a pony and cart and two beautiful black watchdogs, Caesar and Pompey, to which were added in time sundry pet rabbits, squirrels, birds and white mice. All of these possessions, as well as his toys, Willie shared with his pals who included, besides Eugene Lent: Orrin Peck, who was to become a famous portrait painter; Frederick S. Moody, later father-in-law of Helen Wills Moody, the tennis champion; Walter Carey, son of Judge James Carey; and John Spring, son of Francis S. Spring.

Deceptively quiet and soft of voice, Willie Hearst seemed at times two discrete personalities. However, the boy possessed one unique talent which established him as leader of the gang. He could devise and develop pranks far beyond the imaginative reach of his fellows. "As Willie grew older he became inventive in mischief," remarks Mrs. Older. "Squirrels appeared in his pockets. When he was expected to be decorous and reverential he always had a perverse desire to be the opposite. On reception days he gravely snapped a mechanical mouse among the ladies. Mrs. Hearst and her cultured group of women friends grew to be a little apprehensive if Willie entered the room."

By this time, Willie was absorbing the rudiments of education in the nearby North Cosmopolitan Grammar School under a cultured Englishwoman, Miss K. Mullens, who had previously taught him his letters in her private kindergarten. Miss Mullens did not disguise her liking for the boy. For this reason and because of his velvet jacket, knickerbockers and immaculate white blouse, some of his rougher classmates called him Sissy and Teacher's Pet and threatened to beat him up. Cannily, Willie invited the leader of the gang to his big house and stuffed him with jelly and cake, thereby escaping a possible black eye or bruised jaw. Thus early he learned the practical advantages of the velvet approach.

The youngster's reaction was more direct when his mother sought to enter him in Professor Lunt's Dancing Academy, operated by a tall, soldierly gentleman with bristling mustachios. Willie collected some of his cronies and stoned the building. The Professor recognized Willie as the leader and most zealous of the stone throwers and sent word to Mrs. Hearst that under no circumstances would her young barbarian be admitted within the refined precincts of his polka parlor. Willie was highly pleased.

Mr. and Mrs. Hearst celebrated the tenth anniversary of their marriage with a tin wedding party. Among the droll presents were a huge tin watch chain and a tin horn five feet long. Willie promptly possessed himself of these oddities and went calling on his friends, wearing the chain and blowing lustily on the horn.

George Hearst at this time was developing the Ontario mine in Utah and, with his associates, surveying other properties in various states. These activities would keep him on the move for the next year. And so he suggested that Mrs. Hearst and Billy Buster could now go to Europe if they wished. For Phoebe Hearst, it was a girlhood dream come true. Often had she gone to R. B. Woodward's art gallery on Mission Street, studied the reproductions of Titian, Leonardo and other masters and longed to see the originals.

Mrs. William M. Lent and her son Eugene had already left for a European tour and Willie Hearst anticipated with keen pleasure a promised reunion with his chum at Paris some months hence. He kicked his heels in glee at the prospect of quitting school but his joy was tempered somewhat when his mother introduced him to a young man of grave mien and serious manner, Thomas Barry, and announced that Mr. Barry would accompany them as Willie's tutor. The tutor thought Willie a well mannered little boy and looked forward to planting in his burgeoning mind some of the seeds of his own ample classical education. Mr. Barry was Harvard trained.

"The neighborhood was really dead after Willie Hearst went away," recalled Fred Moody half a century later. "Before departing, however, Willie gave a series of parties that lasted for ten days. Ice cream, cake, fireworks, everything!"

Mrs. Hearst, Willie and tutor Barry sailed from Boston on the *Adriatic*. The story of the epochal journey is told in Phoebe Hearst's diary and letters to her husband. Coming at a highly perceptive age, the trip, it is not too much to say, shaped the whole course of young Hearst's future.

In Dublin, where he saw barefooted women and children doing the work of draft animals, the boy was so affected that he wanted to take off his jacket

24

and overcoat and give them away. Mrs. Hearst wrote to her husband: "The poorer classes are so *terribly* poor. Willie wanted to give away all his money and his clothes, too." In Queen's Court, the sight of judges in curled wigs and robes brought a burst of laughter. In Edinburgh, old ruins fascinated him and his mother reported that he was "picture-crazy" and wished to take drawing lessons. Mrs. Hearst observed: "I shouldn't want him to be an artist unless he could be a great one." Explorations in London were interrupted by an attack of whooping cough. Driving through the beautiful grounds at Windsor Castle, Willie remarked: "I'd like to live here."

The young visitor was even more impressed with Germany and the Rhine country. In Dresden, where they tarried, mother and son took a daily lesson in German and spoke only German at meals. It was here that he began collecting the amusing *Bilder Bücher,* as we have recounted. At Hanover, he longed to buy the royal horses, climbed the statue of Hercules, and refought the Battle of Waterloo with tin soldiers. He was interested in everything and everybody. Everywhere they went, mother and son fairly drank in the beauties of art. In a Vienna museum, closed to children, Willie bribed a custodian so that he could inspect three of the rooms. Phoebe Hearst wrote to her husband: "He has a mania for antiquities. Poor old boy, if you could see him studying, prying into everything, birds, fishes, books."

In addition, the boy was a voracious reader, devouring books by the dozen. Like a magpie, Willie collected stamps, coins, pictures, all manner of mechanical toys and contrivances. The wondrously wrought watches, clocks and wood carvings of Switzerland so fascinated him that he wanted to buy them all. Withal, he absorbed history and geography on the spot and with eager facility. Tutor Barry was surprised and delighted. Nevertheless, a blowup was due and it came when Willie and Eugene Lent finally got together in Paris, at the Hotel d'Albe, where Gene's mother had him tethered in the hands of an English tutor.

When the Chestnut Street chums again coalesced, all the animal spirits which had been pent up for months burst into a charivari of mischief and pranks. "They had come from a country where war was still in the air," Mrs. Older tells us, "and now they were invading a foreign land. They marched, countermarched and waved the American flag. A needle-gun with a ramrod was fired off by them. The ramrod drove into the ceiling of the Hotel d'Albe."

The warriors' harassed mothers sent them to a gymnasium for fencing lessons but even this strenuous sport did not absorb all the energies of the irrepressible colts from California. Their next exploit was more serious. Eugene had acquired a toy sailboat, which the boys launched in a wash basin. Then they poured kerosene over the little vessel, set it ablaze so as to simulate a fire at sea.

Willie Hearst, as was his wont, proposed a more exciting adventure. Why not a real fire? They found a quantity of packing straw, dampened it to make a good smudge, bought some red lights at a chemist shop, and tossed matches into the wet straw. Howling like Comanches, the miscreants danced about as smoke filled the halls and red lights flashed from the windows. The dread cry of "Fire! Fire!" ran through the hotel and the street. Soon a dozen firemen arrived in helmets and boots, brandishing axes and spluttering Gallic ejaculations. Pale and coughing, but jubilant over the excitement they had created, the boys aided the firemen in bringing an end to their macabre jest. Only the opportune arrival of their mothers prevented the amateur arsonists from being marched before a magistrate.

Willie and Eugene settled down as quickly as they had erupted and in Italy (for a time) were models of conduct. Willie learned to strum on the guitar in Florence and took art lessons. In Rome, the pre-Lenten carnival was under way and the boys were permitted to dress in bizarre costumes and mingle with the singing, dancing crowds in the streets. Willie bought scores of papal medallions and eagerly absorbed the colorful details of Roman history as collated by his tutor and made more vivid through visits to the Colosseum, the Forum, the Vatican and other storied spots. However, young Hearst was not overwhelmed, or even awed, by what he saw. One day the party was shown an altar light which the guide said had not been extinguished for a thousand years. Willie hovered hungrily about it and whispered to his partner in crime: "Eugene, I'd like to put out that light. Isn't there some way it can be done?" However, the guards were too vigilant and Willie was finally forced to leave the Holy City, his ambition regretfully unfulfilled.

Mother and son returned from Europe in the early summer of 1874 to find people in the doldrums and the country still dazed from the effects of the paralyzing panic of 1873–74. Even George Hearst's talismanic touch seemed to have deserted him. He and his partners were overextended and pressed for funds with which to develop their mining properties. It was necessary to sell the Chestnut Street mansion, with its conservatory, beautiful furniture and remodeled stables and go to live for a time in what was then known as a "refined" boarding house run by their friends, the Winns. Phoebe Hearst assented to the change with a twinge. Yet this second seemingly disastrous blow of fate was to prove more short-lived than its predecessor.

Within six months, as George Hearst was setting out to inspect a site in South Dakota about which he and James B. Haggin had received promising reports, his wife said: "Whatever this mine turns out to be, let's keep it as a home stake."

"All right," her husband agreed, smilingly. "We'll name it Homestake."

26

The sequel is historic. Homestake became the largest and most lucrative gold mine in the country. Hearst and Haggin acquired a heavy interest in it for a mere $80,000. Within a year the partners had obtained complete control, as well as 2,616 acres of adjacent property. They erected a city—Lead, South Dakota—to house their miners and other workmen; operated it like feudal lords, and eventually drew an annual income from Homestake of $4,000,000. Also, through control of water rights for many miles around, Hearst and Haggin obtained profitable suzerainty over the whole district.

Now the wand had really touched George Hearst. He went on to his biggest strike, Anaconda, in Montana. The property had been recommended to Haggin and himself as a possible silver mine by Marcus Daly, a boss foreman for W. A. Clark. Instead, Hearst, the master geologist, turned up the world's richest vein of copper. In one spot the vein was thirty feet wide. Eventually Anaconda, employing thousands of men, was producing one-fifth of the world's supply of copper. In the joint stock company formed to exploit it, Hearst held thirty shares, Haggin twenty-seven and Daly twenty-five.

The Hearsts bought another mansion, the Graves house on Van Ness Avenue, and added an art gallery, which Phoebe Hearst adorned with paintings, sculpture, porcelains. Quickly she took rank as a patron of the arts and philanthropist as well as a social leader. Her salon was often opened for charitable events and once for some resplendent *tableaux vivants,* applauded by Lord Rosebery and other distinguished English visitors.

Willie Hearst, intermittently, attended both the Lincoln and Washington Grammar Schools. Despite that quenchless penchant for mischief, he was in the forefront of his classes in history, geography, English literature. Mathematics he calmly ignored. It was to be ever thus, the formal education of rule and rote anathema.

Willie welcomed his mother's announcement, in the fall of 1876, that she would visit the centennial World's Fair Exposition in Philadelphia and would take him along. They would stop over in New York for a few days. Arriving in mid-October, mother and son found the metropolis seething with excitement over the Hayes-Tilden Presidential contest. Flags were waving, bands playing, red fire burning, men afoot and on horseback parading every night. Billy Buster almost jumped out of his shoes in glee. He could hardly contain himself when he actually met and shook hands with the Democratic candidate, Samuel J. Tilden. Because George Hearst was a prominent Democrat in California and a valued contributor to party funds, the Great Reformer received Mrs. Hearst and her son in the Tilden home on Gramercy Park. Tilden was promptly enshrined in Willie Hearst's private Pantheon, joining a growing roster of personal heroes which included Caesar, Napoleon, Washington, Dickens and, above all, Charlemagne, who, as a boy, tutor Barry had told him artfully, resembled a certain urchin from California. Billy Buster was as disappointed as his father when Tilden first "won," then lost the contested election.

In Philadelphia, Phoebe Hearst and her son missed none of the marvels of the great Exposition and returned home, their luggage crammed with purchases and souvenirs.

Sensing a trend of the future, George Hearst had begun buying up great tracts of land all over the West. The purchase that was to mean most to the family was the 40,000-acre Piedra Blanca ranch in central California, extending from San Simeon Bay on the Pacific back into the Santa Lucia mountains. It cost seventy cents an acre and was to become one of California's prize stock farms. The climate was mild, the scenic beauties unmatched.

At first, before a wharf with docking facilities was erected at San Simeon, the property was reached most readily by horseback over the mountains. Hearst senior made use of these trips to harden up his son and initiate him into the rigors of camp life. Once he sent Willie scouting for butter in a wild region back of Monterey. The boy spotted a curl of smoke and came upon an old sourdough named Pringle, with Scotch terrier whiskers and a wild eye. When he disclosed his mission, the old prospector snorted: "Butter, sonny! What in hell is that? I ain't seen any in twenty years." Never before had Willie envisioned a butterless world.

To compensate for the dietary deficiencies, the vaqueros at the ranch taught the boy to toss a riata, strum a guitar, and sing ditties in Spanish and English. In return, the boss' son taught the cowherders many of the popular songs of the day, of which he possessed an ample repertoire. Already, Billy Buster had become an ardent devotee of the theatre, his taste ranging from the elder Booth's awesome Hamlet and Joe Jefferson's whimsical Rip Van Winkle to Clara Morris' imperishable Camille and comedian Billy Emerson's minstrel songs. The latter was his chief admiration, so much so that he could give a startlingly life-like imitation, with gestures, of Billy Emerson rendering such fetching ditties as:

> The ladies sigh as I go by,
> "Are you there, Moriar-i-tee?"

When the family sold the Graves house on Van Ness Avenue and moved into a huge white stucco mansion of Spanish architecture in Taylor Street, with a pair of stone lions rampant on either side of the imposing entrance, young Hearst embraced the opportunity to become a theatrical "proprietor" himself. He persuaded his parents to fit up a theatre in the great stable. Here he and his chums presented minstrel shows and sometimes essayed more ambitious performances. Willie's singing and his really excellent gift of mimicry invariably brought down the house.

The Hearsts were living in the Taylor Street mansion during the famous

28

"Workingman's Revolt" of 1878. Enraged by the competition of Chinese coolies imported by the Central Pacific Railroad, mobs of unemployed laborers threatened to swarm up Nob Hill and sack the rococo, costly homes of the hated railroad magnates. The mob's bitterness was quickly directed also against other wealthy householders. In her privately printed life of Mrs. Phoebe Apperson Hearst, Winifred Black Bonfils ("Annie Laurie") writes: "The great castles on Nob Hill built by the railroad princes stood— but those who lived in them had to give up their gorgeous entertainment for a while, and one fervid orator tried to get his followers to go up and tear down the lions that stood in front of the Hearst house because, he said, they were a threat and a menace to the freedom of the people below. Gentle Mrs. Hearst was so hurt and astonished at the strange things that had come over the city that she loved so dearly that she would have been glad to go away and never return."

Influenced perhaps by these disturbing events, Mrs. Hearst and her son, again accompanied by tutor Barry, soon left for a full year in Europe. Phoebe Hearst reveled in the art galleries, and her developing boy with her. In fact, this highly perceptive and mystifying adolescent gained a more comprehensive knowledge of art and a love of beauty and the purity of perfect craftsmanship which, with the years, was to grow into ruling passion. Also, he read history and literature with new insight and began to take a deep interest in politics and journalism. He read newspapers, magazines, critical journals and seemed to absorb and retain everything that was poured into his quick mind. He familiarized himself with the noted periodicals of England and of the Continent, even perusing daily the *Times* of London. Nor did he ever willingly miss an issue of *Punch* or of the leading French and German illustrated magazines, which he learned to read facilely.

In the fall of 1879, Will, as the family now called him, returned with tutor Barry to enter St. Paul's exclusive Episcopal school in Concord, New Hampshire, rooming with Will Tevis of San Francisco. Mrs. Hearst remained in Germany to take the baths. That there had been some mischievous episodes and difficult moments in Europe is indicated in a letter to Mrs. Hearst at her spa: "If you get well you shall never have anything to make you sick again, if I can help it. . . . I often think how bad I have been and how many unkind words I have said, and I am sure that when you come back I will be good and never be so bad again."

The young man from California was depressed by the frigid New England climate and the rigorous discipline at St. Paul's, particularly the compulsory attendance at church, once daily, thrice on Sundays. "Camp meetings," Will Hearst called them. Doctor Coit, he thought, enlisted every superannuated ecclesiastical windbag in the country to practice on the boys. "The Doctor preaches pretty well," Will wrote his mother, "but he hollers

29

too much. The only thing that comforts me is that the time is getting shorter every day till you will be here." Mrs. Hearst finally arrived to take the bored fifth-former to New York for the Christmas holidays.

At last the dreary year was over, and the youth was back in his beloved, sun-drenched California. Without much enthusiasm, he fell in with his mother's ambition to enter him at Harvard and promised to bone up under private tutors if only he could escape another penitential term at St. Paul's.

It was a joy to have long talks and pal around again with his father. George Hearst was dipping into politics once more, with wide ambitions, and had become the leading angel of the reviving Democratic Party in California. In furtherance of his ambitions he had taken over, partly for debt, a paper called the San Francisco *Examiner*. It was a poor sheet, at best, and Will Hearst, fresh from acquaintance with the most stimulating journals of Europe, received quite casually the news that the drab, parochial little paper had been added to the family portfolio.

Indeed, the youth was far more interested in a beautiful, temperamental young woman with an angelic singing voice, Sybil Sanderson. Her father was a Supreme Court Justice and the family lived in a large white house overlooking the bay. After a rapid-fire summer romance, the two became engaged, but only momentarily, for Sybil Sanderson's mother whisked her off to Paris for further voice culture. There, and later in America, she enjoyed a meteoric career as an opera singer.

In the fall of 1882, at nineteen, Will Hearst entered Harvard.

Bluff old George Hearst and his gentle wife never dreamed that their tall, gangling, rather silly-looking boy would become a storm center of some rather exciting events, nor that he would return home, sooner than expected, without his sheepskin and with a curious request that he be permitted to take charge of the sickly, practically moribund little newspaper Hearst senior had casually attached to his other holdings.

Harvard—
Birth of a Journalist

For God's sake give me the young man who has
brains enough to make a fool of himself.

Crabbed Age
ROBERT LOUIS STEVENSON

3

WILL HEARST'S three years at Harvard were more vital in his
development than any comparable period of his life.

The tall, pale, loose-jointed youth from California came into exhil-
arating contact with new people and new experiences. His mental processes
matured into a pattern as systematic and as symmetrical as his genius and
extreme individualism were ever to permit. More significantly, Harvard
provided the opportunity which led to his choice of journalism as a career.
This opportunity came as a result of a characteristic act of kindness toward
a friend in distress.

Atrabilious critics have portrayed Hearst the collegian as a notorious rake
and debauchee, a sort of reincarnated Cellini or François Villon. This distorted picture gradually formed because of widely publicized episodes growing out of the young man's unconformability, high spirits and still incorrig-
ible addiction to pranks and practical jokes, one of which, unsavory in
nature, resulted in his expulsion.

A more rounded, and far kinder, portrait of Hearst in his undergraduate
days was painted by his surviving classmates to whom the present writer
talked when he began his researches into the life of the master journalist
more than a quarter of a century ago. This firsthand testimony displays
Hearst as an avid student in subjects which interested him, a natural leader,

31

and always a romantic and extravagant figure. For there was a flair about him. He wore Piccadilly clothes and his scarves were as chromatic as any ever seen on the campus. He could sing songs, both comic and weepy. He could play the banjo and shuffle his feet or give imitations in the best vaudeville manner.

Added to this was the knowledge that his allowance was unlimited. It was rumored that his fabulously wealthy father sent him souvenirs now and then in the shape of solid gold nuggets. Whether or not this was true, Will Hearst certainly spent money as no other Cambridge undergraduate ever had. He gave his friends a continuous and a continuing good time. Withal there was a certain dignity about him, and he ruled the gang quietly and mildly. But he ruled.

In selecting his subjects, student Hearst took full advantage of the wide latitude permitted by a progressive college administration. Latin and Greek were spurned in favor of modern languages, particularly German. Philosophy was quickly dropped, the young man writing his mother: "The Professor got up and began talking about the as-it-wereness-of-the-sometimes, and I lit out. I have taken English instead." English literature, as taught by Professors Le Baron Russell Briggs and Barrett Wendell, enthralled him, as did the distinguished Charles Eliot Norton's humanistic lectures on the History of Fine Arts. Doctor Norton talked to him as to a fellow connoisseur of his friend Ruskin and other famous critics and artists.

Quite fortuitously, and through a desire to help a friend, Will Hearst gained his first practical experience in journalism—and cast the die that was to determine his future. This is how it came about:—

His boyhood chum and companion in mischief, Eugene Lent, had preceded him at Cambridge by a year and had become business manager of the *Lampoon,* the clever college comic weekly. "Lampy's" roster of staff contributors included such future greats as novelist Owen Wister, author of *The Virginian;* William Roscoe Thayer, the historian; and George Santayana, eminent philosopher. But the magazine was threatened with extinction, for the second time, because of lack of funds. Lent, in despair, sought counsel of his friend and idol Will Hearst. In nostalgic retrospect, Eugene Lent speculated years later: "Perhaps if I hadn't been in a hole and Will hadn't tried to help me out, he might never have taken up journalism." Lent recalled his own sigh of relief when Will offered to take over the thankless post of business manager.

The result surprised and delighted the entire *Lampoon* group. For Hearst, the fun-loving wastrel, promptly displayed a business instinct hitherto unsuspected. Beginning with his own tailor and haberdasher, he solicited and obtained advertising from Cambridge merchants. He drew up lists of advertisers in other college periodicals and boned them on behalf of Lampy. Alumni received letters by the score in his sprawling handwriting requesting subscriptions. The response was encouraging. Soon the magazine's deficit began to drop. "Hearst alone took a responsible view of the situation," recalled George Santayana a generation later. "The rest of us cultivated a philosophic disbelief in Space and Time."

It was a proud day indeed when the young business editor was able to report to his mother:—

> We took up the *Lampoon* when the subscription list numbered three hundred. Nine hundred a year came from subscribers and three hundred a year from "ads" making a grand total of twelve hundred. As it takes fourteen hundred to run the thing, we scoured the county for ads. We ransacked the college for subscriptions. In fact, we infused energy into the *Lampoon,* and now we stand on a firm basis with a subscription list of 450 with $900 in advertising making a grand total of $2,250 and leaving a profit of $650 after the debt is paid.*

As a significant footnote to history, the young man in a postscript made first mention of an inchoate idea which was rattling around in his head: "Show this to Papa, and tell him just to wait until Gene and I get hold of the old *Examiner* and run her in the same way."

Young Hearst composed some unsigned comic verses for the *Lampoon* and supplied numerous ideas for cartoons and sketches. In addition to Lent, three other staff men were to accompany Hearst into journalism: Francis Lester Hawks Noble, better known as "Cosy"; cartoonist Fred Briggs, of Springfield, Massachusetts; and E. L. "Phinney" Thayer, future author for the *Examiner* of that deathless classic, *Casey at the Bat.* However, Hearst's warmest friend was a genial, jovial fellow Californian, Jack Follansbee. They became inseparable and were to remain so for life. When the spectacular collapse of his uncle and patron, James R. Keene, forced Follansbee to leave college, Hearst successfully besought his father's aid for his friend.

These and other cronies forgathered almost nightly in Hearst's quarters for oyster suppers, beer parties and bull sessions. They accepted quite as a matter of course the Californian's eccentricity in keeping a baby alligator and gravely calling upon other students accompanied by his pet.

In the Presidential election of 1884, Hearst cast his first ballot and went all out for Cleveland and Hendricks, the Democratic candidates. When their victory was belatedly confirmed, Hearst organized a celebration such as staid old Harvard had never experienced. He hired several bands of music, bought wagonloads of beer, set off fireworks in all directions and raised such a blazing, ear-splitting, rip-roaring, all-night racket as to scandalize Cambridge and almost cause his expulsion. It was the first outburst

---

* Among the assets of the Hearst estate over a half century later were two $100 bonds of the *Lampoon.* They were sold by the executors in 1955 for $200.

of that Hearstian genius for fireworks, brass bands and spectacular demonstrations which afterward were to startle and entertain the populace so frequently.

Some days later, with a cherubic smile wreathing his countenance, Hearst stood before a choleric dean and was informed that the college authorities had decided he might, for a period of some months, be able to give more undivided attention to his studies as a nonresident of Cambridge. This process was known as "rustication." So young Hearst flitted for a time while the campus settled down and sighed for him.

The suspension continued for almost half a year and the young man thoroughly enjoyed his involuntary vacation. There had been great changes in the family fortunes. Constantly expanding in wealth and influence, George Hearst and his associates had acquired mines in Mexico, in Chile, in Peru. Hearst himself took personal title to extensive timber holdings in Shasta and Siskiyou Counties and ranch lands in Tulare, Fresno, Marin and Butte Counties. For his wife he built a lovely hacienda on a rolling tract of five-hundred acres near Pleasanton in Alameda County. Mrs. Hearst was to live here after his death, until her own in 1919.

On frequent trips to Mexico, Hearst had become a warm friend of Dictator-President Porfirio Díaz, who was eager to attract foreign capital. For Díaz, Hearst financed and directed Mexico's first comprehensive land survey, covering the entire country. When the costly job was done and the blueprints were piled to the ceiling, Díaz expressed his appreciation by giving Hearst full and complete title to a thousand square miles of land in the states of Vera Cruz, Campeche, and Yucatan. Later, also through the friendly offices of President Díaz, Hearst was enabled to purchase (at a reported price of forty cents an acre) the great Babicora ranch of a million acres in the state of Chihuahua, only two hundred and forty miles from the Texas border. In 1953 the entire property was re-acquired by the Mexican Government for $2,500,000 to distribute among the peasants.

Meanwhile, "Uncle George" Hearst, as people began to call the convivial old mining bashaw, had become the keystone of the reviving Democratic Party in San Francisco and throughout the state. Ambitious to obtain a seat in the United States Senate, Uncle George succeeded in uniting back of him various snarling and dissident factions of the party. One acidulous political enemy referred to this unique federation as "a sort of Democratic happy family, like we see in the prairie-dog villages, where owls, rattlesnakes, prairie-dogs, and lizards all live in the same hole."

Uncle George's ambition was realized in March, 1885, when California's Senior Senator, John T. Miller, died and Governor Stoneman appointed Hearst to fill the brief vacancy of three months. Subsequently, Hearst was elected for a full term of six years, beginning March 4, 1887, and had served four years of this term at his death on February 28, 1891.

Toward the end of his enforced absence from college, Will Hearst joined his parents in Washington. The capital had never been more interesting, more thrilling a city than during this spring of 1885 which witnessed the inauguration of the first Democratic President since the Civil War. Will Hearst enjoyed a close-up view of the ceremonies and later a personal meeting with Grover Cleveland when his father's stout friend was sworn in as twenty-second President of the United States. The pageantry fired young Hearst with enthusiasm and turned his interest and his reading more intensely upon American and world history. He devoured every detail of the lives of the early and sturdy Presidents and promptly pedestaled Washington, Jefferson, Jackson and Lincoln. When he returned to Harvard he was solidly interested in national affairs.

He also became more than passingly interested while in Washington in a beautiful and talented young woman from San Francisco who was his mother's house guest. She was Eleanor Calhoun, grandniece of the famous South Carolina statesman John C. Calhoun, and already a budding actress of promise. Somewhat older than Will Hearst, she was regally tall and slender, with eyes of deep blue and affected flowing robes when she recited dramatic passages in her rich and resonant voice. The two considered themselves practically engaged when Eleanor, as had the entrancing Sybil Sanderson before her, felt that her destiny called her to Europe to complete her studies for the stage. Hearst and Eleanor Calhoun remained warm friends, although he did not again seriously consider marriage for almost twenty years.

It would be pleasant to record that Hearst, chastened, settled down to a serious routine when back at Cambridge. But it was not to be. He still lived high and wide, still smoked as many cigarettes as a queasy stomach would permit, tried manfully to drink beer, sang comic songs, indulged his passion for pranks and sponsored gorgeous parties. His side-splitting impersonations of Henry Irving and a mock temperance lecture which he committed to memory gained him admittance to Hasty Pudding; and he appeared in one of the club's shows, "Joan of Arc, or the Old Maid of New Orleans," in which he assumed the role of "Pretzel, the German valet of Philip of Burgundy, an interesting cuss with a penchant for legerdemain." The performance won him satisfying applause.

As formerly, Hearst took most interest in the progress of the *Lampoon*. Welcomed back to the staff as business editor, he never failed to rustle up sufficient advertising revenue to pay for the necessary Lampy dinners, with ample moisture included.

The long-legged, soft-voiced Californian and his gang still frolicked evenings. The boys attended every show that came to town, including the rough burlesque offerings, and frequently dated the feminine members of

35

the casts. Of course tales got out and Hearst was set down as a hell-raiser and a wastrel. There was a large amount of libel in this gossip, as we shall presently see. But Harvard men of the class of '86 still recall a box party at the Howard Athenaeum, even before Charlie Chaplin was born, wherein a group of undergraduates, Hearst among them, demonstrated that custard pies were excellent instruments for expressing dissatisfaction with the work of the performers. This novelty delighted one and all—in the audience. It was not checked until a lady soloist, in extreme décolleté, received an entire pie upon her chest; and the trap drummer found another neatly encircling his neck like an Elizabethan ruff. Then the management felt obliged to invite the boisterous young gentlemen to take their patronage elsewhere.

Such episodes, deplorable as they seem in retrospect, merely reveal a surface facet of Hearst's curiously ambivalent nature. Often, while he was running the *Lampoon* and while envious campus gossip had him supping in state with some vestal of the footlights, the gangling youth from California was really indulging a newborn passion for journalism. Although making no attempt to fathom his motivations, he felt himself drawn irresistibly toward the pulsing world of the newspaper.

Instinctively an artist and a perfectionist, Hearst went systematically about the business of equipping himself for the practice of his chosen profession. He subscribed to all the great Eastern and Midwestern newspapers, studied and compared them thoroughly; then obtained entree to the Boston *Globe* through a letter of introduction to its proprietor, General Taylor. He talked with everyone, from oilers to editors, asked questions interminable— and ended with a pretty fair working knowledge of the way newspapers were made and assembled, from the first assignments to reporters to the editing and headlining and the various processes of printing and stereotyping and final distribution. A natural bent for mechanics aided immensely. What most fascinated him, however, was the actual manner in which news was drawn in from the ends of the earth and the way it was played up and made palatable.

It was during this period that the budding journalist expressed the drawling opinion to his cronies that "a man named Pulitzer down in New York" was putting out the best paper in the country and added, half seriously, that he might take over his father's little San Francisco *Examiner* and give them all jobs.

As the idea germinated, he began sending suggestions both to his father and directly to the managers of the Senator's paper. Some of these communications were couched in a tone of lofty condescension. In one letter to his father, the young man complained that woodcut illustrations which had recently appeared in the *Examiner* bore "an unquestionable resemblance to Cuticura soap advertisements," adding: "I am inclined to believe that our editor has illustrated many of his articles from his stock on hand of cuts representing gentlemen before and after using Cuticura. In case my remarks should have no effect, and he should continue in his career of desolation, let me beg of you to remonstrate with him and thus prevent him from giving the finishing stroke to our miserable little sheet." Then followed an expression of historic significance referred to earlier in this book:—

> *I have begun to have a strange fondness for our little paper—a tenderness like unto that which a mother feels for a puny or deformed offspring, and I should hate to see it die now after it had battled so long and so nobly for existence. In fact, to tell the truth, I am possessed of the weakness, which at some time or other of their lives, pervades most men; I am convinced that I could run a newspaper successfully.*

In his notable anthology, *The World's Great Letters,* where this communication appears, M. Lincoln Schuster quotes Hearst as having remarked, somewhat wryly, more than fifty years later: "At that time my father was the only person in the world who, in my modest opinion, knew more than I did, although I have learned since, to my consternation, that quite a number of other people in this surprising world are gifted with thought reservoirs of a more spectacular order than my own."

Senator Hearst considered his son's yearning to operate a newspaper about the silliest thing he had ever heard and expressed himself to that effect in no uncertain terms. However, he responded with his usual open-handedness to a request to send along three thousand dollars for the purchase of some rare issues of Alexander Hamilton's *Federalist* which Will had unearthed in a Boston bookshop and did not categorically forbid him from continuing to pursue what the youth called his "journalistic investigations." Meanwhile, though, the Senator promoted a quick trip to Mexico to see if he could get Will interested in his great new million-acre Babicora ranch. Jack Follansbee and Eugene Lent were taken along. The ranch, an empire in itself, stretched over four vast plateaus, separated by as many ranges of towering mountains. The country was bleak in its grandeur and storm-swept. According to Mrs. Older, Hearst senior offered his son the ranch outright if he would "keep away from newspapers."

Will refused the offer with a shiver of distaste but Jack Follansbee gladly accepted a gift of 100,000 acres and lived on the ranch for many years like a "Mexican grandee, and pleasantly varied his life by long visits to the United States."

As we have indicated, Hearst was always in more or less of a muddle with the Harvard faculty. But it was not until the middle of his senior year, at the beginning of the Christmas holidays of 1885, that he was actually expelled. The specific cause was an unpalatable practical joke, concocted in the early morning hours after Hearst and a few heel-kicking buddies had been over Boston-way until dawn. Similar pranks were common enough in certain European centers of learning but happily had not hitherto reached less effete and possibly more cleanminded American institutions.

Just at breakfast time, messenger boys rang the doorbells at the homes of certain members of the faculty and delivered stout packages gay with ribbons and holly. The scholarly gentlemen, a little thrilled with the mystery of the proceedings, opened their gifts. Each package contained a chamber pot, adorned with the recipient's name and photograph. This was Will Hearst's l'envoi to Harvard.

The inglorious exit did not dampen his spirits in the least. Promptly and happily, he went to New York to learn more about newspapers and their makers, particularly about the "man named Pulitzer," and never thereafter did he cherish the slightest bitterness against Harvard or its authorities. In fact, he made a point of keeping up with the institution and with the *Lampoon* pals with whom he had loafed and joked and worked. That the old college tie was still binding is illustrated by an anecdote related to the writer many years ago by Cosy Noble, the *Lampoon* staffer who followed Hearst to the *Examiner:*—

Late in May, 1886, a little group of youngsters, hardly twenty in all, were gathered in a parlor car en route to New York. They were the members of the Harvard track team on their way to the intercollegiate games in New York. Although Harvard had won for several years in a row, this was not a very cheerful bunch. Yale was reported unbeatable, and Harvard's team was far from strong. Harvard's mainstay was Wendell Baker, '86, who later held the world's record for the quarter mile. Jim Lathrop, the trainer, was plainly worried. At Stamford, a telegram was brought into the car for Baker. The quarter-miler tore it open and exclaimed:

"Hey, fellows, here's a wire from Will Hearst. Listen to this," and he read: " 'Bet all you like for me on Harvard.' "

Baker and Hearst were close friends.

"Don't talk about the huge wagers of 'Bet-You-a-Million' Gates, 'Plunger' Walton or 'Pittsburgh Phil'!" enthused Cosy Noble in relating the episode. "Mere fleabites! Chicken feed! This was the real thing! Our gloom and distrust vanished like morning mist. We felt we must be good, unbeatable, if anyone would back us for 'all you like.' Well, we won the big cup the next day. But it was close, fearfully close, and I honestly think it was that telegram that turned the scale."

At this time Hearst was in New York working as a reporter on the New York *World* under the late Ballard Smith and under the same general arrangement he had had with the Boston *Globe*. Ballard Smith, who could recognize budding talent when he saw it and who quickly fell under the charm of the young ex-collegian's zeal and persuasive personality, let him poke into every corner and paid him more attention than he ever had any other cub. Hearst did not then succeed in meeting the great Joseph Pulitzer, already a part of the national lore, because Mr. Pulitzer, wracked by illness, seldom came to the office. If he had, it is interesting to speculate whether the blinding old autocrat of Park Row would have realized that he was, in a sense, nurturing a viper in his bosom.

After his sudden severance from Harvard, Hearst had definitely determined to go into journalism for the reason that it appealed to him as the "most interesting" pursuit that he could take up. "I didn't want to go into any business that would require a long, dull preparation," he told Huntington Archer of *Printer's Ink* many years later. "The newspaper business seemed to offer more attractions than any other—more immediate attractions, and as many ultimate rewards. I drifted about New York, acquainting myself with newspaper methods, and then went into the *Examiner.*"

The "drifting about" in New York lasted less than a year but it was of primal importance in the young man's development. There had been an upheaval in metropolitan journalism. The keen, frenetic, hawklike Pulitzer, who looked like a titan and acted like a demon—a curious admixture of sensationalism and idealism—had taken over the little Gould-owned toy, the *World,* a sheet held in universal contempt, and by a bold series of forays had raised its circulation from 15,000 to 250,000. Hearst was in New York in September, 1886, when Pulitzer ordered a silver medal struck off to commemorate "the largest circulation ever attained by an American newspaper."

It was natural, then, that Hearst, aflame with big ideas, disregarded the small and scholarly *Evening Post* of Edwin Lawrence Godkin; the temperate *Times* of George Jones and Charles R. Miller; the comparatively moderate *Tribune* of Whitelaw Reid; the sparkling *Sun* of Charles A. Dana and his able coadjutors, Edward P. Mitchell, Chester S. Lord, and Selah M. "Boss" Clarke; even the powerful *Herald* of the younger James Gordon Bennett, which was still a world-wide symbol of personal journalism and newspaper enterprise.

Hearst, like Pulitzer, wanted eventually to talk to a nation, not to a "small coterie" like Godkin and Dana and Reid. So he turned instinctively toward Pulitzer and Pulitzer's method of crusading and "stunt" journalism. His mind, though still groping, sensed instantly that Pulitzer's success was based upon the simple theory: "Attract readers, readers, readers!" He studied and catalogued the methods by which Pulitzer won and held readers: Striking features, bold woodcut illustrations, sensational campaigns, diagrams of the spot where the body was found, and the like.

Evening after evening Hearst would return to his hotel rooms more than ever convinced that the type of newspaper he intended to establish should be modeled definitely on the Pulitzer pattern. As a matter of fact, Pulitzer, after the lapse of half a century, was merely reviving the popular emotional appeal of the crude, blackguardly penny papers of the 1830's. Pulitzer, however, had carried penny paper emotionalism far beyond its original scope, stressing sex, love, jealousy, desire for gain, sympathy—in short, fundamental passions and instincts; and, to give legitimacy to his quest for wealth and power, fearlessly exposed and opposed (to a certain point) corruption and exploitation of the masses.

Pulitzer's fierce antagonism against capitalists as a class sprang from his own harrowing struggles for existence as a common laborer, waiter, coachman, gravedigger, etc., during a cholera epidemic in St. Louis. Hearst had undergone no such warping agonies, yet his generous nature revolted also against the evils and injustices which were everywhere apparent in man's imperfect social and economic system.

During his stay in New York, Hearst made a point of meeting and talking with as many prominent editors and working newspaper men as he could. One of those with whom he fraternized was the famous Sam Chamberlain, formerly secretary to James Gordon Bennett and founder of the Paris *Le Matin.* Witty and urbane, a dandy and a gargantuan drinker although seldom drunk, Chamberlain made his headquarters at the bar of the Fifth Avenue Hotel. He and Hearst knocked about for days on end.

The young Californian's chief admiration, however, was Ballard Smith. When he had definitely decided upon his own career, he asked the *World* editor if he would consider coming with him to take charge of the editorial and news departments of the *Examiner.* "No," replied Ballard Smith, "I am happy here and intend to remain. Do you mind if I give you a bit of advice? Don't hire any of these high-priced New York editors. Be your own editor. In my opinion, you are qualified right now to edit a newspaper." This expression of confidence brought a glow to Hearst's cheeks.

Still remained the task of winning over his father, who was hotly engaged in campaigning for the United States Senate. In a letter from which we have quoted a brief excerpt but which is worth presenting in full, the young man practiced a neat bit of psychology on his sire. Breathing self-confidence and calmly taking it for granted that he was to have the *Examiner,* the letter, undated but evidently written early in 1887, reads as follows:—

> *Dear Father:*
>
> I want to see you about the paper. I shall be through here on the 10th of February, and I shall go immediately to San Francisco if I can catch you before you come here. I am anxious to begin work on the *Examiner.* I have all my pipes laid, and it only remains to turn on the gas. One year from the day I take hold of the thing our circulation will have increased ten thousand.
>
> It is necessary that the *Examiner* destroy every possibility of being considered an organ. I know it is not an organ exclusively devoted to your interests, but there are many people who do not know this, and

so, the influence and accordingly the sale of the paper is thus largely affected.

We must be alarmingly enterprising, and we must be startlingly original. We must be honest and fearless. We must have greater variety than we have ever had. We must print more matter than we have printed. We must increase our force, and enlarge our editorial building.

There are some things that I intend to do new and striking which will constitute a revolution in the sleepy journalism of the Pacific slope and will focus the eyes of all that section on the *Examiner*. I am not going to write you what these are, for the letter might get lost, or you might leak. You would be telling people about the big things that Billy Buster was proposing to bring out in the paper, and the first thing I knew somebody else would have it. No, I will tell you when we meet, but cut out this and paste it on Pickering [owner of the *Call*]. In a year we will have increased at least ten thousand in circulation. In two years we will be paying. And in five years we will be the biggest paper on the Pacific slope. We won't be paying for two years because up to that time I propose turning back into the improvement of the paper every cent that comes in.

Your affectionate son,
W. R. Hearst

When Hearst returned to San Francisco for the final showdown with his father, his luggage contained bound volumes of the New York *World*.

Senator-elect George Hearst was at his desk in the offices of Haggin, Hearst & Tevis when his son, still shy of manner, still gentle of voice, still smiling of mien, walked in. Gravely, the old Argonaut eyed his tall, foppishly attired heir and stroked his gray beard.

"My boy," he said, "I am glad to know that you are not content to live simply as a rich man's son, but that you want to get out and do something for yourself and on your own."

"That's right, Pop."

"You know there's lots of work to be done developing these ranch properties we own? Want to try it?"

The young man shook his head vigorously.

"And our mines?"

Another emphatic shake of the head.

"You are still keen to take over that damned newspaper?"

"Yes, Pop."

The Senator snorted.

"Great God!" he cried, throwing up his hands. "Haven't I spent money enough on that paper already! I took it for a bad debt and it's a sure loser.

41

But if you are still set, Will, and want it, go ahead. Only I want you to promise that you will go into it seriously and earnestly."

Humidly, Will Hearst thanked his father and then he began to unfold his plans. As he talked, the Senator realized that this resolute, self-reliant young man approaching twenty-four was not the immature boy whom his parents had posted off to college. His knowledge of every phase of newspaper making seemed encyclopedic. Craftily, he told how he had filled the *Lampoon's* strongbox and pointed out that the recent surprising growth of department stores would soon make all merchants advertising conscious. With equal guile, he kept to himself some of the more audacious schemes which he had formed.

Half convinced but still skeptical, Uncle George Hearst, his windbeaten countenance a bewildered red, sent for his friend T. T. Williams, editor of the San Francisco *Post*. Williams, who later became manager of the *Examiner,* was jocularly called "Good Tom" to distinguish him from the President of the California Jockey Club who was known, also jocularly, as "Bad Tom" Williams. Good Tom, who will figure later and more than once in this narrative, was a rough and ready sort of person, a genius in his way. Many years earlier he had rolled into San Francisco on a sailing ship, got a job as a streetcar driver, educated himself, and by long, hard tugs had become a successful newspaper man.

"Tom," spluttered Senator Hearst, when the editor made his appearance, "suppose a man made a great success of a newspaper, greater than anybody ever made. How much could he profit?"

"Oh," replied Williams carelessly, "maybe $100,000 a year."

"Hell!" exploded Hearst senior, "that ain't any money. What do you think, Tom? I been saving the *Examiner* to unload on some enemy and along comes my boy Will and says he wants to take it over. He won't take the mines or the ranches or the horses or something useful. But, hell! he's so set guess I better let him have his way."

And thus it happened that March 4, 1887 became a climactic, red-letter day in the Hearst family. For on that day George Hearst took his seat in the United States Senate for his first full term and Will Hearst became proprietor and sole owner of the San Francisco *Examiner*.

The town laughed when word got around that George Hearst's long-legged, soft-voiced dude son was to assume the dignities and responsibilities of editorship. It was a public joke.

But San Francisco was mistaken. Hearst brought to his task a personality and an intelligence hitherto unsuspected. Vigorous, energetic, courageous, he had made plans which he had confided to no one—plans which were to mature and to exert illimitable influence upon his city, his state, his country and the world at large.

"He Multiplies Himself
in Others"

Cromwell, I charge thee, fling away ambition:
By that sin fell the angels; cq

Henry VIII, iii, 2
WILLIAM SHAKESPEARE

4

CONFOUNDING EVEN those who knew him intimately, young Will Hearst, playboy and "wastrel," threw himself into active journalism with a fierce and consuming ambition to make good on his own.

He succeeded magnificently but only after the sort of struggle which tries a man's soul and stamina to the very limit. Indeed, more than once, the young man felt that his physical and nervous organism could not stand up under the strain. With a clarity of judgment which was to distinguish most of his subsequent great career, he prescribed his own antidote by selecting able and loyal subordinates and giving them free rein. Once, at least, he found it necessary to resort to subterfuge in winning further financial backing from his father. Finally, though, the corner was turned and Senator Hearst paid proud tribute to his son's courage, resourcefulness and talent.

Nevertheless, certain phases of the young man's enigmatic character continued to puzzle George Hearst. One day in 1890, when the new San Francisco *Examiner* was an established success, the shrewd and sagacious old miner-politician seated himself at a desk in the public room of the old Astor House in New York and slowly and quietly, as was his wont, wrote down his own private estimate of his remarkable son. The document, in the elder Hearst's careful, close-spaced, distinctive script, is still in existence. It reads as follows:—

If he lacked confidence in himself he might require more ceremony from others; but, doubtless, the very reason why he is so indulgent to those who serve him in various capacities is that it

43

never occurred to him that he was insecure in his own position. He selects his men wisely for the work he wants them to do and so long as they attend to that work he does not bother himself by trying to discipline them. Thus, without much wear and tear, he does a vast deal of work by other heads and hands: he multiplies himself in them.

The success with which he has done this for years and his ability to multiply himself again and again in every new enterprise or requisition upon his intellectuality amounts to nothing less than genius.

His reserve of information: talk at much length and with great particularity, perhaps, upon a subject which you may think he has not given any attention to. He is a good listener. When you get through, maybe, he will, through [throw?] his originality into the matter which you have laboriously presented, and in a few words condense all that need be said about it and give it a life and spirit peculiar to his own thinking. You may talk ever so well but if your ideas or expressions are such as men generally have and use, his will be a contribution to the discourse, because they are distinctly his own and are agreeable on account of his individuality which comes out in them.

Those who make social questions a study and go pretty deeply into the good and evil, the right and the wrong, regarding the relations of people to one another in the complex conditions of our society will find that he, though having but slight regard for mere form or outward appearance, cuts through dress and flesh into the heart of a proposition when a principle or law of manhood or womanhood is involved.

It may be noted that the wise old Argonaut ventured no appraisal of his son's moral or spiritual qualities. However, after three years of close observation, the Senator's earlier skepticism had changed to admiration. Further, he had come to realize the immensity of the task Will had taken upon himself. Drawing upon a hitherto unsuspected range of knowledge and experience, young editor Hearst had succeeded in selecting and placing before his readers material which amused, interested and instructed them. His yardstick was his own insatiable curiosity and eagerness to find out what made things tick. With a prescience far beyond his years, Will Hearst felt that what interested him would interest most people—and he was right a heartening proportion of the time.

Much has been written of Hearst's extraordinary early successes with the bumbling little San Francisco *Examiner*. Some accounts, bathed in the warm glow of reminiscence, would make it appear that a seeming miracle was accomplished by the wave of a wand or a secret alchemy known only to Hearst himself. In reality, his triumph was due to a capacity for taking infinite pains combined with an unprecedented sense of the dramatic and the unusual. Many a genius has gone to the grave unsung for lack of this rare combination of qualities. Hearst was both self-confident and self-contained.

In the aftermath, some of his stunts and spectacular exploits tempt one to quote Dryden's witty reflection that "there is pleasure, sure, in being mad which none but madmen know." But there was, most certainly, a coolheaded method in Hearst's seeming madness, a solid foundation, a definite objective.

The impartial historian of today detects nothing adventitious about Will Hearst's surge to the fore in Pacific Coast journalism. Using the drab little *Examiner* as a laboratory, he devoted almost a decade to improvising, experimenting, perfecting a new and wholly unique technique of journalism. Only after his death was it generally recognized and acknowledged that, beginning in those dim San Francisco days, William Randolph Hearst had changed the practices and standards of American journalism.

Shock, surprise, sensationalism were among Hearst's ingredients, but not the only elements by far. Without social consciousness and a very real sense of public service and responsibility toward its readers and its community, the New Journalism would have faded into oblivion, a mere passing fad.

By 1890, Senator George Hearst was not alone in the realization that an individual of remarkable talent had entered a field for which he was ideally equipped by temperament, inclination and ability.

During the course of three abrasive yet thrill-packed years, Will Hearst had transformed the totally undistinguished *Examiner* into a live, dynamic journal, crammed with news and features, eagerly read, financially successful and of ever-widening influence. The changes and improvements initiated by the young proprietor were so marked and so revolutionary that the new *Examiner* by now was watched and quoted all over the country. A far cry, indeed, from the sheet Hearst had taken over on the evening of March 3, 1887, when he had strolled through a rubbish-strewn alley into a rickety frame building in the unkempt downtown area of San Francisco.

That *Examiner* was a so-called "blanket" sheet, printed on a single web press direct from type. There were four or six pages daily, and eight pages on Sunday. The circulation of twenty-odd thousand was largely of the throwaway or deadhead variety. Advertising was exceedingly meager. All departments were understaffed and spiritless. A couple of men working with the outdated chalk plate process over a coal-oil stove comprised the art department. There was no stereotyping.

Hearst at once ordered sheet-fed cylinder process such as he had seen in the press rooms of the Boston *Globe* and New York *World* and set about acquiring every modern mechanical device as soon as it was perfected.

Later, his own unusual talent for mechanics was employed in many improvements and inventions.

Like every American success story, Hearst's saga, as we have indicated, is tinted with rose-colored legends. Although he scored no overnight victory, the tall young editor with the pale blue eyes and wistful smile moved with a sure, confident touch betokening much thought and careful preparation.

The very first night on the job he devoted himself to sprucing up the paper's typographical appearance, dropping all advertisements from the front page and widening his columns as he had suggested in an earlier letter to his father. He also rearranged his makeup and headings to render them more striking and eye-arresting. In those early months of trial-and-error, before he acquired the art of "multiplying himself in others," the youthful new boss of the *Examiner* punished himself unmercifully. A letter to his mother revealed his daily regimen:—

> I don't suppose that I shall live more than three or four years if this strain keeps up. I don't get to bed until two o'clock and I wake up at about seven in the morning and can't get to sleep again, for I must see the paper and compare it with the *Chronicle*. If we are the best, I can turn over and go to sleep with quiet satisfaction, but if the *Chronicle* happens to scoop us, that lets me out of all sleep for the day. . . .
>
> Thank heaven for one thing, our efforts are appreciated. The great and good people of California want the *Examiner*. They don't want it very bad; they don't want it much harder than at the rate of thirty additional copies a day, but in time this will count. If we can manage to keep ahead we will have in a year from thirty to thirty-two thousand subscribers. That will put us well ahead of the *Call,* and well up with the *Chronicle*.

In a surprisingly short time, Hearst hit his stride and began giving the public what it wanted in large, generous doses.

Within a month after assuming charge of the *Examiner,* the newcomer served notice upon Michael de Young's *Chronicle* that a formidable rival was in the field. On the morning of April 1, Hearst learned from a meager telegraphic despatch that the famous Hotel Del Monte at Monterey, some two hundred miles down the coast, was in flames. While the other papers waited for the news to reach them in the leisurely, traditional way, Hearst chartered a special train at two o'clock in the morning, filled it with such staff writers and sketch artists as could assemble and rushed south. It was the first time in Pacific Coast journalism that a special train had been used to gather news. The party arrived while the fire was still smoldering and created almost as much of a furor as the disaster itself.

The following morning the *Examiner* came out with a fourteen-page extra containing one of the most vivid stories of a catastrophe that had ever been published in the West. There were banner heads, zinc etchings and a typical Hearst make-up. Most of the heads and legends had been written by Hearst himself. Three editions were run off to appease the popular demand.

This was Hearst's opening salvo. It was to be followed by others too numerous to itemize in detail. New and commodious editorial and business offices were fitted up in Montgomery Street. Hearst enlisted some of his old *Lampoon* associates, Eugene Lent, Fred Briggs the cartoonist, and "Phinney" Thayer, who were later joined by "Cosy" Noble as Sunday editor.

The young boss of the *Examiner* induced the famous S. S. "Sam" Chamberlain to come out from New York as news editor and authorized him to recruit a crackerjack reportorial staff without regard to expense. Chamberlain thus became the first of a notable line of hard-hitting, imaginative newsmen whose ideas in the assembling and handling of news paralleled those of their employer.

Hearst himself chose his editorial and feature writers. His one requirement was an ability to write strong, clear, forceful English. Above all, the reader must not be bored. Hearst, as we have noted, personally recruited the crotchety, brilliant Ambrose Bierce and gave him free rein for his editorial columns of comment and satire. The young proprietor of the *Examiner* also had to guide Bierce through recurrent spells of neurosis and talk him out of periodical resignations. According to Bierce's biographer, Carey MacWilliams, the columnist was patiently "pampered, mollified and befriended by Hearst." Incidentally, Hearst's handsome payments assured Bierce the leisure to write some of the most penetrating and mordant short stories in the English language.

A fortnight after his name appeared on the *Examiner's* masthead as "Editor and Proprietor," Hearst made it quite evident that he intended to take a bold and progressive stand in civic affairs. A dizzy series of crusades, campaigns and spectacular exploits was launched with a vigorous attack upon a proposed new city charter. The paper fought, and eventually defeated the charter on the ground that it would entrench the local bosses in power. The charter fight was Hearst's opening blast in long and bitter warfare against the gigantic, scowling superboss, Collis Potter Huntington.

C. P. Huntington's hated railroad combination—Central and Southern Pacific—had long been the real government of California, to such an extent indeed that cynics spoke of the state as "Huntington's plantation." Everyone knew that the railroad offices at Fourth and Townsend Streets, San Francisco, were the state capitol in everything except name. Here came judges, editors, office seekers, bosses and sub-bosses to receive their orders and humbly perform groveling acts of obeisance when the Colossus himself appeared from the East three or four times a year to look over his domain and reward or discipline his minions.

Bill Stow was Huntington's chief political fixer. Under him operated

Bill Higgins, the ungainly Republican boss, and his aides, Martin Kelly and Phil Crimmins. The Democratic machine was dominated by Chris Buckley, the notorious "blind boss," a likeable but corrupt old saloonkeeper. His principal lieutenant was Sam Rainey.

Such men regarded with amused tolerance the ordinary weak-livered reform movement. But Hearst's bold, virile attacks were something else again. When the *Examiner* won a crusade for lower water rates and promptly launched another to force electric wires underground in the downtown district, the bosses and their owners began to look upon Hearst as a mad bull in a china shop. This strange, imperturbable young "dude" actually seemed to be planning a restoration of popular rule. Worst of all, the rapscallion could neither be intimidated nor coerced. So the fixers and the bosses, in something of a panic, appealed to Senator Hearst. Uncle George had a heart-to-heart talk with his son. The latter told him that he intended to oppose both the Democratic and Republican machines when the public interest was involved.

"But, Son," remarked Senator Hearst, "every party must have a leader. Buckley is a pretty good sort."

"Yes, Pop, but he is a thief," returned Hearst.

"Well," observed the Argonaut warily, "do you think you can lick him?"

"I most certainly do."

"All right, Son, go to it and good luck."

The young publisher went to it and soon Buckley and Rainey were fugitives on criminal charges, remaining in exile for three years.

Thereafter Senator Hearst, although a bit bewildered by his son's pyrotechnics, never sought to influence him. And when friends of his father attempted to use their friendship as an argument to call him off in some crusade the *Examiner* was engaged in, Hearst's invariable silencer was: "My father is thoroughly capable of fighting his own battles and taking care of his friends. So am I. We never interfere with each other."

In the fight on Buckley, Hearst learned that the blind boss' saloon on Bush Street was a hang-out for Jimmy Hope, the notorious bank robber. Under political protection and financed by a corruption fund raised by the underworld of the country, Hope openly walked the streets of San Francisco for six months, although there were charges against him all over the Union. Hearst's vigorous exposé of Buckley on this and other counts resulted in the convening of a special Superior Court grand jury. The boss and his henchmen were indicted and took French leave. Then, with Hearst's backing, the New Democracy was formed by Gavin McNab, Franklin Lane, Frederick Lawrence, Judge D. J. Sullivan, Frank H. Dunne and others.

In this experimental period, Hearst was in and out of the office day and night. Without the slightest loss of an ingrown sense of personal dignity, he worked in close and affectionate comradeship with his men. He loved nothing better than to crack a good story himself and then supervise its display. There was little ceremony about the shop and no "high hat" at all.

Despite the strain of what he was trying to do, Hearst's spirit of fun and love of practical joking remained inexhaustible. Outside the office he played like a schoolboy. He'd take some of the staff out to help him fly kites, set off firecrackers and balloons, sail boats and steam launches at Sausalito and over San Francisco Bay. Or they would dash to the San Simeon ranch, ride after cattle, catch trout or shoot at quail.

But somehow, no matter what they were doing, Hearst and his playmates, new and old, seemed always to talk newspaper gossip and plan newspaper schemes, and no one seemed sorry to get back to the office. There the unexpected was always turning up, and there centered the chief excitement and fun of those thrilling days. There was more merriment in Sam Chamberlain's little eight-by-ten cubbyhole of an office than in most theatres. This was where the gang sat around most, laughed most, and made most of its plans. The *Lampoon* office over again! Subeditors wondered how Hearst found time to write (in longhand) the pages of directions or suggestions which they would find on their desks daily.

He had an odd trick in those days: he would come to the door of an editor's office, put a hand on either side of the door frame and, with a perfectly grave face, dance a clog or jig while he was making up his mind just what he wanted to say. This was not a pose. He actually thought better while shuffling his feet.

As we have indicated, Hearst early staffed the *Examiner* with the best reporters, editors and business executives he could find, both on the Coast and in Eastern cities; and purchased the telegraphic news service of the New York *Herald,* Pulitzer of the *World* (perhaps, with a prevision of what was to come) having refused his offer. Distance, cost, labor—nothing daunted Hearst. Superior newspaper men naturally flocked to his banner.

Within a year or two, the *Examiner* had incomparably the best staff in the West: Arthur McEwen, the war horse of the editorial page, a fair-haired goateed Highlander Scot, with a pen of acid; his chief assistant, gentle Sam Moffett, Mark Twain's nephew; Joe Ward, quick-witted city editor and his assistant, A. M. "Andy" Lawrence; statuesquely beautiful Winifred Sweet—"Annie Laurie," first of the famous sob-sisters and who, as Winifred Black, continued for half a century to turn out her throbbing copy; Alfonso "Blinker" Murphy, political man, feared, yet somehow liked and respected by boss and ward heeler; "Big Bill" Naughton, pioneer sporting editor, who could remain unmoved as two pugs hammered each other to a pulp, yet weep unashamed when someone sang *Ben Bolt;* Jake Dressler and Charley Dryden, wizard baseball writers; Edward H. Hamilton, Frederick Lawrence, William N. Hart and Charles Michelson, masters of clear, incisive

English and reporters to the fingertips; Eddie Morphy, the wild Irish boy from Dublin University, and Henry D. "Petey" Bigelow, both flagrantly unreliable in their habits but able writers, hence pardonable; and "Phinney" Thayer, who dashed off the immortal *Casey at the Bat* for his Sunday column in the *Examiner*.

Archibald Clavering Gunter, the well-known California novelist, was so taken with the poem that he sent it to his friend De Wolfe Hopper. The actor recited it at a gathering of baseball men in New York and the sequel became historic. For forty-seven years, until his death in 1935, Hopper was called upon to repeat the poem so constantly that his name became inseparably linked with the tragic tale of Mudville and Mighty Casey.

In the art department, under the pioneer Charles Tebbs, worked and played at one time or another Fred Briggs, Theo Hampe, Homer Davenport fresh from twisting brakes on the Northern Pacific Railroad, Haydon Jones, Jimmy Swinnerton, T. A. "Tad" Dorgan, Harrison Fisher, Robert Carter, "Bud" Fisher and others famous later or deeply mourned.

In the business office there were Senator Hearst's former secretary Edward W. Townsend, creator of Chimmie Fadden; Charles M. Palmer, the "Northwestern miller"; and "Bogey," William F. Bogart, a newspaper cashier actually regarded as human by the staff. If a thirsty reporter wanted to cash an order against his salary at night, and Bogey didn't have the money, he'd trot across the street and borrow it from a trustful bartender at the "What Cheer House"!

During his very first year Hearst began casting his lines for famous special writers and artists as well as young reporters of promise. Thomas Nast of *Harper's,* foremost cartoonist of the day, was persuaded to do staff work for the *Examiner* in 1888. Among other special contributors were Mark Twain, Max O'Rell, Gertrude Atherton and Joaquin Miller. Much later, 1899, Edwin Markham wrote for the paper *The Man with the Hoe*.

Hearst was so full of ideas that they tumbled over each other. His parents had built a splendid mansion at 1400 New Hampshire Avenue, Washington, where they entertained with true Western hospitality. Roguishly, Hearst decided to impress them with his new importance, also to make a bid for national attention.

Accordingly, early in 1888, the *Examiner,* with the usual fanfare, started an agitation to bring the Democratic National Convention to San Francisco. Eastern newspapers opposed, citing the difficulty of obtaining telegraph service from so distant a point. Accepting the challenge, Hearst offered to publish a New York edition and supply gratis more telegraphic news than any Eastern paper could possibly use.

Taking half of his staff with him, he went to the national capital in February and, on Washington's birthday, published the first anniversary edition of the *Examiner* under his management. So convincingly did Hearst demonstrate his point that President Cleveland himself was obliged to step in and save the Democratic convention for the East.

The Hearst seniors were delighted to have copies of the "Washington" *Examiner* placed upon their doorstep, although Hearst experienced some difficulty convincing his father that the stunt was worth the $80,000 it reputedly cost.

Later that year, Will's prodigal outlays really began to alarm the Senator and he threatened to call a halt. Hearst dropped in on his father's old prospecting friend, Democratic National Committeeman Michael Francis Tarpey, and explained the impasse. He was certain another $50,000 would enable him to pull the paper out of the red. What happened next was related by Tarpey many years later to Edmond D. Coblentz and is engagingly recalled by this veteran Hearst editor in his book, *William Randolph Hearst, A Portrait in His Own Words.**

"I assured him that I thought I could induce his father to advance the needed funds," said Mr. Tarpey. "We were in the heat of a campaign. I went to the Senator and told him that the party needed contributions, and that he was down for one hundred thousand dollars for the Democratic cause. The Senator didn't hesitate. I received his check for that amount. Half of the sum went into our campaign fund. The other fifty thousand dollars I turned over to young William for his and the paper's espousal of the Democratic principles. I do not know that Will ever required any more money for his paper. It soon became an outstanding and successful journal."

Soon Uncle George Hearst came to realize that his Homeric son possessed as keen a business instinct as his own. Advertising followed circulation. The *Examiner* established an imposing business office on Market Street at Grant Avenue. By 1889, the paper was showing a substantial profit. However, according to the original plan from which he never deviated, Hearst continued to plow back every penny of profit into the enterprise.

Also, never a day passed without a demonstration of his uncanny sense of news values:—

Thomas Nast was in San Francisco when the *Examiner* was seeking to compel the streetcar companies to put fenders on the trolleys. Nast was asked to draw something for use in the campaign. Unfamiliar with the subject, the renowned cartoonist did not produce a very striking effort. At the usual staff dinner that night in a nearby Italian restaurant, Hearst, however, praised the cartoon highly.

"The cars have been maiming and killing a good many children, Mr. Nast," said Hearst. "Sometimes I look at those cars and see not a gripman but a skeleton at the control. The skeleton, it seems to me, leers at the little children at play as they run thoughtlessly across the path of the approaching Juggernaut."

* Simon & Schuster, New York, 1952.

"By George, Mr. Hearst, that would make a wonderful picture!" exclaimed Nast. "Kill that other drawing. Let me work on your idea."

Nast was so enthused that he labored half the night in his hotel room and next day brought in a graphic masterpiece of the cartoonist's art, worthy of Hogarth himself. Together, he and Hearst titled it, "Death the Gripman." Spread across half of the *Examiner's* front page, the drawing exercised determining effect in forcing the cable cars to attach fenders to their death-dealing wheels. "Death the Gripman" became a legend in San Francisco.

One stormy night in January, 1890, word came in that five fishermen were marooned on a rock outside Golden Gate and that attempts of Government lifesavers had been thwarted by the treacherous sea and high gale. Hearst led a party of rescuers from the *Examiner* aboard a Luckenbach ocean-going tug. Among his volunteers was Henry R. Haxton, an Englishman and a notable swimmer. Haxton shed his clothes, leaped into the boiling sea with a line and got close enough to the buffeted men to toss them his rope. All were rescued. Fed and warmed, the grateful fishermen were taken to the *Examiner* office, interviewed and photographed galore. To complete a satisfactory night's work, Hearst gleefully noted that competing morning papers had the men still stormbound on the rock.

Under the lash of the *Examiner's* prompt crusade, the lifesaving service was reorganized. The paper then turned its attention to complaints of laxity in lifesaving drills on the Southern Pacific ferryboats plying between Oakland and San Francisco. Haxton volunteered to jump overboard from a ferryboat and note the time taken to rescue him. Followed a sweeping reform in apparatus and drills. Haxton later returned to England and was elected to Parliament.

And so it went. Presaging a lifelong interest in aviation, Hearst took his first airborne flight in a balloon with Harry B. McDowell and wrote a lively description of San Francisco viewed from the sky. When Kaiser Wilhelm I died, the *Examiner* appeared in both German and English.

While posses hunted the notorious train bandits Sonntag and Evans in their mountain fastness, Petey Bigelow, star *Examiner* reporter, found them and brought back an interview. A railroad train was stalled in the snowshed in the mountains and the *Examiner* sent to the rescue a special engine, equipped with a snowplow and laden with food and clothing. Another staff man, Allen Kelly, naturalist and hunter, went into the mountains and captured a live specimen of the almost extinct California grizzly bear for the Golden Gate Zoo. The bear was christened "Monarch" and the *Examiner* used the exploit to proudly proclaim itself: "The Monarch of the Dailies." Reporter Fred Lawrence made a long journey on horseback over the Canadian border and discovered the leak through which thousands of Chinese and great quantities of opium were pouring into the United States.

During Hearst's first year as an editor occurred the atrocious Haymarket murders in Chicago. Foreshadowing subsequent tremendous and effective campaigns against communism and other subversive doctrines, the *Examiner* on September 1, 1887, printed the following editorial under the heading, "The Chicago Anarchists":—

> There is little doubt that the seven Chicago anarchists will suffer the extreme penalty for their atrocious crime. There should be no sympathy for them. They are the worst types of a class that scares capital away from legitimate pursuits, and smirches honest industry with the soot of their fiendish mechanisms. It is not likely that any attempt will be made to stay the executions by violence. If, however, this mode should be adopted, we trust the authorities will know how to deal with its advocates. We have plenty of room in this country for honest, hard-working immigrants, but for those who delight in plotting murder and destruction our homestead tracts measure just six feet by two.

This editorial, of course, reflected prevailing opinion at the time. However, there are other striking and significant parallels between 1887 and today.

For example, the parent Hearst newspaper took an undeviating stand for adequate national defense. It revealed pitiful weakness in our Pacific naval defenses, a disclosure which reached a grim crescendo at Pearl Harbor. At the same time the *Examiner* appealed for a greater navy and an interocean canal either in Nicaragua or Panama, a campaign which finally succeeded with the construction of the Panama Canal.

From the beginning the paper championed union labor. It fought the menace of Oriental competition by sending out special labor trains and establishing free employment bureaus for white workmen.

In 1889, the longest cable message that had ever been received in San Francisco told of the dramatic double suicide of the Crown Prince Rudolph of Austria and the Baroness Marie de Vetsera. Later that year a staff writer was sent to China to investigate the causes and describe the ravages of the great famine. In 1891 a special correspondent was in Japan covering the tremendous earthquake that ravaged the Mikado's kingdom.

Winifred Black did some great reporting for the *Examiner*. She "fainted" in Market Street and was taken to the City Receiving Hospital in the Hall of Justice Building at Kearny and Washington Streets. Two mornings later the town was shocked by a sensational exposé of conditions in this emergency first-aid institution, to which victims of street accidents were carted in ancient, dirty, straw-lined wagons and where women were subjected to insult and indignity by rowdy and drunken male attendants. Miss Black was so treated. Her shocking account cleaned out the gang and brought about regular ambulance service.

At this time, also, Hearst made the first of many hundreds of subsequent appeals for public funds for public projects. The initial appeal resulted in the famous Little Jim Hospital for Crippled Children. The institution drew its name from an infant born shortly before Christmas to a drunken prostitute in the noisome underground City Prison Hospital.

In all of these enterprises, Hearst's right bower was Sam Chamberlain, a newspaper man of bold initiative and of international experience.

Scion of a well-known Eastern family, Chamberlain had been secretary to James Gordon Bennett; founder of *Le Matin* in Paris with John W. Mackay's backing; and editorial director of the *Evening Telegram* and other metropolitan papers. Hearst and Chamberlain were cut from the same bolt. "The story's the thing" was their creed. In San Francisco, and later in New York, they carried personal journalism to the very limit of its development.

Until the end of his racing life a big story could always lure Sam Chamberlain from his desk. During the political upheaval in the Sandwich Islands (now Hawaii) that resulted in the overthrow of Queen Liliuokalani, Chamberlain bobbed up along with numerous other American correspondents. A lordly, impressive figure of a man, impeccably attired, he mingled with the people of the court, gave wine suppers and so ingratiated himself with the Queen that she passed pleasant hours with the magnetic American and told every detail of what would now be termed her "true life story."

Chamberlain, they say, wrote the interview in the presence of the Queen and remained with her until the steamer, San Francisco bound, was ready to warp out of the dock in Honolulu. Whereupon he rushed down to the vessel and, as the gangplank was being pulled in, exultantly waved his manuscript at his disconsolate rivals.

Chamberlain was in a class by himself at playing up a big story. During the Hopkins-Searles will case in Boston, he ordered a complete verbatim report for the *Examiner*. The paper paid telegraph tolls on 17,000 words in a single day and the people of California devoured the story. It was an irresistible combination, Hearst and Chamberlain, each challenging the other in daring schemes. There was great affection between the two. Chamberlain met Hearst's two standards of ability and personal loyalty. Like most newspaper men of the day, Chamberlain delighted in the flowing bowl. Once, when Hearst was abroad, his general manager cabled: "Chamberlain drunk again. May I dismiss him?" Hearst promptly returned a characteristic response: "If he is sober one day in thirty that is all I require."

In the hectic competitive atmosphere of those days, the process of creating the news as well as gathering it led to much outright faking, a misdemeanor of which Hearst and Chamberlain were of course aware but chose blandly to ignore. One of the *Examiner's* biggest human interest hits, "The Last of the McGintys," is a case in point. Star reporter Eddie Morphy's lively imagination was responsible for this tear-jerker about a small, bedraggled newsboy supposedly left to care for an orphaned brood of younger brothers and sisters. Mrs. Phoebe Hearst was so touched that she wrote Morphy a note enclosing five twenty-dollar bills to be used to buy food and clothing for the orphaned youngsters.

"I was in a dilemma," later recounted Morphy. "There *were* no McGintys. When I told the city editor about the problem, he suggested we'd better go over to the Mint, a neighboring saloon, break one of those twenties and talk things over. This we did. Other reporters joined us. By the time we'd spent the greater part of a twenty-dollar bill we found a solution to the problem. Some of the boys rounded up five or six dirty, ragged kids from the street. We photographed and sketched them in all their dirtiness. Then we took them out, bought new clothes for them and cleaned them up. Once more we photographed them. For several Sundays thereafter we ran feature stories about the young McGintys. It was great stuff for the *Examiner*. But some young reporter of the San Francisco *News Letter* heard the real story and printed it.

"After that, for many weeks, I made it my business to keep out of sight whenever Mrs. Phoebe Hearst was around. One day she caught me. 'Oh, Mr. Morphy,' she said, 'how could you do such a thing!' I was trying to think up an adequate apology when she added, 'Well, anyway, Mr. Morphy, that was a wonderful story you wrote about the McGintys. It had me weeping for several hours.'"

Such episodes of those incredible happy-go-lucky days, however, were fillips compared to the big and important things the *Examiner* was accomplishing.

When the Federal census of 1890 was announced, Hearst happened to be in Washington. He sent his paper the entire census of the Coast, filling a complete page, giving the figures for every state and city, down to the smallest towns.

Similarly, the persuasive young editor wangled an exclusive copy of the new McKinley Tariff Bill from Congressman, later Mr. Justice, Joseph McKenna, chairman of the Congressional Tariff Committee, and wired the entire document to the *Examiner*. It was the longest dispatch which had ever gone over the wires, occupying three pages of close type. Foreshadowing as it did drastic changes in business, Hearst always considered this one of his most notable scoops. However, the target of his most sustained battle in the early days was, of course, the Southern Pacific Railroad. That fight lasted for years.

Collis P. Huntington's malign railroad combination, as we have pointed out, held the state in a vise, buying legislators en bloc, votes wholesale. Its grip was broken finally by Hearst's dramatic and telling use of the so-called "Colton letters."

David H. Colton, an eminent California attorney, was the legal mind behind C. P. Huntington's original railroad organization schemes. After Colton's death his widow sued the Central Pacific Railroad. The suit brought to light astonishing letters from Huntington to Colton revealing almost unbelievable corruption. Employing this ammunition, Hearst leaped to the attack and thundered against Huntington. The railroad despotism and its methods—"Public Plunder by Pirate Privilege" it was termed by the mordant Hearst editorial writers—became an issue in every state campaign for twenty years. The people profited on a dozen fronts, as did the *Examiner,* which was enabled to boast at the end of 1889 that its circulation already exceeded 60,000 daily and was gaining at the rate of 1,000 copies a week.

In his second year with the *Examiner,* Hearst happened upon a man who was destined to be of inestimable value to him as he proceeded to enlarge and expand his publications. This was George E. Pancoast, an itinerant printer from Boston, a mechanical jack-of-all-trades, and with extraordinary gifts of Yankee inventiveness and of dry wit. Pancoast drifted into the *Examiner* office in 1888 and got a job from Ike Allen, then chief copyreader in the editorial department. One night Pancoast wrote what he considered a snappy head on a story about a young man acquitted by a jury on a robbery charge.

The boss copyreader didn't like Pancoast's effort and changed the head to read: "It's All Right Now." When the paper had been put to bed, Pancoast ran off a handbill and posted it in the ad alley. It read: "Ike Allen's Patent Adjustable Head: 'It's All Right Now.' Will fit any story by changing one letter: 'It's All Right Not.' "

Everyone laughed, including Hearst, who asked, "Who's the comedian?" Next day Hearst sent for Pancoast and asked if he could operate a typewriter which had just been installed. The Yankee allowed that he could learn soon enough. "All right," Hearst grinned, "then you're my secretary." Thus began a warm and affectionate association that endured for more than half a century, until Pancoast's passing. Stimulated by Hearst's backing and wealth of mechanical ideas, Pancoast became an outstanding inventor, earned a substantial fortune for himself and many millions for Hearst. He designed the beveled linotype slug, experimented first with motor-driven presses and invented the Pancoast color press, first of its type. But to him the proudest of his titles was that of mechanical superintendent of the Hearst papers.

Like his employer, Pancoast was a nighthawk, available at all hours, and ever ready to tackle anything new and exciting. The secretary was experimenting with amateur photography and Hearst joined in with eager enthusiasm, an interest which was to prove of tremendous practical value in the development of Hearst's newspaper plants.

One morning Pancoast succeeded in making a remarkable camera study of the bay, showing masts of ships and the top of Angel Island and Belvedere rising out of the fog. Hearst went wild with enthusiasm, ordered the best available photographic equipment, and worked for hours and days on end in a specially constructed darkroom at his house in Sausalito. Soon he was expert. "He wasn't satisfied until he could take pictures better than they had ever been taken before," remarked Pancoast years later.

In the late '80's and early '90's Hearst and Pancoast dashed off on trips to Europe and the Near East, taking pictures wherever they went. They photographed celebrities and strange animals, explored the battlefields of Italy and France and the byways of the British Isles and sent back hundreds of photographs to be etched and stories to be printed by Chamberlain in the *Examiner*.

In 1893 Hearst and his secretary were at the Hotel Wagram in the Rue de Rivoli on their way to Egypt. The rich Parisian food had given them indigestion, but one night they came upon a tiny restaurant run by an American, where beans, codfish and chowder were served. The proprietor admitted these "delicacies" were shipped to him in cans from the United States.

"George," said Hearst, "we've a three-month trip up the Nile ahead of us. I don't see how we can make it without some good plain American grub. Suppose you cable Ike Allen to send us a shipment of beans, chowder and codfish." Ike, by this time, was Eastern representative of the *Examiner*.

Just at closing time, next afternoon, into Allen's imposing suite of rooms in the new Pulitzer Building in New York, came this cable:—

> Rush dozen cans Boston beans dozen cans clam chowder two codfish Alexandria Egypt **HEARST**

Ike shook his head in perplexity. He took the strange message around and about town with him that night. Next morning he dropped down to the Wells, Fargo & Company bank on lower Broadway.

"Mr. Parsons," he asked the dignified gentleman who received him, "what cable code is Mr. Hearst using?"

"Why the regular ABC code, Mr. Allen."

"Well, here's a message in a new code," replied Ike, displaying the cable.

The Wells, Fargo man puzzled over it and could offer no solution. After wending his way back to the Pulitzer Building, Allen cabled the Boss: "What code are you using?" The reply was quick and decisive: "No code. Want beans chowder codfish."

Thus were Hearst and his boon companion Pancoast liberally supplied with cans of New England's favorite food when the steam dhahabiyah *Nitrocris* set forth on a cruise up the Nile. The trip was a photographic orgy; 3,200 negatives were made. For the first time in history the tombs of the ancient Egyptian kings were flashlighted. The tombs were carved out of solid rock. The Americans set up two cameras and had their dragomen hold candles so that they could reproduce the depths of the tombs and the beautiful wall carvings. Undisturbed for thousands of years, the great crypts reverberated throughout the sound of the flashlights. The visitors were disturbed only by bats which swooped down upon their pith helmets.

Hearst, indulging the passion for art which had gripped him from childhood, picked up some wonderful mummies. Experts pronounced two of these as perfectly preserved as any in existence. When the British Government learned of the activities of the harum-scarum Americans, cameras were barred from the tombs of the kings. But Hearst got safely away with his trunks full of photographs and he had Lévy of Paris color his lantern slides.

"W. R. knows as much about photography as any man in the world," remarked George Pancoast, relating these anecdotes many years ago as we sat on his lovely porch in the Jersey highlands. "Furthermore," he added emphatically, "he knows more about printing presses and all manner of technical equipment than anyone else."

Told of this opinion, Hearst commented with a smile that Pancoast overestimated his mastery of mechanics, "perhaps because the ordinary publisher knows nothing about blueprints or presses. An inventor like Pancoast is always surprised to find that I know a little."

Hearst's onrushing career was saddened by the passing of his father in Washington on February 28, 1891. He was at the bedside. The Senator was in his seventy-first year.

San Francisco buried its distinguished citizen with unaccustomed pomp and panoply and genuine sorrow among all ranks of the populace. Before the coffin in Grace Episcopal Church stood a unique floral tribute from the *Examiner*. A bank of white flowers represented the front page of the paper. The columns, rules and headings were in blue violets.

George Hearst left his entire estate to his wife. The old miner evidently considered it wise to continue a financial checkrein upon his exuberant, still comparatively inexperienced son. Besides, the latter owned outright the flourishing *Examiner* and the great Babicora ranch.

Will Hearst was not in the least disturbed at the provisions of his father's will. Some years later, when his mother wrote that she in turn had made him her sole heir, he indicated his feelings in a letter to her:—

> My father never did a better thing than when he made the will he did. I have admired him for it and have been happy to concur in it, and I have never told you how many times I have been advised by fools and scoundrels otherwise. This is the kind of thing for our own kind of people, and I hope to so live that you will have as much confidence in me as my father had in you. I hope too that I will never live to read your will, and that you will live as long as I do and that we both shall be as happy as I am now.

The *Examiner* continued to gain both in circulation and in advertising revenue. So, in 1894, Hearst purchased a choice central site at Third and Market Streets and began the construction of a splendid new building. The structure incorporated features never before attempted in a publishing plant. The innovations were Hearst's own and were worked out in detail with the prominent architect, A. C. Schweinfurth.

The building was so arranged that the public, especially school children, could stand on a U-shaped top floor mezzanine and watch the actual process of making a newspaper in unbroken sequence: linotyping, proofreading, make-up, photoengraving, the making of "mats," stereotyping, etc.

With certain technical refinements, later perfected by Hearst with the aid of many experts, this progressive process became known as "straight line production." It meant immense conservation in time and labor, and promoted all around efficiency.

As may well be imagined, Hearst had no intention of cabining his genius in a comparatively small and unimportant Western city. He yearned to spread out and make his imprint felt in the nation at large. New York, the domain of the great Joseph Pulitzer and his *World,* was the young Californian's natural focal point. One day, while crossing the bay to Sausalito with his *fidus Achates* George Pancoast, Hearst pulled out a railroad map of the country. With nervous pencil, he drew rings about the principal cities and remarked: "George, some day, a paper here and here and here." A double ring, Pancoast noted, was drawn about New York.

As early as 1892, Hearst had sent his able business manager, Charles M. Palmer, to make a survey of the metropolis. Palmer reported that conditions at that time did not seem favorable. Those newspaper properties which were for sale were held by their owners at ridiculously inflated valuations. So Hearst decided to bide his time.

In 1895, with his new plant a reality, Hearst determined definitely to invade New York. Again, Charles Palmer was entrusted with the scouting mission. Neither man had any illusions. They knew that violent and expensive collision with Hearst's well established natural rival, Joseph Pulitzer, was inevitable.

Great sums would be needed, as well as an infinite resourcefulness, to attain leadership in the difficult metropolitan field. Hearst took the problem to his mother. Phoebe Hearst had already arranged to sell the Hearst interest in the Anaconda mine for a reputed $7,500,000. Without hesitation, she offered to advance any sum required for the New York venture.

In Paris that summer, where they were both vacationing, Hearst gave his agent Palmer instructions to resurvey the situation in New York and report upon newspaper properties for sale. Palmer sailed for America late in July.

New Blood in Park Row

To be devoted to one thing and to make all other things subservient to it, to persist to the finish although not necessarily to the logical end, is to become something and someone, to acquire a character adequate and necessary to master circumstances. Finally, it is to be able to steer a course through the otherwise mysterious fluid of events, because there is a constant point of reference in view.

The Forest and the Fort
HERVEY ALLEN

5

IN 1895, when William Randolph Hearst, like Lochinvar, rode out of the West to woo New York, metropolitan journalism was dominated by Dana's *Sun,* Bennett's *Herald* and Joseph Pulitzer's *World.* Although each was a giant in its specialized field, the crusading, enterprising *World,* housed in its own massive skyscraper with a golden dome, was the acknowledged pacemaker.

Far behind the Big Three lagged the *Tribune* and *Times,* both in sad decline from former great estate; the *Press, Recorder, Advertiser* and *Morning Journal.* The latter was easily the least distinguished of all.

Founded in 1881 by Albert Pulitzer, estranged brother of the great Joseph and a direct opposite in character and temperament, the *Journal* based its appeal upon backstairs gossip and salacious tidbits from the lives of the wealthy. For a time these methods paid so handsomely that Albert Pulitzer was enabled to freely indulge his predilection for the fleshpots of Europe.

Then he raised the *Journal's* price to two cents and attempted to compete with his far abler brother who had taken over the *World* from Jay Gould in 1883. The result was a disastrous decline both in circulation and in advertising revenue. Imagine then Newspaper Row's astonishment when, late in 1894, wily Albert Pulitzer persuaded hardheaded John R. McLean to pay him $1,000,000 for the wobbly property.

McLean, a resident of Washington, D. C., and a millionaire many times over, was owner of the exceedingly valuable Cincinnati *Enquirer.*

60

Why so experienced a trouper as McLean fell for the deal was a mystery. In his eagerness to close the transaction and catch the first steamship for Europe, Albert Pulitzer is said to have overlooked $70,000 in the treasury. However, this was small consolation for McLean, who soon discovered that the most expensive toy in the world was a metropolitan newspaper.

McLean tried to make a more respectable sheet of the *Journal,* introducing the methods and approach of his Midwestern property, but New York would have none of it. Circulation and revenue dropped almost to the vanishing point. Week after week, McLean sat in the *Journal's* shabby offices in the Tribune Building at 154 Nassau Street, gazed ruefully at his cost and balance sheets—and wrote out another check to cover his losses. By late summer (1895) he was in a panic, his mood of indigo blue in no whit assuaged by an attack of gout which kept him confined to his temporary leased quarters in the Perry Belmont house on Fifth Avenue.

At this juncture and under these circumstances, McLean received a visit from Charles M. Palmer, Hearst's heavy-set, genial business manager. In the front drawing room, bare of furniture save for an unpainted kitchen table and three chairs, McLean was endeavoring to conduct the *Journal* by telephone. His gouty foot, swathed in bandages, was carefully propped on a corner of the table. Mr. Hearst's representative came to the point at once.

"John," he said, "Mr. Hearst is back from Europe. He wishes to close a deal right away for a New York newspaper, yours or some other. Have you decided upon your final terms?"

"Yes," responded McLean. "I am willing to have Mr. Hearst come in with me as a partner. He can have a half interest in the *Journal* for $360,000. Without taking account of the purchase price, that's the amount I have put into the paper these last eight months."

Palmer laughed and reached for his hat.

"If that's the best you can do the deal is off," he said flatly. "Mr. Hearst believes in going it alone. If you knew him as I do, you'd realize you and he could never team up in running a newspaper. Why, man, when he is out to accomplish something gold pieces are like so many grains of sand with him. But don't think for an instant that he's a sucker. Lots of people have found that out to their cost. No use wasting your time. Guess I better be going."

McLean raised his hand and asked cautiously: "Well, what is the best offer you people will make for the *Journal?*"

Palmer's reply was prompt: "One hundred and eighty thousand dollars for the property exactly as it stands, lock, stock and barrel. You'll get your money in cash immediately. And let me tell you, John, you're lucky. Three months from now, the way things have been going, you wouldn't be able to give the *Journal* away."

Groaning with financial as well as physical pain, McLean rubbed his chin a moment, and then surprised Palmer by yielding without further parley.

"All right," he said, "a hundred and eighty thousand it is. I'll meet Mr. Hearst tomorrow and we'll close the deal."

An hour later, in a suite of the Hoffman House, Palmer sat opposite his sphinx-faced young employer and remarked ruefully: "Mr. Hearst, I feel I have made a bad bargain. We could have gotten the property for a hundred thousand."

"Never mind," countered Hearst happily. "We're in the big picture now," and he celebrated by dancing a jig and cracking his heels together. Then he sent a jubilant wire to Sam Chamberlain in San Francisco directing him to come to New York at once and to bring with him Homer Davenport, Arthur McEwen, Charles Tebbs, Winifred Black, "Cosy" Noble and the cream of the *Examiner's* staff of brilliant reporters.

Although title was passed on September 25, 1895, formal announcement of the *Journal's* change of ownership was not made until November 8 when the paper appeared as the "New York *Journal,* W. R. Hearst, Proprietor." The new owner did not learn for some time that he had also acquired a German edition, *Das Morgen Journal.* "So I bought a frankfurter too," he remarked with a chuckle.

Weeks in advance of an indifferent public, the news reached the omniscient ears of Joseph Pulitzer in his soundproof study at Bar Harbor.

"So that young dude from California is coming to New York," he smilingly remarked to a house guest, Arthur Brisbane, a former secretary and now one of his favorite younger executives. "How fortunate for us McLean has quit the field! Mac's fault was that he didn't know what do with the *Journal.* But he had $60,000,000 back of him and he might have built up another Cincinnati *Enquirer* in New York. I'm afraid young Hearst won't last long. He will find the going tougher than in his home town."

For once Uncle Joe's uncanny gift of prophecy was to fail him. He was, however, merely reflecting the general opinion that Hearst's remarkable success in San Francisco was freakish and ephemeral. He did not then realize that this particular "dude" was tempered steel behind a façade of bright suits, beribboned hats and chromatic scarves. Further, as the arrogant overlord of the *World* and others would soon discover, Hearst had mastered every tool of his trade. One is reminded of the incomparable Richard Wagner who possessed the unique gift of being able to compose for as well as play every instrument in his orchestras.

Within a few months, Pulitzer was forced to revise his hasty estimate of Hearst. The interloper from the West was doing the fiddling on Park Row, and if the *World* and its indomitable proprietor were not exactly dancing to the dude's tunes at least they had shaken the dust from their own fiddles and were lustily sawing away on the G strings. Years later Pulitzer, generous always, placed upon paper a spontaneous tribute to Hearst: "An able, independent man." Hearst, too, developed enormous admiration for Pulitzer's fighting qualities and resourcefulness.

Hearst's invasion of New York launched the most sanguinary and debilitating newspaper war in the history of American journalism. It was fought without scruple. And it produced a phrase, "Yellow Journalism," that was to become a symbol for certain newspaper practices which, as we have remarked earlier, are best forgotten.

Yet from Yellow Journalism's bitter and virile competition, nay even from its very vulgarities, rose the truly independent, crusading newspaper, standing militantly upon its own legs and beholden to no patron, no pressure group save a single client, the public. In this epochal and healthy transition, William Randolph Hearst led the way. Therein lies his greatest glory.

At the onset of his career, as we have seen, Hearst tramped the trail blazed by Joseph Pulitzer. But like so many imitators he so widened and extended the trail that the original pathway became lost to sight.

Destiny, it seemed, willed that Hearst should catch his cue and enter upon the American scene just as Pulitzer was stumbling into the lowered lights of the wings. When the battle was joined, Hearst almost unhorsed Pulitzer at the first onslaught. But, aging, tired as he was, the gallant old warrior of the *World* caught up his spear, buckled on his shield, and fought so valiantly that his foeman was glad eventually to declare the combat a draw. Peace with victory, a double victory, and with enormous mutual respect. The bitter struggle, however, halted the onrush of the *World,* forcing it into a different channel and into eventual oblivion.

In 1895 the young proprietor of the New York *Journal* was still diffident, almost shy, and he shrank from personal publicity. Although he bowed to the conventions to the extent of joining two clubs, the Metropolitan and the Union, social affairs, as such, bored him. However, he was an inveterate theatregoer and seldom missed an opening night at Daly's, Wallack's or Booth's or a new bill at such variety houses as Weber & Fields.

In those formative days he evidenced no desire for political leadership or public office. The excitement and romance of newspaper life satisfied him. In fact, as though purposely, he avoided political attachments, reveling rather in the society of working newspaper men.

In the *Examiner,* however, two years before coming to New York, young editor Hearst had taken delight in debunking the ponderous utterances of President Cleveland, haloed chieftain of a Democratic Party newly restored to power. Hearst predicted, and monotonously repeated the warning, that the Democrats would be swept from office unless they had the courage to be "really democratic." Few party members either in California or in Washington paid much attention to the personal views of the young "freak journalist." Hence, the nervously demure Will Hearst of 1895 concentrated upon a single encompassing ambition: to conquer New York in a newspaper sense, to make a grand splash, build up "the biggest circulation in the world," and become the acknowledged master of "striking" journalism.

For the accomplishment of this purpose he was prepared to risk every dollar of his prospective ample inheritance and every penny of the substantial income the *Examiner* was earning. He had lost well over $500,000 in San Francisco before the *Examiner* began to pay. Before he could turn the corner with the New York *Journal* he was to sacrifice practically all of the $7,500,000 advanced by his mother over the bitter protests of her most trusted business advisers. Years later, when he embarked upon his ambitious motion picture projects, it is interesting to note that he suffered losses approximating the amount sunk into the *Journal*.

As evidence that he had deliberately selected Pulitzer as his antagonist, Hearst adopted the general format and typographical appearance of the *World,* followed its news treatment with some innovations, and dropped the price of the *Journal* to one cent. His reasoning was simple: he would give the public a better bargain for a penny than the *World* did for two cents.

The inscrutable young Californian at once launched a blitz campaign such as the newspaper world never before had witnessed. While Sam Chamberlain assembled a staff of star reporters and artists, doubling and redoubling salaries, Hearst took personal charge of his layouts, news presentations and promotion schemes. The *Journal's* dingy quarters, but a stone's throw from the imposing Pulitzer Building, hummed with activity.

Hearst himself worked around the clock. Each afternoon he went over the high spots of the news with his editors. Each night, in shirt sleeves, he pored over dummy drafts of each page of tomorrow's paper, "the little papers" he called them. While the make-up men were at work in the composing room down cellar, Hearst upstairs was attacking stacks of proof sheets, a blue pencil behind each ear. Improvements, changes, rearrangements were ordered right up to the split second before the forms were locked. A favorite observation was: "There is always time to make it better." Ceaselessly Hearst studied type books, creating effective designs. He even designed a new type which Palmer & Little called "the Hearst."

The *Journal* early adopted as a slogan: "There Is No Substitute for Circulation." Nor was there any limit upon the circulation to which a newspaper could aspire in view of newly perfected mechanical improvements. By 1891, for example, a quadruple Hoe rotary press would print, fold, cut, paste and count 72,000 eight-page papers an hour. The linotype, or mechanical typesetting machine, apotheosis of delicate mechanism, soon followed.

Thus publishers now commanded facilities capable of handling any imaginable increase in circulation. It was necessary only to enlarge basement space and install as many of the new and expensive presses as the publisher could afford. At the same time retail business, particularly department stores in the larger cities, had become convinced that the newspaper was a far more effective salesman than advertising by circular or signboard. Accordingly, since advertising rates depended upon circulation, the quest for readers became a mad race among the newly enlarged newspapers.

Within a few weeks, under Hearst's drive and energy, the *Journal* bounded from 30,000 to 100,000, the highest circulation it had ever attained. There it hung, despite saturation promotion advertising in trade papers, billboards, etc. The *World,* with almost half a million daily circulation and even larger on Sunday, seemed more remote than ever.

Hearst decided that the fault lay with the *Journal's* Sunday edition. Indeed, the entire matter of Sunday circulation was a continuing vexation to newspaper proprietors. With most of the courts and many other official agencies in adjournment, important sources of news are dried up on Saturdays. Sporting events had not then attained the wide vogue since achieved.

In the drab fare spread before readers of the Sunday papers in the mid-1890's, there was but one exception.

A remarkable young man from Maine, Morrill Goddard, had been appointed editor of the *World's* Sunday supplement. He began to offer the public bizarre and sensational stories of fundamental human appeal, illustrated with flaring zinc etchings.

One Sunday, Goddard shocked and amazed the town by devoting the entire front page of his magazine section to the grinning features of a chimpanzee, newborn in Central Park Zoo. This was the first full-page picture which had ever appeared in a metropolitan newspaper. The daring young editor's simultaneous smashing of column rule and of tradition became a seven days' wonder to a citizenry accustomed to viewing with a yawn the mutton chops of Wall Street bankers or the well-fed jowls of Senator Chauncey Depew or Bishop Henry Codman Potter.

As Goddard continued his sensational layouts, the more timid editors of the *World* sought to curb him. Pulitzer peremptorily summoned him to Paris under threat of dismissal. Years later Goddard amusingly described the encounter to the writer. He found Mr. Pulitzer in a darkened hotel room, seated in an armchair, in robe and slippers. His fringy beard was gray, his left eye already sightless.

Goddard, who had come prepared to fight for his professional life, was amazed when Uncle Joe climbed to his feet, took both of Goddard's hands in his and beamed a welcome.

"Dear boy," he cried, "I am so glad you found it possible to accept my invitation. I have just received reports by cable of our Sunday circulation. It's going up, *up*, UP! Most encouraging."

Goddard braced himself while the squeaky, exultant voice went on:

"I knew when I appointed you that you were just the man for the Sunday job. Remember how opposed you were to leaving the city desk? Ah, you do, don't you?"—waving a long, bony, admonishing digit. "Well, let's forget all that. There are other pleasant tasks I have in store for you."

Mr. Pulitzer received Goddard every day for a week, and at parting pressed upon him two lovely Grecian urns and a check. Back in the *World* office, now courted where he had been scowled upon, Goddard continued with marked appeal to readers his flaring type of journalism, and was soon given an opportunity to make it more flamboyant and successful.

A prophetic Sunday feature page gotten up by Morrill Goddard for the New York Sunday *Journal* when neither successful submarines nor wireless controlled weapons existed.

Pulitzer, upon hearing that a competitor, the New York *Recorder,* had contracted with R. Hoe for a four-color rotary press, immediately ordered one for the *World*—and offered a premium to the builder to complete it before the *Recorder's* machine. The *Recorder* won the race, and in April, 1893, started a Sunday series of color pages, "Cosmopolitan Sketches." The innovation attracted nothing except adverse comment, the initial results were so bad. The stage was set for Goddard.

When the *World's* color press was given its test runs in the newspaper's plants, its results were little better. A plan to reproduce famous works of art was abandoned, and the press stood idle, awaiting a more practical idea. Goddard got one. *Puck, Judge,* and other humor periodicals featuring cartoons had growing circulations. There was no doubt that editorial cartoons and "gag" cartoons clipped from humor weeklies got attention from the readers of newspapers able to engrave and publish them. *Puck* used editorial cartoons in color. Why not cartoons in color in the *World?* Cartoons would not emphasize the crudities of the newspaper color process as much as serious drawings would, Goddard reasoned. Pulitzer agreed to the idea being given a try.

The first full-page newspaper comic printed in color was drawn for the *World* by Walt MacDougall, its editorial cartoonist. Goddard wanted more than one cartoon in color, and he thought there should be something that would appeal to readers not interested in the political themes of Mac-Dougall's cartoons. MacDougall was responsible for Goddard's hiring Richard F. Outcault, a draftsman for the *Electrical World* who had also done some cartoons for *Judge.* Outcault was put to work on comics for the *World's* Sunday color section. The first subject was the adventures of a clown and a dog. Outcault and Goddard experimented with a variety of ideas before Outcault concentrated on a series depicting events in a fictional "Hogan's Alley." One of its characters emerged as the "Yellow Kid," as recounted before.*

The color press also enabled Goddard to give more striking effects to illustrations of feature stories he devised. In any news story, he believed, there was an inherent element of human interest, usually lost sight of in the hurry of the moment. Detecting this note of appeal in a story, he trained his magnifying glass upon it. Sunday *World* illustrators were taught to visualize, strikingly, the central theme of the story, to portray this theme in graphic lines. Feature writers were similarly schooled. Thus it often happened that Goddard and his men, working up a suggestion contained in a single casual sentence of a routine news story, would produce a page feature of enthralling human interest.

Hearst, engrossed in a thousand problems, had observed Goddard's pio-

* This account of the origin of the Sunday newspaper color comic is from a pamphlet, *Fifty Years of the Comics,* published by King Features Syndicate in 1948. See Appendix.

neering experiments with keen interest. And he detected an opportunity to direct the young editor's energy and fertility into broader channels. Hearst visualized a magazine which would not only challenge, surprise and entertain, as Goddard was doing on the *World,* but would also educate and enlighten, a sort of People's University.

This magazine, as Hearst turned the idea over in his mind, would be based primarily upon reality—people, what they did, said and thought. It would seek out the latest discoveries in all branches of science, Biblical lore, astronomy, archeology, etc., and present its findings in plain, simple, understandable English. The whole wide world would be combed for material of vital interest without regard to expense.

In sum, the new magazine would give its readers out of *reality* what novelists were offering them in fiction. This child of Hearst's imagination ultimately became the fantastic and uniquely successful *American Weekly,* bellwether and forerunner of our present-day popular magazine press. With a circulation exceeding 10,000,000 families its readership today, and for many decades past, comprises approximately one-fourth of the entire population of the United States.

While Hearst's ideas were crystallizing, Goddard one Sunday published in the *World* a sensational double-page feature which became famous as the "Girl-in-the-Pie" story. This described in lurid detail a stag supper given by Stanford White and James L. Breese during which, as a climax, a nude model stepped out of a huge papier-mâché pie. Because of the prominence of the men involved, the story created a staggering sensation and boosted the *World's* Sunday circulation that day by more than 100,000.

Hearst read the Girl-in-the-Pie story late Saturday night, chuckled in his almost soundless way and sent for Goddard. The men met about noon Monday in Hearst's hotel suite. George Thompson, the head bellhop to whom Hearst had taken such a fancy that he later made him a permanent member of his household, produced a bottle of vintage wine and fetched in a silver dish of kidneys sauté and eggs.

As Goddard's almost photographic memory recalled the scene for the writer years later, Mr. Hearst outlined much of his personal philosophy, saying that he hoped to build newspapers which would inform and educate, as well as amuse and entertain the masses. Then he outlined his ideas for a new popular Sunday magazine based upon his conviction that truth is indeed stranger than fiction and offered his visitor the editorship at double whatever salary he was receiving from the *World.*

Goddard, who had listened in fascination, pondered. Then he spoke, his eyes as coldly blue as Hearst's own: "Your proposition is tremendously interesting, Mr. Hearst, if you can carry out your plans. But some of the shrewdest men on the *World* claim that you can't possibly last longer than three months more in this town."

The youthful proprietor of the *Journal,* but a year older than Goddard's thirty-one, smiled that inscrutable smile with which his visitor was soon to become so familiar. Without a word, he fished about in the pocket of his vest and pulled out a paper carelessly crumbled. This he tossed across the table. Goddard opened it and discovered a Wells, Fargo & Company draft for $35,000.

"Take all or any part of that," said Hearst quietly. "That ought to convince you that I intend to remain in New York quite some time."

Thus a bargain was struck and Hearst had found another ace coadjutor who aided him mightily in establishing and developing one of the most influential and lucrative ventures in all publishing history. For a full forty years these two men worked as a team, with Goddard as editor.

Goddard brought all of his staff men with him. They reveled in their new surroundings. The *Journal's* circulation began to snowball, cutting down the *World's* lead, sometimes by many thousands each week. Pulitzer was so enraged that he ordered the San Francisco *Examiner* to vacate its office in the Pulitzer Building.

Then he gave even more drastic evidence that he was feeling the pressure, for on the evening of February 7, 1896, Pulitzer turned to his trusted advisers John Norris and S. S. Carvalho, riding with him toward Jekyl Island, Georgia, and said: "Gentlemen, I agree with you. On Monday the *World* will reduce its price to one cent."

Hearst grinned cheerfully, sensing that he had his rival on the run, and opened his financial throttle still wider. In colorful advertisements which greeted the public everywhere, in "El" and streetcars, busses and billboards, on wagons and sandwich signs, the *Journal* proclaimed it merits. "You Can't Get MORE Than All the News; You Can't Pay LESS Than One Cent."

Pulitzer's price cut signalized Hearst's greatest triumph during that hectic first year. Pulitzer's move was designed to crush the three-cent *Herald,* stop Hearst. It seemed that he would succeed when the *World's* circulation jumped 88,000 in a single day. Yet the pinch was felt entirely by the smaller, weaker papers. The *Herald,* darling of the cotillion and club sets, was unaffected and Hearst actually gained.

The *World* was forced to increase its advertising rates. Big advertisers, disgruntled, promptly reduced their linage. Profits fell disastrously. Years later Pulitzer remarked musingly: "When I came to New York, Mr. Bennett reduced the price of his paper and raised his advertising rates—all to my advantage. When Mr. Hearst came to New York, I did the same. I wonder why, in view of my experience."

Meanwhile, Goddard and his men, under stimulus of a free hand and Hearst's constant applause, were outdoing themselves in sensationalism. Full streamer headlines and blazing pen-and-ink drawings dealt with subjects which came to be known satirically as "Crime and Underwear." These were balanced with jazzed-up Biblical tales and reports of startling new scientific theories and discoveries. Solid nuggets of fact were often embedded in the lurid treatment. Prehistoric monsters, who roamed the American Continent, "The Jumping Laelaps of 50,000 Years Ago," were shown in florid copy and half-page or full-page sketches.

Stephen Crane, the boy wonder of literature, wrote a series based upon "real life" in New York's notorious Tenderloin district. Murderers, especially pistol-packin' mommers, were prevailed upon to Tell All, with illustrations. Alan Dale, the *Journal's* dramatic critic, interviewed the French comedienne Anna Held—"Mlle. Anna Held Received Alan Dale, Attired in a 'Nightie' "—and a page pen-and-ink sketch showed the lady thus robed. Winifred Black wrote under such headings as "Why Young Girls Kill Themselves" and "Strange Things Women Do for Love."

Returning from his assignment, and doubtless bemused by its earth-shaking import, critic Dale, spats, cane, striped trousers, pencil mustache and all, was bitten by a delivery wagon horse. Editor Goddard remarked drily: "I didn't know you'd ever covered the Horse Show."

Hearst and his editor recognized instinctively that man's primary interests are, in the order named: (a) Himself; (b) Other people; (c) The world around him; (d) Where he came from; (e) Where he is going. Practically all of the vital material published in the *American Weekly* each Sunday for almost sixty years can be classified under one of these five headings.

The formula eventually was adopted bodily by other magazines in the course of building up nation-wide mass circulations.

Under such enticing stimuli, the *Journal's* circulation went forward in spectacular bounds, attaining almost 400,000 the first year. Although every paper in the city was feeling the hemophilic effect, Pulitzer was the only rival who really fought back. He and Hearst continually raided each other's business and editorial staffs to the vast joy of innocent bystanders and to the financial advantage of reporters, cartoonists, editors, advertising men and others.

The leap in circulation was especially noticeable when the *Journal* installed a markedly improved color press, a product of the combined inventive skills of George Pancoast, experts of R. H. Hoe & Company, and of Hearst himself. Pancoast smashed three machines in an effort to perfect a motor-driven press. Horrified at the loss, Hoe & Company advised Hearst to halt the expensive experiments. Hearst merely grinned and told his mechanical superintendent: "Smash as many presses as you have to, George. Only give us what we need."

The result was that by the fall of 1896, the *Journal* possessed a special Hoe color press capable of printing from four to sixteen pages in colors, "something," the *Journal* proudly quoted the makers, "that had never before been attempted." The *Journal's* blaring announcements of it sneered at the *World's* color supplement as "black and tan," "weak, wishy-washy," four pages of "desolate waste of black."

Richard Outcault and his "Yellow Kid" had come over from the *World* with Goddard, to be one of a gay, historic company of artists in, as the *Journal* boasted, "eight pages of iridescent polychromous effulgence that make the rainbow look like a lead pipe." Hearst was one reader to whom "the Kid" had a compelling interest before it caught the fancy of the general public. As indicated earlier, Hearst was a collector in his boyhood of the comic picture books which the Germans called *Bilder Bücher*. He had been a devoted staff member of the Harvard *Lampoon*. Sketch-art and editorial cartoons had been important elements of the San Francisco *Examiner* from the start of his editorship. He had been responsible for Jimmy Swinnerton's development of "Little Bears" as continuing characters in the *Examiner*. He naturally took up color comics with enthusiasm. Remembering the "Max und Moritz" cartoons of Wilhelm Busch in books he collected as a child, he had Rudolph Dirks start a series with similar characters: the Katzenjammer Kids. He took Frederick Opper, the most versatile and inventive cartoonist since Thomas Nast, from *Puck's* staff to draw for the *Journal*. For it, Opper created "Happy Hooligan," "Uncle Si and Maud the Mule," "Alphonse and Gaston," and a gallery of other comic page immortals. Jimmy Swinnerton, brought on from San Francisco, transformed his "Little Bears" into "Little Tigers" and went on to create "Mount Ararat," "Mr. Batch," "Professor Noodle," and "Little Jimmy." Louis Wain evolved a series of winsome pictures involving tabbycats. Horace Taylor, H. W. Haworth, Carl Anderson, followed these to the *Journal*. With these and others ably abetting him, Hearst did more than any other man to establish the comic page as the most successful circulation builder for newspapers ever invented.

As indicated in a previous chapter, Outcault's switch to the *Journal* did not stop the *World* from printing the "Yellow Kid"; it continued the original "Hogan's Alley" series with another artist, George Luks. The *World* added other comics and tried to outdo the *Journal's* sensational promotion of Sunday color comics. No imagination was required of the editor who started the phrase "yellow journalism" circulating as a description of the tactics of Pulitzer and Hearst.

During his tumultuous first year in the East, Hearst, as we have mentioned, closely imitated the *World* in his headlines and treatment of news.

Both papers played up accidents and disasters, sex aberrations and enticements, criminal trials and suicides. Diagrams marking the spot where the body was found were common. Yet single-column headlines were the rule and there was no marked extravagance of type except in the Sunday feature sections. The *Journal,* like the *World,* sought eye-catching drop-lines, alliterative heads. As a curious sidelight upon his anomalous nature, Hearst always winced at huge, heavily-leaded headlines, although he used more of them than anyone else.

Within a short time, the *Journal* had built up an unexampled array of features; and circulation was rolling in as fast as money was rolling out. Advertisers, as usual, were chary of quickly acquired circulation. A visitor in the cluttered, crowded quarters of the paper was told by business manager Charles Palmer: "Open any closet and you will find money burning." Palmer and a few other close advisers knew that Hearst had dropped more than $2,000,000 in a few months; yet they caught no outward sign of worriment.

In fact, as the first summer drew to a close, Hearst ordered a move which, for boldness and self-confidence, perhaps has never been equaled in journalism. Deliberately doubling his outlay, he established an evening edition of the *Journal.* It appeared first on the streets of New York on September 28, 1896, sold also at a penny, and was intended to rival Pulitzer's *Evening World.*

The *Evening Journal* would be an even more "striking" organ than its morning counterpart. Hearst purposed to compensate for its lack of an Associated Press franchise by presenting through such well known writers as Alfred Henry Lewis, Edward W. Townsend, Julian Hawthorne, Arthur McEwen, Rudolph Block and many others "news novelettes from real life; stories gathered from the live wires of the day and written in dramatic form." This treatment of the news was the herald of the present highly melodramatized form of portraying current events.

Following a disagreement with Pulitzer, S. S. Carvalho had come over to Hearst in April, 1896. This man, of ancient Portuguese-Jewish lineage, had long been one of Pulitzer's right bowers, his last posts being those of publisher and business manager of the morning *World.* A blocky man of satanic appearance who walked with a limp and bred Russian wolfhounds as a hobby, Solomon Solis Carvalho carried in his head encyclopedic knowledge of the publishing business. He had been a fine reporter and city editor, an exceptional managing editor trained under the late Charles A. Dana. As news editor of the *Evening Journal,* he added solidity and strength to the entire organization.

Hearst peered about for another able executive, a circulation builder, and preferably a writer of wide appeal.

By a curious concatenation of events he found his man in Arthur Brisbane, whom Pulitzer had placed temporarily in charge of the *Evening World.* Brisbane, later famous as the "highest salaried editor in the world,"

72

was to prove Hearst's most valuable viceroy, most popular writer, trouble shooter for ailing newspapers, partner in innumerable business ventures and, save for certain periods of estrangement, an intimate friend and confidant.

Brisbane came over to Hearst originally for a mere $200 a week plus a simple little bonus arrangement. This arrangement and the alliance with Hearst was in its fortieth year at Brisbane's death on Christmas Day, 1936, at seventy-two. It proved most profitable for both men. Brisbane's talent for attracting attention and for putting newspapers over with the people and with advertisers was second only to that of Hearst himself. They differed, however, in one vital respect. As his fame and fortune swelled, the pursuit and accumulation of money became a ruling passion with Brisbane; with Hearst, never.

Arthur Brisbane's father was Albert Brisbane, wealthy and erratic follower of Charles Fourier, the eminent French social reformer also, with other idealistic and impractical Americans, a member of the Brook Farm colony. In 1841 Albert Brisbane paid Horace Greeley $150 a week for the privilege of expounding Fourier's theories in a bi-weekly column in Greeley's newly established New York *Tribune*.

Following the death of his mother when he was but two, Arthur Brisbane was raised and educated in unconventional, rather helter-skelter, fashion both in this country and in Europe by his visionary though kindhearted father and the latter's second wife. From his thirteenth to his eighteenth year he lived in Europe, attending a variety of schools, principally in France. His keen, alert mind mastered languages, literature and history with amazing rapidity. His father encouraged intellectual curiosity and talked with the precocious boy for hours on the problems of science and the character of the cosmos. Soon the handsome, athletic youth was discoursing learnedly and without abashment with many famous men. Blessed with an exceptional memory, he stored away a Voltairean array of fact and fable upon which he drew freely in later years. Strangely enough, he displayed no early fondness for writing. This indifference continued for a time even after his father's friend Charles A. Dana had given him a job at $15 a week as a reporter on the *Sun*. Young Arthur reported for work on December 12, 1883, his nineteenth birthday.

"He sat around," recalled one of his contemporary reporters, "like a fellow who didn't understand what it was all about—and then he came out of his trance like a shot from a gun and seemed to know everything about everything."

After two years of reportorial work, the energetic young sophisticate with the penetrating blue eyes and unusually high forehead returned to France to continue certain studies, later becoming London correspondent of the *Sun*. Here he soon became a popular, dashing figure, living in an expensive suite at the Victoria Hotel, riding every morning on Rotten Row, hobnobbing with political bigwigs, and lionized by some of the most highly placed ladies of the Victorian era.

When the gruesome Jack-the-Ripper murders occurred in London, Brisbane's realistic word pictures thrilled and horrified *Sun* readers. They were equally fascinated by his descriptions of the misery and drunkenness in Whitechapel, a slum even more sordid than New York's Bowery or lower East Side. The young man was equally facile in covering Parliamentary debates, and traveled widely on the Continent. In Rome he met and interviewed Pope Leo XIII, then almost ninety years of age. The venerable Pontiff presented him with a poem of his own composition in which he advocated the use of red wines in moderation.

In March, 1888, when John L. Sullivan and the Englishman Charley Mitchell met at Chantilly, France, for their celebrated prize fight, Brisbane was at the ringside and wrote one of his most effective stories. His account contained never a word of pugilistic slang but a great deal else of interest. He saw the human side:—

> Deeply interested were the handfuls of Frenchmen who gathered and watched from such a safe pavilion as we would select to look upon a hyena fight.

And when the other reporters were deafened by the sound of the battle, Brisbane heard the plaintive appeal of Baldock, Mitchell's tough second, to his losing principal:—

"Think of the kids, Charley, the dear little kids a-calling for you at home and a-counting on you for bread. Think what their feelings will be if you don't knock the ear off him and knock it off him again!"

At twenty-three Brisbane was made managing editor of the *Evening Sun*. In 1890 he went to the *World,* where he wrote in the same simple, clear style which had endeared him to *Sun* readers. Joseph Pulitzer was so taken with his versatile recruit that he induced him to become his companion-secretary and for a year they traveled in many waters aboard Pulitzer's yacht. Uncle Joe taught his favorite many things but he could not improve Brisbane's style of writing which had a natural terse, cutting quality, avoidance of all but the simplest words, and direct drive at the object to be attained. Also, Brisbane had early absorbed the Dana principle of editorial writing, iteration and reiteration, incessant drumfire.

After Goddard deserted to Hearst, Brisbane was made Sunday editor of the *World.* Followed a battle royal, with Brisbane and Goddard seeking to outdo each other in freak ideas. Some of their stories and sketches were so lurid that both the Sunday *World* and the Sunday *Journal* were excluded from many homes and clubs. "I had no objection to being barred from the clubs," reminisced Brisbane long afterward, "since it compelled club members to buy the paper individually. However Mr. Pulitzer, as sometimes happens with owners, had an attack of 'respectability.' I remember he once sent me this message: 'Please have on the front page of the magazine in next Sunday's *World* the fine portrait of General O. O. Howard, head of the army, done by Mortimer, and an interview with Howard.' Mortimer made fine portraits in pen and ink. General O. O. Howard would have talked fine platitudes. The following Monday I sent Mr. Pulitzer this telegram: 'Sorry we did not have that O. O. Howard picture and interview. Instead, on the front page, I had a wonderful picture of Kate Swan in the electric chair and circulation is up 15,000.' Mr. Pulitzer telegraphed back: 'You know perfectly well I am blind, and must rely on you. Congratulations.' "

However, Pulitzer soon wearied of the bizarre features concocted around crime, sex and pseudo-science, and ordered them toned down. Goddard kept on and the *Journal* continued to bound forward. Pulitzer, cruising abroad, cabled for Brisbane to take charge of the *Evening World*. Now Brisbane sensed an opportunity to carry out an ambition which he had nursed for years. He wanted above all else to do a daily editorial column under his own signature to be set boldly on page one, column one. It would consist of pithy comment, opinion, and reminiscence along the line of his later tremendously successful "Today" column.

Several times Brisbane had broached the subject personally with Pulitzer but invariably that acidulous genius had replied: "No. You may do big features, news stories, assignment in any part of the globe, but no man, so long as I live, will express independent editorial opinions in my newspapers."

Now, however, Pulitzer was thousands of miles away and, daringly, Brisbane wrote one column, a second, a dozen, which he placed each day on page one, column one in the *Evening World*. Weeks went by. Brisbane was beginning to congratulate himself. Then came a furious cable from a European port: "Stop that column at once. I don't want the *Evening World* to have an editorial policy. If you want good editorials, rewrite those in the morning *World*."

Brisbane, of course, obeyed orders. But he was disgruntled. A few days after the Pulitzer explosion had blown his column off the front page of the *Evening World*, Brisbane wandered into the Cafe Martin. By chance he there ran into Hearst. They chatted and Hearst said: "Mr. Brisbane, I wish you were with us. If you will come over, you may name your own salary. Suppose we talk it over tomorrow?"

Brisbane agreed. Next day he met Hearst in the latter's bachelor apartment adjoining the Hoffman House. It is worthy of note that Hearst's rooms were beautifully decorated with tapestries, bronzes and paintings. Also, that George Thompson, the former bellhop, had been advanced to major-domo. Brisbane said: "If your offer is still open, Mr. Hearst, I'll come with you. But I don't want Mr. Pulitzer to think I am leaving for more money." Hearst, in his usual indolent fashion, asked: "How much do you want?" "Just what I am earning now," replied Brisbane. "Two hundred dollars a week. If, in addition, you want to add a small bonus, I have worked out a plan: Give me one dollar a week for each thousand in circulation I put on the *Evening Journal.*"

Hearst laughed. "That's only a fleabite," he said. "Suppose we make it fifteen dollars a thousand." "No," said Brisbane with remarkable prevision, "I'll make enough at one dollar a thousand." So Hearst sat down at his desk, pulled out a sheet of his pigeon-blue stationery and, in the informal way in which he was accustomed to do business, wrote out a contract in the form of a note to Brisbane. The contract was of doubtful legality, there being no consideration, no witnesses, but (despite many contrary versions which have seen print) that's how Arthur Brisbane went to work for Hearst.

Brisbane's tiny two hundred a week went up to twenty, thirty, forty thousand dollars a year. The informal contract was based upon a survey of circulation every six months. After a year or two Hearst and Brisbane got together and revised it. Then Brisbane was paid $52,000 a year salary. Eventually he received $260,000 a year plus extras.

Arthur Brisbane burst into the dingy *Evening Journal* office like a whirlwind.

Reporting for work at 4.30 in the morning, he insisted that the rest of the staff check in at the same time. Consequently, the paper was on the street hours before the rival afternoon papers, and scored many important news beats as well as multiplying circulation. The other papers were forced to follow suit. The situation took on an *opéra bouffe* complexion when confused newsboys began hawking evening papers at six in the morning, while morning papers appeared as early as six in the evening. Indeed, not until 1935 was an agreement reached between metropolitan publishers regulating the respective hours of sale.

When Brisbane took over, the *Evening Journal* had 40,000 readers; the *Evening World,* 325,000. The new editor prophesied that the *Journal* would overtake its rival "within seven years" and vowed that he would drink nothing stronger than tea or milk until the feat had been accomplished. To the amazement of Newspaper Row, the *Evening Journal* pulled even within seven weeks.

During his second month, Brisbane earned a commission of $9,000. Hearst paid this cheerfully but winced at some of his new editor's double-truck pictures and the huge smash heads on the news stories, which Hearst considered disfiguring. Brisbane pointed to the astronomical rise in the circulation graph and gleefully ordered new type, seven inches high. A picture of concentrated industry, Brisbane sat upon an elevated platform protected by a wire screen, mapping out his campaigns, directing assignments and layouts and, amid the bedlam, pecking out his amazing editorials on an old-fashioned invisible action Remington typewriter.

At night, in his Hempstead, Long Island, home, he would try out his writings on his German housekeeper and, if she did not immediately grasp a point, would reframe sentences and paragraphs in clearer form with fewer big words. To his staff men he constantly preached the virtue of simplicity:—

"There is no need ever to use a word of more than three syllables in a newspaper. Remember that a newspaper is mostly read by very busy people, or by very tired people, or by very uneducated people, none of whom are going to hunt up a dictionary to find out what you mean. And never forget that if you don't hit a newspaper reader between the eyes with your first sentence, there is no need of writing a second one."

Eventually, Brisbane's edicts covered so wide a range that one eminent savant, David Starr Jordan, coined a new word—"sciosophy"—to describe the intellectual farrago which daily poured from the cocksure columnist. Sciosophy, Dr. Jordan defined as "systematized ignorance, the most delightful science in the world because it is acquired without labor or pain and keeps the mind from melancholy."

Arthur Brisbane as caricatured by the man who dubbed him "Big George," T. A. "Tad" Dorgan, in a Hearst organization house organ. The cartoonist is Tad himself.

Fortunately for Brisbane, millions of readers seemed to take issue with the distinguished critic. For they read the Great Thinker of the Hearst Press so avidly and in such constantly increasing numbers that Arthur Brisbane won and held for many years unquestionably the largest personal following of any writer in the world.

In Goddard and Brisbane, Hearst now had under his direction the two most effective circulation-building editors in the country. The figures proved it.

Further, the twin *Journals* were staffed with more and better feature writers and reporters than had ever before been assembled by any American newspaper organization. To name but a few: Julius Chambers, Julian Ralph, Stephen Crane, Richard Harding Davis, Edgar Saltus, James Creelman, Alfred Henry Lewis, Robert H. Davis, Mark Twain, Murat Halstead, Henry W. Fischer, Julian Hawthorne, W. J. Henderson, James L. Ford, A. C. "Nym Crinkle" Wheeler. There was, also, and not least, a group of women writers headed by that incomparable trio: Winifred Black, Dorothy Dix and Ella Wheeler Wilcox.

Richard Harding Davis went to St. Petersburg and reported the coronation of the Czar exclusively for the *Journal*. Ralph was sent to London, Fischer to Berlin, Halstead to Cuba. Mark Twain became a Yankee at Queen Victoria's court and reported the Queen's Jubilee for the *Journal*. As "Dan Quin" Alfred Henry Lewis wrote for Hearst the best Western stories since Bret Harte bade farewell to John Oakhurst.*

Now, with both massive circulation and national influence assured, William Randolph Hearst could devote himself to carrying forward his ideas for the social betterment of the people. The bold, brave crusading days were dawning.

* Collected in the volumes "Wolfville," "Wolfville Nights," "Wolfville Days." The series originated in the Kansas City *Times* in 1890.

Crusader Extraordinary

Your every voter, as surely as your chief magistrate, exercises a public trust.

Inaugural Address, 1885
GROVER CLEVELAND

6

WITH A MAYOR misnamed Strong and a grafting Hibernian called Croker as undisputed boss of Tammany Hall, civic virtue in New York in the mid-1890's was chiefly noticeable by its absence.

On every side ruthless, amoral men were reaching for quick millions. Predatory business and predatory politics were in firm, and for the most part, frictionless alliance. Particulary was this true in the field of public utilities, where silk-hatted harpies such as Thomas Fortune Ryan, William C. Whitney, Jay Gould, and their ilk were exploiting the sprawling, mushrooming metropolis with obscene eagerness and on a massive scale.

With immigration at a peak, the city's population was increasing by tens of thousands annually. Factories, business buildings and miles of dreary tenements and almost equally drab apartment houses, with dark "railroad" flats, were pushing up both sides of Manhattan Island, dispossessing squatters and herds of cows and goats long accustomed to look upon Harlem and Washington Heights as favorite browsing grounds. Jay Gould's elevated railroads, spewing dirt and live cinders upon those below, had reached the Harlem River. Like a spoonfed, starving giant, New York was begging for transportation, water, gas, paving, housing.

The exploiters stepped into the breach—at a price—and then the people discovered that they were being doubly victimized. Facilities of a sort were furnished but at exorbitant tariffs. In mingled rage and frustration, New Yorkers cried out for relief.

As though that anguished petition reached a higher power, there suddenly stepped forward a spokesman and a champion. This was William Randolph Hearst.

Behind a mask of smiling cynicism, the young proprietor of the New York *Journal* and the San Francisco *Examiner* was genuinely sympathetic and protective toward the underdog. From childhood, instances of oppression, injustice or cruelty to the weak, whether man or animal, had aroused not only his compassion but his fighting spirit.

Now, from the steaming crucible of a decade's observation and experience, there had crystallized within him a determination to further a transcendental change in the country's political and economic conditions. He would do what he could to bring about true democracy in America: actual rule by, of, and for the people. In his lexicon, to think was to act.

In December, 1896, just as a graft-ridden Board of Aldermen was complacently preparing to grant a new gas franchise in Brooklyn to a gang of insiders, Hearst went into court, as a citizen and a taxpayer, and obtained an injunction alleging fraud and illegality. The *Journal* labeled the transaction "a $10,000,000 steal" and gave facts and particulars. Within three days the application for the franchise was withdrawn and Hearst composed a significant scare head for page one: "While Others Talk the *Journal* Acts."

This victory was to be followed over the years by innumerable others equally spectacular, many of them waged both in the columns of the paper and in the courts. The targets were rapacious entrepreneurs and combinations of capital in traction, oil, sugar, beef, gas, coal. Accompanied by furious excitements, these battles awakened the people and aroused support and enthusiasm comparable only to the fervor, and sometimes the fanaticism, of a religious movement.

Hearst has been roundly damned, from many angles, for these campaigns. Yet one overriding fact remains. Whatever his motivation, he did succeed in arousing and informing the inarticulate and hitherto unrepresented masses; and his activities bore lasting fruit in legislation and in improved conditions for the plain people. These achievements cannot be ignored or minimized by any impartial present-day critic.

Hearst himself, who was never much given to self-analysis, contented himself at the time with coining a new catch phrase—"What Is Everybody's Business Is the *Journal's* Business"—and with printing an editorial summation of his purposes:—

> Within the past year a new force has appeared on the side of good government in New York. It has been a simple matter for unfaithful servants to squander the resources and trample on the rights of the public. Complaints and denunciations in the press have been as idle as the breeze from a lady's fan. There seemed to be no remedy. But suddenly the jobbers have discovered that the control of a corrupt or careless or stupid board is not enough to carry through a scheme of plunder or of oppression. Above the boards and counsels

and commissions stands the new journalism ready to touch the button that sets the ponderous machine in motion. . . . The *Journal* has adopted the policy of action deliberately and it means to stick to it. It thinks that it has discovered exactly the engine of which the dwellers in American cities stand in need.

These lines appeared at the close of the epochal, emotion-charged Free Silver campaign of 1896 in which Hearst backed the loser, William Jennings Bryan, but won literally hundreds of thousands of new readers and invaluable personal prestige. Since it marked a vital milestone in the publisher's expanding career, it merits recounting in some detail:—

During his second administration, President Grover Cleveland was bedeviled, indeed almost engulfed, by grave financial problems. These centered about powerful movements, in both political parties, to enshrine silver with gold as the nation's basic currency. The resultant drain in gold reserves dangerously weakened the Treasury.

With the silver-producing West and the agrarian South arraying themselves against the banker-dominated East, the agitation for free silver rapidly assumed the fervor of an ethical uprising. Wall Street, with its interlocking web of great banking houses, was accused, with considerable logic, of every crime in the calendar because of the financial community's determination to perpetuate the single standard (gold) upon which its power was largely based.

As the clans gathered in Chicago early in July for the Democratic National Convention, it was evident that a titanic struggle would be waged over the issue of free silver. The Republicans had already nominated an undistinguished party hack, William McKinley, following his belated conversion to gold. William C. Whitney and his stealthy, catfooted partner Ryan led the "sound money" men in Chicago. Hearst and several of his crack correspondents were on hand to see the fun.

They stepped into a flag festooned city, seething with heat, excitement and partisanship. With state delegations and marching clubs arriving hourly, each with its distinctive costumes, banners, bands and slogans, the general atmosphere was that of a mining camp upon which a gigantic revival meeting had descended. Pitchfork Ben Tillman, the South Carolina fire-eater, his single eye gleaming balefully, trumpeted his intention of burying Cleveland, Whitney and the gold standard in the same grave. Picturesque Richard P. "Silver Dick" Bland of Missouri, Horace Boise of Iowa, and other free silver leaders expressed themselves with equal emphasis.

Hearst and his fellow observers from the *Journal* could almost see a handwriting on the wall when the Committee on Credentials threw out the entire Nebraska gold delegation of sixteen, seating in their stead the silverites, in whose ranks was a comparatively unknown young lawyer politician from Lincoln, Nebraska, William Jennings Bryan. When the Nebraskans marched to their places, the silver men went wild, flinging flags, hats and newspapers into the air.

Session by session, the fratricidal struggle continued amid growing tension. The massed thousands in the great hall, many of whom clung to their seat for days, recognized that they were witnessing not only a political but a social revolution. By a vote of 33 to 15, the Committee on Resolutions presented a platform calling for the free and unlimited coinage of silver at a ratio of 16 to 1. Other planks assailed Cleveland's policies and, in effect, labeled the President a tool of the "plutocratic" and the "parasitic" East.

Now came the climactic moment of the convention.

A stoutening young man, with beaked nose, flashing eyes, and shock of dark hair, rose from his seat with the Nebraska delegation and walked with purposeful stride to the platform. This was William Jennings Bryan, come to keep an appointment with destiny.

In his pocket was a manuscript, but he had no occasion to refer to it. For weeks and months he had labored over this speech until he was not only letter-perfect but had carefully rehearsed, over and over again, every gesture, every nuance, every inflection. Blessed with the organ tones of the true orator, Bryan held the delegates and the packed galleries spellbound as he pleaded the cause of free silver and denounced the alleged oppressors of the farmer and the laboring man. His famous closing words, "You shall not crucify mankind upon a cross of gold," carried an indescribable emotional impact.

In the mad pandemonium that followed, one countenance remained impassive. Hearst, sitting a few feet away, observed that wild scene with scientific detachment. However, he realized that Bryan's nomination was now practically a foregone conclusion. The Nebraskan won on the fifth ballot on Friday, July 10.

A few days later the proprietor of the New York *Journal* called a conference of his editorial and business advisers. "Gentlemen," announced Hearst, "I have asked you in to discuss our attitude in the coming campaign. Shall we support McKinley and the gold standard or Bryan and free silver?"

Each man spoke his opinion. And each man was outspoken. "You must either remain on the fence or support McKinley," advised Sam Chamberlain, news editor. "I personally favor Bryan and the Democratic platform," chimed in Arthur McEwen, whose editorials were a dominating factor of the rising newspaper, "but of course we can't support Bryan here in the heart of the gold country." Business manager Charles M. Palmer was even more emphatic. "Any other course than support of McKinley would be suicide," he asserted. "Why, Chief, we have worked like slaves getting advertising contracts. Come out for free silver and every ad of any importance will be taken out of the paper automatically."

Hearst whistled softly and listened carefully. After half an hour, he said very calmly: "I am sorry to disagree with you, but I have made up my mind. Mr. McEwen, write a good strong editorial for Bryan and silver. Get it into tomorrow's paper. Have it played up right, Sam. Good day, gentlemen." He fingered his scarf-pin, fashioned from the first twenty-dollar gold piece taken over the counter of the San Francisco *Examiner,* picked up his gaily beribboned straw hat and walked out of the room, still whistling softly.

In the issue of the following morning the editorial—"The *Journal* for Bryan"—was of course featured and advertisements began to drop out of the paper by the dozens. They stayed out for some time. Hearst lost over a million dollars by that performance, a result which he had anticipated. But the *Journal* was placed on the map once and for all, and established as the leading Democratic paper of the country. Furthermore, a growing army of readers became convinced that America could boast of at least one powerful organ which would place principle above profit. By this single act of courage and independence Hearst won thousands of adherents whose loyalty remained steadfast over the years.

While the great Eastern newspapers, led by the New York *World,* bolted the Democratic ticket in a body, the *Journal* was hailed and eagerly read by the masses. Circulation jumped like a scared rabbit, not alone in New York but throughout the South and West. Within a few months the *Journal* was the best known and most faithfully perused paper from Maine to Texas and from Florida to the Rockies.

The ensuing campaign hit a new high for sound and fury. Hearst the matchless showman at once took up the cudgels for the journalistically-abandoned Democratic cause and put on a display which startled the country by its dash and audacity. Bryan proved an apt performer.

The *Journal's* espousal of Bryan threw the other metropolitan newspapers into a froth of indignation, real or assumed. Hearst was showered with such bitter names as "anarchist," "Jacobin," "socialist," and accused of attempting to destroy all that he should have stood for by birth and training. The editor and his gay young crew enjoyed the fight and proved no green hands at tossing verbal clods.

"I am supporting Mr. Bryan because he is his own man," asserted Hearst. "No syndicate controls him. He came to his nomination by no tricks or dark methods. Slanders and abuse showered upon him after his nomination hastened and heated my judgment to support him. Bryan is not an anarchist, not a public menace. The convention which selected him was not moved by lunacy nor made up of Satan-inspired traitors seeking the overthrow of American institutions."

In the campaign Hearst began unleashing the terrific attacks upon McKinley which were to continue, with brief intermissions, until the latter's

"Wall Street's New Guardian," a caricature of Mark Hanna by Homer Davenport in the New York *Journal,* 1899. Davenport is termed a Hearst major discovery in *A History of American Graphic Humor* (Macmillan, New York, 1938). Hearst hired Davenport for the San Francisco *Examiner* directly from a job as brakeman on the Northern Pacific Railroad. He took him to New York when he bought the *Journal.* (See opposite page.)

assassination in Buffalo five years later. The *Journal* and *Evening Journal* featured cartoons by their self-taught genius Homer Davenport, spread over five or more columns, depicting Mark Hanna, McKinley's mentor, as a gross, bulging figure attired in suits or dresses covered from neck to ankle with dollar signs. Hanna was shown clutching his moneybags to his bosom. A puny little figure labeled "McKinley" was dandled upon the Hanna knee, like the dummy of a ventriloquist, or permitted timidly to grasp the Hanna skirt. The cartoons were savage and effective. Almost all of them were the ideas of Hearst, Chamberlain or Alfred Henry Lewis, Davenport being strong on execution but weak on originating.

Afternoons the big, hulking cartoonist, who had come to Hearst fresh from twisting brakes on the Northern Pacific Railroad, would drop into Chamberlain's or McEwen's office, listen to the talk and pick up his ideas. Then he'd work feverishly at his board for an hour, and bring back a drawing that would be shown to everyone from office boy to proprietor. If the verdict was favorable, and it was, nine times out of ten, Hearst or Sam Chamberlain would supply a snappy caption.

As the campaign progressed, the *Journal* hit upon a new plan to raise funds. Asserting that Wall Street and the interests, generally described in capital letters as "Boodle," had raised a huge McKinley corruption fund, the *Journal* opened its columns for a popular subscription "for the education of the voters of the United States," and offered to duplicate every dollar so subscribed with a dollar of its own. More than $80,000 was contributed, a sizable sum for those days. It was, however, a mere drop in the bucket compared with the money poured into the Republican coffers by the thoroughly frightened leaders of capital and industry.

As for the election itself: Bryan drew the crowds, McKinley got the votes. The final tabulation of the popular vote was McKinley 7,035,638, Bryan 6,467,946; in the Electoral College, McKinley 271, Bryan 176. Overturn of a few tens of thousands of votes, properly distributed, would have reversed the result. Bryan, however, captured the Democratic Party and, save for brief intervals, was to remain its master for sixteen years until the rise of Professor Woodrow Wilson. An even more lasting result was that Bryan and Hearst popularized such "wild" heresies as the income tax and the popular election of United States Senators, which later found place upon the statute books without causing the stars to fall.

The day after the election the *Journal's* presses ran continuously around the clock, without a second's pause, in an effort to supply the demand for papers. Election extras were rushed by chartered special trains to Boston, Buffalo and Washington. The *Journal, Evening Journal* and *Das Morgen Journal* printed 1,506,634 copies—"an achievement," it was declared, "not only unparalleled in the history of the world but hitherto undreamed of in the realm of modern journalism."

As in the early days on the Coast, Hearst was still strictly one of the gang. While he maintained a large office in the front of the building overlooking City Hall Park, he was to be found most of the time in the city room where he knew everyone.

The young boss' enthusiasm for being in on a big story had diminished not a whit. A flash from police or fire headquarters caused a mass exodus from the *Journal* office. Sam Chamberlain's boys leaped into action aboard bicycles, hansom cabs, or any other available contraption. With the knowledge that luscious tips and a lot of fun might be in prospect, daredevil cabbies gravitated toward the *Journal* building, their horses fit and panting.

When a story broke, a motley procession followed pell-mell after the Hearst legions, messenger boys, stray dogs, excited bystanders. To the clamant warnings of bells, the cracking of whips, the strident shouts of leather-lunged cabbies, the lanes of traffic parted, pedestrians scurried for

With his acquisition of the New York *Journal,* Hearst was able to extend into the Eastern States the campaign he had begun in the San Francisco *Examiner* for a new, non-isolationist U.S. policy in the Pacific. The *Examiner* had been the first to point out the "Yellow Peril" to U.S. interests. In 1898, the Hearst papers urged annexation of Hawaii as a bastion against the growing Japanese power. They pressed for construction of an interoceanic canal as a defense measure. In 1905, when the Japs emerged victorious from a war with Russia, the Hearst papers published this prophetic cartoon. The Hearst papers were pleading for strengthened fortifications in the Pacific when the Japanese attacked Pearl Harbor.

cover. Hearst himself often led his "wrecking crew," particularly if the occasion was a fire. He would come leaping from his office, long legs covering the ground like a champion runner, eyes gleaming and a little wild, and jump into a hansom, to be whisked like a field marshal to the scene of action.

The proprietor of the *Journal* ruled with a tolerant hand. Yet none of his brilliant, temperamental crew was ever permitted to doubt for an instant who was boss. One night he came into the composing room and looked over the make-up of the first page. He thought a story being played down was worthy of top billing and suggested a remake. "I agree with you," said the make-up man, "but I am afraid there is no time to reset."

Hearst smiled, without mirth, pushed the whole form off the table, making a beautiful pile of pied type, then remarked with no change of expression: "Now, perhaps, there is time to reset," adding: "There is always time to make a thing better." He was uttering a code from which he was never to deviate in the decades to come.

While conquering tremendous mechanical difficulties, Hearst bent over his paper like an artist over his picture. So canalized and controlled was his cool energy that he seemed to direct the most minute details about the plant and editorial rooms. Yet, miraculously enough, he found time to loll in the park and on Fifth Avenue, to attend art exhibits and theatres, to dine leisurely and well, and to play host at sprightly parties where the food and wines were of the best and the entertainment most enjoyable, though, as has been noted, Hearst drank none of the wine which flowed so copiously for his guests.

Not for a moment, even when his bankroll was melting like morning dew, did he admit discouragement. Always his mother heartened him. Often, in the midst of a crisis, he would stroll with an intimate up the Bowery in the early morning hours and scarcely utter a word. The two would pass the blinking lights of Fifth Avenue, turn in at Hearst's rooms. Then the proprietor of the *Journal* would spread the *World, Herald, Times, Press, Sun* and *Tribune* upon the carpet, spurn them with his toe and remark: "This story isn't so badly handled by the other papers, is it? But our story is a lot more striking!"

On November 8, 1896, one year to the day after Hearst took over, the *Journal* boasted proudly of its "amazing and wholly unmatched progress":—

> The *Journal* has made it its business to reach out for news wherever it is to be had, considering neither precedent, difficulty, nor cost. When the ordinary news channels are blocked or inadequate, the *Journal* despatches its own correspondents to the points, however distant, where the news is to be obtained, and even presses monarchs and statesmen into its service. And these dignitaries are

87

often graciously obliging. His Holiness the Pope and the Queen of Spain and her Prime Minister are among those who have been kind enough to respond to the *Journal's* cabled request for news.

The following September 26, 1897, the *Evening Journal* was host to a first anniversary birthday party at Delmonico's. Among the distinguished guests was the noted toastmaster Senator Chauncey M. Depew, who asserted that the success of the *Evening Journal* was the most startling phenomenon in journalism he had witnessed during his forty years in New York. Hearst and his new young editor Arthur Brisbane, each a phenomenon in his own way, took bows.

In its second year the morning *Journal* reached out for the news even more eagerly than before. December 6 and 7, 1896, it provoked an international sensation by printing exclusively the full text of the Anglo-American treaty of arbitration regarding the boundary between Venezuela and British Guiana, a dispute which the previous year had threatened war between the United States and Great Britain.

The inauguration of President McKinley on March 4, 1897, gave Hearst an opportunity for an exploit that boosted circulation many tens of thousands. A flying special train leased to the *Journal* by the Pennsylvania Railroad set a new record for speed between Washington and New York, 228 miles in 249 minutes. Staff writers pounded typewriters and "lightning" artists made their sketches while the train traveled a mile in thirty-four seconds. In his spare moments Hearst had been experimenting with vitascope motion pictures, and he and his operators took pictures of inauguration scenes. In its account of the exploit, the *Journal* announced that these early motion pictures would soon be on view in every city in the country. Meanwhile, the paper was content with presenting huge double-truck line drawings by artist De Lippman and others showing such impressive spectacles as trials, conventions and horse shows. Some of these drawings, awesome in detail, were spread across two entire inside pages.

Events followed each other with bewildering rapidity. Despite a personal aversion for professional pugilism, Hearst conceived the idea of "sewing up" the championship battle between Bob Fitzsimmons and James J. Corbett in Carson City, Nevada. He purchased exclusive rights to all photographs, interviews and signed statements by the principals for his expanding sports pages, and sent Robert H. Davis and other staff men to the battleground. The versatile Davis pulled a sweater over his head and became "secretary" and sole spokesman of Fitzsimmons. Deliveries were speeded up so smoothly that the *Journal's* fight extras beat competitors to the street by a full fifteen minutes. Such triumphs were of great moment in those pre-radio days.

In March, 1897, the Sunday *Journal,* steadily soaring in circulation under Morrill Goddard, used the first half-tone photographs printed on newsprint.* This indeed was a milestone in newspaper production and Hearst's own expert knowledge of photography was a determining factor in bringing it about. The process was later perfected so that it became possible to reproduce photographs almost as speedily as newsprint itself.

The improvement presaged the end of the graphic sketch artist as sole kingpin of the art department. By the turn of the century, practically every reporter was equipped with a heavy, boxlike camera and competition to obtain exclusive pictures became feverish.

The *Journal* made no attempt to hide its light under a bushel. Mayors, governors and prominent citizens were importuned for endorsements of the paper's action in going to court to remedy local abuses, and symposia printed under such modest spread headlines as "Journalism That Acts; Men of Action in All Walks of Life Heartily Endorse the *Journal's* Fight in Behalf of the People" and "The Development of a New Idea in Journalism," followed by two banks which read: "The Value and the Propriety of the Action of a Newspaper in Invoking the Courts When Public Interests Are in Jeopardy," and "First Employed by the *Journal*, the Novel Conceit Seems Likely to Become an Accepted Part of the Function of the Newspapers of This Country."

When Hearst bought the tottering *Morning Advertiser* April 2, 1897, in order to obtain an Associated Press franchise, he accused the *World* of deliberately plotting to deny the *Journal* membership in the A. P. Joseph Pulitzer was denounced as "a journalist who made his money by pandering to the worst tastes of the prurient and horror-loving by dealing in bogus news, such as forged cablegrams from eminent personages, and by affecting a devotion to the interests of the people while never really hurting those of their enemies, and sedulously looking out for his own." This was the opening salvo in a battle of personal invective between Pulitzer and Hearst that was not to end until after the Spanish-American War.

With the possibility of a Greco-Turkish war looming, Hearst sent James Creelman to Europe as a sort of roving commissioner. As the forerunner of many notable achievements, Creelman interviewed King George of Greece and even succeeded in persuading the monarch to send a cable message to the *Journal*. When the war broke out, Hearst put seven correspondents in the field, including Stephen Crane and Julian Ralph, and sold their exclusive cables to other newspapers. Thus he laid the foundation for his later enormous news and feature services which eventually blanketed the globe.

On April 27, 1897, the *Evening Journal* came out with its first page in colors, and printed five editions to celebrate the dedication of Grant's Tomb on Riverside Drive. Two expeditions, jointly representing the *Journal* and

* *Journalism in the United States,* by Robert W. Jones (Dutton). The New York *Daily Graphic* and other papers had printed photos by a zinc-etching process.

the San Francisco *Examiner,* joined the gold rush to the Klondike, and on August 22, 1897, the Sunday *Journal* devoted a special twelve-page section to articles and pictures of the Klondike.

Under the constant prodding of the proprietor, the paper's editors and reporters outdid themselves in enterprise and sensationalism. A mobile "murder squad" was formed to solve criminal mysteries independent of the police. Liberal rewards were offered. The first pay dirt was struck when the *Journal* men, single-handed, unraveled a mystery which became famous as the Guldensuppe murder case.

The drama began in June, 1897, when the torso of a man, headless, legless, armless, was found floating in the East River. It was carefully wrapped and tightly tied in oilcloth. At intervals, while *Journal* men bayed up and down the town for clues, other parts of the corpse were washed ashore, an arm here, a leg there—all wrapped in oilcloth and tied with swollen, ordinary package twine. Among hundreds who viewed the grisly remains at the Morgue was George Waugh Arnold, a *Journal* staff man and a barrel-chested athlete despite his diminutive stature. Arnold kept himself fit through exercise and frequent Turkish baths at the Murray Hill Baths in midtown Manhattan. His favorite rubber was a hulking man named Charles Guldensuppe.

When Arnold learned that Guldensuppe had not reported for work for some time, his reporter's mind flashed back to the corpse at the Morgue. The corpse's dismembered hands were curiously calloused and the toes on one foot splayed and twisted. Where had he noticed such physical peculiarities before? The reporter returned to the Morgue accompanied by two employees of the Murray Hill Baths. An hour later the *Journal* was on the street with a positive identification and little George Arnold was waving a thousand-dollar bonus from Mr. Hearst up and down Park Row. Simultaneously, the *Journal* reproduced the pattern of the oilcloth in its own colors and assigned thirty men to find the purchaser.

A storekeeper, Mrs. Max Riger, came forward to assert positively that she had sold a bolt of the oilcloth to an East Side midwife, Mrs. Nack. This woman's estranged husband told the *Journal* news hawks that she had been living with a man named Guldensuppe. Eureka!

Mrs. Nack brazened through a denial but investigation proved that she and Guldensuppe had parted after a quarrel and the woman had taken up with a new paramour, one Martin Thorn (real name Torsewski). Mrs. Nack and Thorn were promptly taken into custody. The woman broke under questioning, confessing that she and Thorn had killed Guldensuppe from jealousy, dismembered the body, and threw it piecemeal into the East River. Meanwhile, the missing head had been dragged from the water, completing the identification. Thorn was electrocuted. Mrs. Nack escaped with a sentence of fifteen years.

Although the characters in the drama were lowly and drab the *Journal,* by its treatment, lifted the story to the level of a fascinating fiction mystery and for many days thousands clutched eagerly at the paper's extras.

While rival editors squirmed, the *Journal* boasted that the case had been solved by its great news gathering machinery "under the personal direction of the best editorial brains in the world," and offered its conception of the New Journalism's function in criminal cases: "Time has been when the utmost art of the literary man or the journalist has been employed in making a criminal a heroic figure in an engrossing romance. This was in the era of the old journalism. The New Journalism strives to apprehend the criminal, to bring him to the bar of justice and thereafter not to convict him but to show him as he is."

Again, the New Journalism proudly asserted that it did not await "the cautious handling of professional detectives" but "investigated along its own lines, examining every clue, tracing every rumor and unraveling every theory . . . the *Journal* has made itself the most efficient ally of justice in this city. By the terror it has inspired among criminals it has added materially to the safety of human life. Not only has its staff of reporters constituted a detective force at least as efficient as that maintained at public expense by this or any other city but by enlisting its millions of readers in the work it has created a new instrument of detection of incomparable power."

The paper was insatiable in its search for features, especially those with "woman appeal." On one occasion the entire third page was given over to "Stories of Love and Romance Gathered from the News of the Day." Each of the seven columns was topped by a heart-shaped illustration.

Soon "Letters from the Lovelorn" blossomed out. Beatrice Fairfax, Dorothy Dix and other pioneer menders of broken hearts would write replies to requests for advice from young girls, wives, and, on occasion, young men. Their field was soon broadened to encompass general personal and family problems, thus tapping a rich new vein. From these columns, dripping with sentiment, undoubtedly stemmed a later flood of mawkish "heart-throb" and "confession" magazines, intimate radio and television programs, etc.

The twin *Journals* of those days became a training ground for men Hearst later sent to various parts of the country as executives of papers purchased or founded. Among the men famous in the newspaper world who developed or flowered under Hearst in the late nineties and early years of this century were Charles Edward Russell, Alfred Henry Lewis' brothers, Charles E. and Irving, who later became the owners of the *Morning Telegraph;* Joseph Johnson, Reginald Foster, Charles Michelson, Robert H. Davis, Thomas Vivian, Foster Coates, John L. Eddy, James J. Montague, Clinton B. Fisk, Joseph Mulcahey, Robert McCabe, Martin Dunn, Victor A. Watson, Roy

Daniel, William A. Curley, P. L. "Pete" Campbell, and Fred E. Eldridge.

At that time, with America's *nouveaux riches* striving to outdo each other in prodigality and garish spending, Astor, Vanderbilt and Gould balls were events of the social season. Most of the newspapers treated these functions rather decorously. Hearst showed his rivals how to cover them in a way that would interest the masses. On February 11, 1897, the *Journal* devoted its first five pages to a fancy dress ball which, it declared, cost $369,200. The entire front page contained a sketch drawn by Archie Gunn. There were additional elaborate drawings by E. W. Kemble, Granville Smith and other popular illustrators. Kemble's seven-column sketch portrayed "Some of the Four Thousand Who Were Not in the Cotillion," as contrasted with the four hundred who were.

Hearst's society columns have always been chatty, intimate, satirical and a little bit naughty, aimed to catch below-stairs as well as drawing-room readership.

Under Hearst's insistent leadership and unabated energy, the pace in the *Journal* shop was terrific. Everyone except Hearst himself showed the strain at times and each reacted differently. One morning Sam Chamberlain came down to the office arrayed as usual like a lily of the field. But he seemed restless. He rang his desk bell and said to the head office boy: "Joe, get me a list of sailings for Europe." A Dutch boat was sailing that afternoon. Chamberlain rose, locked his desk, put the key in his pocket, took his hat down from a nail, donned his smart London overcoat, pulled on his smart London gloves, stepped gaily out of the office—and was gone.

Two or three days later Arthur McEwen was looking for Chamberlain. No one knew where the news editor was. McEwen called the head office boy. Joe told his tale of the steamer lists. "Ah," said McEwen, "get me a list." McEwen read the steamship schedules, drew a deep sigh of satisfaction, grabbed his broad-brimmed Western hat from the top of his desk, pulled it down over his eyes, thrust his arms into his rough overcoat—and was gone.

A few days later Mr. Hearst, returning from a trip to Washington, sought out Chamberlain. No news editor. Then he tried to find McEwen. He also was a "mysterious disappearance." Finally Joe came and told his tale. "Ah," said Hearst. He went to the city desk and said: "Give me your brightest young man." And to the brightest young man, Jim Farrelly, he said: "Go down to the business office and get some money. Take the first steamer for Europe. I think you'll have to get one to England. From England go to the Hook of Holland and get to Amsterdam. When you arrive in Amsterdam, walk for about three blocks along the big street where you land. Turn to the left in a little side street. There you will find a small, low house with a green door. Open the door and walk in. There will be a fat, good-natured Dutchman in the room you enter. Ask him where the two tall Americans are, and when he tells you, go and find Mr. Chamberlain and Mr. McEwen and ask them to be kind enough to take the next boat home."

Young Farrelly did as he was bid: arrived in Amsterdam, walked along the broad street, turned to the left up the narrow street, located the little low-roofed house, met the stout, good-humored man smoking a large Dutch pipe. The stout man regarded him attentively, marked well his pantomimic description of the two tall Americans, blew a gust of smoke from his pipe, nodded and threw open a door into a small inner apartment. There, with a glass of schnapps in his hand, on one side of the tall porcelain stove, sat Samuel Chamberlain, news editor of the New York *Journal,* and on the other side sat Arthur McEwen, chief editorial writer for the same interesting publication.

Both started to their feet. Mr. Hearst's emissary delivered his message. The gentlemen nodded courteously. "Arthur, it was a fatal mistake to describe this place so accurately to Hearst," remarked Chamberlain sadly.

"Are you in need of funds?" asked the young man from the office.

The answer was miraculously "No," and in a very short time the missing editors were on their way back to New York, the *Journal,* and William Randolph Hearst. When they arrived there was a new man in charge of the editorial page and a new editor sat at Chamberlain's desk.

"Pardon me," said Chamberlain, "just a moment."

He hung up his smart English overcoat, seated himself at the suddenly vacated desk without disarranging a petal of the flower in the lapel of his smart morning coat, opened his mail and telegrams and stepped into the local room, inquiring as was his wont: "Well, what is this array of talent and beauty doing to make the world brighter and better this morning?"

McEwen's substitute also dutifully evaporated and life resumed in the *Journal* office its hectic, customary course. When Mr. Hearst came in, he greeted the returned prodigals politely, without a word of reproof or admonition, just as though he had seen them every day for the past month.

Similarly, the singular owner of the *Journal* would go to any lengths to conceal acts of charity and personal benefactions. Indeed, to the end of his career, the most striking individualist of his time maintained confidential and discreet almoners to take care of old employees or former supporters who had fallen upon evil times and his personal charities were enormous. Details of some of them inevitably leaked out, to Hearst's unfailing irritation.

When he learned that a schoolteacher in San Francisco had sacrificed for a sick pupil's family funds she had saved to take her mother on a frugal Cook's tour of Europe, he sent the teacher and her mother on a de luxe trip as representatives of his paper "inspecting foreign school systems." The teacher was provided with a batch of blue envelopes in which she faithfully mailed back weekly reports. But not a line of her essays was used.

A stenographer in the *Journal* office suffered a stroke of paralysis one day and was taken home. She was a lighthearted girl, and well liked. Hearst sent her to Europe to take a famous cure and, when this failed, supported her in an expensive sanitarium here.

One day word reached him that what appeared to be the final tragedy had occurred: "She has fallen in love with a man she met in the sanitarium." Hearst was told: "They are both hopeless cripples." The publisher whistled his soft little tune between his teeth and directed: "Find out about the man, what sort he is and what are his circumstances."

The report on the man's character was favorable, but he was poor. Hearst had an apartment fitted up in Brooklyn and, after they were married, moved the two invalids there. The girl's sister and the man's sister went to live with them. The former was provided with a position in Manhattan, the latter kept house. The cripples played chess, read together and eventually died in peace and happiness.

When Bill Hart, one of his star *Examiner* men, was stricken with cancer, Hearst wired Hart's mother to take a drawing room on a fast train and bring her son from San Francisco to New York. Then he cabled to France and brought over a Pasteur specialist who had won a great reputation in Europe through the treatment of cancer. Unfortunately, help came too late. Hearst paid all the bills and timidly exacted a pledge from Mrs. Hart that she would never reveal his part in the affair.

There was nothing timid, however, about the *Journal's* decisive intervention in the exciting New York City campaign of 1897:—

Republican state boss, Thomas C. Platt, had extended the mayor's term of office to four years and was supremely confident of electing his man, General Benjamin F. Tracy of Brooklyn. Tammany nominated Robert A. Van Wyck. Independents rallied behind President Seth Low of Columbia College, who had twice been chosen Mayor of Brooklyn. Henry George was the choice of the more pronounced radicals and his own single-taxers.

Joseph Pulitzer and the *World* beat the drums for Low. Early in the campaign, the *Journal* had many kind words for Henry George and his theories but at the last moment swung its support to Van Wyck, who was elected. Thus began a long series of alliances and misalliances between Hearst and Tammany Hall.

The election over, the *Journal* and its sensation seeking proprietor turned their attention to the Caribbean island of Cuba, where various groups of patriots were agitating, with renewed vigor, for freedom from Spanish rule. With singular lack of foresight, Spain had ground the natives into a state of peonage, denying them even starvation wages for their backbreaking toil in the sugar canefields.

94

The result was that unrest had flamed into open revolt. The movement was secretly financed by a few Cuban plantation owners and American sympathizers, who established a junta in New York and appealed for support to prominent publicists and other leaders of opinion. Only Hearst responded sympathetically.

Already the Cuban patriots knew him as a friend. As long before as the abortive rebellion of 1893–4, the San Francisco *Examiner* had called for American intervention in Cuba. Now, three years later, Hearst, with his extraordinary perceptiveness, recognized in the Cuban situation a great human drama, and rose to it. Soon *Journal* men were pouring into Cuba. Murat Halstead, Richard Harding Davis, Charles Michelson, Frederick Lawrence and others were instructed to expose Spanish oppression. At the same time Governors of all states were asked:

First—Do you favor on the part of the United States such interference in the Cuban revolution, by recognition or the giving of material aid, as would promote the war of independence?

Second—How many volunteers would your state probably furnish for the sea and land forces respectively in case of a war with a foreign power?

Soon atrocity stories of the most harrowing kind, bulwarked by photographs, some real, some faked, bloomed in the columns of the *Journal*. Its readers were told that "the daily practice of the Spanish jailers is to take several captives from the forts and prisons and shoot them"; that Spanish troops reveled in "beating Cuban prisoners to death"; that unarmed peasants, women and children were murdered indiscriminately. In the United States, public indignation and circulation boomed simultaneously. Pulitzer, belatedly sensing that he was missing the boat, sent his ablest correspondents, Sylvester Scovel and William Shaw Bowen, to Cuba.

The Spanish commander, General Valeriano Weyler (the *Journal* promptly christened him "Butcher" Weyler), expelled some of the Hearst representatives. Others were sent and the *Journal* managed to get the news, and to make it. One of the special correspondents was Frederic Remington, the eminent artist, who drew notable sketches of Spanish cruelty. After a short time Remington sent this telegram from Havana:—

W. R. Hearst, New York *Journal*, N. Y.:
Everything is quiet. There is no trouble here. There will be no war. I wish to return.   REMINGTON

Hearst's alleged reply, perhaps his most quoted single utterance, was:

Remington, Havana:
Please remain. You furnish the pictures and I'll furnish the war.
                                                        W. R. HEARST

95

Hearst later privately denied that his telegram was couched in the epigrammatic form quoted. It is doubtful whether so inflammatory a message would have been permitted to pass the rigorous Spanish censorship at Havana. But there is no question that the sentiment expressed accurately reflected the attitude, the desire and the hope of the owner of the New York *Journal.*

Fifteen months later the United States and Spain were at war over the issue of Cuban liberation; and to this day patriotic Cubans of long memory gratefully single out William Randolph Hearst as the chief individual factor in the winning of their country's independence.

THE acts of the terrible savages, or irregular troops called "guerillas," employed by the Spaniards, pass all understanding by civilized man. The American Indian was never guilty of the monstrous crimes that they commit.

Their treatment of women is unspeakable, and as for the men captured by them alive, the blood curdles in my veins as I think of the atrocity of the cruelty, practiced on these helpless victims.

My picture illustrates one case where the guerillas saw fit to bring their captives into the lines, trussed up at the elbows, after their fashion.

FREDERIC REMINGTON.

Guines, Cuba, Jan. 15, 1897.

Fredric Remington —

A Frederic Remington drawing from Cuba in the New York *Journal,* 1897. "The acts of the terrible savages, or irregular troops called guerrillas, employed by the Spaniards, pass all understanding by civilized man," the caption says. "My picture illustrates one case where the guerrillas saw fit to bring their captives into the lines, trussed up at the elbows, after their fashion." This and another Remington drawing were given a full page in the *Journal* on this occasion.

96

A Journalist
Liberates a Country

"This is an official and public recognition by the Cuban people of the enthusiastic and exceptionally useful efforts performed by this eminent citizen of the United States when he defended, through all the instruments of the press at his disposal, the right of the people of Cuba to independence. We Cubans do not forget that when it seemed difficult to obtain the support of the government of the United States to the cause of our independence, Mr. Hearst's New York *Journal* was the flag and instrument in his policy of sympathy for free Cuba"—His Excellency Oscar Gans, Ambassador of the Republic of Cuba to the United States, on Sept. 30, 1949.*

7

IT HAS BECOME a generally accepted axiom that wars are brought about by events, not men. This is unquestionably true today in the infinitely complex pattern of forces which govern international relationships.

Yet, well within the span of memory of many living Americans, one major war *was* brought about by a single individual, William Randolph Hearst, thirty-five years old, who in a brief decade had swept over the surface and depths of journalism, revolutionizing manners and methods, making and changing rules as he pursued his meteoric way.

For the first time, in a matter of supreme national importance, Hearst demonstrated the preponderant effectiveness of intelligently directed newspaper propaganda. Stepping into a fermentative situation, chiefly upon his own initiative, young Mr. Hearst so stirred and marshaled American sentiment in behalf of Cuba's struggle for freedom from Spain that a reluctant President and Congress were forced into war; and the proud flag of Castile, after centuries of dominance, was permanently lowered in the Western Hemisphere, as well as in the Philippines.

"The conclusion seems justified that without W. R. Hearst there would have been no Spanish-American War," it is declared in *Hearst, Lord of San Simeon,* by Bates and Carlson. After conceding "there is little reason to accuse Hearst of deliberate insincerity in the beginning," they then credit him with no higher motivation than a desire to sell papers. Others

* In presenting to Hearst, *in absentia,* Cuba's highest decoration, the Grand Cross of the Order of Carlos Manuel de Cespedes.

echo this accusation. Hostile critics usually overlook the man's congenital aversion to injustice and oppression of the weak. This observation may strain the credulity of those unacquainted with the complex nature of the man from California. Yet time and again, as will become apparent in the course of this narrative, our protagonist deliberately sacrificed the sale of papers in furthering causes in which he believed.

Recalling those brave days, in which he heard the whine of enemy bullets, wrote stories from the actual battlefield, and saw two of his men shot down practically at his side, Hearst commented reminiscently in an interview with the late Damon Runyon on the publisher's seventy-fifth birthday: "Ah, well, we were young. It was adventure."

Historically, the Spanish-American War was a tonic for the United States. With the Blue and the Gray again fighting side by side, it went far to heal the terrible wounds of factionalism left by the Civil War. It unveiled our Navy as a first-class fighting force. It kindled an enthusiasm for expansion which was to sweep us into a tide still running. This latter result was one released genie which Hearst subsequently would have been pleased to chase back into its bottle! *

The New York *Journal* and its proprietor, as we have seen, were far in advance of their rivals in support of the Cuban insurrectionists. Even before President Cleveland turned over his office to William McKinley on March 4, 1897, the *Journal* demanded complete recognition of Cuban independence. Making no pretense of impartiality, it published a flood of atrocity stories, some illustrated by graphic Frederic Remington sketches. One devastating Remington drawing showed a group of lustful Spanish officers brutally stripping the clothing from a Cuban girl at a search point. A wave of indignation swept the country.

Up the street the *World* and *Evening World* sought to ignore the combustible Cuban situation. Joseph Pulitzer's brief service as a cavalryman on the side lines in the Civil War had engendered in him a burning hatred of war. Nevertheless, both his journalistic and highly sensitive commercial instincts soon combined to force him into following Hearst; and for many months the bitter rivals edified the public with a pyrotechnical display of warfare which equaled the struggle in Cuba for sensationalism, blatant disregard of ethics, and ferocious in-fighting. The sanguinary journalistic conflict reached the limit of absurdity after the editorship of the *Evening Journal* was taken over by Arthur Brisbane, glowingly eager to prove to his new boss that he could hit bulls'-eyes and boost circulation to the skies.

With the coming of warm weather in the summer of 1897, the humid island of Cuba was enveloped in a state of siesta. Lethargy gripped both

---

* It might well be wondered what would have been the consequences to the United States in World War II if Cuba had remained a Spanish possession, or if Hawaii had not been annexed in the wake of the Spanish-American War.

the news hounds and the dogs of war. Then, like a bolt of electricity, came an event which under Hearst's dexterous handling was rapidly built into a *cause célèbre*.

One sultry day in August, Hearst was languidly fingering a sheaf of wires and cables in the *Journal* office when an item, filed by correspondent George Bryson, from Havana, caught his eye: "Evangelina Cisneros, pretty girl of seventeen years, related to President of Provisional Cuban Republic, is to be imprisoned for twenty years on African coast for having taken part in uprising of Cuban political prisoners on Isle of Pines." *

The man at the desk sat perfectly still, reading and re-reading the brief despatch. Then he pushed a bell. "Ask Mr. Chamberlain to come here a moment." Chamberlain, quick, energetic, and appearing cool despite the blistering heat, popped in. "Sam!" cried Hearst—and this was one of the few occasions when his news editor had caught a note of real excitement in his voice—"Sam, we've got Spain! Look at this! Get every detail of this case from Havana. Let's draw up a petition to the Queen Mother of Spain for this child's pardon. Enlist the women of America. Have them sign the petition. Wake up our correspondents all over the country. Have distinguished women sign first. Cable the petition and the names to the Queen Mother. Notify our minister in Madrid. We can make a national issue of this case. It will do more to open the eyes of the country to Spanish cruelty and oppression than a thousand editorials or political speeches." The staccato voice went on, rising to a falsetto of excitement: "The Spanish Minister can attack our correspondents, but we'll see if he can face the women of America when they take up the fight! This girl must be saved, if we have to take her out of prison by force or send a steamer to meet the vessel carrying her to Africa—but that would be piracy, wouldn't it?"

Hearst's orders were executed with the precision of exploding firecrackers. Petitions poured in upon the Queen Regent and upon the Pope. Signatories included the mother of President McKinley, the widow of Jefferson Davis, Clara Barton, the adored Julia Ward Howe. Within a few days little Evangelina Cisneros had become a symbol. Thousands of American women had signed the petition and the *Journal,* devoting two or three pages a day to the crusade, announced in a banner headline: "The Whole Country Rising to the Rescue." Adding fuel to the flames, the paper disclosed that Miss Cisneros had been forced to defend her honor from the "bestial" Spanish commandant on the Isle of Pines, then had been removed to the notorious

---

* The history of Cuban rebellion against Spanish rule began long before this. Many from the United States were volunteer soldiers in uprisings of Cuban patriots. One of them is immortal for his last words, facing a Spanish firing squad. Captured by the Spanish while aiding the Narciso Lopez revolt in 1851, William Logan Crittenden of Kentucky refused to obey his executioners' instructions to kneel with his back to the firing squad. "A Kentuckian kneels to none except his God," Crittenden told them.

Recojidas Prison in Havana pending deportation to a "pestilential" penal colony off the coast of Africa. Graphically the girl's situation was described:—

> This tenderly nurtured girl was imprisoned at seventeen among the most depraved negresses of Havana, and now she is to be sent in mockery to spend twenty years in a servitude that will kill her in a year. . . . The unspeakable fate to which Weyler has doomed an innocent girl whose only crime is that she has defended her honor against a beast in uniform has sent a shudder of horror through the American people. . . . She was reared in seclusion and, almost a child in years, is as ignorant of the world as a cloistered nun. . . . This girl, delicate, refined, sensitive, unused to hardship, absolutely ignorant of vice, unconscious of the existence of such beings as crowd the cells of the Casa de Recojidas, is seized, thrust into the prison maintained for the vilest class of abandoned women of Havana, compelled to scrub floors and to sleep on bare boards with outcast negresses, and shattered in health until she is threatened with an early death.

Frantic with jealousy, the *World* sought to stem the tide by minimizing the *Journal's* eagerly read disclosures. It asserted that the Hearst heroine, far from being "ignorant of the world as a cloistered nun," had in fact tried to lure the commander of the Isle of Pines to her quarters where a group of fellow conspirators, concealed behind curtains, waited to assassinate him. Only by chance had the plot been discovered and the ringleaders, including the fair Evangelina, removed to Havana. Further, insisted the *World,* the girl was lodged in a comfortable apartment of her own in Casa Recojidas and was being treated by her jailers with marked consideration. The *World's* counter allegations were indignantly rejected by the romance-loving American public.

While the other papers ignored the harrowing case of the pretty captive as much as they could, the energetic exemplar of the "new journalism" plainly revealed that he had no intention of awaiting the slow processes of diplomacy.

With public fever at its apogee, Hearst called in Karl Decker, his star Washington man, and told him he had determined to rescue Miss Cisneros at any hazard. He asked Decker if he wanted to undertake the mission. Decker, a strapping, courageous Virginian, jumped at the chance. Plans were laid.

The specially selected commissioner arrived at Cienfuegos late in September and met other men employed by the *Journal,* who had carefully worked out a plan to break into Casa Recojidas. The *Journal* men had managed to lease a house directly adjoining the prison. The subsequent course of events has ever since been veiled in an incredible farrago of melodramatic fact-and-fancy.

However, in its issue of Sunday, October 10, 1897, the *Journal* startled the country by announcing in a front page banner head, with seven-column pyramid bank beneath: "Miss Evangelina Cisneros Rescued by the *Journal*. An American Newspaper Accomplishes at a Single Stroke What the Best Efforts of Diplomacy Failed Utterly to Bring About in Many Months." Sub-headlines read: "Taken from Her Loathsome Havana Prison by a Courageous Correspondent," and "Now on Her Way to New York Under the Shelter of the Stars and Stripes."

The front page contained a sketch of "the rescued martyr in her prison garb"; a facsimile of the *Journal's* petition to Her Majesty Maria Christina, and two pen-and-ink drawings showing Miss Cisneros "before and after fifteen months' incarceration." In his first despatch, filed under the *nom de guerre* of "Charles Duval," Decker wrote:—

> Evangelina Cosio y Cisneros is at last at liberty, and the *Journal* can place to its credit the greatest journalistic coup of this age. It is an illustration of the methods of the new journalism, and it will find an endorsement in the heart of every woman who has read of the horrible sufferings of the poor girl who has been confined for fifteen long months in Recojidas Prison. . . . I have broken the bars of Recojidas and have set free the beautiful captive of monster Weyler. Weyler could blind the Queen to the real character of Evangelina, but he could not build a jail that would hold against *Journal* enterprise when properly set to work. . . . A plot had been hatched right in the heart of Havana—a desperate plot as shown by the revolver found on the roof of the house through which the escape was effected. . . . I came here three weeks ago, having been told by the editor of the *Journal* to go to Cuba and rescue from her prison Miss Cisneros, a niece of the former President of the Cuban Republic, a tenderly reared girl, descended from one of the best families in the island, and herself a martyr to the unsatisfied desires of a beast in Spanish uniform.

Disguised as a boy, Evangelina was smuggled aboard an outbound steamer and brought to New York. Decker followed by a roundabout route. For weeks the *Journal* played up its feat to the limit. A half-page sketch showed President McKinley and his Cabinet discussing the rescue. McKinley was represented as reading from the *Journal* Secretary of State Sherman's statement that "everyone will sympathize with the *Journal's* enterprise in releasing Miss Cisneros." "Well, Mr. Secretary," the President was quoted, "I think that you have correctly voiced the unofficial sentiment of the Administration. It was a most heroic deed."

The climax of the exploit (perhaps even of Hearst's resourceful early journalistic career) was an open air reception in Madison Square—another typical Hearst stroke—where more than 100,000 New Yorkers welcomed the slender, dark-eyed little beauty who had come to symbolize her country's struggle, and her dauntless rescuer. Red fire, military bands, such a demonstration that the press of the world was compelled to take note, and it needed but another spark or two—soon to come—to bring on the war Hearst is alleged to have promised.

The dainty and dazed little Miss Cisneros was taken to Washington to meet the President, following which she toured other cities. Everywhere she was lionized and hailed with a wellspring of emotion. Congratulatory messages from governors, senators, prominent women, flooded the *Journal*. For three months a serialized version of the case was featured in the Sunday magazine section. The novelized script was preposterous in many of its imaginative episodes but the public ate it up.

The campaign to compel intervention obtained tremendous impetus when the *Journal's* Washington bureau intercepted a private letter written by the Spanish Minister, Senor Dupuy de Lome, to one José Canalejas, an unofficial Spanish agent in Cuba. The letter described the growing war fever and referred to President McKinley as "a low politician, catering to the rabble."

Hearst pounced upon the phrase. The *Journal* printed a huge facsimile of the letter under a screaming head, "The Worst Insult to the United States in Its History," and a bold-face editorial three columns wide demanding instant recall of the hapless Spanish diplomat.

The next day, February 10, 1898, triumphant headlines proclaimed: *"Journal's* Letter Gets De Lome His Walking Papers" and "Spanish Minister Couldn't Deny the *Journal's* Fac Simile Reproduction of His Infamous Letter, So He Makes a Confession by Silence." Exultant over its victory in the affair, the paper even broke into doggerel verse:—

Dupuy de Lome, Dupuy de Lome, what's this I hear of you!
Have you been throwing mud again, is what they're saying true?
Get out, I say get out before I start to fight.
Just pack your few possessions and take a boat for home.
I would not like my boot to use but—oh— get out, de Lome.

Five days later, on February 15, 1898, came the event that made war inevitable—the destruction by a mystifying explosion of the United States battleship *Maine* in Havana Harbor with an ultimate loss of over 250 American seamen.

Despite two ex parte and asthenic investigations, the cause of the explosion that destroyed the *Maine* is still a matter of naval speculation.*

One of William Randolph Hearst's most acidulous critics, by a tortuous process of questionable logic and guesswork, arrives at the weird conclusion that the publisher himself was responsible for the sinking of the *Maine*. Charles Edward Russell, who was city editor of the *Journal* at the time, correctly characterized this pipe dream as "preposterous and beneath the dignity of serious authorship."

Yet the very theory itself is a reflection of the frenzy and hysteria which swept the country following the disaster. Needless to relate, the New York *Journal* and its indefatigable proprietor pulled out all the stops. The issue of Thursday, February 17, was a masterpiece of Hearst's evocative art. Seizing a pencil, he wrote out an offer of a reward of $50,000 which was played up in boxes and streamer headlines. The boxes read:—

$50,000!

$50,000 REWARD!

For the Detection of the

Perpetrator of

The *Maine* Outrage!

The New York *Journal* hereby offers a reward of $50,00 CASH for information FURNISHED TO IT EXCLUSIVELY, which shall lead to the detection and conviction of the person, persons or government criminally responsible for the explosions which resulted in the destruction, at Havana, of the United States warship *Maine* and the loss of 258 lives of American sailors.

The $50,000 CASH offered for the above information is on deposit with Wells, Fargo & Co., and will be paid upon the production of the convicting evidence.

No one is barred, be he the humble but misguided seaman eking out a few miserable dollars by acting as a spy, or the attaché of a government secret service, plotting by any devilish means, to revenge fancied insults or cripple menacing countries.

This offer has been cabled to Europe and will be made public in every capital of the Continent and in London this morning.

The *Journal* believes that any man who can be bought to commit murder can also be bought to betray his comrades. FOR THE PERPETRATOR OF THIS OUTRAGE HAD ACCOMPLICES.

W. R. HEARST

* A board of inquiry convened by the United States Navy in 1911, when the *Maine's* hulk was raised from Havana harbor to remove it as a navigation menace, concluded that a form of explosive exterior to the ship had caused the first explosion. The source of this explosive was not pinned down. Spanish authorities stuck to their story that an internal explosion, perhaps spontaneous combustion in the coal bunkers, had been the primary cause. The *Dictionary of American History* lists the destruction of the *Maine* as an unsolved mystery.

From the beginning the *Journal* took the position that the *Maine* had been blown up by the Spaniards. The lead headline in the city edition asserted flatly, "Destruction of the War Ship *Maine* Was the Work of an Enemy"; while a "6 a.m. extra" proclaimed: "The War Ship *Maine* Was Split in Two by an Enemy's Secret Infernal Machine." A seven-column sketch, placed in the center of the first of eight pages devoted to the disaster, showed the ship anchored above mines connected with a Spanish fort ashore. It was captioned: "Naval Officers Think the *Maine* Was Destroyed by a Spanish Mine." A sub-caption read in part: "The Spaniards, it is believed, arranged to have the *Maine* anchored over one of the harbor mines. Wires connected the mine with a powder magazine, and it is thought the explosion was caused by sending an electric current through the wire. If this can be proven, the brutal nature of the Spaniards will be shown by the fact that they waited to spring the mine until after all the men had retired for the night. The Maltese cross in the picture shows where the mine may have been fired." Another sub-head announced: *"Journal* Sends Divers to Havana to Report Upon the Condition of the Wreck."

The *Evening Journal* printed the first Sunday extra of an evening newspaper on February 20. It featured a Brisbane creation, a two-page illustration purporting to show "How the *Maine* Actually Looks as It Lies, Wrecked by Spanish Treachery, in Havana Bay." Circulation for the three days following the loss of the *Maine* totaled 3,098,825 copies, setting a new all-time mark for an American newspaper.

In a Broadway bar an unknown man raised his glass and solemnly said: "Gentlemen, remember the *Maine!"* thereby furnishing a slogan that was to ring around the world. At 154 Nassau Street, Hearst and his men produced great double-page color spreads, pen-and-ink sketches and provocative news stories under such heads as: "No North, No South, One United Country!"; "Sections Widely Apart Welded by a Common Impulse to Avenge Heroes of the *Maine!"*; "The Union Ablaze with Patriotism— Every State Ready to Spring to Arms at a Moment's Notice!"; "Desperate Work to Hold the United States Senate in Check"; "No War—But Night and Sunday Work on Big Guns Goes On, Sabbath Toil and Rush of Soldiers to All Seaside Forts."

On February 24, the first eight pages of the *Journal* appeared as the "Maine News Section." The Sunday *Journal* jumped 200,000 in circulation in six weeks. The *Evening Journal* reached 519,032, "a record," it proudly boasted, "never before equaled by any afternoon paper published in the English language or any other language." Dynamic Arthur Brisbane was well on the way to his first million under his generous bonus arrangement with Mr. Hearst.

The entire front page of the "Maine News Section" was taken up with sketches of the *Journal's* "War fleet, correspondents and artists." George

Washington's calm and imposing features appeared in the "ears" of the paper, at either side of the title, looking down upon the "two fast yachts *Buccaneer* and *Anita* and tug *Echo;* War Correspondents Julian Hawthorne, Karl Decker, James Creelman, A. H. Lewis, George E. Bryson and William E. Lewis; artists Frederic Remington and William Bengough." Hearst, assuredly, was ready for war.

The administration delayed, however, and all through March and early April Hearst hammered away hotly. The *Journal* roundly berated President McKinley, the Cabinet and Mark Hanna, charging boldly that the purpose of the procrastination was to enable speculators to pile up profits in Wall Street.

McKinley's advisers were dubbed the "Wall Street Cabinet." A Davenport cartoon showed Mark Hanna as the Goddess of Liberty in a robe covered with dollar signs. Hanna's avaricious eyes, glued to ticker tape, were eagerly watching quotations on the Stock Exchange. "McKinley and the Wall Street Cabinet are ready to surrender every particle of national honor and dignity," read one *Journal* attack. The paper quoted Theodore Roosevelt, Assistant Secretary of the Navy, already chafing to get into battle, and who was doing a little jingoing on his own account: "It is cheering to find a newspaper of the great influence and circulation of the *Journal* tell the facts as they exist and ignore the suggestions of various kinds that emanate from sources that cannot be described as patriotic or loyal to the flag of this country."

Roosevelt indignantly denied the alleged interview, characterizing it as "an invention from beginning to end" and adding: "I never in public or private commended the New York *Journal*. . . . I have never given a certificate of character to the *Journal*." This was the first of many occasions when these two masters in the art of swaying the public were to refuse "certificates of character" to each other. Yet each had a concealed respect for the other's great abilities. Colonel Roosevelt once told the writer that Hearst excelled any one he had ever known in his facility at "cutting across lots and anticipating public opinion."

Joseph Pulitzer, whose own chauvinism was swelling in direct proportion to his circulation figures, played up Roosevelt's rebuff of the *Journal* and snarled that Hearst's war news was "written by fools for fools." Ex-President Cleveland also took occasion to rebuke Hearst. Refusing to serve upon a committee formed by the *Journal* to raise funds for a *Maine* memorial, Mr. Cleveland wrote: "I decline to allow my sorrow for those who died on the *Maine* to be perverted to an advertising scheme for the New York *Journal*."

The scholarly Edwin Lawrence Godkin in the *Nation* and the *Evening Post* was even more caustic, roundly denouncing both the *Journal* and the *World*. He asserted that the multitude "have already established a regime," in which "a blackguard boy [Hearst] with several millions of dollars at his

105

disposal has more influence on the use a great nation may make of its credit, of its army and navy, of its name and traditions, than all the statesmen and philosophers and professors in the country. If this does not supply food for reflection about the future of the nation to thoughtful men, it must be because the practice of reflection has ceased."

Godkin went on to declare that nothing so disgraceful as the behavior of the *Journal* and the *World*—"newspaper firebrands scattered broadcast throughout the country"—had ever been known in journalism, adding: "Their business is not to promote public happiness or morality but to 'sell

SAILORS GIVING THE DOLPHIN A COAT OF WAR PAINT.

Front page of the New York *Journal,* Sunday, March 27, 1898. The headlines were small compared to those the *Journal* used after war was declared a month later. (See text, next page.)

106

the papers.' The resources of type have been about exhausted. Nothing in the way of larger letters can be used, unless only a single headline is to be given on the first page. Red ink has been resorted to as an additional element of attraction or terror, and if we had a war, the whole paper might be printed in red, white and blue. In that case, real lunatics instead of imitation lunatics should be employed as editors and contributors. . . . A yellow journal office is probably the nearest approach, in atmosphere, to hell existing in any Christian state. A better place in which to prepare a young man for eternal damnation than a yellow-journal office does not exist."

However, sober voices such as Godkin's were but whispers upon the gale. With a roar and a whoop, war was declared on April 11, 1898.

Then came a new outburst of typographical violence. Brisbane introduced block letter headlines into the *Evening Journal,* some seven inches high. The itchingly ambitious Boy Wonder of Park Row also enticed the pennies by concocting a new type of headline in which the huge first line gave a very different impression from the second line in tiny type, as:—

BIG BATTLE (96 pt)
Is Expected (agate or small pica)

However, there was plenty of real and tremendous news in the brief three-month campaign and Hearst, as was his wont, poured out more than $500,000 above ordinary expenses in covering it. So thoroughly were his newsgathering and communications facilities organized (even carrier pigeons were used), that beat after beat was scored over rivals. At one time the Hearst papers had under charter two yachts, an ocean-going tug, six steam vessels, a Brazilian cattle boat and a Red Cross boat. The Hearst news service functioned so beautifully that competitors resorted to filching news from *Journal* bulletin boards. After this practice had gone on for some weeks, Arthur McEwen of the *Journal* put a temporary stop to it through a hoax that became a Park Row classic:—

An item posted on the *Journal's* bulletin board told of the death in gallant action of a brave volunteer with our Cuban allies, an Austrian officer, Colonel Reflipe W. Thenuz. An hour later the *Evening World* blared the story on its front page. The *Journal* was hard on its rival's heels with the revelation that the heroic colonel was a mythical character, the letters of whose name, rearranged, spelled out: "We pilfer the news." The *Evening World* dropped the story amid laughter by *Journal* readers (see next page).

At the beginning of the war, Hearst was aflame with the idea of equipping a regiment of cowboys, including some of the men from the family ranch with whom he had roamed California woods and streams, but the government politely declined. The editor was told that Theodore Roosevelt had already been authorized to organize a regiment of rough riders.

NEW YORK JOURNAL COLORED SUPPLEMENT, SUNDAY, JULY 10, 1898.

HOW "THE NEW YORK WORLD" GETS ITS NEWS.

THE JOKE

The Journal knew that the New York World was stealing its war news, but made no protest until the World, in addition to stealing, became "sassy." Then the Journal decided that the whole world should know of these daily thefts. So one bright morning the Journal took the words "We Pilfer the News" and arranged half the letters backwards to read "Reflipe W. Thenuz," and saddled the name on an Austrian colonel who had never lived. In the Journal that day appeared the notice that "Col. Reflipe W. Thenuz was killed."

The World snapped at the bait as a hungry dog snaps at a bone, and after dressing it up in the form of a special cable dispatch, forging to it the name of a war correspondent and dating it "On board the World's dispatch boat," announced boldly next day that "Col. Reflipe W. Thenuz was dead."

So that if you read these letters properly you learn from the World's own mouth "We pilfer the news."

Ha! Ha! Ha!

THIS IS THE PRIZE JOKE OF THE CENTURY.

A full-page cartoon in the New York *Journal,* Sunday, July 10, 1898 following the *Evening World's* entrapment as a news-stealer. (See previous page.) One careless biographer of Hearst got mixed up and made it appear that the *Journal* stole the "Col. Reflipe W. Thenuz" story from the *Evening World.* Others picked up the mistake from him.

Hearst then offered the government his yacht, the *Buccaneer,* without cost. This offer was accepted and Hearst was given an honorary commission of ensign in the Navy.

The editor chartered the British steamer *Sylvia* and a whole fleet of tugs and led twenty correspondents, artists and photographers to the war zone, including J. C. Hemment, pioneer motion picture photographer. A crew of printers with hand presses helped to get out a Cuban edition of the *Journal* which was distributed gratis among the camps and the fleet, thus becoming a forerunner of the latter-day *Stars and Stripes.* Also aboard was Hearst's genial chum Jack Follansbee who, with Arthur Brisbane and the host, shared bachelor quarters in the new house Hearst had purchased at Lexington Avenue and Twenty-eighth Street. The sedate brownstone mansion, formerly the home of Chester A. Arthur, was always referred to by its irreverent new occupants as "the Shanty."

At the actual scene of war, Hearst was in his element. He fed raw meat to his men and roused them to extraordinary efforts. Edward Marshall, one of the *Journal's* most brilliant correspondents, was shot twice in the spine at El Caney. Before a young army surgeon, Dr. William C. Gorgas, later of Panama fame, amputated his left leg in the rude field hospital, Marshall dictated his story of the battle to a colleague. Hearst got the narrative out in time to score a beat which boosted circulation a hundred thousand in New York, and then hurried back to hover tenderly over the sorely stricken man. Marshall lived thirty-five years longer, surviving three train wrecks, two hotel fires, a lake steamer sinking, and the torpedoing in 1916 of the English Channel steamer *Sussex.*

While the struggle raged, people throughout the country were ecstatic with patriotism. In *The Martial Spirit* (1931) Walter Millis catches this atmosphere excellently:—

> The war extras followed one another through the streets in a torrential outpouring; and the war correspondents, flocking into every camp, every naval station, and into every possible or impossible theatre of action, loaded down the wires with detailed accounts of every move made or contemplated. Any feeble opposition put up by the browbeaten authorities on the score of secrecy was imperiously brushed aside. After all, if it was not the newspapers' war, whose war was it? When the Navy fitted out a vessel as a hospital ship, she was immediately stormed by whole battalions of reporters, who calculated that as she would have to hurry from the scene of battle to land the wounded, she would be the first to reach the telegraph wires. Mr. Long [Secretary of the Navy] managed to keep them off; not, however, because they might reveal military secrets, but because he believed news to be "contraband of war"

and thought that their presence might destroy the ship's neutrality. . . . Already, by April 26th, Mr. Pulitzer was selling 1,300,000 copies of the *World* a day; and as the editorial writers of the country settled to the serious business of conducting operations, a triumphant journalism was definitely in command. Even the sedate *Atlantic Monthly* stunned its readers by appearing, actually, with an American flag upon the cover and after that it seemed that patriotism could indeed go no farther.

Journalistic insolence reached a peak when the *World's* irascible correspondent Sylvester Scovel, becoming embroiled in a quarrel with General Shafter, struck the commanding officer in the face and was saved from court-martial only by the intervention of President McKinley.

Although ubiquitous in their pursuit of news, no such disgraceful episode marred the work of the Hearst expeditionary force. In one of his earliest letters, Hearst bespoke the confidence of the people in their military leaders:—

"General Shafter and his officers have accomplished almost a miracle in landing sixteen thousand soldiers with food, arms, ammunition and equipment in small boats through a rough surf on the steep, dangerous beach, between ugly reefs in almost killing heat. . . . The work was all done and well done in four days. . . . The spirit of the army is high."

Gay as a schoolboy, spurning danger, Hearst rode from camp to camp and battlefield to battlefield and often visited the fleet. His hurriedly written despatches, although few in number, contained some exceptionally fine descriptive passages. General Shafter was a "sort of human fortress in blue coat and flannel shirt." General Calixto Garcia, venerable Cuban insurrecto leader, received Hearst in spotless white and presented him with a battle flag in commemoration of the journalist's long fight for Cuban independence. Tears coursing down his bronzed cheeks, the gnarled old warrior said with emotion:—

"The colors of this flag are faded, and it is pierced with bullet holes, but brave men have died under it. This flag is the best gift the Cuban Republic can offer its best friend."

Hearst sent the flag to his office in New York, then from the improvised parade ground described what he saw:—

From the top of the ridge where I write I see the monstrous form of Sampson's fleet lying in semi-circle in front of the entrance of Santiago Harbor, while here at our feet masses of American soldiers pour from the beach into the scorching valley. Vultures wheel lazily above the thorny, poisonous jungles. They have already fed on corpses of slain Spaniards. Santiago and the flower of the Spanish fleet are ours, although hundreds of men may have to die before we take possession of them.

Hearst's most notable article, which has often been cited as a graphic example of war reporting, was a full-page account of the Battle of El Caney:—

> With the army in front of Santiago, July 1, midnight, via Kingston, Jamaica.
>
> Tonight as I write, ambulance trains are bringing wounded soldiers from the fierce battle around the little village of El Caney.
>
> Siboney, the base of the army, is a hospital and nothing more. There is no saying when the slaughter will cease. Tents are crowded with wounded, and hard worked surgeons are busy with medical work. There is an odor of antiseptics, and ambulances clatter through one narrow street.
>
> Under the fierce firing of far heavier artillery than it was supposed the Spaniards had, the American infantry and dismounted cavalry have done their work and done it nobly.
>
> I have been at the artillery positions all day to see what our guns could do. There is no question of the skill and courage of American gunmen. Their work is as near perfect as gunnery gets to be. The War Department furnished the necessary heavy guns, but they remained in the rear because of the difficulty of transporting them from the coast.

Hearst described an early morning ride on horseback with Honore Laine, a Cuban colonel, who accompanied him as a guide. They rode for miles over rough terrain, dodging bullets and viewing the surging combat at close range:—

> We found that a shrapnel ball had passed clean through one of our cans of pressed beef which our pack mule was carrying.
>
> We turned to the right toward our battery on the ridge. When we were half way to the battery, the second shell which the Spaniards fired burst over the American battery not ten feet over the heads of our men. Six of our fellows were killed and sixteen wounded. The men in the battery wavered for a moment, then rallied and returned to their guns, and the firing went on.
>
> We passed to the right again where General Shafter's war balloon was ascending. Six shells landed in this vicinity, and then our battery ceased firing. The smoke clouds from our guns were forming too plain a target for the Spaniards. There was no trace to be seen of the enemy's battery because of their use of smokeless powder. . . .

Through glasses our infantry could be seen advancing toward the fort.

As the cannon at our side would bang and the shell would swish through the air with its querulous note, we would watch its explosion and then turn our attention to the little black specks of infantry dodging in and out between the groups of trees. Now they would disappear wholly from sight in the brush, and again would be seen hurrying across the open spaces, over the grass-covered slopes or across plowed fields. . . .

The Spaniards fired in volleys whenever our men came in sight in the open spaces. Many times we heard this volley fire and saw numbers of our brave fellows pitch forward and lie still on the turf while the others hurried on to the next protecting clump of trees. For hours the Spaniards had poured their fire from slits in the stone fort, also from their deep trenches and from the windows of the town. For hours our men answered back from trees and brush and gullies. For hours cannon at our side banged and shells screamed through the air and fell upon the fort and town.

And always our infantry advanced, drawing nearer and closing up on the village, till at last they formed under the mangrove tree at the foot of the hill on which the stone fort stood. With a rush they swept up the slope and the stone fort was ours.

Hearst ended his despatch with a poignant personal note:—

Laine and I hurried up to the stone fort and found that James Creelman, the *Journal* correspondent with the infantry column, had been seriously wounded and was lying in the Twelfth Infantry Hospital. Our men were still firing an occasional shot. From the blockhouse and isolated trenches from which the Spaniards could not safely retreat, flags of truce were waved. Guns and side arms were being taken away from such Spaniards as had outlived the pitiless fire, and their dead were being dumped without ceremony into the trenches after Spanish fashion.

When I left the fort to hunt for Creelman I found him bloody and bandaged, lying on his back on a blanket on the ground, but shown all care that a kindly, skillful surgeon could give him. He was pretty well dazed and said, "I'm afraid I can't write much of a story. If you will write it for me I will describe it the best I can."

Creelman had been painfully wounded in the shoulder by a dumdum bullet and spent weeks convalescing in hospital and aboard the *Sylvia*. Hearst took down his story and added a point related to him by others, that Creelman had charged up the slope with the first wave of infantrymen, seized a Spanish flag and waved it in encouragement of the oncoming American troops.

112

During the decisive naval battle of Santiago Bay, the *Sylvia* edged as close to the combat as possible. In a couple of hours Admiral Cervera's proud fleet was completely destroyed, either sunk or lying upon the beach, burning hulks. At one spot on the sand was huddled a group of survivors from the gutted Spanish flagship *Vizcaya*. After being all but swamped, a heavy naval boat manned by marines had given up an attempt to make them prisoner.

Hearst, his eyes dancing, turned to George Pancoast and exclaimed: "Let's get them!" "All right," replied Pancoast, "those fellows don't know how to beach a boat." The *Sylvia's* small boat was lowered and succeeded in negotiating the breakers. Wet, bedraggled and miserable, the enemy sailors, twenty-nine in number, were huddled together for warmth. Hearst pulled off his pants and shoes and leaped into the surf. Brandishing a huge revolver, he shepherded the quite willing prisoners into his boat.

Back on the *Sylvia,* Jack Hemment made the frightened and dripping prisoners kneel and kiss the flag while he photographed them to his heart's content, after which they were clothed and fed. From the lanyards blossomed a signal, "We have prisoners for the fleet," and the *Journal* yacht proceeded majestically through the re-formed line of American warships, seeking to deliver their captives. She drew up first alongside the *Oregon,* whose bluff old Captain Clark was on the bridge. Through a megaphone, Hearst shouted: "We have twenty-nine Spanish prisoners on board. What shall we do with them?"

"Keep 'em," barked the skipper. "You took 'em. You can take care of 'em."

"But, Captain, think of the glory."

"Think of the yellow fever," rejoined the captain.

Hearst did, and the thought increased his desire to get rid of his captives. Finally, the converted cruiser *Harvard* reluctantly agreed to accept the men. Writing whimsically of the incident many years later, Hearst observed:—

"We knew that no one would ever believe that we had taken twenty-nine prisoners. So we demanded a receipt. We got it, signed, sealed and delivered. 'Received of W. R. Hearst 29 Spanish prisoners.' We have it framed."

Hearst was not the only personage whose dignity was slightly dampened on that historic day. On board the *St. Louis* he encountered Admiral Cervera, an imposing figure in full dress uniform, gold braid, decorations and all. But the courtly Spanish commander's trousers were still wet as a result of wading ashore from his burning flagship.

At the inception of the war, James Creelman was in London for the *Journal*. There was grave apprehension in America lest Admiral Camara's powerful Mediterranean fleet should move by way of the Suez Canal to

113

attack Dewey in the Pacific. Two American monitors with ten-inch guns were steaming across the Pacific to the Philippines to reinforce Dewey. It was a critical situation. Had Camara's fleet reached Manila Bay before the arrival of the slow monitors, Dewey might have been overwhelmed.

In this exciting and perilous hour, Hearst addressed to Creelman one of the most remarkable communications ever written by a private citizen in time of war. Carefully preserved by Creelman and reproduced in his book *The Broad Highway,* the letter reads:—

NEW YORK JOURNAL
W. R. HEARST.

Dear Mr. Creelman:-

I wish you would at once make preparations so that in case the Spanish fleet actually starts for Manila we can buy some big English steamer at the eastern end of the Mediterranean and take her to some part of the Suez Canal where we can then sink her and obstruct the passage of the Spanish warships. This must be done if the American monitors sent from San Francisco have not reached Dewey and he should be placed in a critical position by the approach of Camara's fleet. I understand that if a British vessel were taken into the canal and sunk under the circumstances outlined above, the British Government would not allow her to be blown up to clear a passage and it might take time enough to raise her to put Dewey in a safe position.

Yours very truly,

W R Hearst.

Camara's fleet actually entered the Suez Canal on its way to attack Dewey, but the attempted execution of Hearst's daring maneuver was averted by the hasty return of the Spanish warships to the threatened coast of Spain. Hearst, of course, was aware that his scheme would be a grave breach of international law, but to him it represented a combination of practical patriotism and a truly Napoleonic stroke of advertising for the New Journalism.

It is interesting to note that the young naval constructor, Richmond P. Hobson and his daring crew of seven, employed precisely the same strate-

114

gem on the night of June 3, 1898, when they sank the collier *Merrimac* in the channel entrance of Santiago Harbor in an unsuccessful but heroic attempt to block the egress of Admiral Cervera's fleet.

During the frenzied war period, all known records for newspaper sales were broken by the *Journal*. The day Dewey's victory at Manila was announced, May 2, 1898, the paper issued a stream of extras that followed each other as fast as the huge octuple and quadruple presses could turn them out. Circulation reached a new mark of 1,600,000. During the war approximately 1,500,000 papers were printed and sold each day, and even at the close of the year sales averaged 1,250,000. The influence of the typographical extravagance brought about by the *Journal's* use of spread-eagle type is shown in practically every American newspaper today.

Hearst's quarrel with Spain ended with eminent satisfaction to him. Cuba was free. Its first President, Tomas Estrada Palma, cabled him, "I do not believe that we could have secured our independence without the aid which you rendered." Hearst was voted the Cuban Grand Cross.

As for Evangelina Cisneros herself, there was a romantic epilogue.

She married young Carlos Carbonel, a member of Karl Decker's rescue party. Their only daughter, studying art in New Orleans, died tragically at seventeen. Later, widowed, Evangelina remarried and lives with her present husband and two daughters in Havana. "My country and I," she said with simple conviction after learning of the award of the Grand Cross, "owe everything to Mr. Hearst and the American people."

It is one of the ironies of Hearst's massive career that in later years he grew increasingly fond of Spain and of Spanish art. More than one of the numerous treasures on his great California estate were purchased in Spain and transported to America. Over the years he made several visits to Spain and was cordially received by the late King Alfonso, who was a mere lad playing on the beach at San Sebastian when Hearst wrote his surprising letter to James Creelman. The publisher also enjoyed more or less cordial relationships with subsequent Spanish regimes, including that of Francisco Franco.

Back at his desk in the *Journal* office, Hearst found that things were going well. Circulation was holding its own. Brisbane was beginning to build up advertising for the evening edition. Joseph Pulitzer was glad to declare a truce "by mutual consent" in the debilitating personal warfare which had caused him to draw upon his working capital for the first time since he had taken over the *World*. Deficits were being reduced. Hearst could see daylight ahead.

Accordingly, he posted off on a brief pleasure trip to Italy. In Verona, he was welcomed as the Grand Signore who, a few years before, had so admired a wonderful old Roman wellhead that he had purchased it for

One of the "Little Willie and His Pa" cartoons by Frederick Burr Opper
in the Hearst papers in the Presidential campaign of 1900 (see page 117).
"Little Willie" was President McKinley; "Pa," Mark Hanna. "The most
fecund and popular of the newspaper cartoonists of the new century," is
the tribute paid to Opper by Thomas Craven in *Cartoon Cavalcade* (Simon
& Schuster, New York, 1943). Craven reports having polled comic artists
"on the relative merits of their brethren, dead or alive, and without a dis-
senting vote, all proclaimed Opper the 'funniest man ever connected with
the daily press in America.'"

116

a fancy price and had it transported to his mother's ranch in California. Mrs. Phoebe Hearst was so delighted with the unique gift that she installed the wellhead in her garden and changed the name of her place to "La Hacienda del Pozo de Verona." Now laughing, dark-eyed women gathered about the munificent visitor and showed him with vast pride their new well and runways which permitted them to let down their buckets and draw water up to the second floor balconies.

With the twin *Journals,* the mixture was as before, based upon a realization that the mass mind must be shocked or amused before it could, or would, assimilate more mature material. In the winter of 1898–9 a crusade against polygamy was launched. Winifred Black went to Utah and interviewed Mormon women. "Crush the Harem; Protect the Home!" read a headline over one of her stories. Robberies and murder mysteries were still played up, rewards offered for the apprehension of criminals.

Headlines continued to be snappy and striking: "She Fell in Love with a Man's Face in a Soap 'Ad' "; "Fight for Fair One; Both Lads in Limbo."

On January 1, 1899, the *Journal* exclusively printed the full text of the Spanish-American peace treaty and protocols—"a journalistic achievement," it asserted, "believed to be entirely without precedent. Such enterprise makes senatorial secrecy an absurdity." Soon the Senate made public both the treaty and the protocols.

The inimitable Frederick Burr Opper had been brought in to become creator of an amazing array of comic characters, including "Happy Hooligan" and "Maud the Mule," which delighted two generations of youngsters and grownups. Opper's "Willie and His Pa" depicted President McKinley as the creature of the trusts. In contrast with the blasting attacks of Homer Davenport, these hilarious slapstick sketches were without venom. No one seemed to enjoy them more than the President himself who, with Opper's aid, collected a set of signed originals.

Editorially, the *Journal* campaigned for the annexation of Hawaii, a larger navy, establishment of West Indies bases, construction of a Nicaraguan canal to link the Atlantic and Pacific, and enlargement of the "great national universities at West Point and Annapolis." On February 5, 1899, Hearst enunciated a far-reaching domestic policy including public ownership of public franchises; destruction of "criminal trusts"; popular election of United States Senators; and greater development of the public school system.

The sponsor of these measures was in deadly earnest. Yet he realized that not one of them could be accomplished without a hard struggle. Perhaps he could fight best inside the government. Hearst was turning the idea over in his mind as the Presidential campaign of 1900 approached.

In the Political Arena

8

OFTEN, IN ATTEMPTING to reconstruct a life, the biographer is balked by the sheer multiplicity of events. Blending these into a smooth pattern is about as simple as bottling smoke.

Hence one must resort to chronological narration to obtain an unblurred picture of Hearst's prodigious, variegated activities and achievements in the years immediately clustering about the turn of the century.

Early in 1900, it became apparent that the Democratic Party would again nominate William Jennings Bryan for the Presidency. Bryan and other leading Democrats joined in urging Mr. Hearst to establish a newspaper in the Midwest, where the party was without an influential organ.

Hearst hesitated. Chicago was a notoriously tough newspaper town, strewn with failures. Of its eight papers, only the powerful *Tribune* and Victor Lawson's *Daily News* were successful. H. H. Kohlsaat was on the ropes with his *Times-Herald*. John R. Walsh was sinking large sums in the *Chronicle*. Joseph Dunlap had abandoned the unlucky *Despatch*. Charles T. Yerkes' traction swollen fortune could not pull the *Inter-Ocean* out of the red. Even the able Scripps-Booth outfit, after four years, was eager to sell its *Journal* and return to Michigan, as it did in 1904. This was the dour prospect any newcomer faced.

After a struggle which had taken heavier toll than he had ever admitted to anyone, Hearst felt that his metropolitan newspapers were no longer a financial gamble but that moving on to Chicago was a hazard to say the least, and premature. At this juncture, around Decoration Day, 1900, Bryan renewed his plea that a Hearst paper be launched in Chicago. "All right," said Hearst, "if the leaders will recognize that I am doing it for the party's sake, not for the money."

Bryan, Senator Jones, chairman of the Democratic National Committee, and other leaders gave the assurance gladly and, as a token of gratitude, made Hearst president of the National Association of Democratic Clubs. The publisher's acceptance marked his personal entrance into practical politics.

Hearst called in S. S. Carvalho, publisher of the New York *Journal,* and asked him to leave at once for Chicago. "The new paper must appear in thirty days," he said. "Let's plan on getting out the first issue on July 4. We'll call it the Chicago *American.*" The assignment was herculean but Carvalho was equal to it. Three large octuple presses, with color and "fudge" attachments, were shipped from New York by express freight. Lino-type machines were transported in Pullman cars.

Eschewing Newspaper Row, Carvalho leased a dingy but substantial and commodious old building belonging to the Steuben County Wine Company in West Madison Street, between Fifth Avenue and Franklin Street. Within an incredibly short time, eight hundred men were working around the clock in three shifts and the whole run-down neighborhood was humming with activity. Arthur Brisbane came out from New York to edit the first edition and Hearst himself, of course, was everywhere.

Early on the morning of July 4, William Jennings Bryan wired "Start the presses" and instantly was audible the deep, rhythmic sound, unlike any on earth, and pure rhapsody to compositor, printer, pressman, and every ground-at-the-stone newspaper man. Again Will Hearst was making history.

The first issue carried the following message from Bryan:—

> *Dear Mr. Hearst:*
> Chicago, Illinois, and the States of the Upper Mississippi Valley are to be congratulated upon the establishment of the *American,* a name admirably suited to a paper which will represent an American policy for the American people on all questions domestic and foreign.
> The fact that your paper was established not merely to make money, but because of your desire to aid the Democratic Party in the fight in the Central States, and because of the expressed desire of the Democratic leaders that you should duplicate in Chicago this year the splendid work done by the *Journal* and the *Examiner* in 1896, ought to commend the paper to the friends of democracy, and I am confident that a large circulation awaits the Chicago *American.*
>
> *Yours truly,*
> *William Jennings Bryan*

Bundles of papers were rushed to the Democratic Convention Hall in St. Louis, where the delegates waved them in triumph. On the next day, July 5, Bryan was nominated to make his second race for the Presidency.

The established Chicago newspapers did not make the mistake of denying Hearst credit for rare intelligence, unbendable will, and dashing, if sometimes bewildering, methods. They knew a dangerous rival had come to town and they gave him a rough reception. Broad-shouldered, big-fisted fellows were employed to discourage newsboys and newsdealers from selling the new paper and to discourage the public from buying it. It was a kind of competition Hearst had never before encountered. But he quickly adjusted himself and discovered that not all the husky, brine-fisted men in Chicago had enlisted with the opposition. Many of the others were soon drawing pay from Hearst.

There ensued a short, decisive guerrilla warfare, marked by sharp clashes between Hearst and anti-Hearst drivers, delivery men and guards. Balinghooks were brandished and a number of heads were broken. Brawny vendors were sent out from the Hearst plant in squads. These took positions at strategic points and fought with knuckles and billies for the privilege of selling the *American*. In the Loop district the police were kept busy quelling incipient riots.

"After a few days I noticed an inclination on the part of the opposition to cease hostilities," Hearst chuckled in an interview with the New York *Herald* on July 24, 1900. "That was agreeable to me, and the large-fisted gentlemen have gradually drifted back to their old vocations, and Chicago citizens are now able to buy whatever papers they want without creating a riot. Our circulation has gone up from 115,000 to 150,000. We get our first 'afternoon edition' on sale soon after sunrise. That's doing pretty well for a youngster, and the people of Chicago seem to think an evening paper at six o'clock in the morning is a pretty good joke. There are six regular later editions, with a few extras thrown in as occasion requires."

Subsequently there were other long and bloody circulation wars in Chicago, sometimes intermingled with the rivalries and blood feuds of gang overlords. For many years Hearst's numerous enemies sought to blame him for initiating Chicago's scandalous saturnalia of crime, a canard which by now has been thoroughly exploded. However it must be added that Hearst and his men have never been accused of backing away from a fight with unseemly celerity.

In fact, the Chicago *American* and its morning counterpart, the *Examiner*, which came along in May, 1902, quickly became known as the most uninhibited of the Hearst papers. Its daredevil staff men and its able, hard driving (and thoroughly unscrupulous) editors became legendary. The picture, in all its rowdy nakedness, is accurately presented in the Hecht-MacArthur melodrama, *The Front Page*.

120

In the election of 1900, Hearst and Joseph Pulitzer, surprisingly, found themselves on the same side. Foxy old Joe had learned his lesson from the gains coming to Hearst in 1896 and this time deemed it expedient to forego his earlier apostasy of Bryan. But not all the thunderings of the *World* against "imperialism" and the shouts of Hearst against "plutocracy" could put Bryan over. The Commoner was defeated by 137 votes in the Electoral College; his popular vote 150,000 smaller than in 1896. Free silver as a pivotal issue had passed.

In that campaign, Hearst listened and learned. With lines sharply drawn between Haves and Have Nots, he foresaw the rise of a new democratic movement in America where the people, under stronger leadership than Bryan had given them, could be induced to combine and shake off their economic shackles. He began to feel the time would soon come when he himself could personify the new movement.

"My early ambition," he explained years later, "was to do my part in newspapers. This I still intended to do. But when I saw mayors and governors and presidents fail, I felt that I'd like to see if I couldn't do better. I felt I'd like to go into office, almost any office, to see if I couldn't do the things I wanted to see done."

A ready instrument in Hearst's astute hands was the National Association of Democratic Clubs. The publisher appointed his Washington correspondent, Max F. Ihmsen, corresponding secretary of the leagued clubs and for years the organization was in a sense a Hearst property, supported and absolutely controlled by him. In the second Bryan campaign these clubs acquired an enrolled membership of nearly 3,000,000 and were to prove of immense value four years later when the master of "striking" journalism judged the time ripe to strike out for the White House.

Like so many of his innovations, Hearst's idea of a one man political organization was unique. The officers would be his employees; the workers in his pay; the committees to be of his choosing; his word to decide policies and platforms. He would treat with other parties, for he wanted their votes, but he would not be bossed by their bosses. He would be his own boss.

Hearst had no illusions either about the intellectual limitations of the masses or about the character and capacity of the politicians, although he had sympathy for the former, cold contempt for the latter. Deepening experience convinced him that political organizations were largely made up of noise and boasting; and that most of the men who did the real work among the voters could be controlled by anyone with sufficient audacity to proclaim himself leader and pay for the printing, music and red fire.

Early in 1901, leaving his simmering political moves in the hands of lieutenants, Hearst sailed away for a leisurely photographing and art buying trip to Europe and the Near East.

Even on this holiday, his uncanny journalistic sixth sense led to his becoming a decisive factor in a matter of great international import. This concerned forcing through Congress vital amendments to the Hay-Pauncefote Treaty between the United States and Great Britain dealing with a proposed isthmian canal.

When the pact was in final negotiation, Hearst was traveling up the Nile, his third visit to a land that always held much enchantment for him. His eye caught a paragraph in a fortnight-old English newspaper stating: "The treaty has been signed and ratified by the British Cabinet. All that remains is ratification by the American Senate. The United States and Great Britain agree the proposed canal *shall not be fortified.*" The phrase italicized exerted a galvanic effect upon the American publisher.

He scribbled a note upon the back of an envelope, summoned a native messenger and rushed the courier to the nearest cable office, seventy miles away. The following night the message reached Hearst's executives in New York: "Better no canal than an unfortified canal. Marshal every resource at your command. Fight ratification of the Hay-Pauncefote Treaty."

The newspaper proprietor's words detonated an explosion which became historic. The battle lasted a year: on the one side Hearst and the public sentiment he was able to arouse, on the other President McKinley, John Hay, the British Government and practically the entire non-Hearst press of the day.

Hearst was victorious, the American Senate refusing to ratify the original draft of the treaty. Hearst's position was powerfully supported by Theodore Roosevelt, who had been swept into office as Governor of New York on the strength of his Spanish War record. Roosevelt wrote his old friend Hay: "You have been the greatest Secretary of State I have seen in my time—Olney comes second—but at this moment I cannot, try as I may, see that you are right. Understand me. When the treaty is adopted, as I suppose it will be, I shall put the best face possible on it, and shall back the Administration as heartily as ever; but oh, how I wish you and the President would drop the treaty and push through a bill to build *and fortify* our own canal!"

When the Senate Committee on Foreign Relations also adopted the Hearst viewpoint, Secretary Hay, bitterly disappointed, sent a letter of resignation to President McKinley containing a significant phrase: "I cannot help fearing also that the newspaper attacks upon the State Department, which have so strongly influenced the Senate, may be an injury to you if I remain in the Cabinet." McKinley refused to accept the resignation and the Hearst-Hay battle was still on when tragedy prematurely ended McKinley's term.

The treaty was to come again before the Senate. Theodore Roosevelt, now President, called his eminent Secretary of State to the White House. Placing his arm about the shoulder of his friend, Roosevelt said: "John, I love you and I despise Hearst. But, dammit, this time Hearst is right! We must have a fortified canal."

The treaty was modified and ratified, all because the vigilant Hearst in Egypt almost two years before had caught sight of a short paragraph in an old English journal! Stating unequivocally that Secretary Hay was wrong, William Roscoe Thayer, Hay's biographer, writes: "Secretary Hay himself was converted to the need of fortifying the canal; and no doubt the advent of Mr. Roosevelt to the Presidency hastened his conversion."

While this triumph was developing, fate dealt Hearst a devastating blow on September 6, 1901, when President McKinley was shot by a psychopathic anarchist at the Pan-American Exposition in Buffalo, N. Y. He died eight days later in a Buffalo hospital.

At once, a wave of hatred against Hearst and his papers swept the country. They were charged with direct responsibility for the assassination. In many communities, as though by spontaneous design, Hearst was hung in effigy, sometimes in concert with a grotesque figure representing Emma Goldman, the country's most notorious anarchist.

Passers-by pelted the dangling dummies with various missiles. Small boys hooted and jeered. When the authorities cut down the effigies, bonfires fed by Hearst papers were lighted north, south, east and west. A cry of rage sounded across the continent. The Hearst organs were boycotted by many church groups and business organizations; the papers were cast out of numerous homes, clubs and libraries; thousands signed pledges to patronize no cafe, barber shop or public resort subscribing to the "anarchist sheets." Meeting Charles Edward Russell in the composing room of the Chicago *American,* Hearst remarked, "Things are going to be very bad." He kept a loaded revolver in his desk.

Yet, ironically, the Hearst papers had scored a notable scoop on the shooting itself:—

Pete Campbell, the *Evening Journal's* head office boy, whose brain was as nimble as his legs, received the fateful bulletin over the phone through a message relayed from the only wire open near the actual scene of the tragedy. He threw open the door of his phone booth and yelled across the city room to Foster Coates, managing editor: "McKinley shot at Buffalo Exposition by a crank. Bulletin from Publisher's Press." Mr. Coates yelled back: "Verify it by phone," and while Campbell was doing this called the Fudge room and dictated a bulletin and story.

Half a century later, Mr. Campbell, beloved veteran of many posts in the Hearst organization, described swift-moving subsequent events as though they had happened yesterday.

"The bulletin came to Publisher's Press and to us through John Tremain, an Albany correspondent," he said. "Being a good reporter he had quietly spotted the only telephone on the grounds while walking about with the

Presidential party. The flash came in to us at 3.32 p.m. and the paper was on the street exactly twelve minutes later with a huge red line across the top of the page and a story set in a two-column box. The time element favored the *Evening Journal* which had an agreement with the *Evening World* not to release the presses until 3.45 on the 'Sports Special' edition. Each paper had a man in the other's press room to enforce the agreement. Both papers had gone to press, it being a dull day for news, and were just waiting for the release of the presses. Then came our smash head and story. In Buffalo, Tremain's phone went permanently dead. The confusion was indescribable. Our story could not be verified for more than an hour. During that time, every other paper in the world had to content itself with quoting our account."

It is doubtful if any American ever faced a wilder and more concentrated storm of abuse than that which burst over Hearst and his organs following the shooting of President McKinley. Murderer, anarchist, scoundrel were among the milder epithets. Leon Czolgosz the assassin was even offered $10,000 "for his family" if he would state that he had been inspired by the Hearst papers. Stolidly Czolgosz replied that he had never seen or read a Hearst paper. He went through his trial and execution unwavering in this denial.

Rival newspapers and other enemies used with telling effect an editorial attack upon President McKinley by the *Evening Journal* on April 10, 1901, in which it was asserted: "If bad institutions and bad men can be got rid of only by killing, then the killing must be done." Widely quoted also were lines written by Ambrose Bierce in 1900 following the assassination of Governor Goebel of Kentucky:—

> The bullet that pierced Goebel's breast
> Can not be found in all the West;
> Good reason, it is speeding here
> To stretch McKinley on his bier.

Although Hearst's castigations of McKinley had been biting, as has been amply noted, these specific attacks had been printed without his personal knowledge. Indeed, when the first papers containing the "assassination" editorial reached his desk, Hearst ordered the presses stopped and the editorial "toned down." However, a sufficient number of *Journals* had gotten into the hands of the critics to furnish deadly ammunition in the current crisis.*

Hearst himself evidently realized that he had gone too far in his assaults

* In *Art Young: His Life and Times* (New York: Sheridan House, 1939), the well-known Socialist cartoonist said, "But to hold him [Hearst] responsible for the killing of McKinley because of a bitter editorial, a poem, and Frederick Opper's cartoons of 'Willie and his Papa'—Willie being the President and Papa being Mark Hanna, both favorites of the overfed trusts—was far-fetched."

upon the President. Months before McKinley was shot, the owner of the *Journal* sent James Creelman to McKinley to express regret that his newspapers, in the heat of political warfare, had indulged in excessive personal attacks.

"Mr. Hearst offered to exclude from his pages anything that the President might find personally offensive," said Creelman years later. "Also he pledged the President hearty support in all things as to which Mr. Hearst did not differ with him politically. The President seemed deeply touched by this wholly voluntary offer and sent a message of sincere thanks. These facts are given as an explanation of the actual terms upon which Mr. Hearst and Mr. McKinley were living when Czolgosz fired the fatal shot."

Bierce explained afterward that the purpose of his famous quatrain was to warn of the danger of "this particularly perilous precedent if unpunished," and said Hearst never knew of the verse until after it was published. Bierce added for the record that Hearst never rebuked him nor even mentioned the matter. The charge, though, was to stalk Hearst for many years.

Indeed, President Theodore Roosevelt, who in private was wont to refer to McKinley contemptuously as "chocolate eclair," went out of his way in his first message to Congress to describe his predecessor's assassin as "a professed anarchist, inflamed by the teachings of professed anarchists, and probably also by the reckless utterances of those who, on the stump and in the public press, appeal to the dark and evil spirits of malice and greed, envy and sullen hate. The wind is sowed by the men who preach such doctrines, and they cannot escape their share of responsibility for the whirlwind that is reaped."

When Hearst was running for Governor of New York in 1906, Roosevelt authorized Elihu Root, his Secretary of State, to declare that the President when uttering these words "had Mr. Hearst specifically in his mind." Hearst's reply was to redouble assaults upon Root, whom he always portrayed as a "jackal of the interests," and sedulously sought to couple Root with the latter's former star client, "Boss" Tweed.

During the entire uproar, which lasted for weeks, the Hearst counterattack was sharp, and never defensive. The *Journal* asserted: "The sum of the *Journal's* offenses is that it has fought for the people, and against privilege and class pride and class greed and class heartlessness, with more and varied weapons, with more force and talent and enthusiasm, than any other newspaper in the country." In a signed editorial, Hearst himself summed up his position and epitomized a journalistic philosophy from which he was never to recede:—

> From coast to coast this newspaper has been attacked and is
> being attacked with savage ferocity by the incompetent, the failures

of journalism, by the kept organs of plutocracy heading the mob. The Hearst papers are American papers for Americans. They are conservative papers, for the truest conservatism is that radicalism which would uproot revolution-breeding abuses. . . . All the enemies of the people, of the democratic people conscious and unconscious—all who reap where others have sown, all the rascals and their organs, and many fools caught by the malignant uproar, are yelling at the *Journal*. LET THEM YELL.

In New York, the *Sun* led the anti-Hearst pack. Hearst recalled that he had supported Dana's printers when they were locked out. He quoted letter and text of the vituperation heaped by the *Sun* upon Bryan during both of the Commoner's campaigns. The *Sun* also had assailed Grant, Garfield and Hayes as "boodlers," "frauds" and "corruptionists," carrying its hatred of Garfield and Grant beyond the grave. Another critic, the *Evening Post*, Hearst asserted, had referred to McKinley as a "liar," "renegade," "traitor." President Cleveland had been accused by the *Post* of permitting his unfortunate illegitimate child to languish in a Buffalo almshouse, although he himself was well-to-do. The *Sun* had once demanded that Cleveland be buried under such an avalanche of votes that never again would he dare aspire even to the office of hangman.

"The Hearst papers," their founder wrote, "rely on the plain people as did Lincoln. The people understand the Hearst papers."

Apparently the people did, for they soon returned Hearst to his mountain top.

When the tempest had subsided, the *Journal* still boasted the largest net paid circulation in the world, having gained 100,000 in September, 1901, over the preceding year. Also, in August and September it had gained almost four hundred columns of display advertising, while the *World* showed a loss.

However, although he had remained outwardly placid throughout the storm, Hearst found it expedient to change the name of his morning newspaper in New York; and on October 17, 1902 it blossomed forth as the New York *American*.

With the White House as a possible end of the road, Hearst realized that he must make a beginning as an active officeholder. Accordingly, in the fall of 1902, he entered into an alliance with Charles F. Murphy, leader of Tammany Hall, thus initiating an association which was to be characterized by alternate periods of peace and discord for twenty years.

Murphy had become the sole boss of Tammany, succeeding a triumvirate of which he was one and which had been dubbed "Sport," "Two Spot" and "Joke" by "Big Bill" Devery. The Republicans had control of the city, Croker having deserted New York for the more lenient precincts of his native Ireland; and Tammany's fortunes and coffers were low. In the state, David B. Hill, arch foe of Tammany, still aspired to be Democratic state leader. However, the former Governor's star was waning. Men high in the councils of the party were openly advocating throwing him overboard as a Jonah.

Charles Francis Murphy, dour, silent, deep, wanted to cut his eyeteeth as a boss grandly by forcing the nomination for Governor of Bird S. Coler, New York's "honest Comptroller." He therefore welcomed an offer of Hearst's support and gladly promised to nominate the publisher for Congress from the midtown district in which Hearst resided.

Thus it came about on the afternoon of October 6, 1902 that a delegation of old-line Tammany leaders, whose rough-hewn faces showed their curiosity at meeting the young "hellraiser" for the first time, called upon Hearst at Democratic headquarters in the Hoffman House, and solemnly informed him that "the Democratic voters of the Eleventh Congressional District of the City of New York, in convention assembled on the second day of October, 1902, by unanimous choice, named you as their candidate for Representative in Congress."

In a voice which scarcely carried to the corners of the small, private room, and with a stenographer from his newspaper present, Hearst read a speech of acceptance that was to launch him upon a long and tempestuous career as an office seeker. Peter Dooling, James J. Frawley, George Washington Plunkett and the eleven other Tammany Hall war horses comprising the Notification Committee looked at their youthful candidate wonderingly. Could this pale, nervous person flutteringly fingering his manuscript be the bold crusader who was employing his papers like a Thor's hammer in support of John Mitchell and the anthracite coal miners and who had bluntly called the leader of the mining interests "Divine Right" Baer and informed the coal-carrying railroads they ought to be fined and their directors jailed for rebating?

Hearst's timidly uttered words in that speech of acceptance crystallized the social and political theories which had been forming in his mind ever since he had begun his assaults against "pirate privilege" in the tiny San Francisco *Examiner* fifteen years before. He said in part:—

> I believe that of the eighty millions of people in this country, five or six millions (the most prosperous five or six millions) are ably represented in Congress, in the law courts and in the newspapers. It would be immodesty on my part to imagine that I could add much to the comfort or prosperity of the few who are so thoroughly well looked after. My ambition is to forward the interests of the seventy millions or more of typical Americans who are not so well looked after. Their needs seem to offer a wider field for useful effort.

127

At the same time let me say that I do not seek to divide the nation into classes or foster unreasoning dislike of one class by another. I can recognize the genius and generosity of the great captains of industry; of Mr. J. Pierpont Morgan, for instance, who gives a splendid hospital for poor women, educational buildings to Harvard University and treasures of art to the Metropolitan Museum, but I feel that Mr. Morgan can take care of himself. My interest is in the average American citizen. The welfare of the country demands that he too shall secure a fair share in the advantages of prosperity. . . .

I do not mean to say that the genius of the great captains of industry is not of much benefit to the community in many ways; I do not mean to say that their charities are not highly commendable— but I do say that a situation such as the present one brings into strong contrast the difference between the enormous power of the trust magnate and the helpless position of the average citizen. . . . A real danger threatens the country today in the great power and arrogance of the trusts that defy the laws and laugh in the face of the President of the United States when he begs them to avert a public calamity.

Nothing is so important to the people as the regulation of this financial power which has suddenly overshadowed the power of the government itself. The means of controlling these great industrial giants must be discovered and applied before the power of the trusts gets absolutely beyond control. There is no objection to legitimate organization in business. But there is every objection to the injurious, illegitimate, illegal organizations known as the trusts which absorb and suppress all competitors in order to establish a monopoly and exercise that monopoly—as in the case of the Beef Trust—to compel the payment of extortionate prices by the helpless public.

Congress must deal with the matter through law, and therefore Congress first of all must be made to represent the people and not the trusts. The people will never be protected against the trusts by a Senate in which the trusts occupy many seats and control a majority. A first step, therefore, will be "The Election of United States Senators by the People."

Given the election of a truly representative Congress, the next step will be such modification of the tariff as will permit outside competition with illegal combinations and will prevent the trusts from selling their products dearly at home while they sell them cheaply abroad. With the regulation of the tariff there must come wise application of the principles of "Government Ownership of Certain Public Utilities." It is not advocated that the government engage in all the branches of industry which the trusts have managed to monopolize. A natural beginning will be the government ownership of railroads and telegraphs. These are as legitimate objects of government today as the post office was when that was first taken over by the government.

Adequate laws must be passed to punish criminally trust owners and officers for criminal infractions of the law. The whole complicated system of civilized society, from policeman to President, was devised to prevent the powerful and unscrupulous individual from overriding the rights of his weaker brethren. The laws must now be applied and where necessary must be strengthened to protect the people against that powerful and unscrupulous criminal combination known as a trust.

In a district always safely Democratic, Hearst was elected by a record-breaking plurality. On election night he held open house at the Hoffman House and the *Journal* sponsored a mammoth display of fireworks in Madison Square Park. While the photograph of the Congressman-elect was being flashed on a stereopticon screen and the crowd was yelling or hooting good-naturedly, a mortar used to set off rockets exploded and turned part of the park into a shambles. Almost a hundred persons were killed and injured. There was consternation in the *Journal* office. The paper was hastily made over and the story of the rally relegated to an inside page, without illustrations or a drop of red ink.

The young man from the Eleventh New York District went into a national law-making body dominated by old-line Republican stalwarts, such as Quay, Platt, Penrose, Hanna, "Uncle Joe" Cannon. Bourbons all, they believed in privilege and protection and the divine ruling right of the dollar.

These men got along nicely with their Democratic counterparts on a *quid pro quo* basis. A cozy little arrangement, but it was not for Hearst. In politics as in journalism, he would operate strictly by his own code; and he quickly decided that he could best further his own interests by steering clear of undercover intrigue. Thus, though nominally a regular Democrat, he became in effect a one man party; and aimed his sights at no less bold a prize than the capture in 1904 of the Democratic nomination for the Presidency.

In general, Hearst's congressional technique consisted in sponsoring bills popular with the people and advertising them widely in his newspapers. He leased a house in Lafayette Square from Admiral Ludlowsen and entertained frequently. Often at his table were two guests of whom we shall hear again: Champ Clark of Missouri, whom the Democratic leaders were already grooming as a future Speaker of the House, and young John Nance Garner, a freshman colleague from Texas.

The new member was too flowing with vitality to fetter himself to the monotonous routine of the House. He spent much time with the men in his Washington bureau, yachted in the Atlantic and the Caribbean, dropped into his newspaper offices unexpectedly, dashed across the continent two or three times a year to visit his mother at Pleasanton. With her small, capable young architect friend Julia Morgan, who had mastered her craft in Paris, Hearst joyed in supervising alterations at the Hacienda del Pozo de Verona. In 1903, he journeyed to Berkeley to dedicate a lovely outdoor Greek amphitheatre presented by him to the University of California. The happy suggestion came from his mother, who had already endowed the institution with immense sums for buildings, scholarships and archaeological expeditions. Phoebe Hearst was called the University's "Fairy Godmother" not only because of these gifts but because of her warm personal interest in students and faculty.

Examination of bills introduced by Congressman Hearst and fought for in his newspapers shows how often he outran his hour. His railroad rate measure, strengthening the Interstate Commerce Commission and creating an Interstate Commerce Court, was abruptly suppressed by the Republicans, only to be adopted later as the basis of their entire legislation in this field. Hearst offered bills to promote construction of good roads; to increase the salaries of U. S. Supreme Court Justices; to establish the eight-hour day on government work; an amendment to the Constitution providing for the popular election of United States Senators; a bill authorizing the government to acquire, maintain and operate electric telegraphs; a bill making railroad rebating a criminal offense; various measures aimed at the trusts, with particular application to Standard Oil; a bill authorizing the government to acquire and operate the Panama Railroad Company; and, perhaps most useful of all, an act extending the postal system to the delivery of merchandise (parcel post).

Although professing to ignore him, Representative Hearst's associates watched him warily. The man was as ubiquitous as the weather; and the tough old butternuts of both parties did not discount his resourcefulness.

Despite the hectic course of his life, Congressman Hearst seemed to find ample time for play and diversion. Almost every summer found him in European art centers purchasing paintings, sculpture, tapestries, fine furniture and bibelots of every description to the very limit of his means. As usual, he was an indefatigable theatregoer and delighted to entertain the men and women of the footlights.

A musical comedy called "The Girl from Paris" was playing at the Herald Square Theatre. In the company were two comely young dancers known as the Willson sisters. Millicent and Anita Willson were the daughters of George Leslie Willson, of a substantial Maine family.

Reversing the usual Down East custom, George Willson in his youth had run away from the sea and, as George Leslie, became a popular eccen-

130

tric dancer in vaudeville in the nineties. In those days the rat-tat-tat of George Leslie's clogs entertained audiences all over the country. He sang also. "I Met Her by the Fountain in the Park" was one of the compositions he popularized. He would tip his old white hat, swing his cane merrily and go into his famous medley of coon dances, the "Pasa-ma-la," "Mobile Buck" and "Mule in the Sand."

George Willson married an Irish-American girl whose parents had emigrated from County Cork. Mrs. Willson possessed a keen business instinct and had invested shrewdly in properties lining fast-growing Harlem's leading thoroughfare, 125th Street. The Willsons lived on Gramercy Park. A neighborhood real estate agent, to whom Mrs. Willson took a liking and often consulted, was an engaging young man named Martin Huberth, who will come into our picture later.

The proprietor of the *Journal* was attracted by the beauty, gaiety and charm of Millicent Willson. Night after night Hearst and George Pancoast occupied aisle seats at the Herald Square Theatre; and night after night, after an introduction had been achieved, there were laughter-laden midnight suppers chaperoned by Anita Willson and Pancoast. The *Morning Telegraph* put on a popularity contest. Votes for Millicent Willson piled up so fast it was soon evident that someone was interested in her success. She won the crown, thanks to Hearst's votes.

At that time Hearst was more active than ever raising hob with precedent on Park Row, and in Chicago and San Francisco. He was spending thousands to prove the sugar and other trusts guilty of rebating. He had launched a fight for eighty-cent gas, a battle that was to go victoriously through the Supreme Court of the United States. The long, drawn-out anthracite strike placed coal beyond the means of the poor. Hearst shipped bargeloads of coal to the city and had his reporters sell it from carts at nine cents a pail. He established coffee wagons in the parks; filled the lodging houses with the homeless; and got under way a Christmas and relief fund which was subsequently copied by hundreds of organizations. He was campaigning for a thousand and one things.

Yet one observing his courtship of Millicent Willson would have set him down as a young dilettante whose whole time and attention was devoted to making more joyous the days of his lady fair. Notes, flowers and gifts flew between the *Journal* office and the theatre. The couple were often seen strolling about Gramercy Park arm in arm. The courtship was long, principally because of a disparity of more than twenty years in age.

Yet Hearst persisted, discerning in the vivacious young actress qualities which were to develop her into one of America's outstanding women. Millicent Willson thought later that her suitor's sense of humor had carried the day for him. He called one icy afternoon, only to be told that she was out. It was a white lie and the Willson sisters, hidden behind a drawing room curtain, tittered as they saw the tall, disconsolate caller slip and measure his length upon the sidewalk. A few minutes later a bouquet and a note arrived: "It was bad enough to find you out but to have all of Madison Square Garden fall on me also—that was too much!"

Finally, on April 28, 1903, on the eve of Hearst's fortieth birthday, George Willson, proud in a frock coat with a gardenia in his lapel, stood in the chancel of Grace Church and gave his daughter into the keeping of William Randolph Hearst. Orrin Peck was best man. Bishop Potter performed the ceremony.

After a breakfast for the wedding party of thirty at the Waldorf-Astoria, Mr. and Mrs. Hearst in mid-afternoon boarded the S. S. *Kaiser Wilhelm II* for a long honeymoon in Europe. A beautiful new motorcar of foreign make, Hearst's first, was delivered to them at Bremerhaven. The groom quickly mastered its technique and drove it through many countries.

While Hearst was in Europe his boom for the 1904 Democratic Presidential nomination got under active headway.

There was ample evidence that the publisher had touched a popular note. More than two hundred newspapers throughout the country commended his candidacy. Hearst clubs and the William Randolph Hearst League were organized. The legislature in far-off Nevada by resolution thanked him for his fight against the Coal Trust. Tennessee and Arkansas invited him to address their legislatures. Union labor was almost a unit for him. His agents used tellingly "Divine Right" Baer's carping criticism of Hearst's activities in the coal strike: "Hearst has raised wages and shortened hours of labor throughout the coal regions." Emanating from such a source, this was vote pulling manna from heaven for Hearst.

It has been said that Hearst spent more than $2,000,000 in that attempt to be nominated for President. The fact is that outside of the salaries and ordinary expenses of his regular employees he paid out not more than $150,000—practically all for printing, fireworks, hall hire, banners, badges, music and transportation. He had spent as much for Bryan. Hearst did not have the money to spend. His inherited fortune, rather that part of it upon which he had drawn through the generosity and faith of his mother, was depleted. The comfortable surpluses all four of his papers were earning by now he put into another organ, the Boston *American,* which was launched as an evening paper in 1904.

The Hearst regional political managers were often hard put for funds. One afternoon, shortly before the convention was to convene in St. Louis, A. M. Lawrence, director of the Hearst campaign in the Middle West, went to John Eastman, publisher of the Chicago *American,* and asked for a few hundred dollars to send to Indiana where the Hearst forces were engaged in a bitter contest with Tom Taggart, state Democratic boss. "Andy, I haven't got a nickel to spare for politics," said Eastman. Lawrence appealed to Harmon Campbell, the cashier. Campbell scratched around and dug up four hundred dollars' worth of stamps in denominations of two, fives and tens. Frederick Lawrence, the political manager's brother, and one or two other fellows on the paper spent the rest of the day disposing of the stamps to friends. Thus was the Hearst pre-convention movement in Indiana financed during the latter stages.

Despite the lack of the most potent sinews of modern political warfare, the homemade Hearst boom was worked up so effectively that candidate Hearst carried the Democratic conventions of California, Illinois, Iowa, Idaho, Kansas, Nebraska, Nevada, Rhode Island, South Dakota, Washington, Wyoming, Arizona, New Mexico and Hawaii, with parts of the delegations of Maine, Minnesota, Oregon, West Virginia, Indian Territory, Oklahoma and Puerto Rico. The power of the new Hearst paper in Chicago was demonstrated when the candidate got an instructed delegation from Illinois over the heads of Roger Sullivan, George Brennan and other Democratic bosses. He had similar success in California, where his father's old friend Michael F. Torphy led his forces.

The result was that Hearst, one of the most fanatically admired and cheerfully hated men in the country, went into the convention with 104 instructed delegates; and on one ballot his vote reached 263.

Although he was too much of a realist to overestimate his chances for the nomination, Hearst was anxious for a test of strength. He was quoted privately as stating that he went in "because Roosevelt was stealing my thunder." The valorous Teddy, with a mighty to-do, had already begun to swing his "big stick" at the trusts. Amusedly, Hearst rather admired Roosevelt's very comfortable, fur-lined brain and his ability to project fervor and emotionalism across the footlights. These qualities would have carried Hearst far. Hearst's political methods smacked more of the "plutocrats" he loudly denounced. As Lincoln Steffens pointed out at the time, he used force as they did, as a substitute for charm, humor, persuasion, pleadings. He was an autocratic boss who was willing to give the people democratic government just as others of his class "gave" them colleges, libraries and—good, plutocratic government. Steffens thought Hearst was cold, unmoral, self-seeking.

A quarter of a century later, in his autobiography, Lincoln Steffens completely reversed himself, writing: "I did not understand then what a part dictatorship has to play in democracy. And I found, as his chief fault, that he was not moral; I was just getting over my own righteousness, but I had not yet arrived where Hearst was born, apparently, at the point of view whence one sees that it is economic, rather than moral forces that count. . . . He is so far ahead of his staffs that they can hardly see him; and so, of course, they cannot make either this remarkable man or his perfectly

133

JAPANESE FIGHT THE WARFARE OF THE UNEXPECTED, SAYS JACK LONDON

REVISED MAP OF THE FIELD OF THE FIGHTING WHEN THE JAPANESE CROSSED THE YALU.

Executes Apparently Careful Movements in the Open While the Real Work is Proceeding Elsewhere.

BY JACK LONDON.

Author of "The Call of the Wild, and Special Commissioner of the New York "AMERICAN" at the Front.

Copyright, 1904, by W. R. Hearst.

JACK LONDON.

ANTUNG, Manchuria, May 10.— The Japanese, following the German model, make every possible preparation, take every possible precaution and then proceed to act, confident in the belief that nothing short of a miracle can prevent success. Opposed to their three divisions on the Yalu was a greatly inferior Russian force, but the Japanese had to cross a river under fire and attack an enemy lying in wait for them.

By the manipulation of their three divisions, not of their ruses, they must have sadly befuddled the Russians. At the mouth of the Yalu the Japanese had two small gunboats, torpedo boats and four small steamers armed with Hotchkiss guns. Also, they had fifty sampans loaded with bridge materials.

These were intended for a permanent bridge across the Yalu at Wiju; but they served another purpose—first, further down the stream.

The presence of the small navy and the loaded sampans led the Russians to believe that right there was where the bridge was to be built.

So right there they stationed some three thousand men to prevent the building of the bridge.

Thus a handful of Japanese sailors kept three thousand Russian soldiers occupied in doing nothing, and reduced the effectiveness of the Russian strength by that much.

BUILT BRIDGE IN UNPROTECTED SPOT.

Another ruse was the building of a bridge in front of Wiju. This was in plain view of the Russians, on the Conical hill, opposite, and just east of Kiulangcheng, and they consumed much time and powder in shelling it. This was precisely what the Japanese intended for the bridge.

While it held the Russian attention, a little further down the stream the Japanese were at work on another bridge, screened by small willow trees on the intervening island, and which, when completed, had never a shot fired at it.

Have you ev·· ···d in ········age wherein there was a monkey sing·ing ·····—so in··· ·tly and reasonably ··· ·w ·· with ···· ·····

Make Every Possible Precaution and Then Act Confident That Only a Miracle Will Block Them.

about 4,000 men. The Russian line, extending some six or seven miles, was not intact. In fact, because of the lay of the land, the Russians really occupied two positions—one on and about the conical hill at Kiulang-Cheng; the other on the Ai-Ho from its mouth, several miles up.

Against these two positions, each occupied by about two thousand men, was hurled an army of three divisions, probably 35,000 men actually on the spot, backed by a powerful artillery in field guns and Howitzers.

Prevented by shell fire and shrapnel from doing their best to repel the general attack, in process of being flanked by the immensely superior force, the Russian left on the Ai-Ho broke first and fled in the direction of Hamatan.

Used Reserves to Clinch Victory.

The Russian right, on the conical hill, fought more tenaciously, the survivors in turn fleeing toward Hamatan.

The Japanese understood the utility of things. Reserves they consider should be used, not only to strengthen the line or to protect the repulse line, but in the moment of victory to clinch victory hard and fast.

The reserves, fresh and chafing from inaction, will to take part in a glorious day, received the order for general pursuit. Right, left and centre they took after the Russians.

The field guns, delayed by the Ai-Ho, followed at a gallop. The retreat became a rout. The Russian reserves, two regiments, fled without firing a shot. At least, the Japanese have no record of these two regiments.

Hamatan is at the conjunction of three roads, six miles to the rear of the conical hill. Down these three roads the Russians ran coming together and passing into the main road—the Pekin or Mandarin road. And down these three roads, from right, left and centre, came the fresh reserves, and after them the artillery.

In the meantime, however, far from the Japanese right and stripping the rest of the pursuit, arrived one company of men in time to cut off fifteen Russian guns and eight Maxims. The remnants of three battalions rallied around the guns.

A hasty position was taken. The rest of the pursuing Japanese did not arrive.

But one company of men stood between the Russians and the Pekin road. And it stood. Its captain and three lieutenants were killed. Only one officer remained. The last cartridge was fired.

Russians Assailed from Three Sides.

Those that survived fixed their bayonets, ready to receive a charge. And in that moment, left, right and centre, their pursuing comrades arrived.

The Russians were assailed from three sides. The day was lost; they knew it; yet they fought on doggedly. Night was falling. As the Japanese drew closer the Russians turned loose their horses, destroyed or threw away the breech-blocks of their guns, smashed the breeches of the Maxims, and then, as bayonets countered bayonets, drew white handkerchiefs from their pockets in token of surrender.

One other noteworthy thing occurred in the Japanese pursuit. Mid to Hamatan, flying on the heels o· ···ut, in the very heat and swee· triumph, they dropped a line o· ······t them they ···ried t ·t brok· ···irb·

rational ideas comprehensible to his readers, the people Hearst would like to see served."

In the convention city the Hearst candidacy of 1904 was accompanied by the latest electrical stage effects, by noise, oratory and general furor. The entire second floor of St. Louis' handsome Hotel Jefferson was used as headquarters with a legend across the main entrance spelling out in electric lights in letters two feet high: "Hearst Headquarters." From this, extending upward, were colored electric-light streamers, caught above to an American flag, wavy in multicolored illumination.

A band of stump speakers addressed throngs of the curious by day and night in a hall formed by throwing large suites together. Literature telling of Hearst's services to the people, of his liberal intentions when he should reach the White House, and invariably bearing his picture in a pensive pose, was passed out by the ton, together with buttons and other campaign knickknacks.

In the building of a nearby newspaper a regiment of editors, reporters and telegraph operators sent endless words to the Hearst newspapers telling of daily accessions to the ranks and prophesying that Hearst would sweep the convention; that the Hearst movement was then strong but hidden under a current later to be turned into a resistless tide. The "resistless tide" did not develop and Alton B. Parker of New York, a safe, sane and colorless conservative, received the nomination.

Parker ran haltingly against Roosevelt. Hearst supported him limply, for he believed the corporations controlled both parties, and then accepted another term in Congress at the hands of Tammany.

Hearst bided his time, like a canny boxer, confident his turn would come. It came the following year, and was marked by such a gale of passion as to make all previous political battles seem like mere summer zephyrs.

←

During all the demands on his time in the 1904 Presidential campaign, Hearst gave close attention to all details of his papers' operations. Upon its becoming apparent that a Russo-Japanese War was imminent, he arranged for thorough coverage. Jack London, who had just scored his first big success as a novelist with *The Call of the Wild,* was one of the correspondents whom he hired. This is a prophetic London dispatch from Antung, Manchuria, May 10, 1904.

The People's Champion

We are all at the mercy of a falling tile.

JULIUS CAESAR

9

IN 1905 AND 1906, William Randolph Hearst initiated and led two cyclonic campaigns for public office. Although neither was officially successful, Hearst employed them to introduce his own exciting brand of political thermodynamics and made himself the most widely known living American, with the possible exception of Theodore Roosevelt.

If he had won either contest, and there is not the slightest doubt that he was defrauded of one, Hearst's path to the White House would have been smoothed. Instead, he joined a long list of Might Have Beens, with unusually fascinating conjectures as to his possible influence upon history.

In 1905, without a party and with a mere pretense of an organization known as the Municipal Ownership League, the publisher came within a fraction of being elected Mayor of New York. Subsequent revelations of widespread ballot box tampering, of which he was the victim, indicated clearly that Hearst had defeated his Tammany opponent by many thousands of votes. Hearst paid his own expenses, which ran to $65,000.

In 1906, under the dictated nomination of his own incorporated political party, the Independence League, and the reluctant endorsement of the Democrats, Hearst ran for Governor of New York, losing to Charles Evans Hughes by less than 60,000 votes. This struggle cost him $256,000.

In these two campaigns, New York went through an entirely new political experience. For fervor and emotionalism, no one ever saw anything quite like them before or since. Stirred by economic and political inequities the plain people everywhere, but peculiarly in New York, were eager to slay bosses. With almost religious fanaticism, they hailed as their defender

136

and champion the man who for years had fought the "robber barons of gold" and used his newspapers and the courts as a lash to sting the "saffron sides of the pirates of special privilege."

There never has been such a popular fury as attended Hearst throughout these campaigns. Commonly a crowd means no more than curiosity and as great a multitude will come to see you hanged as crowned. The Hearst crusades were an exception. Not curiosity but a cause drew the throngs singing and shouting about his carriage wheels. The frenzy was intoxicating and Hearst in his new role of statesman, in black slouch hat and long-tailed coat, enjoyed it to the full, although his tongue at times may have been in his cheek. More than once a roguish smile would break through the austere mask of the great reformer appealing to "Lincoln Republicans" and "Jeffersonian Democrats" to seek shelter beneath his fluttering banners.

The campaigns of 1905 and 1906 were unique in that they were absolutely in charge of men who had been in the candidate's employ for years as editors, reporters, legal advisers, secretaries or private investigators. The show was directed and produced by a natural master in the art of arousing crowd emotion. Hearst on a campaign was like a Hearst afternoon newspaper—there was a new edition every fifteen minutes, with frequent extras. The Hearst political technique emphasized the striking, picturesque features of the struggle just as the Hearst newspapers accentuated the picturesque, striking features of the news. What Hearst didn't say to the advantage of his candidacy on the stump, Hearst papers said in glaring headlines on the journalistic stump, morning, noon, evening, midnight and in between. Generally spellbinders and newspapers, working as smoothly as the twin barrels on a double-barreled shotgun, simultaneously enfiladed the bosses and their financial overlords.

Himself, ironically enough, a boss of bosses, the People's Defender broke through and scattered party lines like chaff. Men took sides in 1905 and 1906 not as Republicans or Democrats but as Hearst or anti-Hearst. Was the phenomenon man-made or a product of the times? Everyone took a hand at guessing.

"The significant thing is not so much Mr. Hearst himself as the Hearst movement," pontificated the distinguished *Review of Reviews*. "This movement stands for every phase of social and economic discontent. It has its tinge of fanaticism. In the minds of many adherents of it, the movement is idealistic and Utopian." The magazine, although hostile to Hearst personally, continued:—

"It would be useless to minimize the plucky and aggressive fights that the Hearst newspapers have made against corporate monopolies and kindred evils of all sorts. There is wide difference of opinion as to the motives that have impelled this policy. But merely to disparage it as 'yellow journalism' cannot alter the fact that it has brought to the Hearst movement a tremendous following of workingmen and plain citizens."

The machine politician nurtured no delusions. He was not fighting for the memory of Lincoln or Jefferson, or the glory of Roosevelt or Cleveland. He was fighting William Randolph Hearst—"an able, independent man of extraordinary boldness," as Joseph Pulitzer described him in a confidential memorandum to the directors of his editorial pages.

In the White House, President Theodore Roosevelt watched the Hughes-Hearst struggle for the Governorship with mounting interest. The national Republican managers knew that a Hearst victory in New York that fall would mean that the same battle, forty times more vital, must be fought on a scale forty times as large two years from 1906. Hence that amorphous but no less real element known as the Money Power unleashed all its minions against Hearst. Roosevelt sent three members of his Cabinet into New York State and exerted every ounce of Federal pressure in behalf of Hughes.

When Hearst ran for Mayor of New York in 1905 revelations of corruption in almost every large American city were tumbling over each other on the front pages of the newspapers and in the magazines. It had required just a decade for the seed planted by Hearst to flower into the cauterizing exposés of such brilliant, misnamed "muckrakers" as Ray Stannard Baker, Lincoln Steffens and Ida M. Tarbell.

With undiminished vigor the Hearst organs were battling for municipal reform in New York, San Francisco, Chicago, Boston and Los Angeles, where Hearst had just established another newspaper, destined to become his most profitable, the Los Angeles *Examiner*. In New York the publisher had carried his spectacular fight for eighty-cent gas into the courts. The devastating insurance scandals had been exposed under the merciless scalpel of Charles Evans Hughes. Hearst was stridently demanding municipal ownership of public utilities, including interborough subways for transit-starved New York.

Hearst had quarreled with Charles F. Murphy, leader of Tammany Hall, and the Tammany sponsored Mayor, George B. McClellan. Boss Murphy had abandoned his lamppost forum near the Anawanda Club, at Second Avenue and Twentieth Street, and taken to deciding matters of import from a corner table in the plushy atmosphere of Delmonico's restaurant on Fifth Avenue. He was outspoken in his contempt for Hearst's "Populist ideas" and predicted the Californian would be "licked hands down" if he had the temerity to run for Mayor against McClellan. In the three weeks of his slashing campaign Hearst quickly forced Murphy to change his tune. Mayor McClellan had intended making but half a dozen perfunctory speeches—he made sixty-four.

The 1905 campaign marked Hearst's definite emergence as a public speaker. Until then, and despite his brief appearances on the floor of Con-

138

WHO'S ZOO IN AMERICA

By WALLACE IRWIN

WILLIAM ALSO-RAN-DOLPH HEARST

WILLIE runs a supplement which always beats the news;
  Willie runs for President, with nothing much to lose—
Willie's always running, whether by request or not.
Whenever there's a vacancy, it's Willie-on-the-Spot.

Frisky Willie, risky Willie, feverish for speed,
Prints a rapid journal, so that he who runs may read.

Willie runs for Governor quite regular of late,
Willie runs the Government (or tries at any rate).
Willie looks on Politics with serious intent,
As a sort of annex to his Comic Supplement.

Willing Willie, wanton Willie, can he, will he quit?
Willie's always playing tag—and yet he's never It!

Willie ran for Mayor once, but when he realized
That he was defeated he was not at all surprised.
In this land, which (Willie says) by grafters is accursed,
Almost everybody has defeated Willie Hearst.

Dreaming Willie, scheming Willie, hitting of the pipe;
He's one type of journalist—his Journal's mostly type.

When he saw that Puddles were the topics of the hour
Willie got a Muck-Rake of a hundred-donkey power,
Started up a geyser, shrilly shrieking all the time:
"Don't you touch my mud! I've got a scoop on this here slime!"

Frantic Willie, antic Willie, always on the jump,
Willie found the Muck-Rake slow, and so he bought a pump.

Brimstone is to Willie quite the mildest of emulsions—
Dowie multiplied by fits and Lawson in convulsions;
Any great calamity that comes the world to curse,
Read it in the "Journal"—and you'll find that it is worse.

Bumptious Willie, gumptious Willie, running for a prize,
Keeps his circulation brisk by constant exercise.

In the first quarter of the 20th century practically every newspaper or magazine had a doggerel writer who took his subjects from news or political events. Naturally, Hearst was a frequent subject. This example appeared in *Collier's Weekly* in September, 1906. The writer, Wallace Irwin, became memorable chiefly for his comic *Letters of a Japanese Schoolboy.*

gress, he would tremble and grow pale at mere thought of making a speech. His devices for avoiding platform appearances excited laughter and jeers; and gave rise to canards that were long in dying. It was said that everything appearing over his name was written by employees, that he was too shallow to think and too dull and shamefaced to talk. But in his fight for the Mayoralty he developed surprising powers of oratory and of slashing, give and take attack. He even learned to joke good naturedly with the crowds and to capitalize upon the high notes which crept into his voice at moments of excitement, a peculiarity similar to the falsetto "break" in the voice of his distinguished foeman, Colonel Roosevelt.

Hearst was nominated for Mayor at a mass meeting of the Municipal Ownership League on October 4, 1905. While Clarence J. Shearn, the Hearst lawyer, J. G. Phelps Stokes, John Ford, Max F. Ihmsen and other orators denounced Charles F. Murphy, Mayor McClellan, August Belmont, Thomas F. Ryan, the Standard Oil Company, the Gas Trust and the "plunderbund" generally, Hearst walked up and down behind the stage, occasionally strolling to the bar for a sip of seltzer. Resolutions were passed calling for the nomination of "a man honest and independent" to lead the fight of the people against "the gas interests, the life insurance swindlers, the crooked corporation owners and franchise grabbers." Then Hearst was introduced. For some moments the tall, gawky giant stood with downcast eyes, manuscript in hand, while the crowd cheered and the band played "The Star-Spangled Banner," "There's a Hot Time in the Old Town Tonight," and "Waltz Me Around Again, Willie." Hearst said in part:—

> Have we left any government by the people? You have your votes and the privilege of casting them, but for whom? For Mr. Murphy's puppet, or for Mr. Odell's puppet. If you want gas that will burn and not merely poison, you can vote for Mr. Murphy's puppet and you won't get it. And if you want a reduction in your extortionate bills, you can vote for Mr. Odell's puppet and not get it.
>
> If you want decent treatment for your heroic firemen, your brave police, your conscientious clerks, your hardworking street cleaners, you can vote for Mr. Murphy's man and you won't get it; and if you want to retain the small portion of your public property still unstolen, you can vote for Mr. Odell's man or Mr. Murphy's man and you won't get that.
>
> I do not believe the corporations are at fault. I do not believe that Mr. Murphy or Mr. Odell or Mr. Murphy's man or Mr. Odell's man is at fault—I am afraid you are at fault. You are a sleeping majority, pledged by pygmies. Wake up! Nominate independent men. Men who will lead you to victory and restore this city to a government of the people, by the people . . .

Fifty men leaped to their feet to nominate Hearst for Mayor. The nomination was made unanimous. As soon as he could escape the cheers and the handshakers, the chief actor in the drama slipped away. He would say nothing as to accepting. Next day he wrote declining the nomination. The following Monday Charles Evans Hughes declined the Republican nomination. Then Hearst reconsidered, saying that he had decided not to shirk a task that presented itself as a public duty. This was on October 10.

"The situation in this city is so grave," explained Hearst, "and the condition of the public in the face of organized bossism is apparently so helpless that no man has a right to consider anything else, least of all his private affairs or personal inclinations. The one thing to be considered is the necessity of giving to the people an opportunity to vote for some man of whom it may at least be said that he would, if elected, represent those that voted for him and not any boss or corporation or selfish private interest."

The campaign consumed only twenty days but it pulsed with excitement.

Hearst's photographs and his insistent cry of "No bossism!" blossomed from the billboards and his newspaper delivery wagons. His printers and stereotypers and office boys and stenographers got into the fight. Hearst personally directed the cartoon wizardry of Davenport and Opper and T. E. Powers and T. A. "Tad" Dorgan, a new self-taught young genius recently arrived from the San Francisco *Examiner*. The editor addressed a dozen meetings each evening and his measured emotions warmed visibly amid the red fire, the band music and the thunderous endorsement greeting his promises of cheaper and better transportation, more and better schools, better wages and lower taxes. He insisted that if there was one man between the oceans who was not radical, not extreme, but wholly conservative, that man was himself.

There was a suggestion of the Norse, something Bismarckian, about the young giant who drove about the city to the blare of bands, the glare of red fire, accompanied by flag waving retinues, denouncing the bosses and pouring vitriol upon the "rogue millions of the moneychangers"; something that set the crowd's blood to pulsing.

From all quarters reports of a drift to Hearst poured in upon Tammany Leader Murphy. He promptly forsook his corner table in Delmonico's and sent every spellbinder that could be enlisted out upon the cart-tails. These glib fellows were the Judas goats of the Hall, depended upon to keep the voters marching sheeplike to the polls. They could not call Hearst "rascal" so they called him "radical," "destructionist," "socialist" and raked up the old McKinley charge. And Tammany made other and more stealthy preparations: "Big" and "Little" Tim Sullivan, who controlled the Bowery and the lower east side of Manhattan, gathered their clans and grinned when asked how many votes the independent candidate would garner in their bailiwicks. The election machinery was in their hands, completely.

Amid the storm Hearst, as usual, remained tranquil. One afternoon Max Ihmsen, his chief political lieutenant, dashed into the house at 123 Lexington Avenue upon a mission of importance. The candidate was sprawled upon a bed, holding the bottle of his baby son George, born in April of the previous year. Every time the lusty youngster squalled his daddy would yell loud enough to be heard a block away, "Extry! Extry! Extry edition!" Not until the infant sank into gurgling slumber could Ihmsen gain the boss' ear.

The campaign reached a frenzied climax on Sunday evening before election with a mammoth rally in Madison Square Garden, largest the metropolis had ever known. Long before twilight the Garden was jammed to capacity, with more than 100,000 people vainly seeking admittance. Pandemonium broke loose when Hearst and his wife entered the auditorium. Hats, coats, handkerchiefs, flags, even folding chairs were held high and waved. Rattles were shaken, horns blown, a roar from 40,000 lungs drowned out the orchestra of 120 pieces. After a twenty-minute ovation, the candidate was able partially to still the clamor. His face flushed with pleasure, eyes sparkling, his voice vibrant with genuine feeling, Hearst launched into his brief talk:—

> My friends, I do not desire to make a speech. I only want to thank you for your kindness and your friendship. I greet you tonight not as Democrats or Republicans, but as friends. I greet you not as partisans, but as citizens deeply interested with us in the welfare of our citizens and in the progress and prosperity of our great city. I greet you with hope and confidence in the result because I believe implicitly in the wisdom and the patriotism and the conscience of the people. . . .
>
> I am proud of the friends that have rallied around us. They are the people's friends. I am proud of the enemies who oppose us. They are the people's enemies. We will fight those enemies together and triumph over them, no matter how powerful and unscrupulous they may be. . . . We shall say with Jackson, "Let us ask nothing but what is right and submit to nothing that is wrong." We will fight the battle along those lines, and we will win a glorious victory if we will only trust the people.

Hearst spent most of Election Day in his headquarters. His watchers, beaten and bleeding, staggered in with reports of thugs in control at the voting booths. Ihmsen and the other managers were wild. But Hearst kept perfectly cool, outwardly. "Let's fix these men up and put others in their places," he directed. That evening, as incomplete returns showed a neck-and-neck race, he drummed on the wainscoting in the Lexington Avenue home. He sat in the high ceiled drawing room, the green walls copied from the Chateau de Blois—Bourbon lilies and crowned porcupines daintily picked out in gold. A score of costly paintings stood on the floor, leaning against the walls. Here was a wonderfully painted and gilded Egyptian mummy-case standing on end under glass; there a complete suit of ancient German armor. On a pianola stood a gilded bronze statuette of Caesar crossing the Rubicon and one of Napoleon as First Consul. In a corner gleamed Frémiet's golden St. George and the Dragon and under a window a beautiful porcelain Eve with Cain and Abel, as infants, playing at her knee. Through an open door could be seen the quaint oak dining room with deer antlers for chandeliers and picturesque groupings of Delft and old glass.

Presently Mrs. Hearst passed through the dim, wide hall. "Come on, let's go out to dinner," called the candidate, and they left the house together.

The official vote was so close that a recount was necessary to determine the result. Charges of blatant and cynical frauds against the independent ticket were made and amply proven in a long, drawn out investigation. Many ballot boxes had actually been thrown into the river. Hundreds of floaters and repeaters had been imported from various Eastern cities. Registered from vacant lots, public parks, even gas tanks, they had been herded to the polling places in droves under police and judicial protection. One thug confessed that he had cast a dozen ballots under names written out for him by a Tammany bagman. In one voting district alone hundreds of Hearst ballots had been invalidated and voided on various pretexts. Although only two or three nobodies were sent to prison, the exposure of the frauds stirred the legislature into enacting a law requiring personal signatures on registration and voting lists.

Despite the lack of experienced workers and the short tally, Hearst succeeded in carrying two counties—Kings and Queens—and the final returns showed McClellan victor by the narrow margin of 3,472 votes. The city-wide figures were:—

McClellan, 228,397

Hearst, 224,925

William M. Ivins (Republican candidate), 137,193.

For weeks and months the Hearst papers made the welkin ring with shouts of fraud and crime. In editorials and cartoons Boss Murphy was placarded as a thief and grafter. Beginning a day or two after the election the *Evening Journal's* cartoons showed Murphy in prison stripes. "Look Out, Murphy! It's a Short Lockstep from Delmonico's to Sing Sing," read the caption over a cartoon by Tad Dorgan. The cartoon showed a stout, scowling figure, with closely cropped hair, a monocle in one eye, and was embellished by an editorial in bold-face type reading:—

Every honest voter in New York WANTS TO SEE YOU IN THIS COSTUME. You have committed crimes against the people that will send you for many years to State prison, if the crimes can be proved against you. Your dull mind cannot conceive of any REAL public opinion. But an awakening is ahead of you. YOU KNOW THAT YOU ARE GUILTY. The PEOPLE know it. You have swindled the poor as their employer; you have swindled the voting public as political manager of your miserable little gas tool. The people have found you out. If you persist in your effort to rob the city, your friends will soon find you in State prison.

Don't be such a fool as to repeat Tweed's question. He only stole MONEY. You have stolen VOTES. There could not be found in New York at this moment a jury to acquit you. YOU KNOW THAT.

Look out! If you ever sit in the prisoner's dock you will not come out, except in striped clothing. You were warned before election. Be warned now—or follow Tweed and the men BETTER THAN YOU that have worked for the State prison after working against it in public office.

The following year, when Tammany was supporting Hearst for Governor, Murphy threatened action for criminal libel against anti-Hearst newspapers and political committees guilty of reproducing the "Murphy-in-stripes" cartoons. A crony of the Tammany leader explained the apparent inconsistency: "Last year Murphy pictured Hearst as the assassin of McKinley and Hearst pictured Murphy as a convict. That was a private quarrel and each man expected to be called names by the other. But now other papers are trying to steal Hearst's thunder and Charlie won't stand for that."

In later years Hearst found much to admire in Murphy. Once he remarked privately that "a few more Murphys" would effect a complete and permanent reformation of Tammany. Hearst said he had found that the stolid former grogshop proprietor made good on personal pledges. For instance, Murphy wholeheartedly lived up to his promises of co-operation with John F. Hylan, Hearst's handpicked Mayor, in crusades against gambling and prostitution.

While his political managers and attorneys were battling unsuccessfully to overturn the result of the Mayoralty election, Hearst scribbled a note to Morrill Goddard, his Sunday editor:—

Dear Goddard:
I got it here [sketch showing a chicken being axed and an arrow

pointing to the neck]. But that's that. Come on down to New Mexico with me for a month.

Hearst

On the trip the candidate lived in the open, rode horseback and reveled in his release from the toil of a hard campaign. During the entire month Hearst carried no watch. He seemed totally free of time and responsibility except on one dramatic occasion when cool shooting saved his life. Hunting in the hills, the party's dogs flushed a mountain lion at dusk on the evening of January 9, 1906. Hearst, out ahead, wounded the big cat, which sprang from a tree in which it had taken refuge and rushed at him. Hearst managed to fire another shot when the animal was only a few feet away and the big snarling cat fell dead at his feet. It was a moment of real peril.

Meanwhile, the Hearst lieutenants were far from inactive in the equally fascinating game of Tiger hunting in New York. Orders had been given to keep pounding into the public consciousness that both old parties were corrupt and unfit to rid the state government of grafters. Hearst intended to make full use of the prestige gained in the Mayoralty campaign and set in motion an industrious effort to capture the Governorship of New York in 1906. Hardly had his managers set to work throughout the state when the signs of Hearst's strength caused even the bitterest anti-Bryan leaders in the Democratic Party to unite in a loud cry for Bryan, who was traveling in Europe, to return and "save the country," meaning the conservatives, from that bold, bad Hearst.

The bold, bad man meantime kept his finger closely upon the pulse of his newspapers. His cool ability to focus his mind upon the particular problem at hand was illustrated the day of the earthquake and fire in San Francisco.

During the morning of that tremendous April 18, 1906, the fate of Hearst's properties on the Coast had been in doubt. No definite word had come out of the confusion. One of his executives who had an engagement to lunch with him appeared at the *American* office to keep the appointment. The previous summer the plant had been moved to the Rhinelander Building at William and Duane Streets. The executive was quite certain that Hearst would cancel the luncheon. However the publisher not only appeared but disposed of the problem upon his executive's mind with no more than cursory mention of the catastrophe. This done, he showed his guest a telegram which had been handed to him during the meal and at which he had glanced casually. It told of the two-million-dollar ruin of the *Examiner* plant in San Francisco. "Do you think," he asked quietly, "that it would be fair to put our men there on half pay until we can get started again?"

Hearst calmly returned to his office. There, however, things happened. He communicated with R. H. Hoe & Co., leading manufacturers of printing presses. Did it, by any chance, have a press nearing completion, that he could buy? No? Were any presses in transit anywhere? It developed that a paper in Salt Lake City had recently purchased a press. Hearst communicated with the Utah organ, bought the press for twice its original cost, enlisted the aid of the railroads in locating the cars in which the parts were packed, ordered these cars attached to an express train bound for California and arranged to have a staff of mechanics capable of assembling the machine board the Overland Limited at Chicago—all before dinner. Within a matter of days the *Examiner* was operating again from temporary headquarters in Oakland.

As soon as possible Hearst made a personal inspection of the ruins which were caused far more by the fires than by the earthquake. He found that his early hillside home had miraculously escaped the holocaust. Overwhelming as was the disaster, he was heartened by the spirit of the tens of thousands of refugees crowded into tents. He filed a despatch to his newspapers: "Everything has been destroyed except that indomitable American pluck, that unconquerable American spirit which will not be subdued. In a month there will be the beginning of a new and splendid city; in a year it will have assumed shape; and in three to five years it will be built and busy, greater than ever."

Hearst always had a particularly warm spot in his heart for the newspaper workers who carried on so heroically in 1906. A few months before his death he sent felicitations to the Late Watch, an organization of newspaper veterans, addressed especially to those who had served San Francisco papers in 1906. Hearst proudly numbered himself among the "Pre-Quakers," elder statesmen of the Watch who entered newspaper work in San Francisco before 1906.

That summer the publisher purchased the old farm homestead of Abraham Lincoln in Salem, Illinois, and committed the sixty-two acres into the keeping of the Chautauqua Association of that state. The homestead has since been developed into one of America's most hallowed shrines.

The District Attorney of New York at that time was William Travers Jerome, an independent Democrat who aspired to the Governorship. The Hearst papers attacked him bitterly for his alleged failure to prosecute traction manipulators. Hearst tagged Judge Jerome with one of his apt coinages: "The Brass-Buttoned Bellhop of the Trusts" and printed a photograph snapped by an audacious Hearst photographer showing the District Attorney enjoying a nap at his desk, with feet elevated and mouth open. You may imagine to what use the fertile minds in the *Evening Journal* and *American* offices put that picture!

Hearst and his editors employed both the polished rapier of irony and the bludgeon of invective upon the hapless Jerome. One evening the District

146

Attorney, whose salty vocabulary was itself not at all timid, delivered a biting personal attack upon Hearst. Shortly before midnight the Chief softly padded up to the desk of Louis J. Lang, the *American's* veteran political reporter, and asked, as was his almost nightly custom: "What's doing in politics, Louie?"

Lang showed him a copy of Jerome's speech and remarked that the managing editor had set aside two sticks on an inside page for it. Hearst ran over the mimeograph copy, chuckled, and slipped into an adjoining room, where he busied himself with pen and paper. When the city edition came steaming from the press it contained Jerome's speech in full, in bold-face, and prominently displayed on the the first page.

Just above the opening paragraphs of the District Attorney's blistering words was a drawing of a seedy, sprawling individual labeled "Jerome," patently intoxicated, leaning dizzily against a lamppost, beneath the screaming caption, "HIGHBALL HYSTERIA!" It was the handiwork of Hearst himself. But no one outside the *American* office knew it; and when Jerome ran into Lang in the Fifth Avenue Hotel that afternoon, the District Attorney grinned and remarked: "Brisbane thinks he's a pretty smart duck, doesn't he?"

Hearst's political thought and the style and tone of his writing during this period is mirrored in messages to his editors. A letter to Brisbane from Washington gives this excellent pen picture of the American Government:—

Feb. 21, 1906

Dear Mr. Brisbane:

Don't you think it would be a good Sunday editorial on corporation government, not to make it political, but sort of historical? Ask if a republic really exists today, if this country is governed by the republic. . . .

We still maintain a republican form of government, but who has control of the primaries that nominate the candidate? The corporations have. Who control the conventions? The corporations. Who control the machinery of elections? Who count the votes to suit themselves? The corporations. Who own the bosses and the elected officials? Are they representatives of the people or of the corporations? Let any fair-minded man answer that question truthfully.

If the corporations do all this—and they surely do—can we maintain that this is any longer a government by the people? It is a government by a distinct class, and a government not for the greatest good of the greatest number but for the special advantage of that class. Laws are passed for the benefit of the corporations, laws are interpreted for the benefit of the corporations, and such laws as are not to the advantage of the corporations are ignored. The people are neglected because they have ceased to be important as a factor in the government. . . .

W. R. Hearst

In another letter Hearst referred to both old parties as obstacles: "It is time to think and act. There is no question of party politics involved. The Democrats are as bad as the Republicans. The problem must be met and solved not by partisanship but by patriotism." A long telegram from Los Angeles to Brisbane directed a fight "for honest Judges":—

Brisbane, N. Y.: Must be cautious in attacking courts, but nevertheless necessary to explain to the people the fact that they are governed by the judiciary. The corporations realize the importance of the Judges, and have secured most of them. The people do not yet understand the situation. The legislatures make laws, but the Judges interpret them, and they seldom fail to interpret them as the corporations desire. It is true, as Jerome said, that the Judges go hat in hand to Mr. Murphy, but it is also true that Mr. Murphy goes hat in hand to Mr. Ryan, and Mr. Ryan, who instructs Mr. Murphy and appoints the Judges and governs the people, keeps his hat on all the time.

The fight must be made for honest Judges, and it is only a phase of the fight against boss rule and corporation rule which is the great issue of today. We do not want the Judges appointed either by legitimate executives or by corrupt bosses or by criminal corporations. We want them elected by the people, responsible only to the people, and replaced at sufficiently short intervals to make them realize their responsibility. The people must appreciate the importance of the judiciary as well as the corporations realize it. They must own their Judges, limit their power and make their impeachment easy. . . .

The one thing that hampers the progress of reform is party prejudice. Party prejudice is used by clever schemers to divide the people and overcome them while divided. The people must unite for the interest of themselves and their fellow citizens, and united they will be irresistible. HEARST

Early in 1906 it became evident that Hearst intended to run for Governor as an independent. His agents went through the state establishing branches of the Independence League. At League headquarters in the Gilsey House, New York, could be heard a clatter and hum and a strife of voices which was like nothing in the world except the office of one of Hearst's newspapers. Hearst was out to give the people good democratic government according to his exclusive definition of same.

148

One evening at the Hotel Ten Eyck in Albany, State Senator Patrick H. McCarren paused at a table where Louis Lang was dining alone. McCarren, a tall, thin, silent man, had succeeded Hugh McLaughlin as Democratic boss of Brooklyn. "Louie," said McCarren quietly, "I thought you might be interested to know that the next Democratic candidate for Governor will be William Randolph Hearst. And you may tell him from me that the Kings County Democratic organization will support him." Leaving Lang gasping over his coffee, Senator McCarren passed on.

Lang caught a late express for New York and next morning presented himself at the Hearst home. After an hour he was admitted to the Chief's bedroom, and delivered his message. Hearst, attired in a bathrobe, strolled about the room for a moment or two and looked out of the window. Then he wheeled suddenly, turned the coldest of eyes upon his visitor and said without raising his voice a particle: "Louie, tell Senator McCarren I do not want his support and I would not accept it under any circumstances. Thank you for coming down. Good morning."

Hearst's decision and the manner of it cost him the Governorship. From that moment McCarren whetted a knife for Hearst and influenced sufficient votes in Kings County alone to insure his defeat by a plurality of 58,000. Later, when Charles F. Murphy forced the Democratic state convention to endorse the Independence League candidate, Hearst said bluntly: "Murphy may be for me but I am not for Murphy and never will be." Yet subsequently Hearst unaccountably consented to a fusion of forces which resulted in the election of a mixed ticket of Independence Leaguers and Democrats to all state offices save that of Governor.

Murphy was astute enough to realize that Hearst, as an independent, would either win or run second to the Republican nominee. So the boss swallowed personal prejudices, made Hearst a "regular" Democrat and insured the retention by Tammany of vitally important election machinery. Privately he may have yearned for the defeat of the man who had "put him in stripes" a year before.

When the Democrats met at Buffalo, Murphy pushed through Hearst's nomination by brute force in a convention which sat sullen, ugly and defiant. It was a weird situation. The Hearst managers had obtained about one-third of the delegates. Murphy's manipulation of the Membership Committee gave him another one-third. State Senator Thomas F. O'Grady, an old-line Tammany leader to whom Hearst was anathema, was chairman of the Membership Committee. After he had seated a number of Hearst delegates, riding roughshod over contestants, Grady mopped his dripping brow and delivered himself of a remark which has become a classic in state politics: "Boys, I have done the dirtiest day's work of my life."

A fortnight before, Hearst had been nominated for Governor by a wildly enthusiastic convention of the Independence League in Carnegie Hall, New

York, on a platform calling for municipal ownership of public utilities, election law reforms, and war to the hilt against "criminal combinations of capital."

The Republicans put up a formidable candidate, Charles Evans Hughes, whose success in exposing the insurance frauds had been lavishly praised by Hearst. Those who supposed this would embarrass Hearst underestimated the man's surprising dexterities. Overnight, Hughes became not a fearless scourge of grafters but a mere tool of the "plunderbund." When the austere Hughes was needled into attacking Hearst as a demagogue and into denying that his own income flowed chiefly from the hated corporations, Hearst retorted: "I define a corporation attorney as a man who served the corporations before he went into politics and who expects to serve the corporations after he has gone out of politics. If Mr. Hughes will stop lying about me, I will stop telling the truth about him."

As usual, the Hearst papers employed the inimitable wizardry of their caricaturists against the boss' political opponent. The risibilities of even the most humorless individual were stirred when the dignified, heavily bearded Hughes was portrayed as an animated "featherduster" behind which the Pirates of High Finance hid. Soon the irreverent man in the street was referring openly to the Republican nominee as Featherduster. It was one of those universal though ridiculous thrusts of satire which no one could forget.

When Hearst appeared in the big cities upstate he was received by enormous crowds and almost fanatical evidences of devotion. Puzzled and concerned by the obvious inroads Hearst was making in traditional Republican territory, the *Outlook* assigned experienced observers to analyze the Hearst following.

Their report was interesting:—

> In one of the large cities a man sat in a cobbler shop with his stocking feet on a newspaper while the cobbler repaired his shoes. He was evidently a small tradesman. He was not a Party man, but he might be termed normally a Republican. He predicted, rather vindictively, that Hearst would "sweep the state." He put his support of Hearst on the ground of the increase in the number of swollen fortunes, idleness of rich men's sons and the difficulty of competing with big concerns. . . . A mild-faced, quiet-voiced working man, a Republican all his life, confessed his adherence to Mr. Hearst and predicted the vote for him would be a surprise. A deaf old man, excited by the Hearst meeting, walked along the street shouting so that he could be heard a block away: "That's the man! I've been a Republican all my life and I've been voting for a lot of rottenness. Talk about a square deal! What we want is a new deal—all round!"

Even in rural sections great audiences listened to Hearst attentively. Record attendances greeted his numerous appearances at county fairs. Critics sneered that farmers came to see him as they would have come to see any "other circus freak." This may have been so in the early days of the campaign. Soon, however, the farmers and upstate citizens generally were listening to him eagerly. Babies were named for him in batches, a sure barometer in politics. Pleased as Punch, Hearst directed a secretary to take down the names; and each gurgling and promising young voter-to-be received a commemorative silver cup. The candidate's own stout youngster George, now thirty months old, appeared often beside his father, waving his country's flag like a trained campaigner and crowing his delight at the excitement.

At the big meetings in New York City thousands were turned away. The editor repeated over and over again that he was running as an independent and that if elected he would drive Boss Murphy and his ilk out of politics.

"I decline to fuse with Tammany Hall," he exclaimed in his high yet penetrating voice. "I repeat now that I am unalterably opposed to the Murphys, the McCarrens, Sullivans and McClellans and to the kind of politics they represent. The old parties are infested with the vermin of bossism, corruption, and rascals in office who mouth empty words about civic righteousness while the dollars of their corporate masters are jingling in their pockets."

Hearst crossed the bridge into Brooklyn, bailiwick of McCarren, and amid turbulent scenes denounced the Kings County boss as "a corrupt scoundrel and tool of Standard Oil." Everywhere his cavalcade went there was a racket and roar that could be heard for blocks. Hearst loved it. By contrast the unemotional Hughes meetings held all the percussive effect of a Sunday school picnic. From his retreat in Ireland, where he was leading the life of a country gentleman, old Dick Croker, abdicated boss of Tammany, added to the gaiety of the campaign by denouncing both Hearst and Murphy. Old Dick, without cracking a smile, allowed that it was downright "unprincipled" for Murphy and the other Tammany boys to support a fellow who was "allus" portraying them as jail bait.

Arthur Brisbane, with his facility at coining apt phrases, said:—

"The plutocrats and the anarchists are against Mr. Hearst. The first class because they want to plunder the people; the second class because they want no law. The richest men of this country owe Mr. Hearst a debt because he is trying to solve the problems of civilization by persuasion and helpful discussion."

On November 1, Secretary of State Elihu Root delivered the major speech of the campaign for Hughes at Utica. He quoted with telling effect Theodore Roosevelt's denunciation of the "reckless utterances" of the "deliberate demagogue" who had inflamed the assassin of McKinley and thundered:

151

"I say, by the President's authority, that in penning these words, with the horror of President McKinley's murder fresh before him, he had Mr. Hearst specifically in his mind. And I say, by his authority, that what he thought of Mr. Hearst then he thinks of Mr. Hearst now."

The struggle seemed to come to an emotional climax with Root's appearance in Utica. The Secretary's speech had been given out in advance and as he and Hughes rode from the railroad station to the hall newsboys confronted them with copies of the New York *Evening Journal,* its front page ablaze with a great cartoon showing "Root the Rat" gnawing away at the rights of the people. Fist fights broke out along the street and in the auditorium, where the speaker was heckled and cheered in turn. Trembling with rage, the usually controlled Root poured upon his tormentor Hearst such epithets as "insincere demagogue" and "revolutionist."

Hearst closed his campaign with a roaring meeting in Madison Square Garden, where once again thousands flung themselves against the police lines in a fruitless effort to gain entrance into an already jammed arena. A *World* reporter gives us a graphic description of the forty-three-year-old man who had turned New York and a large part of the country topsy-turvy:—

> Hearst presented a striking figure, the predominant notes of which were the clear, pink-tinted complexion of his face, a white Ascot tie knotted under a high, turned-down soiled white collar in which nestled a little brown pin that looked as if it might have cost as much as forty-five cents. His light tawny hair was sleek and brushed over his forehead, a stray lock reaching almost to the brow of his left eye. His tall straight figure was encased in a long Prince Albert coat that was shiny at the elbows and was long at the sides. His trousers of dark gray stripe had not been recently creased. Mr. Hearst's first act upon reaching the platform was to rub the back of his left hand over his mouth. Then he picked up a beer glass and poured into it a drink of water from a cracked white pitcher that stood on the reading stand.
>
> He turned to Henry A. Powell who had called the meeting together, made a remark, and the corners of his mouth turned up in a broad smile of almost childish pleasure. Then he faced the audience, gripped the rail in front of him with both hands and drummed upon it with his fingers. His right foot tapped in unison with the crash of the band of one hundred and fifty pieces behind him. He bowed as each succeeding wave of cheers bellowed at him from the front.

At Tammany Hall Murphy stolidly ignored Hearst's continued attacks and predicted the publisher's election by a 100,000 plurality. Hearst's executives, untrained in politics, poured equally pleasing prophecies into his ears. The day before election the candidate called a conference of his principal subordinates. Brisbane, S. S. Carvalho, T. T. Williams ("Good Tom" of the *Examiner*), now business manager of the *American,* and others assured the Chief of his certain election, but Louis Lang, the veteran reporter who had the ear of every politician in the state, edged toward the door.

Hearst called him back. "What is your opinion, Louie?" he asked. "I'd rather not say," replied the reporter. Hearst insisted. "Chief, you're licked, licked by at least 50,000," explained Lang, bluntly. "You sealed your own warrant of defeat when you turned down Pat McCarren. He and Tim Sullivan are going to knife you. So are many Tammany district leaders. You will carry the city but Mr. Hughes' vote upstate will defeat you and the election won't be particularly close." There were murmurs of dissent and incredulity. Hearst's own expression was one of bewilderment and displeasure. No one sought to halt Lang this time when he again headed for the door.

The prediction proved accurate. The vote in the state was: Hughes, 749,002; Hearst, 691,105. For New York City the figures stood: Hughes, 261,455; Hearst, 338,513. Hearst carried every borough in the city but ran far behind the rest of the ticket. The entire Democratic-Independence League slate was elected with the exception of the candidate for Governor. The McCarren knife had been effectively employed.

Hearst was deeply hurt but expressed no public regret, saying merely: "I congratulate the bosses on their foresight in defeating me, for my first act as Governor would have been to lift the dishonest officials by the hair of their unworthy heads." Then he took his wife and son on a trip to Mexico to inspect his mining properties and ranches. On the way back he wrote to his mother on a double post card:—

> We have just arrived in God-blessed California. The light is real sunlight—not artificial light. The heat is real sun heat, not steam heat. The Colorado River is real mud. The Yuma desert is real dirt, and the Indians are mostly real dirt, too.
>
> Some people may object to the horned toad, the cacti and the tarantula, but I like them. I like them, not for what they are, but what they may become. The horned toad will soon be replaced by the Eastern tourists, and the cacti by orange groves, and the tarantula by the real estate agents. Most old Californians prefer the horned toad, the cacti and the tarantula, but I am for progress and reform. I think California is the best country in the world, and always will be, no matter who comes into it or what is done to it.
>
> *Vive le ranch!* I am going to save up and build a cabin down at the ranch just big enough for you and Millie and the baby and me.

That winter, after Mr. Hughes had taken office, Hearst happened to be in Albany. He said to his representative at the capital: "Think I'll walk up the hill and see 'Featherduster.' Wonder if he will be glad to see me?" The meeting was most pleasant. Hughes piloted his visitor into his private office and the quondam rivals chatted for half an hour. "The Governor is a pretty human sort of fellow," remarked Hearst later.

During the struggle in 1906 Hearst's most caustic critic and bitterest journalistic enemy was James Gordon Bennett, owner of the New York *Herald*. At that time Bennett was under Federal indictment, charged with using the mails for the circulation of indecent reading matter. The indictment grew out of attacks by the Hearst papers upon the *Herald's* notorious "Personal" column. Bennett, voluntarily "exiled" in Paris, wrote Hearst a letter enclosing cuttings from the *Evening Journal* and the *American* and stating: "I shall never forget you in this matter." Hearst replied succinctly: "I hope you never will." Upon order of Bennett, Hearst's name was excluded from the *Herald* for many years.

The Hearst-Bennett feud had its beginnings in 1899 when it became evident that the *Herald's* "Personal" column had become an adjunct of the red-light district and the white-slave trade. The *Herald* was reaping a dollar a line from advertisements inserted by "chic Parisian ladies with cosy suites," "masseuses with highly magnetic manners" for "jolly sports" desiring the acquaintance of "witty, affectionate ladies possessing beautiful figures, hair, teeth." "Pleasant possibilities" were promised. A "wealthy, retired bachelor" advertised for "a fifteen-year-old Miss as secretary. Must be pretty and good figure. Splendid opportunity. Write particulars in own hand. MATINEE."

Such ads as these evoked gales of laughter in certain circles in New York: "LADY loyal, lovable, loving, with famished heart craves devotion of but one man financially worth while. FAITH, HOPE, CHARITY." "Is there a TRUE man who would help and care for a SWEET girl?" "A woman finds paddling own canoe dreary task; seeks manly pilot." "Refined young lady desires immediate loan." "The little girl cannot meet expenses this month. Hopes Mr. W. will see this and embrace opportunity he requested at lunch. THE FASCINATING BABY."

Under the direction of Victor A. Watson, a *Journal* reporter, Hearst investigators rented a post-office box under an assumed name and obtained evidence that the "Personal" column was being used for vicious purposes and that the *Herald* knew and pandered to this employment of its columns. The *Herald* and its proprietor were indicted in October, 1906. Bennett kept out of the jurisdiction as long as he could. Finally he traveled to New York by a roundabout route, pleaded guilty as charged on April 10, 1907 and paid a fine of $25,000 in cash. Thereafter he shunned the city of his birth.

154

Standard Oil Letters

> An honest politician is one who, when he is bought, will stay bought.
>
> SIMON CAMERON

10

"I WON'T LOOK at a paper, not even French papers," Hearst wrote his mother from Paris in the summer of 1907. "I don't know what is happening anywhere. I have telegrams from the office saying that everything is all right there, but I am not interested in the 'news.' I have the same aversion to news that I once had for stewed pears after having got sick from them. My mental gorge gags at the thought of news."

It was a confession to the person who understood him best that even his preternatural energies required replenishment at times. Accordingly, with his vivacious, humorful young wife, he poked by motor into quaint and odd corners of the Continent, mingling with the people, reveling in their unhurried way of life and constantly searching out and purchasing rare and beautiful objects.

This idyllic journey was marked also by an item of family news which thrilled and delighted the travelers: assurance that after an interval of almost four years they were again to become parents.

The baby, a blue-eyed boy who was named for his father, arrived on January 27, 1908; and his birth was attended by a circumstance so poignant that his parents were plunged into despair. For ten days it seemed impossible that he could live. A closed pylorus, the tube connecting the stomach with the small intestine, entirely prevented the newborn infant from retaining nourishment.

With the child wasting away day by day physicians, including the famous baby specialists Drs. Jacoby and Holt, advised an operation as a last resort, although admitting that the chance of survival was infinitesimal.

At this most critical juncture Mrs. Jessamine Rugg Goddard, wife of the *American Weekly's* editor Morrill Goddard, came to the Hearst home on Lexington Avenue. She was then experimenting with Christian Science. With her was Miss Hughes, a Science practitioner, who, Mrs. Goddard said, had healed her baby of double pneumonia after the doctors had yielded hope. All that night the healer prayed over the child. In the morning the emaciated infant took and retained milk and started on the road to recovery.

Metaphysical speculation is seldom very profitable. Yet, looking today at W. R. Hearst, Jr., with his six-foot plus, 190-pound frame, in the full flush of mental and physical vigor, one wonders at the mystery of the benign fate which spared from extinction a life that has proved of growing importance to the Hearst organization and to the nation.

The miracle—if miracle it was—was indirectly responsible for what the late Arthur Brisbane often cited as perhaps his finest piece of reporting: his interview with Mrs. Mary Baker Eddy in her Concord, New Hampshire, home June 8, 1908. Mrs. Eddy and her cult were under attack in *McClure's* magazine and Hearst assigned Brisbane with instructions to defend her. Afterwards Hearst, born an Episcopalian, and his wife, a Catholic, demonstrated a friendly interest in the faith which they believed had healed their son by sending him and two of his brothers to a Christian Science Sunday school.

Although plagued frequently by recurrent illnesses, young Bill Hearst grew into a fun-loving, game-playing youngster.

That year of 1908 is memorable for Hearst's production and devastating use of the so-called Standard Oil Letters. These were intimate papers of John D. Archbold, executive vice-president of the Standard Oil Company. Archbold was also a deacon in the Methodist Church.

The documents produced by Hearst, as though conjured out of thin air, proved that Archbold had for many years acted as political manipulator for the powerful oil group and, by liberal employment of secret certificates of deposit and other potent allurements, had swayed elections, judicial appointments and legislation in individual states and in both houses of Congress. Men of high influence in both parties were involved, among them Senators Joseph Benson Foraker and Marcus Alonzo Hanna (Ohio), Boies Penrose and Matthew Quay (Pennsylvania), Republicans; and Senator Joseph D. Bailey (Texas), Democrat.

Nothing in the entire course of his throbbing career is more indicative of the unique reaches of Hearst and his genius for violently stirring up things at the dramatic moment than the manner of his Standard Oil exposure. He used the letters remorselessly to drive into the public consciousness his credo that both established parties were corrupt and should be swept from office. He went tumbling about the country crying a plague upon Democratic and Republican machines alike, his ammunition the deadly documents

156

which had strangely popped into his possession from the very letter files of the hated oil monopoly.

During the Presidential campaign of 1908 and at intervals for four years thereafter Hearst entertained and astonished the country, paralyzed the politicians, and tantalized his foemen. Plain as was his purpose, his maneuvers were feline in their ferocity; and without consideration for conventional ethical standards.

The Archbold letters literally walked into the Hearst newspaper offices. This is how it came about:—

Employed in the Standard Oil office at No. 26 Broadway, New York, as messengers, door tenders and file clerks were two young men, William Winkfield and Charles Stump. The former was a stepson of Mr. Archbold's negro butler, James Wilkins, a trusted employee of twenty years' service. Stump was a white man.

Willie Winkfield played the races and "galloped" dice with sporty members of his race in a dive called the Little Savoy in West Thirty-fifth Street.

Frequently he found himself in need of funds. He therefore conceived a plan of abstracting letters from the Standard Oil files and selling them to newspapers. Using Stump as a go-between, Winkfield got into communication with editors of the New York *American*. This was shortly after the Presidential election of 1904.

Soon Winkfield and Stump began to loiter about the Standard Oil office after other employees had left. They made foray after foray upon Archbold's letter-books and carried away many bundles wrapped in newspapers. Important letters were photostated during the night and returned to the files early the following morning. No suspicion attached itself to the messengers, although both were discharged for other causes within a year. It never became known exactly how many Standard Oil letters were "borrowed" by Winkfield and Stump. The total sum obtained, it is said, was $20,500.

Initialed for identification purposes by three Hearst employees—John L. Eddy, city editor of the *American,* Charles Tebbs, director of the art department and P. L. Campbell, reporter—the photostats remained locked in a safe in New York for more than three years. John D. Archbold went along serenely "protecting," according to his lights, the interests of his supertrust in the government and politics of the country.

This was the situation on the evening of September 17, 1908, when several thousand citizens of Columbus, Ohio, gathered in Memorial Hall to hear an address by Hearst. The publisher, owner of seven newspapers in five cities, was campaigning in behalf of his Independence Party. He had put an independent ticket into the field to oppose both the ubiquitous William Jennings Bryan, making a third bid for the White House, and William Howard Taft, whom President Theodore Roosevelt had selected as the Republican candidate.

The Independence Party's candidate for President was Thomas L. Hisgen of Massachusetts, a manufacturer of kerosene and axle grease, whose chief claim to fame was that he was one of the pitifully few business men who had fought the Standard Oil octopus and survived.

A bluff, forthright sort of fellow, Hisgen had made a good though losing campaign for Governor in Massachusetts, traveling about in an old-fashioned carryall and talking with the farmers in their fields. He was the type of plain, pioneer American that Hearst most admired. Hisgen's running mate was John Temple Graves of Georgia, a florid orator and Hearst special writer.

Hisgen and Graves had been nominated in Orchestra Hall, Chicago, on July 29. The gathering was an interesting political phenomenon, a national convention in miniature. Among the five hundred delegates were many printers and stereotypers from the Hearst papers in Chicago. Andy Lawrence, Hearst's chief viceroy in Chicago, supplied a "wrecking crew" of circulation department huskies to drown out any possible temerarious shouts for Hearst's former ally, Bryan. The word had gone forth that there was to be only one boss so far as dictating nominations was concerned. His initials were "W. R. H."

When Hearst came to Columbus stumping for his ticket, the people welcomed the great nonconformist avidly. His picturesque methods of fighting and audacious launching of a new national party "on nothing except nerve" had aroused eager curiosity concerning both himself and his principles. There was standing room only in Memorial Hall that warm September evening. The crowd came prepared for a colorful exhibition of campaign rhetoric. It listened, it is interesting to note, without sensing the importance of Hearst's disclosures. The audience was plainly disappointed when the speaker, without emphasis of voice or gesture, said gravely:—

> *Gentlemen:* The Independence Party claims that the corruption fund in American politics has become more powerful than the people's vote. We claim that political machines and corrupt bosses and criminal special interests control the government for their own advantage and that we no longer have either a government of the people or a government in the interest of the people. . . . We claim the Democrats are today eagerly competing with the Republicans for trust favor. We claim that when Theodore Roosevelt whipped the Standard Oil out of the Republican Party the Democratic Party welcomed that convicted criminal with open arms. We claim that the Democratic Party killed for Mr. Rockefeller the fatted calf. . . .
>
> I am not here to amuse you and entertain you with oratory, but I am here to present to you as patriotic American citizens some facts

that should startle you and alarm you and arouse you to a fitting sense of the genuine danger that threatens our republic. I am not here either with empty assertions but with legal evidence and documentary proof. I ask you to rally to your country's needs, to rescue your country from the greatest danger that can threaten a republic —the danger that is within the gates—the corrupting power of unscrupulous and criminal wealth.

I am now going to read copies of letters written by Mr. John D. Archbold, chief agent of the Standard Oil, an intimate personal representative of Mr. Rockefeller and Mr. Rogers. These letters have been given me by a gentleman who has intimate association with this giant of corruption, the Standard Oil, but whose name I may not divulge lest he be subjected to the persecution of this monopoly.

26 Broadway, New York.
March 9, 1900.

My dear Senator:
I have your favor of last night with enclosure, which letter with letter from Mr. Elliott commenting on same, I beg to send you herewith. Perhaps it would be better to make a demonstration against the whole bill, but certainly the ninth clause to which Mr. Elliott refers should be stricken out, and the same is true of House Bill No. 500, also introduced by Mr. Price, in relation to foreign corporations, in which the same objectionable clause occurs.

Am glad to hear that you think the situation is fairly well in hand.

Very truly yours,
Jno. D. Archbold.

Hon. J. B. Foraker,
Senate Chamber,
Washington, D. C.

26 Broadway, New York.
March 26, 1900.

Hon. J. B. Foraker,
1500 Sixteenth St.,
Washington, D. C.

Dear Senator:
In accordance with our understanding, I now beg to enclose you certificate of deposit to your favor of $15,000. Kindly acknowledge receipt and oblige.

Yours very truly,
Jno. D. Archbold.

159

26 Broadway, New York.
February 16, 1900.
(Personal)

My dear Senator:

Here is still another very objectional bill. It is so outrageous as to be ridiculous, but it needs to be looked after, and I hope there will be no difficulty in killing it.

Am anxious to hear from you as to the situation as a whole.

Very truly yours,
Jno. D. Archbold.

Hon. J. B. Foraker,
1500 Sixteenth St.,
Washington, D. C.

April 17, 1900.

My dear Senator:

I enclose you certificate of deposit to your favor for $14,500. We are greatly at a loss in the matter, but I send this, and will be glad to have a very frank talk with you when opportunity offers, and if you so desire.

I need scarcely again express our great gratification over the favorable outcome of affairs.

Very truly yours,
Jno. D. Archbold.

Hon. J. B. Foraker,
1500 Sixteenth St., City.

There, my friends, is some documentary evidence of how bills are declared to be unwise and unconstitutional and some intimation of the causes that lead to the defeat of such bills. I will read you the conclusion of a letter written by Mr. Sibley, a Representative from Pennsylvania—that is his title. But, in fact, he is, I believe, a representative of the Standard Oil Company. The letter was written to Mr. Archbold and relates how Mr. Sibley told Mr. Roosevelt that he should be careful how he offended the Standard Oil and that he could not afford to depend merely upon the support of the people. This is the conclusion of the letter: "For the first time in my life I told the President some plain if unpalatable truths as to the situation politically, and that no man should win or deserves to win who depended upon the rabble rather than upon the conservative men of affairs. I don't know as he really liked all I said, but he thanked me with apparent heartiness. Anything you may desire here in my power, please advise. Sincerely yours, Joseph C. Sibley."

Facsimile of a letter in which Mark Hanna told John D. Archbold, "I am 'holding the bag' and this is going to be an expensive campaign. I can see where I will land before this thing is over. So I have no doubt, I will have to CALL AGAIN," i.e., ask for more money. It concludes, "Should Johnson carry the Legislature, Corporations will catch it as I am as their representative, so-called." Tom L. Johnson, a Democrat, was the reform Mayor of Cleveland and a power in Ohio.

You gentlemen, I, Mr. Hisgen—all of us are the rabble. Seekers after office cannot depend upon us: they need the conservative citizens, these magnates of the great criminal trusts!

Mr. Roosevelt did not seem to heed Mr. Sibley's well-intentioned advice and he prosecuted the Standard Oil and the Standard Oil went out of the Republican Party and into the Democratic Party. Mr. Bryan appointed Mr. C. N. Haskell, political paymaster of the Standard Oil, to be chairman of the Committee on Platform. Mr. Bryan made Mr. Haskell treasurer of his national campaign fund to collect from Standard Oil substantial evidence of the great monopoly's appreciation.

Here are two more letters that will interest you:

New York, December 18, 1902.
My dear Senator:

You of course know of Judge Burket's candidacy for re-election to the Supreme Court bench in Ohio. We understand that his re-election to the position would be in the line of usage as followed in such cases in Ohio, and we feel very strongly that his eminent qualifications and great integrity entitle him to this further recognition.

We most earnestly hope that you agree with this view, and will favor and aid his re-election. Mr. Rogers joins me most heartily in this expression to you.

With kind regards, I am,
Very sincerely yours,
Jno. D. Archbold.

To Senator Foraker.

26 Broadway, New York.
March 20, 1903.
(Personal)

My dear Senator:

To our amazement, it is reported that Smith W. Bennett is making a canvass for the Attorney Generalship in Ohio. Mr. Bennett is a brother-in-law of F. S. Monnett, recent Attorney General, and was associated with Monnett in the action against us in that state. If there is any possible danger, which I cannot believe, of Mr. Bennett's candidacy assuming serious proportions, I would like to tell you something of our experience and impressions of the man in connection with that case. I am sure, however, that you will agree that Ohio is not so poorly off as to take that sort of timber for its

Attorney General. I will be very glad to hear from you on the subject.

Sincerely yours,
Jno. D. Archbold.

Hon. M. A. Hanna,
Washington, D. C.

Thus, in this simple, undramatic manner, Hearst released the first of the
letters with which he was to dumfound the country for four years. The
correspondence not only injected life and interest in the campaign but it
served as a determining influence in stimulating reform. Many laws requiring publicity for campaign expenditures grew directly out of it, as did
various state and national corrupt practices acts.

No coup ever stirred more excitement or pleased Hearst more. The publisher once wrote that "a President of the United States" had said to him
that "the value of the Standard Oil letters was not so much that they revealed anything new but that they proved what everybody suspected but
had not before been able to prove."

By presumption Hearst was quoting Theodore Roosevelt. A fortnight
after the election, and while Hearst was still exploding his Archbold bombs
in the camps of both parties, the President asked the publisher to visit him
in the White House. They talked for forty-five minutes. The President, according to Washington despatches which were never denied, asked Hearst
if any "gossip" in the Archbold letters referred to him. "Nothing that I intend to publish at this time," replied Hearst blandly.

As we have indicated, the first batch of letters created no excitement
among the Columbus audience or the newspaper men covering the meeting.
It was not until Hearst arrived in St. Louis on the following afternoon that
the press and public had fully realized the vital nature of the disclosure.

"When I got off the train at St. Louis," Hearst wrote in 1912, "it seemed
to me that all the newspaper men in America were there to inquire about
the Foraker letters and to ask how many and what kind of letters still remained to be read. Foraker had admitted the genuineness of the letters
published. Not knowing, however, that there were other letters to further
convict him, he had attempted explanations which, in the light of the other
letters, were obviously false. These statements of Foraker I refuted with
documents at hand, and Foraker retired from the discussion overwhelmed
by the evidence of his own correspondence. It was unfortunate for any one
during that campaign to attempt to deny or explain the implication of those
Standard Oil letters because the evidence contained in them was generally
sufficient to refute all denials or explanations."

In Memphis, on September 20, 1908, Hearst read a letter from Congressman Sibley—"the miserable little Standard Oil spy in the House"—to

Archbold informing the oil magnate that "Senator B, a Democrat," would be a "tower of strength and safety" and advising a conference with "B."

"Mr. Sibley does not say who Senator B is," remarked Hearst waggishly. "We'll have to do a little Sherlock Holmes work. Let's see, the vowels of the alphabet are a, e, i, o and u. It can't be Senator Bully as there is no Senator Bully. It can't be Bolly for the same reason. It can't be Billy unless Mr. Sibley is calling some Senator by his first name. It can't be Senator Belly. Can it be Senator Ba—? Why, to be sure there is a Senator Bailey and we have heard his name mentioned before in connection with Standard Oil. Another thing that makes me suspect the Senator referred to may be Senator Bailey is this letter from Mr. Archbold asking Senator B to come down to New York and step up to the captain's office quick," and he read an undated letter from Archbold to Sibley beginning: "We are anxious to have a talk here at as early a date as possible with Senator Bailey of Texas."

Returning East, Hearst released additional Foraker-Archbold correspondence showing payments of large sums to the influential Republican Senator. On September 22, President Roosevelt jumped in and rough-rode Foraker out of the Taft campaign. Foraker retired denouncing Roosevelt and Taft as ingrates. He was to have Samsonian revenge in 1912 when Hearst published a letter showing that Archbold and H. H. Rogers had been welcome guests at Oyster Bay before Roosevelt turned upon the "malefactors of great wealth" and ordered the proceedings against the trust which resulted in Federal Judge Landis' famous $29,000,000 fine.

It was then that John D. Rockefeller closed his steel trap of a mouth and remarked: "Judge Landis will never see this fine paid." It wasn't. Archbold took the witness stand that same year before a Senatorial investigating committee and testified with mixed emotions that Standard Oil had contributed $100,000 to the $2,100,000 Roosevelt campaign fund of 1904.

Hearst observed that Roosevelt's method with the trusts was to "hold a big stick in one hand, a contribution box in the other." The mercurial Teddy added to the gaiety of the times by actually praising Hearst in a left-handed sort of way for his Standard Oil revelations. "I have in times past criticized Mr. Hearst," said the President, "but in this matter he has rendered a public service of high importance. I hope he will publish all the letters which he has in his possession. If Mr. Hearst or anybody else has any letter from me dealing with Standard Oil affairs I shall be delighted to have it published."

In the 1908 campaign Archbold testily attacked Hearst as an exponent of nosegay journalism. He denounced Hearst's bit of white fiction that a "friend" had given him the letters and bemoaned his attorney's advice that he could not replevin the facsimiles or originals in the publisher's possession. Archbold was sorely handicapped in his comment and explanations because for all he knew Hearst might have obtained copies of his butcher

164

bills and household check-stubs. In answer to his critics, Hearst published a tart reply:—

> If I discover any more letters which tend to show that the people's representatives are in the pay of the privileged interests, and are traitorously betraying the people to these privileged interests, I will certainly inform the people of these dangerous and disgraceful conditions.
>
> There has been a good deal of hypocritical cant, chiefly from those whose rascality has been exposed, about the impropriety of publicly reading private letters. I do not consider that letters written to public men on matters affecting the public interests and threatening the public welfare are private letters. I do not consider that the offer of a $15,000 bribe by a privileged corporation to a public servant to betray a public trust is a private transaction.

For the remainder of the Taft-Bryan campaign at least the corporations cut down upon their customary lavish contributions to politics. Mark Hanna, that remarkable wholesale groceryman from Ohio, had elevated the collection of campaign funds to a fine art. Hanna did not collect funds, he levied them after the manner of the Algerian pirates. Banks and corporations were assessed on a cold-blooded *quid pro quo* basis. When the campaign was over the books were burned. It was an open secret that Hanna had disbursed more than $10,000,000 in each of the two McKinley campaigns of 1896 and 1900.

After the Hearst attacks the Democrats changed national chairmen and pledged themselves to make all contributions public by October 15, while the Republicans were forced to beg fifty-dollar contributions for the first time since the Civil War. However, so deeply engrained was the two-party system that despite the fanfaronade and the shouts of the populace, the Independence Party vote was negligible. The sovereign State of Georgia, for example, gave its doughty son John Temple Graves just seventy-seven votes. Nevertheless, keen observers agreed that Hearst had done some valuable subsoil ploughing.

Solid, friendly Tom Hisgen had exacted a promise that Hearst would speak during the campaign in Hisgen's birthplace, a remote Indiana village. To carry out his pledge and also to keep other engagements the schedule makers found that a special train would have to be hired at Indianapolis. Hearst stood the expense without demur and went bumping over a rough roadbed for two hundred miles. He threw his long legs over a seat in the none too clean day coach and chatted cheerfully with the trainmen.

A couple of hundred curious countrymen were gathered in the village hall. Hearst warmed up to his subject and pitched into both parties just as vigorously as though his forum was Madison Square Garden. Response was faint. The Hearst ideas were slow to percolate in the minds of men whose only contact with the outside world came through the weekly farm paper. But the tall, loose-jointed man in the frock coat and striped trousers waved his arms, stamped his feet and kept a-going. After three-quarters of an hour came the blast of train whistles. Fred Lawrence, one of his political managers, had arranged the signal.

"Toot, toot!"

Lawrence pulled at Hearst's coattails. "What is it, Fred?" whispered Hearst. "We've got to get away, Chief, to catch the Big Four. Haven't a minute to spare."

"Toot! TOOT!"

Hearst brought his peroration to a close. The farmers moved silently toward their hitched horses. Hearst and Lawrence dashed for the train. In the dimly lighted day coach, Hearst turned to Lawrence and remarked roguishly: "Splendid meeting, eh, Fred?"

"Yes, splendid, Mr. Hearst."

"Good speech, too, Fred. We ought to get many votes in this county, Fred, many votes."

They grinned at each other. At Indianapolis, the Big Four flyer was waiting. Hearst swung aboard and, as the train gained headway, shouted: "Oh, Fred, give the conductor a hundred. And don't forget the engineer. A hundred for him too, Fred. Don't forget. Good-bye. Fine meeting!"

The election returns showed a big round zero for the Independence Party in the county of its candidate's birth.

Commenting after the election upon the Independence Party's slogan, "Vote for Hisgen, Graves and Principle," the eminent "Fingy" Connors, Democratic boss of Buffalo, commented feelingly: "People don't want no principle; they want to be on the winning side."

The campaign concluded, Hearst threw himself with zeal and energy into the execution of large and comprehensive plans for his various newspapers. He seemed happy in his complete divorcement from politics and told his followers, amid shouts of dissent, that he would not again run for office. The occasion was a banquet tendered him in April, 1909.

Smiling somewhat sadly, the great dissenter told the cheering company:—

"I shall keep on fighting but for someone else. The Independence Party is like the rod hanging conspicuously in a schoolroom. The very sight of it makes bad political boys better. Do you not realize that almost every progressive measure that is before our lawmaking bodies, or that has actually passed into law, found its main source and first strength in the agitation of our Party?"

Events soon induced the speaker to change his mind.

At the next Mayoralty election Hearst favored Supreme Court Justice

166

A Hearst
Family
Album

The publisher's mother,
Phoebe Apperson Hearst.
She died in 1919 at the
age of seventy-six.

Phoebe Hearst and son, aged six months. He was her only child.

Master Willie, going on nine and a rebel against going to dancing school.

ator George Hearst

his sixties. He

d in 1891, aged seventy-one,

r years after W. R. had

t Harvard and

rsuaded his father

let him run the

n Francisco *Examiner*.

W. R.'s Harvard activities included being an actor.

distinctive, new kind of

rnalism made its appearance in

Examiner. This is an 1890 issue.

W. R. made cameramen coequal in importance with reporters in the coverage of news. Pictorial journalism got its biggest impetus from the coverage given the Spanish-American War in the *Examiner* and in Hearst's second paper, the New York *Journal*. This is W. R. as war photographer on the despatch boat he chartered in 1898.

After the war, Hearst was persuaded to take to the political platform. He was elected to Congress from New York in 1902, the year before he married Millicent Willson. In the 1904 Democratic Presidential Convention, he got 263 votes for the nomination.

W. R., Jr. and John with their father on the *Olympic* in 1922. About this time, young Will wrote his father, "I realize us kids are handicapped by too much money." John reassured his father, "I think we both will turn out to be hard workers." Hearst treasured the letters.

Mr. and Mrs. Hearst in 1923 with the first Kerry blue terriers brought into the U. S. Unbeknownst to Hearst, they had been trained by Irish republicans. The dogs caused him trouble in New York by jumping at any uniformed police, including Irish cops.

Hearst's enormous art collection was started in his youth with stamps, coins, medallions, porcelains. He became the world's foremost private owner of tapestries, armor, Hispano-Moresque ceramics.

A circular basin in Hispano-Moresque faience from the Hearst collection. The decoration is blue with red copper metal reflections. The back (below) has a belled ox. Auction price of this piece: $17,000.

[←] One of many superb full suits of Gothic armor W. R. amassed. It was made at Augsburg about 1480. Part of a Hearst Foundation gift which placed Detroit's Institute of Fine Arts among the foremost possessors of XV, XVI and XVII century armor.

Hearst kept a large part of his armor and other art treasures in his historic St. Donat's Castle in Wales [→]. This view of St. Donat's is from one of its tiers of centuries-old gardens.

Hearst was more at home at San Simeon, and spent most of his later years there. One of its old master sculptures from the Old World is the background of a picture of him with "Helen"—the dachshund about which he wrote a famous column in 1942.

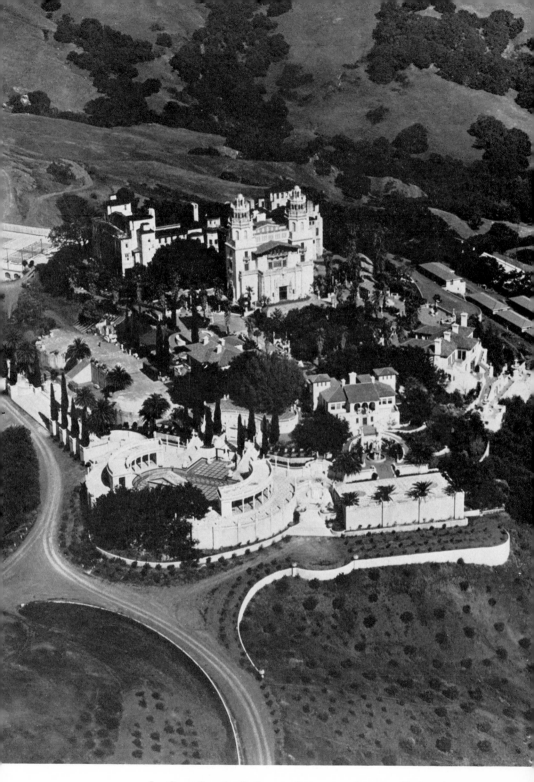

La Casa Grande, Italian gardens, guest houses, office, and open swimming pool (left) at San Simeon. Hearst, his wife and sons gave it a grand opening on Christmas Eve, 1925. Subsequent additions included an enclosed swimming pool in a gymnasium and a theatre.

Hearst sought work as avidly as other men pursued pleasure and sport. Wherever he was—San Simeon, New York, at sea, Europe, he gave his daily personal attention to the management of his far-flung enterprises. Associates remember his frequently working eight hours without a halt.

He played as vigorously. He teamed up with son Bill (background) against sons George and John in tennis on his seventy-first birthday at San Simeon.

The enterprise he encouraged and expected of his newsmen resulted in many scoops as notable as the publication of this historic picture in 1914. It proved the cruiser *Audacious* had been sunk by a German submarine—a fact denied officially by the British.

...awarded the W. R. Hearst communication enterprises. Front

Their mother, Mrs. William Randolph Hearst, Sr., one of the great ladies of New York society, was hostess to King Paul and Queen Frederika of Greece at the Metropolitan Opera in 1953.

A third generation is getting ready to continue the
Hearst tradition. John, son of John Randolph, has
won prizes as a go-getter news photographer.

William J. Gaynor as the anti-Tammany candidate. Gaynor was an independent Democrat who in his younger days had broken up the so-called "Coney Island Graft Ring." Although tart of temperament and notoriously fond of the bottle, he was a man of scholarly attainment.

Judge Gaynor had attacked Tammany Hall as vehemently as any man in public life. But Charles Francis Murphy, who never permitted personal feelings to sway his political judgment, persuaded Gaynor to accept the Tammany nomination. Through Gaynor's popularity he hoped to gain control of a Board of Estimate which would have the letting of valuable subway contracts and expenditure of almost $1,000,000,000 in the ensuing four years. Also Murphy reasoned that Hearst was too deeply committed to Gaynor to withdraw his partly promised support. The boss guessed wrong.

After personally failing to induce Gaynor to repudiate Tammany, Hearst himself accepted an independent nomination for Mayor tendered him by the Hearstites' new local organization, the Civic Alliance. The publisher stood on the rostrum at Carnegie Hall and for fifteen minutes smilingly responded to the old chant of the Independence League: "Hearst! Hearst! Hearst!"

The Civic Alliance endorsed all anti-Tammany candidates (the Fusion-Republican ticket) below the rank of Mayor, thus, as it turned out, insuring the election of a Board of Estimate opposed to the Hall. Hearst put just enough energy into the campaign to accomplish his purpose as shown by the final Mayoralty vote: Gaynor (Dem.), 250,387; Bannard (Fusion-Rep.), 177,304; Hearst (Ind.), 154,187.

Quite ignoring the mild-mannered Otto T. Bannard, Hearst and irascible old Judge Gaynor centered their attacks upon each other. And the fur flew as in an encounter of Kilkenny cats. The Judge enlisted the testimony of a Hearst editor to prove that Hearst had promised to support Gaynor. Hearst read his employee's statement with a grin and remarked: "Oh, Mr. Rudolph Block is my comic editor," and added: "It is true that Mr. Gaynor came humbly up to my house once, twice, thrice, hat in hand to beg my support. I refused it. Judge Gaynor is not a lifelong friend, or a deeply loved brother to whom a blind devotion is due. He has been to me merely a representative of certain ideas, an exponent of certain principles. While he was supporting those principles, I supported him."

As election neared, Gaynor's vituperation reached a new low in scurrility. One night, obviously so intoxicated that he could scarcely stand, he shrieked at hecklers, "Shut up you slanderers, you blackguards!" Again he shrieked that Hearst's face was one "which almost makes me puke." In the words of his biographer, Mortimer Smith, it was difficult to believe that this man "held a studious and intellectual social and political philosophy."

Six weeks after the election, Hearst threw the town into an uproar when he began publishing a batch of letters to Charles F. Murphy—notes written by the leader's lieutenants to him while he was resting at Mount Clemens, Michigan. Murphy charged that a maid had been bribed to turn over to a Hearst agent the torn contents of Murphy's wastebasket.

The letters to a boss at ease showed that Murphy and Mayor-elect Gaynor were working in harmony. The Mount Clemens basket yielded much of the inside game of getting jobs for more or less deserving Tammany men. The letters, holding no surprises to insiders, were a revelation to laymen.

Mayor Gaynor and Hearst were in vivid, roaring feud during the former's entire stormy term. Gaynor, with a tongue like acid biting into an etching, was one of the few foemen who ever got under Hearst's skin. Upon every occasion, in public and private, the Mayor bitterly attacked Hearst and his "claptrap, ragbag newspapers." Once, after a particularly vigorous assault at a public dinner, T. T. Williams, business manager of the *Evening Journal,* pushed forward, shook his fist in the Mayor's face and challenged him to make good his charges. Twenty minutes of uproar and excitement followed "Good Tom's" outburst.

Professor Woodrow Wilson was one of the diners and he kept his ears open. Two years later, when Wilson had entered the rough arena of politics and become Governor of New Jersey, he and Mayor Gaynor exchanged letters denouncing Hearst.

After the attempted assassination of Mayor Gaynor by a disgruntled city employee as the Mayor was boarding a ship for Europe, every newspaper editor in town naturally recalled the McKinley episode. Herbert Bayard Swope and Henry Stansbury, star men on the *World* and the *American* respectively, arrived simultaneously at the door of the Hoboken, New Jersey, cell where the dazed, mauled prisoner, a man named Gallagher, was confined. Both reporters were panting.

Gallagher sat slumped on his cot, head in hands. Swope, recovering his breath, spoke first. "Listen to me, Gallagher," he barked. "You read the *Journal* and the *American,* don't you? You have read attacks on Mayor Gaynor in the Hearst papers? Now, haven't you!"

Swope's commanding, insistent tones reached the brain of the dazed man on the cot. Gallagher looked up. Stansbury and Swope stood taut. "Hell, no!" said Gallagher, "I read the *Times."* Gallagher never knew why his visitors fell weakly into each other's arms and laughed until they rattled the rust on the bars.

Between, and even during his various excursions into politics, Hearst kept in closest personal touch with every detail of his expanding organization. His genius for evocative strokes in journalism bubbled out constantly. One Sunday evening—his visits to the office of the New York *American* were frequent on Sundays— he strolled over to the night city editor's desk, looked over a dull news schedule, then called for the proofs of two stories.

One was a despatch from William Hoster, in Georgia, narrating futile efforts of the Pujo Money Trust Committee agents to subpoena William Rockefeller for a Washington hearing. Rockefeller was hidden away on Jekyl Island. All of special counsel Samuel Untermeyer's ingenuity could not lure the Standard Oil magnate into accepting service. The capitalist had no desire to undergo one of the public trepanning operations that so delight the souls of our most notorious legal exhibitionists.

The other story in which Mr. Hearst seemed interested was a short despatch from Tarrytown on Hudson briefly quoting one of John D. Rockefeller Jr.'s saccharine addresses before a local Bible class. Hearst fussed over the proofs. Then he seized a blank sheet of copy paper and rapidly wrote this "telephone wire" head, as it was dubbed in the shop:—

WILLIAM JUMPS OVER THE BACK FENCE WHILE JOHN D. JR. PRATES MORALITY

Hearst's men, particularly Arthur Brisbane, were not far behind their chief so far as inventiveness and bizarre ideas were concerned.

One day A. B. called in Hugh Fullerton, an able sports writer, and disclosed that he had thought up a sure-fire method which would enable the *Evening Journal's* handicappers to pick winning horses for their clientele.

"Hugh," explained the great editor, "I want you to hire an X-ray expert and a machine and X-ray the heart and lungs of every horse entered in Saturday's big race. Get the pictures from every possible angle and bring the plates to me. The horse with the stoutest heart and biggest lung development will be your winner!"

Fullerton dutifully accepted the assignment, although he well knew that the race track authorities would ban so radical an experiment. Accordingly, he persuaded the owner of an ancient, broken down horse to permit pictures to be taken ad-lib of the animal's heart and lungs. The X-ray technician did his work so cleverly that each picture looked different. To each, Fullerton attached the name of an entry for the big race, and marched with them into Brisbane's office.

The latter, not suspecting the hoax, looked over the collection and, after careful study, beamed in triumph. "Here's your winner," he said with finality. "Science beats guesswork every time. This horse is a cinch." And Big George, as the irreverent Tad had dubbed Brisbane because of his bulging forehead, leaned back in his chair with infinite satisfaction.

The epilogue, as related by Fullerton, may afford wry amusement to inveterate horse players. "When I got out of A. B.'s office I laughed till I cried," said the would-be hoaxer. "But what do you think happened? The horse the old man picked actually won the race!"

With the arrival in 1909 of a third son, John Randolph, Grandmother Phoebe Hearst pressed her son and his wife to bring the children to California for a long visit. The family managed the trip early in 1910. Mrs. Hearst senior was so pleased that thereafter she claimed as much of the youngsters' time as circumstances would permit.

Summer vacations and often long periods between were passed by the lively lads either at their grandmother's hacienda near Pleasanton or at Wyntoon, near Mount Shasta in northern California, where she had built a German castle on the rushing McCloud River. Here Indians still roamed the wilderness of pine and spruce and the boys, as they grew up, swam, fished and hunted with the red men.

When mere babies the children were taught to ride by sitting first in a basket chair on a beloved pony, Brownie. At five, William Jr. was able to ride Brownie alone. At six he was given his own mount.

Before long Phoebe Hearst built a structure in a grove of oaks near her hacienda which she called the "Boys' House." The upper floor contained thirteen large rooms for the youngsters, their nurses and, as time went on, tutors and governesses. Downstairs was a playroom spacious enough to stage races on tricycles. In the yard were games, sand piles, swings. When the time came for the children to return East, their adoring grandmother preserved the illusion of their presence by directing that their toys be left just as they had dropped them.

In 1910 the Los Angeles *Examiner* was sponsoring the first international aviation meet. The star of the show was the daring Frenchman, M. Louis Paulhan, and his Bleriot monoplane. The Hearsts sat spellbound in the grandstand. The publisher promptly accepted when Paulhan offered to take him for a trial spin. Although he had often been a passenger in balloons, this was Hearst's first flight in a heavier-than-air machine.

"The sensations of flying are difficult to describe," he said when he had returned to the airdrome. "For the human mind operates through analogy and is convinced by comparisons, and there is nothing with which to compare the sensations of flying. I felt that great sense of exhilaration which all aviators describe, and in addition to a deep serenity a calm enjoyment of what seemed to be the perfect conditions of a new and better state. The little people below seemed to belong to the past, to a period when man walked miserably upon the earth or rolled uncomfortably in primitive autos over the rough surface. We swept over fields where green grass lay in great square patches on the brown sod. Men were toiling in the fields, toiling below in the workaday world, while we were soaring in the sky. I felt it was a shame that anybody should have to walk when he could fly."

So impressed was Hearst by this experience that he promptly offered a prize of $50,000 for a continuous flight from coast to coast, the first of many awards designed to stimulate and improve the new science. This early interest in aviation and in military air power intensified over the years.

170

The American publisher traveled long and far that year. From London he cabled a signed account of the funeral of King Edward VII. The London *Chronicle* referred to Hearst as "one of the most remarkable of all living Americans. Some go so far as to say 'the most remarkable of all living Americans.'"

British publicists were seldom again to afford him so flattering an accolade.

In 1945, when Hearst newspapers printed this cartoon, Hearst was under fire in Britain again because he had called on the British and American governments to open up Palestine to displaced Jews of Europe, and to transport these people in Liberty ships.

Hearst papers and magazines had attacked the Czarist government repeatedly over horrors suffered by Jews in Russia. In the 1930's they flayed Hitler's persecution of Jews.

171

Potpourri

11

ONE OF W. R. Hearst's most deceptive traits was the appearance of the casual with which he surrounded important decisions.

This facet of his character he thoroughly enjoyed, particularly as it endowed him in the estimation of his subordinates with certain highly useful thaumaturgical attributes. An illustration is the apparently off-hand manner in which he dropped into the magazine field in 1903.

It was late summer. Hearst and his fetching young bride were in London following a honeymoon tour of the Continent in their first motorcar. Both had fallen in love with what they called their "red scorcher." As usual, Hearst, in bathrobe and slippers, was riffling through a mound of newspapers and other periodicals. His attention was attracted by a new publication devoted to automobiles called *The Car*.

A few hours later a message went winging over the cables to George d'Utassy, one of the Hearst executives in New York. It read in substance:

> Have decided to start magazine devoted to motor interests. Would you like to take charge? Please look over copies of *The Car* coming by mail.   HEARST

Thus was born *Motor,* earliest of the seventeen flourishing Hearst magazines which today rank among the first in circulation, number and income of any group under individual ownership anywhere in the world. The automobile was then in the early stage of its gigantic development and Hearst, with a characteristic flash of intuition, foresaw the future. His hunch was of course strengthened by his personal experiences as a motorist. Although his decision, it is interesting to note, was unanimously opposed by his closest advisers, *Motor* was a success from the start.

In 1905 Hearst entered the general magazine field by purchasing *Cosmopolitan,* which for nineteen years had been the pioneer among the cheap, popular illustrated monthlies. The new proprietor promptly ran it to a million circulation by carrying out his announced purpose of presenting "not only that which is best, but that which is universally recognized as best." By sedulous personal attention, which ceased only with his death, Hearst built for "Cosmo," as it soon became affectionately known in publishing circles, a prestige and a reputation which has endured for half a century. Then came *Motor Boating* and, in 1911, a publication called the *World Today.*

Hearst's idea in purchasing the *World Today* was to get out a monthly review somewhat like *World's Work* or *Review of Reviews.* However, when it developed in a discussion one day that the maximum circulation that could be expected from such a publication was 200,000, Hearst immediately lost interest. He then had the periodical changed into a direct competitor of *Cosmopolitan,* renaming it *Hearst's International.* It was impossible to market to readers and to advertisers two publications so nearly alike. Accordingly, in 1925, *International* was merged with *Cosmopolitan.* The combined magazine proved far more successful than Cosmo was at the highest point it had reached previously.

Then came a strike comparable to one of his father's great mineral finds.

The magazine *Good Housekeeping,* stodgy and declining, was purchased from a group in Springfield, Massachusetts, for $300,000 in bonds payable over a period of ten years. The new owner put into it fundamentals which have made it one of the most influential and profitable monthly publications in the world. Factors in *Good Housekeeping's* success included a guarantee to readers that if advertisers did not make good the magazine would; employment of the famous food expert Dr. Harvey Wiley with plenary powers to exclude deleterious food and drug products from the advertising columns; and the launching of what became the notable "Good Housekeeping Institute," a laboratory in which every proffered product was tested scientifically before admittance into the publication. The original idea for the Institute is credited to advertising manager Richard Waldo. It proved a brilliant stroke from every standpoint, exerting enormous influence both upon buying habits and health.

Through *Good Housekeeping,* Hearst came into contact with a man who was to have great influence upon his publications, Joseph A. Moore. Moore was a Canadian who had begun his career in the United States as secretary to an advertising man in Chicago, then had gone into advertising himself. Later he became a partner in a publication known as the *People's Home Journal.*

Shortly after Moore had sold out his interest in the *People's Home Journal,* S. S. Carvalho, general supervisor of the growing Hearst magazines, asked him to take charge of *Good Housekeeping.* Moore said the job appealed to him but when Carvalho tried to talk salary with him, remarked: "Don't let's name any salary for the first six months. If at the end of that time I can do what I think I can do with the publication, we will agree on a figure. If I can't, you may have my services for six months for nothing."

The proposition appealed to the canny Carvalho. At the end of six months Joe Moore had more than made good. Carvalho, in a burst of generosity, put the new man on the payroll at ten thousand a year. A couple of days later Moore dropped up to the new Hearst home and said sadly: "It's too bad but of course, Mr. Hearst, I am not the man you want." Hearst wanted to know why. Moore told him of the Carvalho $10,000. Hearst chuckled: "Some of my executives try to save money at the wrong time." They made a satisfactory arrangement. Moore became Hearst's right-hand man in the magazine field and continued so until 1926, when he and an associate purchased a controlling interest in the Butterick Publishing Company.

The new Hearst menage embraced the three upper floors of an imposing apartment house, the Clarendon, at the south corner of Eighty-sixth Street and Riverside Drive which Hearst had purchased in order to gain a free hand for the removal of ceilings and floors, so that he might properly house some recently obtained tapestries and rare armor. The central motif of the remodeled apartment became a vast high Gothic hall—worthy of a Renaissance magnifico—gleaming with armor, its walls hung with rare tapestries.

Always indifferent in matters of finance, Hearst's affairs had become more muddled than usual by 1914. He had established another newspaper, the Atlanta *Georgian,* two years before and acquired also two more magazines, *Harper's Bazaar* and *Nash's Magazine,* in London. Most of his properties were lucrative, but Hearst's personal expenditures were so enormous that money was flowing out faster than it was coming in. So he asked Moore to supervise the books. Moore soon found that Hearst's affairs were so involved that the publisher couldn't negotiate a personal loan for even a million in the money marts.

Under Moore the finances were straightened out somewhat. Hearst promised to cut down appreciably his huge outlays for antiques and other works of art. One day Moore obtained a loan of $500,000 from a bank in Wall Street and drove jubilantly up to the house to tell Hearst about it. He found the latter several hours later sitting in the front row of an art auction room on West Twenty-third Street bidding away for dear life upon some items which had caught his fancy.

174

On Moore's advice Hearst went to the public for his funds, floating bond issues totaling many millions of dollars. Thus began a weird and labyrinthine series of financial gyrations which will be dealt with elsewhere in this volume.

In 1918, on Armistice Day, Hearst acquired one of his most valuable magazine executives, Ray Long. A dynamic little man, with eyes of iceberg blue, whose letters were models of brevity, Long had won wide acclaim as an exceptional judge of popular fiction. During the time *Cosmopolitan* was bounding toward its 1,000,000 circulation, Long was on *Hampton's Magazine*. It blew up one day with a loud bang, and Long found himself without a job. He went to George d'Utassy. Nothing was open on the Hearst magazines. So Long took a job as editor of *Red Book,* published in Chicago, and began to publish arresting fiction by popular authors. *Red Book* gained thousands of new readers monthly. Then d'Utassy asked Long to edit a magazine Hearst had purchased in England, *Vanity Fair.* The offer was a trifle smaller than Long's *Red Book* salary, so he turned it down, naming, however, a counterfigure which the Hearst people in turn rejected.

Six months later d'Utassy informed Long that Hearst would accept the first Long demand. Meanwhile Long had gone ahead, so he had to name a higher figure. This curious game of financial battledore-and-shuttlecock actually went on for seven years.

Finally, on November 11, 1918, Hearst requested Moore to bring Long to the Hearst home for luncheon. Armistice bulletins were brought to the table every moment or two. Hearst read them and dictated brief instructions to editors of his newspapers while he chatted with Long.

"That meeting made an indelible impression upon me," Ray Long told the writer later. "I had never met an individual whose mind seemed so amazingly compartmentalized, able to handle many matters at once, and with frictionless ease and perfect mastery. Our ideas in magazines traveled pretty much the same paths. So there was no real difficulty in reaching an understanding."

When Moore and Long left Hearst they went to the *Cosmopolitan* office to sign a contract. The salary for two years was the last figure over which both Hearst and Moore had protested. Four months later Hearst summoned Long who came into the Presence wonderingly. Smilingly, Hearst tore up the first contract and proffered a new one at an increase of thirty-three and a third per cent. This also was to run for two years. Before the first half of Contract No. 2 was up, Hearst wired Moore from California: "Please destroy Mr. Long's contract. Give him a new one at twenty-five per cent increase."

Thereafter Long never worked out a contract with Hearst. Always before its expiration Hearst voluntarily readjusted the agreement on terms highly advantageous to the party of the second part. In 1926, when Hearst retired

175

as president of his International Magazine Company, he installed Long as president and editor-in-chief.

In more than a decade but one serious difference of opinion threatened the association. This developed over a manuscript of an English woman novelist now dead. Hearst felt under obligation to this writer because she had defended him throughout the period of bitterness against him in England during the first World War. *Cosmopolitan* had contracted for a novel by the writer in question.

The manuscript was so unsatisfactory that Long refused to run it, although he was perfectly willing to tax his budget for the sum agreed upon. Hearst insisted the serial be printed. After pondering the matter for several days, Long sent a wire to Hearst who was in California: "I do not in any way question your right to order into your magazine any feature you wish, but I think you will be willing to grant me the right to decline to edit a magazine containing something in which I do not take pride. Therefore I must ask you to permit me to resign."

Back came a telegram reading:—

> After all, you and I should not quarrel about a girl at our age—and hers. Don't publish the serial if you feel so strongly about it, but please write her a letter which will soften the blow.

Long finally wearied of his job, and quit. Despite many garbled versions, he wasn't fired. He was in Flower Hospital to have a carbuncle removed from the top of his head. William C. Lengel, his capable and trusted assistant editor, was with him the morning he dictated a brief note of resignation to W. R.   Mr. Lengel happened also to be with him a few days later when he received a reply from the Chief asking him to reconsider and to come and talk things over at the ranch. Long wrote back that he would be glad to visit Mr. Hearst at the ranch, as a guest and not to discuss staying on the job. Characteristically, this splendid editor and man made no mention of his overstrained health or of the personal worries which a few years later led him to take his own life.

After his first venture with *Motor,* Hearst purchased or established more than twenty magazines. Some were dropped, others consolidated. Those in operation today number seventeen, twelve in America and five in Britain, all in flourishing condition. The American properties are: *American Druggist, Cosmopolitan, Good Housekeeping, Harper's Bazaar, Motor, Motor Boating, Sports Afield* (acquired in 1953), *Town & Country, House Beautiful* and three offshoots of the latter: *Guide for the Bride, Building Manual, Practical Gardener*. Published in England are *Connoisseur,* English *Good Housekeeping, She, Harper's Bazaar,* and *Vanity Fair*.

In the early days of experimenting with magazines, Hearst picked up *Puck,* the humorous weekly, in sad decline from its former popularity, and

176

asked Joe Moore to see what he could do with it. Moore was a great admirer of Oliver Herford's work. He wired the artist at Lakewood, New Jersey, and asked him to contribute some of his inimitable sketches to *Puck,* adding that he could name his own price.

Herford replied promptly: "The only enterprise in which I shall ever voluntarily join William Randolph Hearst will be one of self-destruction." Herford was not asked to make the supreme sacrifice and in subsequent years modified his rancor to the extent of accepting and presumably enjoying many fat checks from Hearst publications. Hearst, as usual, was merely amused when he learned of the episode.

After the astonishing success of *Cosmopolitan,* Hearst purchased *Nash's Magazine* and *Pall Mall* in London and combined them. He believed that by producing a duplicate of *Cosmopolitan* in England he could be as successful there as he was here. His theory ultimately proved correct, but sending American editors to London caused him to stand several years of red ink on *Nash's.* Hearst's imported editors, he complained, got out not an American magazine but one that was more English than the Englishman produced.

Finally, Hearst despatched S. S. Chamberlain to England as a trouble shooter. In no time at all, the one and only Sam found a man who put the British ventures on the map. This was a tough little oak of an Irishman named J. Y. McPeake. He and Chamberlain got acquainted over a flagon of Scotch at the Savage Club. McPeake at that time was editor of a daily paper in Dublin. He did not know the first living thing about magazine direction. But he was willing to try anything once or twice. In due course he slipped into an unaccustomed editorial chair and things began to hum. Slowly *Nash's* deficit dropped.

Then the war broke out and anything Hearstian became about as popular as the bubonic plague in England. Hearst was portrayed as the leading Germanophile in the U. S.   And McPeake was an Irishman! Things got so hot it was impossible for McPeake to communicate with headquarters in New York. Moore and some other executives advised Hearst to give up the struggle with *Nash's* and "forget the darn thing." Current copies of the London newspapers, as they came into New York, increased the tension. The *Daily Express,* for instance, was running daily a banner across the bottom of its first page urging loyal Englishmen to boycott *Nash's Magazine* as a menace to Great Britain.

Only Hearst was obdurate in his refusal to scuttle *Nash's* and swallow his losses. "From what Sam tells me," drawled the Chief, "I have faith in that little fellow McPeake. I believe he will struggle through some way or other."

The denouement? You've guessed it. One day McPeake, wreathed in smiles, marched into Joe Moore's office, laid a certified check for $30,000 on the desk and announced as calmly as could be: "That's half of our profits for the last six months and I thought you fellows might have use for it." The opposition had actually been helpful to the magazine because Hearst's enemies had "laid it on too thick," in McPeake's words, and the property was at last making money.

Hearst himself got a tremendous kick out of the whole happy situation, invited the plucky Irishman up to his home and they became chummy. McPeake later started the English edition of *Good Housekeeping* in March, 1922 and established something of a record. It turned the corner on its third issue, and on an investment of less than $100,000 soon yielded a profit of more than $750,000 a year. McPeake died in 1926, his son eventually carrying on in his place. By then he had made a fortune for himself and had spent two or three fortunes for Hearst. Practically every cent of profit on the English magazines went in gratifying Hearst's passion for works of art. As Hearst's agent, McPeake became one of the largest purchasers of antiques in the world.

In London Hearst operated as the "National Magazine Company, Ltd." After the unexpected popularity of *Good Housekeeping,* National Magazine moved from its quiet office at 1 Amen Corner, in the shadow of St. Paul's Cathedral, to a spacious building at 153 Queen Victoria Street, while an institute for the testing of advertised products was set up at 49 Wellington Street, Strand. The innovation won quick favor with the British public. Indeed, it was from the comfortable earnings of British *Good Housekeeping* during its first three years that Hearst was enabled to make the purchase of St. Donat's Castle, Wales, described in the next page.

For years Hearst had been an eager reader of the *Connoisseur,* a splendid art publication which circulated throughout the world among collectors and antique dealers. This magazine was acquired in June, 1927. English *Harper's Bazaar* was established in 1924 and caught on quickly.

Managing director McPeake's interim successor was Alice M. Head, an American. She prepared a list of possible permanent successors, with brief background sketches of each, and presented it to Hearst upon the latter's next visit to England. Hearst examined the list carefully and then remarked quizzically: "I don't see your name here. You seem to be doing pretty well. Why not keep on?"

Despite a reputation for coolness under stress, Miss Head was overcome. "Why, Mr. Hearst," she gasped, "don't you know that no woman has ever been at the head of a large magazine in England?" "Then it's time there was one."

Thus Alice Head stepped into a post which she was to fill brilliantly. She soon learned that her duties included many responsibilities besides editing. Like McPeake, she became an art and real estate agent, and a purchaser of wild animals for her employer's private zoo at San Simeon. Perhaps her biggest assignment is described in her biography, *It Could Never Have Happened:* *

> During one of my conversations with Mr. Hearst in New York he mentioned that he would like to have a country home in England, and that if ever Leeds Castle in Kent or St. Donat's Castle in Wales were for sale, I was to let him know. We had seen pictures of both of them in *Country Life* . . . Soon afterward St. Donat's Castle came into the market and one morning I received the cable from Mr. Hearst: "Buy St. Donat's Castle." I like to do as my employer wishes so I bought it. He hadn't seen it. I hadn't seen it. I made some detailed inquiries through the agents, put up an offer with a time limit for its acceptance, and in a brief space of time was informed that the Castle was ours . . . Mr. Hearst was delighted with the purchase and sent me several cables of congratulation. . . . Mr. Hearst did not come over to see his new possession for a year or two.**

For many years prior to Mr. Hearst's death, the magazines were under the capable direction of Richard Emmet Berlin, a self-made man of remarkable force and ability. A native of Omaha, Nebraska, where he was born January 18, 1894, Dick Berlin enlisted in the Navy in the first World War and won a commission as ensign. Attending parties for service men at the Hearst home in New York, he renewed the acquaintance after the armistice and, at Mrs. Hearst's suggestion, entered the Hearst organization as an advertising salesman for *Motor Boating,* at $25 a week. He proved himself quickly and thereafter his rise was meteoric. Tackling one tough job after another, he became president and general manager of Hearst Magazines, Inc. in his early forties and later president of the top Hearst Corporation. In both posts, he won his employer's admiration by his loyalty and stout independence of judgment. During the last years of Hearst's life, he was one of the old gentleman's most trusted advisers and their personal relationship was almost that of father and son.

For so elaborate a menage, which was also part museum, life in the Hearst household was markedly informal and relaxed. George Thompson, the former Hoffman House bellhop, saw to it that the domestic gears meshed and the wheels ran smoothly. George, a salty, forthright character,

---

* William Heinemann, Ltd., London, 1939.
** St. Donat's, a portion of which dates back to the 11th century, remains in Hearst ownership. Extensive restoration work was done in and around it and many of the Hearst antique and art treasures were kept there.

was major-domo and unchallenged boss below stairs. He was also Hearst's valet, confidential messenger, adoring worshiper and never-failing source of amusement. His speech was larded with malapropisms and his comments on all topics distinctively his own. When Hearst began to collect Madonnas, George invariably referred to the priceless paintings as "McDonoughs." Asked his opinion of a new batch of Christmas ties, George remarked: "Well, Mr. Hearst, I doubt these are any worse than your others." He also fancied himself as a thespian. His take-offs of some celebrated stuffed shirt he had served the evening before often threw his auditors into stitches.

This remarkable character was fond of high living and, as the years passed, his rotundity increased. His once abundant red hair thinned until all that remained was a tonsure encircling a shining, bald pate. As he stood at Hearst's left superintending the service and exchanging asides with the master, he looked for all the world like a beaming, well burgundied padre. As he grew older, he got a bit crotchety and his visits to the wine cellar more frequent, resulting in many exasperating incidents. After one of these Hearst turned on him in a burst of irritation and barked: "George, get out. You're fired." Next morning, no George; and everything went awry. Hearst, by now thoroughly contrite, ordered that he be found and brought back without fail. A couple of days later the ousted factotum was discovered fishing morosely from a pier near his brother's home in Sheepshead Bay. Soon he was in Hearst's presence.

"George," accused the latter, "what do you mean walking out on me?"

"I didn't walk out, Mr. Hearst. You fired me," blubbered the "ex" valet.

Hearst's own eyes became misty as he glided across the room and patted his long-time court jester on the back. "Now, now, George," he said with a lame attempt at sternness. "Where on earth did you ever get such a silly idea? Hereafter, when I tell you that you are fired, it simply means you are fired from the room. Please remember that, George. Glad to have you back."

George Thompson and the other servitors were as delighted as the parents themselves when, in December, 1915, twin boys arrived to join their three older brothers. The newcomers were named Randolph Apperson and David Whitmire. All were lively, spirited and full of pranks. Boylike, they worshiped their slim, understanding mother. Their father was wonderful fun but their attitude toward him was tempered by awe and the realization that he was the final symbol of authority. "He seemed like the biggest man in the world to me and I admit I was a little scared of him when I was a kid," explains David Hearst, called Buddy in the family circle.

Indeed, although relations between Hearst and his sons were always intimate and affectionate, yet they were characterized by weathercockish,

180

alternating outbursts of generosity and attempts at discipline. In one mood he would lavish upon them expensive gifts: mechanical toys, ponies, motorcars. (The youngsters were driving Buicks and Cadillacs almost before their heads could be seen above the wheel.) In another mood he would rigidly hold them to a fixed allowance, constantly preaching the evils of idleness.

"You fellows have all got to work and work hard," he told them repeatedly. "I can't look after you forever and I want to tell you right now that when I am gone none of you will get a cent unless you work for it."

The boys all possessed quick, independent, venturesome minds, and were congenial, generous with one another and singularly free of bickering and jealousy. A common characteristic was a yearning for and capacity for friendship. Each early developed a genuine liking for people and ability to mingle with all sorts of people in a manner quite impossible for their father.

From boyhood the Hearst sons accepted the idea that some day they would "work for Pop." Jack Hearst alone sometimes chafed at the prospect. He wanted to become a geological engineer and those who have seen his books and collections agree that he might have made a good one.

The family early conceded that David possessed the best head for business. This quiet dark lad, now publisher of the *Herald-Express* in Los Angeles, long ago showed a decidedly un-Hearstian appreciation of the dollar and his brothers promptly dubbed Buddy "Rockefeller." When an allowance was overdrawn, it was always "Rockefeller" who had a few greenbacks in his wallet, which he would cautiously parcel out and note in a pocket account book. Even in later life, when one of his brothers was strapped, he would turn confidently to David.

The formal education of the Hearst youngsters can only be described as helter-skelter. All have memories of a bewildering parade of governesses and tutors. Bill Hearst, Jr., for example, attended three private and two public schools, East and West, winding up with a couple of tempestuous terms at the University of California, which ended in a prank.

For the most part Hearst accepted his progeny's distaste for conventional education with his usual agate calm. Once, in a letter to his wife, he offered a thumbnail summation of the character and capacity of their sons. Commenting upon a highly critical scholastic report on the lack of progress of the twins, Hearst wrote:—

> Dear Millicent: These boys are simply behaving as the others did. We may not approve of their behavior, but it is characteristic of the clan. They do not take kindly to education. This is probably a defect but Brisbane says "it takes a good mind to resist education." Anyway a certain kind of good mind does resist education.

181

The boys seem to have active and independent mentalities and perhaps are cut out to be good business men. I wish they would learn
something, but apparently they will not. It is not the fault of the
school. We used to think it was. We sent John and William to
various schools. The lack of result was always the same. . . . The
school is probably too strict with them. They do not submit tamely.
They have no particularly bad habits, no evil tendencies. They are
simply more or less untamed and untamable. I always rather let
John and William have their own way. I thought it would develop
character and self-reliance in them. I imagine we will have to do
pretty much the same with Randolph and David.

The Hearst sons remember their father best as an engaging and exciting
companion. He loved children and reveled in the wonderments of burgeoning young minds. Often he would interrupt weighty matters to read tales
from Grimm or Hans Christian Andersen or to take the boys and Mrs.
Hearst for drives or a sail in the family yacht *Oneida* on the Hudson.

Hearst was delighted when his children early manifested his own passionate love of animals and protective instinct toward them. Once, when
he and William, ten, were traveling from New York to California, Walter
Howey, then editor of the Chicago *Herald & Examiner,* received a telegram from Dodge City: "In a boxcar near a water tank about a mile west
of Kansas City is a bawling, black-and-white spotted calf. Bill wants the
darned thing."

As customary with the Chief's slightest whim, Howey dropped all other
activities, roused correspondents by phone and wire and succeeded in
locating and buying the calf. The little animal, saved from its destined fate
in the stockyards through Hearst benevolence, arrived soon at the hacienda
of Mrs. Phoebe Hearst in California and later enjoyed a long and contented
life on the hills of San Simeon.

Hearst described another memorable transcontinental journey in a note
to his mother: "The children are well and William is entirely over his train
sickness. The old man whom John shot in the eye is not recovering as
quickly. He is a cranky, unreasonable old man, and complained about
John's innocent amusements. He can't see a joke—in fact, he can't see
anything just now. John explained to the old man that he hadn't meant to
hit him in the eye. He was aiming at his nose. The old man is still cranky,
however, and looks worried every time John shoots. Some people don't
understand children."

Granted that the Hearst tongue was partially in the Hearst cheek in this
informal communication, nevertheless the fact remains that children reared
under so peculiarly recusant parental attitudes could not fail gradually to

regard themselves as superior and specially favored human beings. The wonder is that they have been able to surmount this handicap.

The sons' earliest recollections of San Simeon are of a vast camp, centered about a great circus tent with board flooring covered with soft, warm rugs rich as those of a Bedouin chieftain's and lesser tents for sleeping, cooking, storage, etc. They remember their father's passion for the newfangled motion picture camera; how he amused himself by writing, directing and photographing cinema plays, using members of the family, guests, even animal pets as actors, and showing pictures in the Big Top every night to the squealing glee of the youngsters.

In New York, the great Gothic hall was often the scene of elaborate parties, with string orchestras, acts from the Broadway stage, and guest artistes. In this highly professional atmosphere frequently appeared an amateur band organized by the household's second son. Young William himself played the drums and banjo mandolin, John Hearst the saxophone, Billy Mayer their chum and cousin the fiddle, and an older boy—a ringer— the piano. The band compensated in noise and enthusiasm for its lack of musical consonance, and always brought down the house. The brothers also organized a baseball team, which cavorted on nearby vacant lots and occasionally at Van Cortlandt Park.

The three eldest boys made their first trip to Europe in 1922 with their parents and a party of friends. William and John were bored by the rounds of enforced sight-seeing in England and France but cheered up when, after much sly maneuvering, they managed to obtain tickets for the Folies Bergère. However their wilier pop, as always one jump ahead of his progeny, got wind of the proposed outing and promptly confiscated the precious pasteboards.

In the autumn William and John entered Berkeley High School, Berkeley, California, soon transferring to Hitchcock Military Academy in San Rafael. During summer vacation the boys and a party of schoolmates journeyed from Los Angeles to New York in the *Oneida*. From Lower California, the youngsters went up to Mexico City, then back to the shoreline and on to Salina Cruz, the canal, Florida and New York. They had a rollicking time and collected all sorts of souvenirs, including live birds, wildcats and foxes.

Back at Hitchcock Military, William Jr., at fifteen, wrote a letter to his father which not only delighted him but gave him a prevision that here indeed might be the titular successor of whom he dreamed. Hearst Sr. had sent his son a newspaper editorial asserting categorically that "money invariably kills ambition." The boy dissented with equal positivity:—

> Not necessarily. Necessity makes a person work a lot harder, that is true. But if it is a worthy ambition, it takes more than money to *kill* it. I'll tell you what my ambition is. It is to be able to help

you in your business, to be capable to do my part, and then some. I have tried to prepare myself in my school work with subjects that would help me in journalism, such as all the History and English I can get. I read a good deal, as you know, and I try to pick out useful books. You may think I am just saying this to please you, but it really is the truth. All of us kids hate society because those kids are sissies. They wouldn't work if it was the last thing to do in the world. They think people who work are beneath them in "social standing" and therefore, inferior. Out here the kids work all summer, some in lumber camps, others on ships to Hawaii, or to the Orient. And these fellows are real good guys. If they are your friends, they will stick by you. I'll bet that a lot of people in New York wouldn't do a thing for us if we went broke. And how those people stick around and flatter you and Mom. That is kind of off the subject, but what I meant to say was, we don't shirk work. All of us appreciate what you have done for us, and I am sure that we are not made of the stuff of a fellow that will not work if he does not have to.

When he was seventeen, the youth made good his expressions. Obtaining a union card, he worked all summer as a "fly boy" in the Frankfort Street press room of the tabloid *Mirror,* pulling papers from the sextuple Hoe presses. Stripped to undershirt and overalls, he sweated manfully for fourteen weeks through the eight-hour workdays. The tall, skinny youth with the contagious, toothy grin became immensely popular with his rough-hewn fellow employees, who tagged him with the affectionate nickname he has since borne—Young Bill.

During most of the period we have described Hearst was embroiled in the bitterest and most significant struggle of his entire career with none other than Thomas Woodrow Wilson, twenty-eighth President of the United States.

Of all the insubstantial trash which has been written about William Randolph Hearst, nothing is more trashily insubstantial than the "inside" published stuff bearing upon his relations with Wilson and particularly with Hearst's epic campaigns to keep America out of the first European war and from joining the League of Nations and World Court.

For a full decade these strong, stubborn men were locked in combat. Upon its outcome depended the future pattern of American constitutional government; indeed, the very fate of the world.

In this titanic struggle Wilson staked both his own political future and that of his party and his obsessive yearning for immortality. Hearst risked everything he possessed, including his personal freedom, in his implacable determination to keep America free of entangling foreign alliances. As to

184

any prospect of immortality, Hearst was far too much of a realist to give it even passing thought.

As protagonists in the greatest struggle of their time, Hearst and Wilson are properly subject to close psychological scrutiny. Such examination reveals startling similarities as well as glaring divergencies.

Both were lonely men, doomed by some psychic force to travel alone. Each died without having revealed himself fully to a single soul. A thousand men threw a thousand facets upon their character and personality. Yet no one, one feels, really touched the inner core. And like all lonely travelers, each saw many things which remain dark to most. Neither was a god, by many fathoms. Yet each, before his time ran out, developed a very easily traced Messianic complex. Which brings to mind Clemenceau's ironic *bon mot* that the task of making peace was rather difficult when he had on one side an individual (Lloyd George) who imagined he was Napoleon, and on the other side a man (Wilson) who imagined he was Jesus Christ. The indomitable old Tiger had a disconcerting way of touching raw spots.

Like Hearst, Wilson from boyhood was accustomed to having his own way. Bespectacled little "Tommy" Wilson was the swaggercock of whatever group he deigned to join. Games had to be played his way or not at all—an unfortunate quality in boy or man. His playmates were awed and overawed by him. Withal, he never managed to kindle a real spark of love in them. The imagination staggers at thought of what might have happened if fate had placed Masters Willie Hearst and Tommy Wilson in the same boyhood gang.

(Hearst would have grinned over this thought.)

Handicapped all his life by physical frailties, young Wilson early determined to conquer by sheer intellectual force. In this he succeeded admirably. Still he was not content. He wanted to dazzle. So he cultivated certain social artifices aimed to convince others, perhaps even himself, that he possessed a gusty, rollicking spirit. In this role he was never quite natural.

In truth, minute examination of the Wilson saga leads to the conclusion that the man was a humanitarian only in the abstract. His distaste for the usual run of ordinary contact amounted almost to a mania. Yet, when he forced himself, he could captivate most women and some men. Usually, though, some icy volcano within made him retreat just at the moment of melting.

Once, in a White House round-robin chat, a visitor got off a bit of whimsy that pleased the President immensely. Spontaneously Wilson raised his hand to clap the narrator on the back. The friendly gesture was arrested in mid-air by some power or instinct beyond the President's control. Brusquely he plunged his hand into his pocket. "It all happened in a flash,"

185

remarked the eyewitness who recounted the incident. "Mr. Wilson acted as though he had done something disreputable. It was tragic."

By way of quirky contrast, there is evidence that Wilson could and did relax in the intimacy of his home. Sometimes, amid the splashing of water in his bathroom, he could be heard quoting passages from the Lake poets, singing a snatch of song or repeating lusty lines from his favorite play of Shakespeare, "King Henry VIII." He was especially fond of Wolsey's advice to Cromwell:—

> Cromwell, I charge thee, fling away ambition.
> By that sin fell the angels; how can man, then,
> The image of his Maker, hope to win by it?
> Love thyself last: cherish those hearts that hate thee;
> Corruption wins not more than honesty.
> Still in thy right hand carry gentle peace,
> To silence envious tongues. Be just, and fear not:
> Let all the ends thou aim'st at be thy country's,
> Thy God's and truth's; then if thou fall'st, O Cromwell,
> Thou fall'st a blessed martyr!

Wilson had a habit, too, of standing before the mirror and rehearsing his speeches with words and gestures. Whenever he heard a new anecdote or a well turned epigram he tried it out upon the adoring women of his household. If it won their applause he added it to his repertoire. Limericks were his particular passion. His favorite was:—

> For beauty I am not a star,
> There are others more handsome by far.
>   But my face I don't mind it,
>   For I am behind it;
> It's the people in front that I jar.

His moments of exuberance were rare. Much of the time physical ills pressed upon him. During a great part of his life he suffered from indigestion, biliousness and frequent headaches. Although not known until after his death, a retinal hemorrhage had practically destroyed the sight of his right eye. The misfortune was caused by overstrain while he was President of Princeton. During this period, also, he suffered a slight thrombosis, or blood clot, in a leg artery.

In 1913 he brought with him to the White House a stomach pump and old-fashioned tar tablets with which he had sought for years to overcome his balky digestion. Not without difficulty young Dr. Cary Grayson persuaded him to give up this outworn treatment. Grayson, who was later to become almost a son to Wilson, substituted golf and automobile rides. The patient's health improved perceptibly. Until he went down under a stroke of paralysis in 1919, it seemed that Woodrow Wilson might live as long as his hearty Scotch and North Irish forebears. In his last years, indeed, Wilson became pure Scotch, an iron-willed old Covenanter, using every resource he could command to carry out what he devoutly believed to be the will of God. In this phase his prototype was Scott's Balfour of Burleigh who smote the enemies of the Lord and feared not. Old histories of Scotland are full of the same narrow, God-fearing men, ready to slay or be slain for what they believed to be right—as revealed to them alone after long study and fervent prayer.

No crusader since the beginning of time ever laid hold of a finer or more splendid idea—World Peace through a League of Nations—than Woodrow Wilson.

Wilson crashed to failure because he insisted on fighting alone. He simply could not co-operate with equally patriotic fellow Americans. Instead of attempting to persuade his political opponents, he sought to ram his ideas down every throat by denouncing all who opposed him as cowards and traitors. The result was that a bipartisan cabal, often employing nauseous methods of attack, stopped him—plus that quality in all of us that can be convinced by fair argument but will not be bulldozed, even by one who professes, with persuasive assurance, that he has only the welfare of the race at heart.

Although his idolaters have often likened Wilson to Washington and Lincoln, the comparison grows weaker with the passing years. Lincoln and Washington went out to meet life. Professor Wilson on the other hand, although successfully tutoring himself into a brilliant speaker and phrase maker, diluted life to meet his hypersensitive nature.* Clinton Gilbert, an able Washington correspondent who observed Wilson closely over the years, says of him: "When all his personal history becomes known, when his papers and letters have all been published and read, when the memoirs of others have told all there is to be told, there will stand out clear something inadequate, a lack of robustness, mental or nervous, an excessive sensitiveness, over self-consciousness, shrinking from life, a neurotic something that in the end brought on defeat and the final overthrow. He was never quite a normal man with the average man's capacity to endure and enjoy, but a strange, impeded, self-absorbed personality."

Granted all this, Wilson bore his cross without a whimper. There was even something heroic and sublime in the stricken Covenanter's last great fight. The figures of Henry Cabot Lodge and the other irreconcilables of both political faiths, who broke Wilson upon the wheel, are already fading into the mist, while the spirit of the man they destroyed lives on.

William Randolph Hearst, with his superb, devastating realism, early took the measure of Woodrow Wilson, and found him wanting.

Hearst once told a small group of interested listeners (about 1932) why

---

* See *Woodrow Wilson: The Man Who Lives On* by John K. Winkler (1933).

he had distrusted Wilson from the time the Doctor first emerged from the cloistered halls of Princeton to become Governor of New Jersey in 1910.

"I recognized," he said, "that this brilliant, pedantic, inexperienced college professor could become a menace to our country. I saw that a combination of events, already foreshadowed, plus the man's evident self-hypnosis and the massive grandeur of his office if he ever reached the White House, could cause Wilson to lead the country into catastrophe. I have often been wrong"—the soundless Hearst chuckle—"but I do not believe I was wrong about Woodrow Wilson. He involved this nation in terrible and needless complications and the end is not yet."

So confident was Hearst in his own judgment that he dropped all other activities and concentrated upon thwarting Wilson's nomination for the Presidency at the dramatic 1912 Democratic convention in Baltimore. His own candidate was Champ Clark, Speaker of the House, and Hearst's friend and mentor when the latter was in Congress. Clark, a Democratic stalwart, was an old-style Missouri politician who wore suspenders and liked corn liquor. Old Champ was a rock-ribbed isolationist long before the word was coined.

This regular of regulars had worked his way through county offices into Congress. His constituents adored him and brought to Baltimore the famous Missouri hound dog song: "You Gotta Quit Kicking My Dawg Around."

Clark's pre-convention campaign had been managed with great skill, largely by Hearst himself, and Clark came to Baltimore comfortably ahead of the other leading candidates: Judson Harmon, Governor of Ohio; Congressman Oscar Underwood of Alabama; and Woodrow Wilson. An undeclared candidate, but still hoping for the great prize, was thrice-defeated William Jennings Bryan of Nebraska. Bryan, in a mood to pull down any temple in his own interest, was to become a focal point of drama and tragedy.

The convention opened on Tuesday, June 25. On the first ballot for President, Clark received 440½ votes to Wilson's 324. As the balloting continued, he scored the greatest gains. On the tenth ballot his total was 560 votes, ten more than a majority. Wilson had 360½. When New York shifted its ninety votes from Harmon to Clark there was a wild demonstration, and it then seemed that the battle was over.

Dejectedly, William F. McCombs, Wilson's campaign manager, telephoned the Governor at his summer cottage in Sea Girt on the New Jersey coast. McCombs, his voice breaking, explained the situation and asked Wilson if he wished to release his delegates to vote for Underwood. "No, that would not be fair," replied Wilson. "I ought not to try to influence my friends in behalf of another candidate. They have been so loyal and kind to me."

As Wilson turned from the telephone, Ellen Axson Wilson put her arms

188

about her husband and said: "My dear Woodrow, I am sorry indeed that you have failed." With no outward show of emotion, Wilson comforted her. "Of course, dear wife, I am disappointed," he said. "But we must not complain. We must be sportsmen. After all I feel that a great load has been lifted from my shoulders."

Wilson at once penciled a message of congratulations to Champ Clark. It was never sent. For, by one masterly move, William Jennings Bryan changed the whole current of the convention. Amid pandemonium he introduced a resolution declaring the convention "opposed to the nomination of any candidate for President who is the representative of or under any obligation to J. Pierpont Morgan, Thomas F. Ryan, August Belmont, or any other member of the privilege-hunting and favor-seeking class." This followed Tammany Hall's switch to Clark, which had so disheartened McCombs, and was a direct assault upon Ryan, a delegate from Virginia, and Belmont, a delegate from New York. Both were bitter anti-Wilson men.

Bryan's dramatic, well-calculated move succeeded in curling about the Champ Clark boom the sinister tail of the Tammany tiger. After riotous debate the Bryan resolution was adopted, with names deleted, by a vote of more than four to one.

Now Bryan had a plausible excuse to bolt Clark, to whom he was pledged as a member of the Nebraska delegation. In a ringing speech the great Commoner declared in his best platform manner, with practiced pear-shaped tones and appropriate gestures, that he was too pure to vote for any candidate tarnished by Tammany support. This began the swing away from Clark. Thousands of telegrams from all parts of the country poured in upon the delegates beseeching them to support Bryan, apostle of political virtue and deadly foeman of wicked Wall Street.

Both Hearst and Clark saw their cause was badly slipping. Hearst extracted the personal satisfaction of telling the trembling Commoner, in words that lashed and stung, what he thought of his perfidy; then contemptuously stalked from Bryan's hotel room, leaving the man he had thrice supported mumbling excuses and self-serving platitudes. Despite the mortal blow from Bryan, Clark determined to fight on.

As Saturday drew to a close there was a deadlock between Clark and Wilson. It seemed the struggle might continue indefinitely. Suspicion grew that Bryan was jockeying to obtain the nomination for himself. The prospect sent shivers down the backs of certain key leaders. Of the two evils, Professor Wilson seemed to them the lesser. On Sunday Roger Sullivan, boss of Illinois, and his confrere, Tom Taggart of Indiana, decided to jump to Wilson unless the Clark forces could put their man over on the next few ballots.

On Monday morning the New York *World,* the country's leading independent Democratic newspaper, which had declared for Wilson in May, appeared with a hammer-and-tongs editorial with a commanding heading: "WILSON—NO COMPROMISE WITH RYAN AND MURPHY!"

Frank I. Cobb, chief editorial writer of the *World,* and a master of clear, forceful, simple English, was at his best in that plea to the convention to nominate Wilson as a "matter of Democratic life or death." The editorial helped to level the crumbling Clark defenses.

The end came on Tuesday, July 2.

Illinois and Indiana started the stampede. On the forty-sixth ballot Oscar Underwood's name was withdrawn and the Clark delegates released. Wilson was nominated by acclamation. Tom Taggart's genial little Hoosier protégé, Thomas Riley Marshall, was named for Vice-President. Gratefully, the worn and weary delegates departed broiling Baltimore.

"I lost the nomination," asserted Champ Clark, "solely through the vile and vicious slanders of Colonel William Jennings Bryan of Nebraska."

Thus it was that Woodrow Wilson drew nearer the most august elective office in the world, for which he and a few inner counselors had long felt that he was predestined.

A bubbling, jovial Wilson greeted callers at Sea Girt. The nominee surprised by passing around cigars. "That's the first box of cigars Woodrow ever bought," laughed Mrs. Wilson. Wilson's spirits were indeed gay. As a demonstration of versatility, he dashed off the first draft of his acceptance speech while listening to Harry Lauder's drolleries on the phonograph.

For Wilson the campaign was not arduous.

Theodore Roosevelt and his Bull Moosers and President William Howard Taft and his regular Republicans were so busy fighting each other that they had little ammunition left for Wilson. The Professor jogged calmly along in the middle of the road, refusing to get excited about anything his opponents, Roosevelt in particular, said or did. Wilson despised Teddy's sword-rattling tactics. On the other hand Roosevelt, the ruddy, outdoor man, contemptuously regarded Wilson as a bloodless product of the cloister.

When whispers were brought to Roosevelt's attention that Wilson had strayed upon the primrose path and that this might be used against the Democratic candidate, the Colonel ordered his managers to squelch the rumors wherever possible. "We must have none of that gossip," declared T. R. sternly. Then, wrinkling his face into the inimitable puckered expression his friends knew so well, he added with a grin: "What's more, it wouldn't work. You can't cast a man as Romeo who looks and acts so much like the Apothecary's Clerk."

"America First
and Forever"

> . . . the way to end war is to prevent war; by
> dealing with the causes thereof. No treaties, no
> scraps of paper, no partial and no complete dis-
> armament, can hold off very long a war that
> we have planted in our maladjustment of con-
> flicting economic interests.
>
> *Autobiography*
> LINCOLN STEFFENS

12

AN INGRAINED pacifist by training and temperament, Woodrow
Wilson abhorred war with a mighty hatred. However, his deep and eclectic
explorations into history spelled out for him the melancholy revelation
that, generally speaking, where a nation's economic interests lie, there
eventually go its muskets and men to bear them.

Early in 1917, as World War I continued in bloody stalemate, grinding
up the flower of Europe's youth, the American President fought like a
trapped soul to keep his country out of the holocaust. Gradually, under the
terrifying impact of reality, he was absorbing grim truths he had lacked
the knowledge and perspective to teach his adoring young feminine students
at Bryn Mawr or his equally unsophisticated classes at Princeton.

In the bitter school of practical power politics, Woodrow Wilson came
to understand something of the nature and composition of the centripetal
forces, financial, sentimental and otherwise, which tended to draw America
toward the Allies. Yet for weeks following his dismissal of the German
Ambassador, von Bernstorff, the man in the White House prayed and
hoped for a miracle that would avert a declaration of war upon the Central
Powers.

E. M. House, the pussyfooting little Texan, and a dozen other advisers
told him the die must at last be cast. Finally Wilson summoned Frank I.
Cobb, powerful editorial writer of the New York *World,* on whose judgment he had come to rely.

"Cobb," he said, and his voice was freighted with conviction, "once lead
the American people into war and they will forget there ever was such a

191

thing as tolerance. To fight, you must be brutal and ruthless. The spirit of ruthless brutality will enter into the very fiber of our national life, infecting Congress, the courts, the policeman on the beat, the man in the street. Conformity will be the only virtue. And every man who refuses to conform will have to pay the penalty.

"If there is any alternative"—the President's voice almost broke—"for God's sake, let's take it!"

Cobb could see no way out.

When he left, Wilson was still clinging to the possibility of peace.

That night Cobb arrived at his Connecticut farm, low and dejected, and remarked to his wife:

"By Jove, I don't think we're going in. I believe the President is again going to turn the other cheek."

Next day, April 2, 1917, Wilson made a dramatic appearance before Congress and asked the legislative body to recognize the existence of a state of war.

Once in the war, Wilson fought like an inspired prophet—fought with winged words and massed men—for victory. The spirit of his Scotch-Presbyterian ancestors surged in his soul.

Woodrow Wilson's conscience had spoken. He was the Anointed of the Lord.

With the outbreak of the war, multitudes in America turned to Editor Hearst for guidance. To the great urban masses, Hearst was a sort of wonder-worker, a mirific champion foiling the predatory Ice Trust in summer, the Coal Trust in winter, the Milk Trust all the year round.

Thousands of foreign-born made their first acquaintance with a new and puzzling tongue through his bold black headlines and comics colored like Joseph's coat. The Irish and German elements of the population, in particular, followed Hearst's preachment of the gospel according to St. Randolph with fanatical devotion.

Clinical examination of the Hearst publications during the years 1914–18 would puzzle a pathologist. Cellini and Barnum, one would guess from perusing the files, must have returned to earth and fused their brilliant, erratic talents into newspaper editorship—so weirdly fluctuating was the seeming Hearst attitude toward the war before and even after our entrance.

The clearer light of present-day perspective, however, indicates that Hearst was truly "playing a part," adroitly, plausibly, resourcefully. Amid all the camouflage, amid all the inconsistencies, the publisher clung to one definite and inflexible aim: to keep America's men, munitions, money out of the war. The Hearst coinages, "America First" and "No Entangling Alliances," and the massive publicity campaigns built around them possibly postponed for many months our entry into the war.

From the onset of the European conflict, Hearst preached that the war was purely a struggle for the mastery of the world's markets; that England and Japan were more menacing to our neutrality than Germany; that we would be dupes and gulls to permit the shedding of a single drop of American blood upon foreign soil.

This line of reasoning, which was later approved in retrospect by many Americans, evoked panic in the Allied chancelleries; and led them, in the fall of 1916, to deny use of the cables and mails to the Hearst papers and news services. We have already recounted * Hearst's personal reaction to this drastic action, his blazing anger, and his instant and astounding resolution to defy, single-handed, the Allied Powers and their influential American associates:—

> "When I inscribed the watchword 'An American Paper for the American People' over the titles of my newspapers, I meant just what the motto said. I will just add the verses of 'The Star-Spangled Banner' to my editorial mottoes and, like that free flag, continue to wave."

Hearst fought with a tenacity and courage seldom, if ever, witnessed in the long battle for freedom of the press. He printed a series of bitter exposés of British censorship and its effect upon the commerce of neutrals. He encouraged fomenters of revolutionary movements in Ireland and other parts of the British Empire. Canadians and Australians were told that they were silly to journey thousands of miles from their homelands to fight in a cause that did not really concern them.

So sharp were Hearst's shafts, so reverberating his arpeggios of logic and persuasion that pro-Ally sympathizers on both sides of the water sought to bring about a *rapprochement*. The embattled editor spurned any form of conditional peace, with a caustic observation: "The exclusion of the International News Service is not due to any delinquency on its part or on the part of the Hearst papers, but is due to the independent and wholly truthful attitude of these papers in their news and editorial columns."

Men watched in fascination as a single untameable journalist fought a great coalition of nations. When thinly veiled threats reached him that his supply of newsprint would be halted if he did not yield, Hearst wired a Washington representative: "I will not supplicate England for news or for print paper or for permission to issue. I will not permit my papers to be edited in the smallest degree by a foreign power. I would shut down every publication I have first and I do not intend to shut them down. In fact, the more foreign powers endeavor to interfere in America's domestic matters, and the more these foreign powers try to control our American institutions, particularly our free press, the more necessary, it seems to me, that American papers for the American people shall continue to be published."

* In the first chapter.

At this time Hearst had been in almost continuous conflict with Woodrow Wilson since the latter took office.

Even before Wilson's surprising nomination at Baltimore Hearst had termed him a sham progressive, giving mere lip service to the initiative, referendum and recall, and other measures "appropriated" from the Hearst program. During the campaign the Hearst organs tepidly supported the Democratic ticket as a choice of evils; but scarcely had Wilson entered the White House when Hearst opened up with all guns on him for reviving the "ancient Federalist custom" of addressing Congress in person, asserting that this was a phase of Wilson's inordinate admiration for the British system of government.

The theme was further developed in a letter, carefully composed, to the editor of the Washington *Post* and published under date of April 14, 1913:—

> The Federalist method of a speech by the President was a mere adaptation of the British usage of a speech to Parliament from the throne. The aristocratic Adams approved it and practiced it. But Thomas Jefferson, who founded the Democratic Party and introduced into American political life the simplicity which has since characterized it, adopted the modest democratic method of writing a message to Congress, expressing his views and offering suggestion for legislation. . . .

> Mr. Wilson gained his degree of doctor of philosophy by an essay which contended flagrantly in the face of fact that the English parliamentary form of government was superior to the American system. To be sure this essay of Mr. Wilson's was written some time ago and might be considered an early and outgrown expression of a Federalist affection for England were it not that Mr. Wilson has only comparatively recently delivered an address in which he declares that he gets his information on world events from the columns of the London *Weekly Times*.

> Certainly the London *Times* is, or at least once was, an excellent paper, but there is no publication on the face of the earth so completely and absolutely saturated with the English prejudice toward all other countries, and toward America in particular, as the London *Times*. . . . Many thoughtful American citizens will be led to wonder how far Mr. Wilson's attitude toward the American protective tariff is influenced by his Federalistic frame of mind and his English sources of information.

> Mr. Wilson's opposition to the protective principle is not inherently or essentially Democratic. Mr. Wilson is FUNDAMENTALLY opposed to the principle of protection, and his idea of radical, ruthless tariff reduction is but an expression of the English

194

free-trade theories of Cobden and Mill. Mr. Wilson is an English free-trader.

Mr. Wilson's political economy is the political economy of a nation that is passing and of an age that is past. Mr. Wilson's theories are the theories of books, but of British books that are no longer believed in by the patriotic and practical and progressive Englishman of today.

Hearst broke definitely with President Wilson and most of the national Democratic leaders during the President's long fight to repeal the Free Tolls Bill. Zealous to insure preferential treatment for American ships using the Panama Canal, the editor accused Wilson of violent Anglophilia. As usual the Hearst method of attack pulled no punches. Hearst turned loose his star cartoonist Winsor McCay to depict "Professor" Wilson as a schoolmaster perverting to his pupils the outstanding events of American history. The cartoons stung and bit to such an extent that Wilson's chief supporter, the New York *World,* fulminated in its lead editorial on April 7, 1914:—

Day after day Mr. Hearst, in word and caricature, is picturing the President of the United States as a traitor to the United States. . . . Mr. Hearst apparently has learned nothing from the assassination of William McKinley. . . . Indeed, his attacks upon President Wilson are even more malicious, mendacious and incendiary than were his attacks upon President McKinley.

With the outbreak of the war in Europe, the gap between Hearst and the Administration widened. The President ignored the Hearst demands for an embargo upon war loans, foodstuffs and munitions to the belligerents. The two worked as one, though in widely diverging ways, to prevent America's entry into the war.

Hearst's frequent quarrels with the British caused him to be hailed as an ally by the Germans. He insisted that he was merely militantly pro-American. There is no question, however, that his break with the British brought his sympathy closer to the Germans. He sent William Bayard Hale, a former American diplomat, to Berlin as his correspondent and featured Hale's despatches. Presumably he did not know that Hale, as it later developed, had been in the employ of the German Embassy. This was one of the many mistakes which rose to plague Hearst after the U. S. entrance into the war.

Another, and by far the most harmful, was his employment as chief editorial writer during the war years of a squat, glowering, troglodytic little man who called himself Philip Francis. His real name was said to be Diefendorf. Hearst had personally discovered him writing editorials for a Stockton, California, newspaper and promptly elevated him over the heads of his most experienced and dependable executives.

Master of a hammer-and-tongs style of writing, Francis-Diefendorf at once launched daily philippics aimed at belittling the British and glorifying the Germans. These continued even after our entry into the war. Some were so immoderate in tone that one top executive, S. S. Carvalho, resigned; and other veterans signed the round-robin protest, which we have mentioned. Carvalho took umbrage at a Francis laudation of the German Government as a "benevolent despotism inaugurating many of the popular benefits which our government and other democratic and semi-democratic governments have since adopted."

As his influence with his mentor grew, Francis visualized himself as a champion of all "oppressed" peoples and his office swarmed with revolutionists from the Balkans, the Levant, Russia and Latin America. Eventually he faded out of the picture, became entangled in murky stock-peddling deals in Mexico, and died in 1924.

President Wilson showed his personal animosity toward Hearst and the latter's motley following in the famous "O'Leary telegram" sent from the White House on September 29, 1916.

Jeremiah A. O'Leary, an Irish extremist, headed an organization of Irish-Americans and German-Americans called the American Truth Society. O'Leary wired the President charging dictatorship over Congress in the interests of the British Government; cited heavy votes polled by anti-Wilson men in New York and New Jersey primaries as significant of the entire country and asked: "Well, sir, will you respond to popular disapproval of your policies by action?"

On the eve of a campaign for re-election with the outcome in admitted doubt, and with enormous burdens upon his shoulders, Wilson yielded to the irritation of the moment and made the following reply:—

> Your telegram received. I would feel deeply mortified to have you or anybody like you vote for me. Since you have access to many disloyal Americans and I have not, I will ask you to convey this message to them. WOODROW WILSON

The hasty words from the White House furnished Hearst with ammunition. He plunged to the attack with all sails set. A three-column box on the front pages of the Hearst papers, headed "Editorial Comment," warmly championed O'Leary and advocated a strong anti-British propaganda of its own:—

> Now, if these telegrams mean anything, they mean that O'Leary, an American citizen, is opposed to President Wilson's policies of submission to British aggression upon our commerce and British blacklisting of American firms and British seizure of American ships, as well as Mr. Wilson's policy of encouraging huge war loans

and large supplies of munitions to prolong the European conflict—
and that Mr. Wilson regards any American who expresses opposition to these policies of his as a disloyal person, whose vote and
support he would be ashamed to have.

The editorial accused the President of "exercising the power of the Presidency in an autocratic way, which no monarch of Europe, with the sole
exception of the Czar, would have dared imitate." Under a heading: "Wilson Slur Denounced by Leading Men," an expression from Hearst was
quoted: "Mr. Wilson's reply to Jeremiah A. O'Leary is one of the most extraordinary statements that ever emanated from an American President.
. . . To protest against pro-British policies may be disloyal to England,
but it certainly is not disloyal to the United States."

Although the Germans, of course, welcomed Hearst's assaults upon the
British, they recognized that the American publisher's first and only loyalty
was to his own country. A memorandum to the Imperial German Government late in 1916 from Dr. Albert Fuehr, German propaganda director in
the United States, made this abundantly clear:—

> Mr. Hearst has replied to the inconceivably short-sighted action
> of the British authorities against his news service in a series of sharp,
> full-page editorials directed against the British censorship, which
> editorials must have considerably shaken the already weakened
> confidence of the American press in the news emanating from
> England. . . .
>
> It must be emphasized that the Hearst papers are, nevertheless,
> not to be classified as blind champions of the German cause, since
> they print many things which could scarcely be to our taste. For
> example, occasional articles about the "German danger," an idea
> which has received fresh impetus as a result of the exploits of the
> *Deutschland* and particularly of the U-53, and which is being used
> as an argument for the expansion of the army and navy. The fact
> is that the newspapers referred to stand upon the ground of a sound
> American policy, but with their sharply anti-English tendencies are
> much more effective in support of our cause than newspapers with
> pronounced German orientation could be.

The German official's memorandum was incorporated into the records
of the Senate Judiciary Committee which initiated an investigation of war
propaganda a few weeks after the armistice. The same committee received
in evidence a series of confidential telegrams passing between Hearst and
his editors in the early months of 1917. The messages disclosed Hearst's
efforts to avert a declaration of war by the United States and to build up
peace sentiment through the vast avenue of publicity presented by his news-

197

papers. They were obtained by agents of the Department of Justice who in shoals dogged Hearst's footsteps during the perilous days preceding the outbreak of the war—though by what warrant has never become known.

These agents were so inept that they cluttered up the neighborhood. One was actually pulled by the ear from his hiding place in a clothing closet and sent packing. Another was caught attempting to break into an escritoire with a nail file. Others reported mysterious flashings of colored lights from the Hearst apartment, presumably signals to marauding German submarines in the nearby Hudson River. These turned out to be interior illumination, switched on and off, and reflecting through the publisher's superb collection of stained glass windows.

The confidential telegrams given to the public by the Senate Judiciary Committee were of more solid material. Sent to and from Palm Beach, where Mr. and Mrs. Hearst occupied a suite at the Breakers in February and March, 1917, they provided fascinating flashes of the publisher's mental processes, his impatience of restraint, the frequent obliqueness of his judgment, his intrepidity in pursuing a course which was becoming increasingly dangerous.

The Palm Beach messages began on February 21, when Hearst directed Philip Francis to launch a vigorous campaign against the Espionage Bill, containing a censorship clause, then pending in Congress. On February 25, he telegraphed Francis:—

> Please make editorial advocating embargo for America along your own lines. Also kindly make one for *Evening Journal* amplifying and improving following suggestions: "America is not only being starved for the benefit of warring Europe but it is being plundered of its wealth as well. We are sending abroad genuine wealth, the wealth of our mines and our mills, the wealth of our farms and our factories, containing natural resources which God has given us for our development. We are receiving in return counters, media of exchange, which may never be redeemed. Of what use are the I.O.U.'s of a bankrupt?
>
> "Uncle Sam is being gold-bricked. He is being sold a satchel full of green goods in return for his genuine and hard-earned property. We are reveling in mock prosperity and will all wake up some fine morning and find the Sheriff at our doors. And why are we wasting our wealth? If it were for some noble purpose we could afford to go poor for a generation and find comfort and consolation in a worthy deed.
>
> "But no; we are wasting our wealth to continue a carnival of murder, to prolong an era of overwhelming disaster, to encourage the destruction of the white race, to tear down the achievements of civilization which have taken ages to construct, to repudiate religion and violate all established standards of decency, morality and

righteousness, to prostitute the progress of the world to the meanest and basest and vilest of purposes.

"If we persist in doing this we will deserve the heavy penalty which will surely fall upon us. Let us end these shipments of food and ammunition and money to the warring nations of Europe for their sakes and for ours. Let us preserve our property and our self-respect. Let us end the war and the wastage of war and the woe which the war is wreaking. Let us feed our own people, build up our own country, conserve our own resources. AMERICA FIRST AND FOREVER."   HEARST

The tone of William Bayard Hale's extravagant despatches from Berlin increased the tension of the period and added volume to the growing denunciations of the Hearst papers.

On February 26, Caleb R. Van Hamm, managing editor of the New York *American,* wired his chief at Palm Beach:—

> Earnestly urge immediate action to check or stop Hale despatches. They come by wireless and surely are picked up. Despite your well known attitude of neutrality, these despatches are so worded as to permit the inference that Berlin is dictating our policy. I find we are drifting into a situation akin to the false McKinley one, only accentuated manyfold. I urge we check Hale and all agencies that tend to throw discredit upon our declared attitude of sturdy Americanism.

After receipt of the Van Hamm warning, Hearst ordered the suppression of a message to Hale which he had dictated two days before and which had been held up by wireless congestion. This despatch read in part:—

> I firmly believe that the vast majority of the people of the United States are entirely undesirous of war with Germany. I believe also that the people of Germany are equally undesirous of war with the United States. . . .
>
> The course of my newspapers has been fair to Germany not because I am pro-German any more than I am pro-Ally. I am merely patriotically interested in the welfare of my own country and altruistically interested in the progress of the world.

To S. S. Carvalho, his general manager, Hearst gave interesting instructions as to preserving the strictly American tenor of everything appearing in his papers, even to dictating when to print and when to eliminate the Stars and Stripes. One message said:—

> Please keep standing in *American* across top of the editorial page

199

the verses of "The Star-Spangled Banner" as originally written. Please keep standing in the evening paper the verses printed in *America* reproduced from *Harper's Weekly* during the Civil War, and referring to shipment of arms by England to South America.

Carvalho's response:—

Cannot find *Harper's Weekly* poem in *America*. Found one reproduced in *Fatherland* from *Harper's Weekly,* 1863, attacking England for sending arms, etc. Therefore, in consequence of sinking of *Laconia* today, with Americans aboard, and President Wilson's address before Congress, urge that we not use this poem, if it is the one you mean, as under present conditions it is bound to hurt papers. Bulk of public believe country is on verge of war with Germany and this poem prominently displayed will be regarded as our taking Germany's side. "The Star-Spangled Banner" is being run top of column morning. Editorial referendum canvass under way.

Carvalho

Hearst replied at once:—

Why not run the red, white and blue title that we had for last edition through all editions for a few days during these troublous times? I think it will meet popular sentiment. Also please run little American flags to right and left of date lines on inside pages, like Chicago *Herald*. Our editorials should be patriotic without slightest criticism, direct or indirect, of Administration. I guess Germany is going to sink every ship that tries to run the submarine blockade and this means three things—first, that we will get into the war; second, that England will be starved into submission in less than six months; third, that Germany will then have time to devote to us, and this country will soon be in a condition similar to warring European countries. We must prepare in every way. Can we say these things editorially?

In the light of what occurred in the ensuing twenty months, it would appear that the divinations of the Palm Beach prophet went slightly askew.

On February 28, 1917, the State Department exposed the Zimmermann notes, in which a German plot to involve the United States and Japan in a row over Mexico was outlined. Without comment, Editor Van Hamm transmitted to Hearst a copy of the alleged instructions sent by Arthur Zimmermann, German Foreign Secretary, to Minister von Eckhardt in Mexico through von Bernstorff. Hearst pondered over this for two days and then, while the sensation was at its height, despatched a denunciatory telegram pronouncing the Zimmermann document a forgery and expressing

200

the opinion that it had been manufactured by the office of Attorney General Gregory. The complete authenticity of the paper was later substantiated.

Nothing in his entire career more clearly discloses the contradictory elements that made up the man Hearst than this curious despatch:—

S. S. Carvalho, N. Y. *American:*

Agree with Francis. Zimmermann note all probability absolute fake and forgery, prepared by a very unscrupulous Attorney General's very unscrupulous department. Everybody knows that the secret police are the most conscienceless manufacturers of forged evidence in the world. The ordinary police are bad enough with their trumped-up evidence and railroading methods, but the Federal agents, with the government back of them and more or less immune from punishment, are the most reckless converters of evidence and framers of jobs in the world.

Gregory's whole career in office, as Francis showed in recent editorials, has been as a spy-fancier and plot-conceiver. He has not been bound by morals, facts or the Constitution. He has employed the Secret Service to enforce England's unlawful orders. He has attempted to put a bill through Congress to make any criticism of his acts or of the President's acts or of any political move or measure treasonable and punishable as such.

He is possibly violently pro-British. He is possibly violently pro-corporation. He is located where he can do the corporations the most good, and he has been unwilling to be removed or they have been unwilling to have him removed, even for position on the Supreme bench.

Gregory and Burleson are so crooked that, as Alfred Henry Lewis used to say, one of them could lie on a bed on top of the Woolworth Building and the other on the ground floor and look down and up forty-seven flights of winding stairs in each other's eyes and understand each other perfectly.

The object of the Zimmermann forgery was to frighten Congress into giving the President the powers that he demanded, and perhaps also into passing the Espionage Bill. When Wilson wanted to give away the rights of the United States in the Panama Canal, he pretended that he had private information of a dangerous international situation sufficient to justify his acts. He has never revealed his private information and no one now believes that he ever had any.

He could not repeat the false claim on this occasion, so a complaisant cable office this time undertook to manufacture sufficient false evidence to enable Wilson to have his way. It is possible that the British Secret Service co-operated in those plans. The only serious consequence is that the whole people of this country, ninety per cent of whom do not want war, may be projected into war because of these misrepresentations and these forged documents, if they are forged.

I believe in war if the people want war. They have to do the fighting. They ought to do the deciding. I believe in, first, a referendum to the people; and second, failing that, a decision by the people's representatives in Congress assembled. We are getting very far away from democracy and very close to autocracy when we repose all the power of the people's representatives in the hands of one man, whom we thereby create a dictator. It may be the right thing to do, but Rome in so doing drifted from a republic into an empire.

I think the United States should remain a republic in fact as well as in name, and that the people should neither be deceived by the machinations of a tricky Attorney General nor deprived of their right to decide a question of war or any other momentus question. I do not believe that any other individual has any interest in such questions equal to the interest of the great mass of the public, and I do not believe that the wisdom of any individual is equal to the collective wisdom of the people.

If we do not want to say all this editorially, we can say part of it editorially, and get some one to stand for interview as Dr. Hale used to do. Bring all these points out, especially those about the probable forging of the note. We should develop the forgery phase of the note for the Sunday paper if Francis and I seem to be right.

"Francis and I" turned out to be wrong and the "forgery phase" of the Zimmermann note was not developed for the Sunday paper. A further batch of instructions was sent to Carvalho. In one wire, Hearst ordered his editorial writers to "speak highly" of President Wilson:—

If situation quiets down please remove color flags from first page and little flags from inside pages, reserving these for special occasions of a warlike or patriotic kind. I think they have been good for this week, giving us a very American character and probably helping sell papers, but to continue effective they should be reserved for occasions.

And in another telegram of the same date he wrote:—

I feel Congress should remain in continual session and protect the people's liberties. This making a dictator of a President is desperately dangerous business. It may do no immediate harm with a

202

good President, but it may do immense injury with a bad one. Augustus, Rome's first Emperor, was a good man, but Nero, who acted under powers and precedents allowed Augustus, was a fearfully bad one. Eternal vigilance is the price of liberty. Wilson is a Federalist, as I wrote in the first year of his term, and as Francis showed in alien and sedition editorial. The Federalists are autocratic in tendency. Hamilton was accused of trying to make monarchy of our government. "Monarchies are destroyed by poverty, republics by wealth."

It is easier to establish a virtual monarchy in the rich America of today than in the poor America of a hundred years ago. We shy at the name of King but we accept the spirit of absolutism. The Romans would have no King but they accepted an Imperator with more power than any King, and so lost their liberties. President of this republic today has more power than any King in any constitutional monarchy in the world. If he gets more he will be a dictator and possibly a despot. It is the duty of true democrats to be vigilant, especially as all these encroachments on popular right are being made in the name of democracy.

Telegram, March 4:—

McCay could make strong eight-column cartoon, occupying in depth two-thirds editorial page, showing smaller figures Uncle Sam and Germany shaking their fists at each other on left side page and on right side big head and shoulders of Japan, with knife in hand, leaning over into picture and evidently watching chance to strike Uncle Sam in back. Title of picture to be "Watchful Waiting," "Look out, Uncle Sam, your neighbor, Japan, is eagerly waiting an opportunity to strike you in the back."

On the same day, the first of President Wilson's new term, Hearst repeated his plea for a special session of Congress. The second March 4 wire to Carvalho:—

Think beneficial thing Senate not to give President great powers demanded. If my telegram of yesterday explaining my opinion on such powers and advocacy of extra sessions was not printed in Sunday paper, please elaborate it somewhat and make it an editorial approving action of Senate. Speak very highly of Wilson; say he is good President and undoubtedly meant to use power for good purposes, but the precedent is a dangerous one to establish, and Senate did well to retain its powers and rights and protect the liberties of the people. Say that the few Senators who voted to retain the rights and functions of that body constitute a roll of honor. They did not

lack respect for President, but they had a greater respect for the
institutions founded by the Fathers. The day will come when their
action will be commended by all the people. Print their names.

With the declaration of war, Hearst crawled into the conflict crabwise.
His papers blossomed with flag displays and patriotic bathos and declared:
"Let every energy be bent upon preparation for a powerful and wholly victorious war. We are now for the most effective war that it is possible to
make. . . . Let us make ready with all possible haste, counting not cost, to
wage a powerful war, an overwhelming war."

The front page gleamed with the panoply of war. Hundreds of columns
were devoted to Red Cross and Liberty Loan campaigns. Recruiting stations
were set up. Yet the editorial pages reflected the old policy: "Let us keep
our men, money and supplies on this side of the water." On July 27, three
and a half months after the war began, Hearst called for an immediate peace
rather than send "a million of our splendid young Americans every year to
a war which may last from seven to ten years to be offered up in bloody
sacrifice." "Stripping Our Country of Men, Money and Food Is a Dangerous
Policy" read an editorial headline. Later he asserted: "If the Allies should
succumb to the submarine warfare inside of three months—as they certainly may—they are beyond any effective help of ours, and we are simply
wasting sorely needed men and supplies by sending them abroad to perish
or to litter the bottom of the sea." And so he went. By winter, when several
divisions of American troops had run the submarine blockade without loss
of a man, a tide of passion had arisen against the Hearst press.

In November, 1917, a packed mass meeting in Carnegie Hall, New York,
condemned Hearst by resolution and heard the publisher denounced as a
traitor and a menace by James M. Beck, former Solicitor General of the
United States. A boycott, already in force in five Allied nations, began to
spread throughout many widely separated communities in the United States.

The New York *Tribune* in the spring of 1918 ran a series of militantly
bitter attacks entitled "Coiled in the Flag, HEARS-S-S-S-T." The *Tribune*
cited chapter and verse to prove Hearst cold in loyalty:—

> Since the United States entered the war the Hearst papers have
> printed: 74 attacks on our Allies, 17 instances of defense or praise
> of Germany, 63 pieces of anti-war propaganda, 1 deletion of a
> Presidential proclamation—total 155—or an average of nearly three
> a week, while America has been engaged in the life and death strug-
> gle with civilization's enemy.

Kenneth MacGowan was the author of the *Tribune* articles. Years later,
when passions had cooled, he told this writer that he had always been a
little ashamed of the ferocity of the attack and that he had never doubted

Hearst's patriotism. Nevertheless, pamphlets containing the *Tribune* charges were broadcast throughout the country; and the feeling against Hearst rose to almost hysterical proportions. In many cities and towns there were riots and the Hearst papers publicly burned. Elsewhere attempts were made to bar their sale. Usually the courts intervened. Some newsdealers refused to handle Hearst publications. Many clubs, patriotic organizations, war associations and religious societies passed boycotting resolutions. The wildest rumors about Hearst, his family and his key men were circulated and believed.

One rumor had Hearst engaged in dark plots with the notorious Bolo Pasha, a wily Levantine and Parisian newspaper publisher, later executed by France as a spy. The basis for this canard was that Hearst had been a fellow guest with many other prominent New Yorkers at a dinner, publicly reported, given by Bolo; and that the visitor had appealed to Hearst and many other publishers in an effort to obtain newsprint for his paper in Paris.

As he traveled imperturbably about the country, Hearst himself often felt the hot prejudice against him. Once, entering a restaurant, he was greeted by a woman, her face distorted with rage, who hissed at him, "boche!"

"You are right, Madam," replied Hearst with a sweep of his Western sombrero and a polite bow, "it's all bosh."

The Hearst counterattack was swift. Endorsements were solicited from directors of war drives, public officials and prominent citizens. The New York *Tribune* was bitterly denounced as a creature of the corporations and toady of Wall Street. A pamphlet, "Distorted Quotations from the Hearst Papers, a Campaign of Falsehood," was issued asserting:—

> The attack upon the Hearst papers has been carried on by the circulation of pamphlets containing false, distorted or disjointed quotations from the Hearst papers. Most of the statements about the course of the Hearst papers in the war are bald falsehoods. . . .
>
> A few sincere, earnest, well-meaning persons have been deceived by these counterfeit presentments of Hearst editorials. The campaign of calumny and misrepresentation has not impressed or affected the great mass of newspaper readers.
>
> The reason probably is that the Hearst newspapers have been too widely read and their pro-American policies too well known for many years for the public to be misled about them.

The *Tribune* onslaught gave the Hearst cabinet many anxious moments. The attacks, however, finally petered out with little appreciable popular effect. Nevertheless, from the spring of 1918 to the triumphant conclusion of the war, the Hearst editorial pages were careful to wave the flag in unison with the news columns.

The war over, Hearst battered away at the Treaty of Versailles and organized a nation-wide campaign in support of the "irreconcilable" Senators who blocked our adherence to the League of Nations.

In the Presidential campaign of 1920, Hearst advised James M. Cox, the Democratic nominee and his running mate, young Franklin D. Roosevelt, to drop the League of Nations and the Wilson "millstone" that was "dragging them to defeat."

After the overwhelming election of Warren G. Harding, Hearst said rejoicingly: "This historic election is purely and simply a repudiation by sterling American citizens of the Wilson party and that party's pro-British, un-American policies. . . . Mr. Wilson wanted a referendum on the League of Nations, and he has had it."

Damon Runyon by Tad (T. A. Dorgan) and a Tad self-portrait. The 1920's marked the rise of Runyon as star reporter for Hearst papers. Doubling first as baseball writer and Mexican border war correspondent, Runyon handled every kind of big news assignment for Hearst papers while continuing to cover sports. Runyon's first guys and dolls Broadway stories were written for Hearst's *Cosmopolitan* magazine. As was his practice, Hearst continued to collect talented, big name writers upon his papers and news services—Bill Corum, Walter Winchell, Floyd Gibbons, Bob Considine, Westbrook Pegler, George Sokolsky, Dorothy Kilgallen, were some of those added in the Twenties, Thirties and Forties, but as long as he lived, Runyon remained the top star.

Exeunt Political Ambition

13

JUST AS Woodrow Wilson appears as chief protagonist in the extraordinary Hearst saga during the second decade of the 20th century, so events of the third decade were largely dominated by the late Alfred E. Smith.

Alternating in uneasy alliance and snarling collision, Hearst and Smith became embroiled in a vendetta so savage that each succeeded in finally wrecking the other's most cherished political hopes.

In the summer of 1922 Smith, by an artfully conceived and effective piece of histrionics, removed Hearst as an office-seeking factor in national politics. Disheveled, perspiration running in streams from the wilted collar of his soft shirt to his bare feet, Smith backed into a corner of a hotel room in Syracuse, N. Y., and over and over again, for hour after hour, shouted refusal to run on the same state ticket with Hearst.

About the same time, Hearst was dealt a blow in his own field of "striking" journalism where he had been without a peer for thirty years. An illustrated tabloid, established in New York three years before by aggressive anti-Hearst publishers, announced proudly that it was approaching 600,000 in circulation and showing, in addition, a comfortably growing profit.

That amazing son of the slums, Al Smith, went on from his defiance of timid Democratic bosses to an unprecedented triumph in his race for the Governorship of New York without Hearst as Senatorial running mate; and the *Daily News,* an avidly read addition to the journalism of the era, rapidly progressed to a point where its circulation about equaled the combined total of the Hearst papers in New York.

Everywhere people began asking whether the curve of the Hearst fortunes had definitely dipped. Was Hearst aging and tiring, failing in the old sure-fire showmanship? At this juncture the ineffable Bernarr Macfadden came along with a weird and neurotic pictorial tabloid called the *Evening Graphic* and cut sadly into Hearst's once million-plus-a-day *Evening Journal*.

When one has volleyed and thundered and led the pack for many years, it is extremely irksome to find one's self shunted into the receiving-line, thundered and volleyed upon. But Hearst, with his usual buoyant resourcefulness, was far from defeated. After writhing for a time in the unexpected competition, he launched tabloid hybrids of his own in New York and Boston. Later, these papers sought to cauterize the new form of journalistic life by the simple expedient of outjazzing the jazzers.

However, he could evolve no effective antidote for the series of crushing defeats which Governor Smith administered beginning with the state convention of 1922 at Syracuse. Never again would Hearst be mentioned seriously as a candidate for high office in state or nation. Hereafter his influence, still potent in many quarters, would be exercised behind the scenes.

All over the land the tocsins rang for the man who had "licked Hearst." The prediction was freely made that Smith might vault lightly into the White House on the strength of his surprising victories over Hearst in New York State.

The Governor of New York, as the conqueror of Hearst, became almost a cult in certain parts of the country. In his own state half a million enrolled Republicans regularly supported him election after election. He was almost deified by old-line Tammany Hall chieftains, smarting for years under the Hearst knout. The new popular hero was quick to sense the political advantage to himself in using the feared press lord as a whipping boy.

Smith brought to the warfare against Hearst native force, an unexcelled knowledge of crowd psychology and astonishing faculty of self-salesmanship. He seemed able to take his audiences by the hand and walk them across the footlights. Delighting in rough-and-ready debate, he was a splendid actor and a master of sweet, simple, sometimes deliberately uncouth English. An example was his habitual misuse of the noun "radio," pronouncing the "a" as in "radish." The carefully contrived solecism invariably drew gales of laughter, and votes. Unlike most machine politicians, Smith did not lack intestinal fortitude, although he could compromise and wriggle with the best of them.

Racially, Alfred Emanuel Smith was a fusion of German and Irish. The family name, originally, is said to have been Schmidt. His mother was undiluted Irish. The father was employed as a waterfront drayman on the East River near the present site of the Brooklyn Bridge and the family lived in a tenement flat at 174 South Street where Al was born in December, 1873, later moving to nearby Oliver Street. Smith Sr. was scarcely able

208

to read or write and the boy could remember his mother leading her spouse to the kitchen sink and forcing him to remove the grime of his daily toil before putting supper on the table.

Gregarious and high-spirited, young Smith, from earliest childhood, could make people laugh. He could not recall when he was not reciting "The Bells" or "The Face on the Barroom Floor" to the neighbors. Later, after he had conquered elementary grades in parochial school, he played leads with a group of neighborhood players in "May Blossom," "The Confederate Spy," "The Mighty Dollar" and other fine old heart-to-heart comedy-dramas. Memory, he was always frank to confess, was his greatest asset. During the Constitutional Convention of 1915, he astonished Elihu Root and other distinguished delegates by talking for two hours without notes on the history of public-service laws. His mind became a reliable file-index of facts, figures, stories, jokes, names. He remembered the choruses of even the most obscure popular songs of his boyhood and could sing them passably.

Serving subpoenas in the office of the Commissioner of Jurors was Al Smith's first political job. Thomas F. Foley, "Big Tom" Foley, who divided control of the populous districts below Fourteenth Street with the Sullivans, "Big" and "Little" Tim, watched Smith; Foley kept his keen, talent-seeking eye upon every likely young fellow in the section.

One day in 1903, Big Tom summoned Smith to his office almost opposite the grim Tombs prison. Foley had just concluded an interview with Paddy Whalen, an attendant in the District Attorney's office. Paddy had pleaded his family couldn't afford the financial sacrifice involved if he should heed the boss' wishes and go to the State Assembly.

"Al," Foley told young Smith, "I am going to help you to get to the Assembly. When you go to Albany study hard, keep your word and make a howl if the leaders don't let you know everything that's going on."

Al took his patron's advice. He went to the legislature for twelve terms, the Assembly Chamber becoming his high school and his college. With dogged determination he mastered the science of government, won friends by the thousand, and fused his platform personality into the thing of force it later became. By sponsoring as much social legislation as the bosses would permit, he became the most popular Democrat in public life and was hailed even by acrimonious critics of Tammany as the best representative of that discredited organization. His one weakness was a fondness for alcohol but he was too strong of will to permit liquor to get the best of him.

Boss Charles F. Murphy recognized Smith's value to Tammany Hall and made him Sheriff of New York County in 1915. Perhaps in the back of Murphy's astute head was the hope that this adroit and winning young son of Tammany would eventually prove an instrument to destroy the political power of Hearst. Although a suave diplomat as politicians go, Murphy at heart chafed as much as his grumbling lieutenants at Hearst's indirect domination. Tammany had experienced a taste of Hearst's power in 1913 when the publisher supported the Fusion movement that swept John Purroy Mitchel into the Mayoralty. Hearst, however, had broken with Mitchel over the issue of municipal ownership; and Murphy saw a chance to win Hearst's support in the election of 1917. Accordingly he sent Hearst an ingratiating request to name the Democratic candidate for Mayor.

L. J. O'Reilly, Hearst's secretary, recommended John F. Hylan, an obscure worker in the Brooklyn political vineyard. Hylan was a simple, ingenuous man who had come to Kings County from a Catskill village and risen from day laborer to motorman on the Brooklyn elevated lines.

He read Blackstone by night, was admitted to the bar and went into neighborhood politics on a modest scale. Behind a mild manner, limpid eye and sandy complexion lay a certain adhesive quality. He was elected a City Magistrate and later County Judge—almost the identical road, it is interesting to recall, subsequently followed by William O'Dwyer.

When Tammany presented John Francis Hylan for the Mayoralty, probably not one per cent of the enrolled voters had ever heard of him. He declared for municipal ownership of public utilities and Hearst praised him for his "sound Americanism, democratic opinions, and lofty, unselfish purposes." Al Smith was placed on the ticket for President of the Board of Aldermen. The Tammany leaders were grooming their fair-haired boy for the inevitable conflict with Hearst. The latter may have been suspicious but he swallowed the entire slate.

Morris Hillquit was the Socialist candidate for Mayor and, as the campaign progressed, developed surprising strength. Adroit behind-scenes political maneuverings are shown in telegrams passing between Hearst, Arthur Brisbane and S. S. Carvalho. On October 21, Brisbane wired Hearst:—

> There is actual possibility of Hillquit's election in four-cornered fight. Conditions ought to disturb the corporations working for Mitchel. They will sweat and pay taxes on their personal property if Hillquit is elected. Shall I write editorial warning corporations that their effort to get everything from Mitchel may cost them dear through Hillquit's victory? If they understood situation and danger they would drop Mitchel and vote for Hylan. Editorial would describe Hillquit's ability and sincerity. Remarkably able lawyer. Rosenwald, who asks me introduce him Hillquit, says latter one of ablest men in country. Can write editorial in such way as to transfer many votes from Mitchel to Hillquit. Please reply.

Hearst's response demonstrated that, although 3,000 miles away, he held a firm finger upon the political pulse in New York. October 23, he sent this wire to his general manager, S. S. Carvalho:—

> Brisbane wants to write editorial praising Hillquit. Brisbane thinks

Hillquit may be elected. Of course Hillquit will not be elected although government's policy will make Socialists very strong. Editorial of kind Brisbane suggests would be construed as disloyalty to Hylan and upset all our plans. Please prevent it.

As a matter of fact Hearst's personal preference, political considerations aside, might well have been the Socialist leader Hillquit.

Properly characterized in the Brisbane despatch as one of the ablest men in the country, Morris Hillquit was completely sincere and no Johnny-Come-Lately in his advocacy of public ownership and other pet Hearst measures. Also, with Hearst, he was unalterably opposed to America's entry into the war.

While commanding lucrative fees in the practise of corporate law, Hillquit for years had donated his services freely in causes which enlisted his sense of justice; and he was an idol among New York's working class.

Although he knew he was leading a forlorn cause, Mayor Mitchel told a cheering crowd on the steps of City Hall that he would make the fight "against Hearst, Hylan and the Hohenzollerns."

Hearst retorted that Mitchel was hiding behind the flag and asserted that "the Mayor has a silly ambition for social recognition." The Hearst papers caricatured Mitchel as a social climber and printed cartoons and full-page editorials under the heading: "Mr. Vanderbilt Calls Me Jack."

Hylan came before the public timidly, reading his speeches in a voice that was like a monotonous phonographic reproduction. Al Smith, on the other hand, ramped the hustings like a "regular guy" who gets watermelon seeds in his ears every time the boys hold a chowder; and it was generally agreed that the wit, bewitching satire and sound common sense of the candidate for the Aldermanic Presidency contributed largely to the overwhelming victory of the Hearst-Tammany ticket.

During Hylan's eight years in City Hall he and Hearst never quarreled. It was a new experience for Hearst who had broken with every mayor since Van Wyck. Hylan was a faithful proselyte. Indeed, his pronouncements were so strikingly similar in wording to Hearst editorials that an inimical grand jury actually sought to demonstrate that Hearst was the real mayor.

The search for this so-called "overshadowing crime" proved abortive. Hylan continued employing his powerful forum in attacking "the interests," standing firm for a five-cent fare, city-owned utilities and lower prices for the necessaries of life.

The Mayor and his chief supporter developed a David and Jonathan friendship. During the first winter of his term the Mayor purchased a snappy suit of flannels and joined Hearst at Palm Beach. He issued one guileless statement which afforded columnists and cartoonists a lot of fun.

"I want the people to know Mr. Hearst as I know him," remarked the

Mayor. "I had an entirely different impression of him until I knew him. We were on the beach yesterday and a jellyfish had closed about a little toad. Mr. Hearst flicked it away with the end of his cane and said: 'Why let the poor little thing suffer?' I think that typifies what I like in Hearst."

Al Smith did not remain in the Hylan cabinet long.

Although there were some rumblings of dissent in the Hearst camp, the Democrats nominated Smith for Governor in the fall of 1918. The candidate and Boss Murphy realized that Hearst's support was essential. The publisher granted Smith an audience and exacted endorsement of the Hearst public-ownership policies. Smith won the election by the narrow margin of 15,000 votes over Charles S. Whitman.

The new Governor moved his wife, five children and their pet dog Caesar into the Executive Mansion and began the task of wrestling with a Republican legislature. His Excellency was still Al Smith of Oliver Street and discarded none of his homely habits. Each Saturday night, following an old Fourth Ward custom, he helped scrub and bathe his boys and turned the hose on them to the accompaniment of screams of laughter.

Shortly after the inauguration, the Hearst papers began to criticize Smith appointments on the ground that he was favoring reactionaries. In May, 1919, Hearst issued a tart statement concerning published reports that he had recommended a judicial appointment:—

> I have been particularly careful never to ask any appointment or any other political favor of Governor Smith, for I have never been quite convinced of the sincerity of his professions of progressive principles. He has always been too close to certain public-service corporations to make him an ideal public official from my point of view.
>
> I supported him because I felt that he was better than Whitman, or at least not as bad as Whitman, and because he made definite declarations in the nature of pledges for publication in my newspapers in favor of public ownership. But that does not mean that I must support any bad appointment that Governor Smith may make or condone any public act of his that might be a repudiation of his pledges to the public.

During the summer the large milk distributing companies increased the price of their product. The Hearst papers demanded that the Governor take action. Smith retorted that he had no power to regulate the price of any commodity. Hearst promptly began to pillory Smith in editorials and cartoons as a boss-controlled politician. Caricatures showed the Milk Trust Barons winking at him and greeting him with the insidious slogan: "You Know Me, Al!" Finally the *Evening Journal* printed a series of cartoons showing emaciated children of the tenements begging the Governor in vain for milk. This was too much for Smith.

He saw red. He tramped the floor of his office for hours. Then he jumped aboard a train for New York and told Murphy, Foley and the other Tammany chieftains: "I am going to say what I think of Hearst openly and publicly."

The Governor issued a challenge to Hearst to meet him in joint debate in Carnegie Hall. His only stipulation was that Hearst might ask him any questions concerning his public or private life if the same privilege was accorded the Governor in respect to Hearst. He promised to divide the seating space equally between partisans of himself and followers of Hearst. Hearst wrote a letter of declination in which he advised Smith to "answer to the people" and added, "you need keep no tickets for any friends of mine."

Smith went alone to Carnegie Hall on the evening of October 29, 1919. A tense and expectant crowd packed the edifice and milled about the doors. It was generally recognized that Smith was staking his political future in deliberately provoking a feud with the man who for thirty years had been a dominating independent force in American public life.

Speaking slowly and solemnly, Smith delivered an address that was a masterpiece of invective. Denouncing Hearst as a "pestilence that walks in the dark" and an "enemy of the people," he proposed organization of a nonpartisan committee "to protect public servants and citizens generally from Hearst's irresponsible methods of misrepresentation and slander." The speaker took up the Hearst charges against himself in detail and went on:—

> But, in the last analysis, there is nothing very remarkable about the assault upon me. Follow back the history of this man's newspapers since he came to this part of the country and you will have to read out of his newspapers this remarkable fact: That in this great democracy, in this land of the free and in this home of the brave, there has never been a man elected to office yet that has not been tainted in some way. Is that right or is it wrong? That is not a severe statement to make, because that is the truth.
>
> If the Hearst newspapers were the textbooks for the children of our schools, they would have to spell out of its every line that no man can be trusted in this country after he is put into public office; that no man thinks enough about it; no man has enough of regard for his country; no man has enough of real Christian charity to do the right thing; no man that ever held great public office had enough of respect and regard for his mother and his wife and his children and his friends to be right in office. About that, there can be no question, because no public man in this state, from Grover Cleve-

land right down to today, has ever escaped this fellow. We all know that. The children on the street know it.

Governor Smith's defiance of Hearst brought him into national prominence almost overnight. His speech went ringing over the country and met wide approval from the anti-Hearst press. A reflection of his newly attained position in the Democratic Party came at the National Convention of 1920 in San Francisco, when the delegation from New York gave him a complimentary ballot and provoked a demonstration lasting twenty-five minutes.

An even greater uproar was touched off in 1924 by Smith's then bosom chum, Franklin D. Roosevelt, who climaxed a dramatic and appealing nominating speech by lauding his man as the "Happy Warrior." In retrospect this speech and Roosevelt's subsequent relations with both Smith and Hearst combine to form a fascinating montage of history-in-the-making.

Smith's renomination for Governor of New York was inevitable. He was defeated by a mere 74,000 votes—a defeat which added tremendously to his personal prestige. For in the Harding-Coolidge Republican landslide of that year Smith received in New York State a million more votes than the national Democratic candidates, James M. Cox and Franklin D. Roosevelt.

Now followers shouted as fanatically for "Boss Killer" Smith as predecessors had done for "Boss Killer" Hearst in 1905 and 1906. With perfect equanimity, Hearst, a week before the election, wired his editors from Los Angeles:—

> I am concerned for my progressive policies and principles, and I don't care whether Smith is elected or not. He is better than Miller. I want to support Malone as a progressive and a genuine Democrat, and if I could get Smith sincerely to pledge himself to progressive legislation I would not oppose him. His personal attacks upon me are wholly unimportant. I don't consider them at all. The objection to Smith is that he isn't sincere and isn't truthful and probably will not do what he says he will do, but he will have to do some of it if he commits himself strongly enough.

Nathan L. Miller was the successful Republican candidate, Dudley Field Malone running as an independent.

During the two years of Smith's retirement into private life, Hearst and Mayor Hylan sought to maneuver him into a politically negligible quantity, deriding him as a reactionary and attacking him for accepting an honorary post on a state commission from Governor Miller. Smith, however, bided his time.

Summers, he took his family and half a dozen animal pets—dogs, monkeys, parrots—to a large house on the waterfront at Sea Gate near Coney Island. A wealthy friend in the trucking industry had provided him with

214

a well-paid, not too exacting, interim job; and Smith thoroughly enjoyed his fling at business life. The writer, summering also at Sea Gate, frequently encountered the ex-Governor on the jaunty little yacht which plied between the Atlantic Yacht Club and the Battery and had many intimate talks with him. These mid-morning chats were veritable seminars in men, events and politics. Smith was as frank as a child with those whom he trusted. Hence, it came as no surprise when he accepted Boss Murphy's judgment that Hylan must be endorsed for a second term in 1921, and chipped in $500 for the Hylan campaign fund.

Hylan was re-elected by a plurality of 400,000. Then the political jockeying began afresh. Hylan, William J. Connors and other supporters persuaded Hearst that it was his duty to re-enter politics. The publisher bent an attentive ear. He added four upstate New York newspapers to his chain of journals encircling the country and announced that he would be glad to run for the United States Senate in 1922 if John Hylan—"a true Democrat in the broadest sense of the word"—could be induced to campaign for the Governorship. Tammany had no intention of promoting Hylan, however. In August Al Smith announced his candidacy and Hearst sought to spike his guns at once:—

> Mr. Smith is doubtless as well fitted as any man in the state to lead the Democratic Party if it is to be a conservative party and dispute with the Republican Party the support of the great interests now behind Governor Miller. I am a progressive, however, and without any disparagement of Mr. Smith I believe it is the highest duty as well as the best policy of the Democratic Party to make its appeal to the masses of the people rather than to the privileged interests.

The battle was on, the chips were down.

At Tammany Hall opposing forces tugged at Murphy. The Boss had not faced so delicate a situation in twenty years. He remained grim-faced and silent but permitted the word to go forth that he favored Hearst for Senator, Smith for Governor. Smith stated flatly that he would not run on the same ticket with Hearst. There were indications that Tammany leaders, including Murphy, secretly applauded this position, although they feared openly to antagonize Hearst and Hylan.

The Syracuse Convention developed into a battle of primitive savagery. Smith resisted every personal influence brought to bear. A rheumatic foot confined him to his hotel. For three days he received delegations in his room, monotonously repeating: "I will not run on a ticket with Hearst. There is not room in the party for us both. That blankety-blank is no Democrat." Finally, at three o'clock on the morning of September 29, Murphy told Mayor Hylan and the other Hearst agents: "I can't budge Al. The delegates

215

want him and they don't want Hearst. Sorry. I did my best." Notified by phone Hearst dictated a telegram of withdrawal:—

> Please be sure not to allow my name to go before the convention. I certainly would not go on any ticket which would be a betrayal of genuine democracy. My nomination for any public office is not important, but it is important that the party declare for progressive principles and show the sincerity of that declaration by nominating men who can be trusted to make it effective.

Al Smith emerged from that victory a figure of supreme state and great national importance. The drama of his apparently lone stand captured the popular imagination and he was elected by an unprecedented majority of 385,932. Hearst decided to support the ticket, explaining: "Our campaign for genuine Democratic principles and policies must be conducted without personal prejudice. We may entertain regrets that progressive ideals did not have what we consider fullest expression, but we should harbor no resentment."

Hearst's sportsmanship and conciliatory words softened some of his once implacable enemies in Tammany Hall. "Big Tom" Foley publicly buried the hatchet at a meeting in his Downtown Tammany Club with candidate Al Smith, in the sight of friends and neighbors of the Fourth Ward, looking on in approval. Next year, however, the merry war was on again when Hearst opposed the Tammany judiciary slate. Boss Murphy waved good-bye to Hearst forever and was moved to announce that he had excluded from his home "the lying, filthy newspapers under the Hearst management."

Murphy died during the Smith drive for the Democratic Presidential nomination in 1924. Several national Democratic leaders sought to enlist Hearst under the Smith banner. The publisher rejected these unofficial overtures and he and Mayor Hylan did nothing to aid the New York Governor in his long battle of ballots with William Gibbs McAdoo. Across the width of the New York *American's* first page, on the eve of the Madison Square Garden Convention, Hearst printed this blast:—

> In order to answer some reactionary rumors and to make the position of the Hearst papers perfectly clear regarding the various candidates before the Democratic Convention, let me say first that the Hearst papers have no special enemies and no particular favorites in the coming contest; second, that the Hearst papers have made no deals with any individuals or with any machines, and will make none; third, that the Hearst papers will print the news with the utmost impartiality and will support any progressive Democrat; fourth, that the Hearst papers have always been opposed to the

216

booze and boodle element of the party, and will conscientiously oppose any candidate representing booze and boodle.

Wall Street newspapers and Tammany organs please copy.

With the McAdoo and Smith forces hopelessly deadlocked, Hearst urged Senator Walsh of Montana as a compromise candidate. Walsh was a Roman Catholic as was Smith, but as dry as the New York man was wet. When John W. Davis was nominated Hearst announced that the "proud old Democratic Party" had "committed suicide" by proposing to "substitute the house of Morgan for the White House," and dashed off to California with Mayor Hylan. In both state and national elections the Hearst press adopted a middle of the road course, its kindest words reserved for Senator Bob La Follette's surprisingly flourishing third party. Al Smith won the Governorship a third time. Then he set to work to truncate Mayor Hylan and remove Hearst's last vestige of power in New York.

Early in the spring of 1925 the Smith men began grooming James J. Walker for the Mayoralty. Jimmy Walker was one of the younger men who had risen to the fore in Tammany. He had been Democratic leader of the State Senate for years and his personal popularity rivaled that of Smith.

Seeking to save Hylan at any cost, Hearst even dangled before Smith's eyes the possibility of Hearst support for the Presidency in 1928, pointing out that neither Hylan nor Smith would gain by dissension. Nothing in the entire course of the Hearst-Smith feud is more enigmatic than this utterance of Hearst, May 24, 1925:—

> There are a number of great offices that are going to be filled during the next few years, and the Democratic Party is going to fill them if conditions remain as favorable as they now are. The party is powerful and conditions are favorable because of the records of Mayor Hylan and Governor Smith. Consequently these men are naturally in line for some of these offices if the party remains powerful and conditions remain harmonious. . . . The Democratic leaders are not fools. They can see this just as clearly as the Republican leaders can see it; and their interest is just as great to maintain harmony as the interest of the Republican leaders and organs is to create dissension.
>
> Unquestionably Governor Smith went about his business attending to his duties in his characteristic, capable way, without quarreling with Mayor Hylan. And unquestionably Mayor Hylan went about his business without quarreling with Governor Smith. . . .
>
> Who is going to upset the apple cart? Certainly not the gentlemen who are sitting pretty on it.

But the clash of ambition—that sin by which other than angels fall—

217

was destined to rudely pierce Hearst's Pollyanna picture. Smith detected a heaven-sent opportunity to upset the apple cart and scatter helter-skelter the fruits of the long Hearst-Hylan alliance. Accordingly, State Senator Jimmy Walker announced his intention of contesting the Mayoralty nomination with Hylan in the September Democratic primaries.

The primary battle attracted national attention. The rival candidates were all but lost sight of in the bitter clash of personalities between Hearst and Smith. The former fired his shafts from California, the latter from the stump. The advantage of a ringside seat was with the Governor. The editor's opening blast charged Smith with subservience to Wall Street and accused him anew of seeking to mix religion with politics. Smith, replying, read Hearst out of the Democratic Party, declared that he was Hylan's heaviest burden and added: "The fathers and mothers of New York resent Mr. Hearst's interference in the politics of this city because the example of his life is such as to make it undesirable that our youth be impressed with the fact that a man like him can wield any considerable amount of political influence in any community."

Hearst retorted by tacking the sobriquet "Alibi Al" to his foeman, adding:—

"The distinguished Governor of the great State of New York has taken three days laboriously to prepare a vulgar tirade that any resident of Billingsgate or any occupant of the alcoholic ward in Bellevue could have written in fifteen minutes in quite the same style, but with more evidence of education and intelligence. The Wall Street friends of Governor Smith have enabled him to remove his domicile and his refined person from the neighborhood of the Bowery, but he still reverts in manner of thought to the familiar localities of Five Points and Hell's Kitchen, if this may be said without undue offense to these historic localities."

Smith promptly tagged Hearst the "Overlord of the Pacific" and brought tears of laughter from a Bronx audience with these thrusts:—

> Hearst is out of the picture. He hasn't any business to make even a suggestion to the Democratic Party, because he has not got a vote. He was not enrolled. So out with him! The owner of the enchanted palace with a thousand hills and a thousand cows grazing. While he and the Mayor were out brushing the flies off the grazing cows on the thousand hills, they were both engaged in shipping the bull on to New York!

A more serious note was struck by Hearst a week before the primary election. In a letter to the New York *World* he denied categorically that he was Mayor Hylan's boss:—

> I am a sincere friend of Mayor Hylan because I like him and be-

cause I greatly admire his sterling character, his genuine ability, his uncorruptible honesty and his uncompromising devotion to the service of the public . . . he maintained the five-cent fare in spite of the efforts of Tammany and Governor Smith and all the powerful financial interests of the city to make him permit the breaking of the Interborough contract and allow the traction companies to charge a ten-cent rate.

Then Mayor Hylan, after his election, saw that it was desirable not only to maintain the five-cent fare but to build municipal subways in order to treat the traveling public decently and give it adequate transportation facilities. These subways he began to build, and then arose such a hue and cry against him by the great financial interests, and the political and journalistic agencies which they controlled, as I never have heard before in all my experience in politics in any state or city of the United States.

Although he had recognized in advance that it would be practically impossible to beat Tammany Hall in an organization primary, Hearst took Mayor Hylan's defeat much to heart. In a private wire to Joseph A. Moore, one of his chief executives, he burst forth with his real opinion of politics and its professional practitioners. Bidding Mr. Moore inform the Mayor that he would "enthusiastically support" him if he wished to run independently, Hearst asserted that the "Tammany crowd" had crucified Hylan because they resented his honesty:—

They would get rid of him as Aristides was ostracized from Athens because they were tired of hearing him called "The Just." However, there is plenty of opportunity and proper recompense for honesty and able men in law and business, and if Hylan would let me advise him I would tell him to leave politics to the crooks and get into the decent business world. He will feel as if he were coming out of a dark cellar into the fresh air and sunlight. Still, let me repeat that if Hylan wants to run independently, I will support him. Hylan has his ideas of duty to the public. My idea of my public duty is to support able and honest men for any position regardless of party.

Hylan, however, decided to remain regular and Hearst followed the Mayor's lead in endorsing the Tammany ticket. The New York *American,* bellwether of the Hearst chain, announced that it would support Jimmy Walker because he had pledged himself to follow Mayor Hylan's policy on the five-cent fare and on the construction of new subways; and because "if he is a sincere Democrat, he is in sympathy with the Democratic masses." Walker won by an enormous plurality.

Hearst made friendly gestures toward the new Mayor but declared undying enmity for Al Smith, explaining in a newspaper interview: "I supported Smith three times and that was three times too many. Josh Billings says that success consists not in never making mistakes but in never making the same mistake twice. I made the same mistake three times. That is enough."

In 1926 Governor Smith was swept into office for his fourth term, Hearst supporting the Republican candidate, Ogden L. Mills.

Late the following year, with Al Smith again a leading candidate for the Democratic Presidential nomination, Hearst, in an apparently chameleon shift, indicated that his bitterest foeman might actually win his support! This is quoted from the publisher's signed statement in the New York *World* of December 13, 1927:—

> His [Smith's] record as Governor has been notable and his record, plus his popularity, has transformed the State of New York from a state which was formerly almost surely Republican into a state which can now be considered safely Democratic. . . . If Governor Smith is nominated, he should have the united and wholehearted support of his party, and I believe he will have it.

In reality Hearst was playing a characteristic game of cat and mouse.

The Republicans were flirting with him ardently and he was determined to exercise a leading influence in the choice of the Republican nominee, as well as to obtain the insertion of certain pet planks in the Republican platform. His choice finally swung to Herbert Hoover after this eager candidate motored from Palo Alto to Los Angeles and outlined to Hearst a glittering prospect of Federal projects for many of which the latter had been fighting for years: magnificent highways, Columbia River development in the Northwest, a gigantic system of flood control of the Mississippi River and its tributaries, inland waterways, and a general broad-gauged and imaginative program of power and irrigation dams and other conservation measures.

In the crucial campaign of 1928, the Hearst press went Republican hook, line and sinker. Hoover's achievements as engineer, statesman and humanitarian were glorified; Smith again was placarded as a tool of Booze and Boodle and an unworthy son of Rome, seeking to use his religion for selfish ends. Smith went down to humiliating defeat and Hoover wired Hearst a fulsome victory message. Smith's private comments on Hearst and the latter's activities in the campaign were unprintable.

Hearst's amicable relations with Hoover ended abruptly during the economic collapse of the early 1930's when the President refused to follow the editor's drastic suggestions for relief, including a $5,000,000,000 bond issue to finance public works. Hearst's fury knew no bounds when Hoover, faced with open defiance of governmental authority by the so-called "Bonus Army," made a difficult political decision. Back in 1924, Congress had passed, over President Coolidge's veto, an Adjusted Compensation Act. It provided for a bonus to every man who had served in World War I more than sixty days in the form of what was, in effect, a paid up insurance policy on a 20-year endowment basis. The legislation was in addition to provision for wounded men and dependents of men killed in the war. Face value of the compensation certificates was fixed on a per diem basis, $1 a day for home service, $1.25 a day for foreign service, plus 25% of the sum so figured. The total was payable in 1945 or upon the death of the certificate holder prior to 1945. A majority of the certificate recipients had never served overseas or on a firing line. Adoption of the Act was supposed to have settled the soldier bonus question, but pressure was soon begun on Congress to provide for immediate cash payment of the certificates. In 1931, with the business depression having thrown many out of employment, some 10,000 ex-servicemen were incited to congregate in Washington and demand immediate bonus payment from Congress. The participants in the demonstration squatted in old buildings along Pennsylvania Avenue near the Capitol and in shacks thrown up at Anacosta. When an immediate cash payment bonus bill was defeated in Congress in June, the campers were ordered to leave Washington. Congress had appropriated money for train fare home for the demonstrators, which about half accepted. The rest stayed, under hazardous housing and sanitary conditions. Finally, on July 28, 1932—an election year—President Hoover ordered them dispersed by troops. With cavalry horse, tear gas and bayonet, Army regulars * drove the squatters from Pennsylvania Avenue quarters. That night, other troops broke up the shack town on the Anacosta flats and burned the shacks. In the action, two ex-servicemen were killed and a number injured.

"I do not care if every paper in the United States comments favorably on Hoover's action," exploded Hearst in a private wire to E. D. Coblentz, editor of the New York *American*. "I think it was the most outrageous piece of stupidity, if nothing worse, that has ever been perpetrated by the Government . . . this despotic action will tend to precipitate further conflict between Communism and Fascism which is already developing in the country and which threatens to eliminate the patriotic and Republican principles on which this nation was built."

* The Army's Chief of Staff took personal responsibility for carrying out the order. The Chief of Staff was General Douglas MacArthur, later a Hearst favorite. An aide at MacArthur's side during the operation was Major Dwight D. Eisenhower. Years after the incident, Hearst ordered the writer of a Hearst newspaper feature taken off the assignment because the writer had made a bare reference to MacArthur's command of Operation Bonus Army. The compensation certificates were paid off in 1936 over the veto of President Franklin D. Roosevelt.

The break with Hoover ended a period of eight years during which Hearst had often been a welcome guest at the White House. He had lunched several times with President Harding and the latter was on his way to visit him in California when stricken with his fatal illness.

With Calvin Coolidge, Hearst developed a friendship and a personal understanding that was even closer, and which mystified most observers. These apparently dissimilar personalities passed harmonious hours together in the White House, on the Presidential yacht and at Hearst's seat in California. The friendship was so inexplicable that one discerning Washington correspondent, T. R. B. of the *New Republic,* characterized it as "one of the most significant and remarkable political phenomena of the period. That Mr. Hearst, whose journalistic talons have been deeply sunk in the back of every national administration, regardless of party, since he became a figure in the publishing world, should turn his twenty-odd newspapers into almost pro-Administration organs, and have the brilliant Brisbane regularly and frequently anoint and glorify the President, instead of assailing him with his customary ferocity, is an interesting and amazing thing."

The friendship remained unruffled despite a mighty international uproar caused in the fall of 1927 by Hearst's publication of what became famous as "The Case of the Forged Mexican Documents."

These documents, the Hearst papers claimed, had been abstracted from the confidential files of President Calles and other Mexican officials. They purported to show that the Mexican Government and the Japanese Government had conspired against the security of the United States. Also that $1,215,000 had been withdrawn from the treasury of Mexico for the purpose of bribing four U. S. Senators and some publicists and clergymen.

A Senatorial investigating committee quickly developed that the documents were tarnished; and that Hearst and his editors, before launching them upon an excitable world, had made no impartial effort to establish the authenticity, although deleting the names of the four Senators—Borah, Heflin, Norris and La Follette. Hearst was summoned before the committee and seemed to be treated very tenderly. In his testimony and in subsequent statements the publisher insisted that the documents were "apparently quite authentic."

During Christmas week the Senate committee's experts examined the exhibits and reported that they were obvious forgeries. The signatures were fraudulent; the language was fraudulent; the typewriting was fraudulent. Hearst then called in handwriting experts of his choosing. All this, of course, was many weeks *after* the original publication.

On January 4, 1928, William A. De Ford, the Hearst attorney, amiably presented a report from the Hearst experts branding the documents as a fraud from first to last. That same morning, evidently having been advised in advance of the findings of his experts, Hearst published a message to the editors of his newspapers. Its wording would appear weirdly fantastic to the average reader:—

"If the handwriting experts should all agree that the documents we have produced bear evidence of having been fabricated, I will not dispute that decision further than to maintain persistently, and I believe patriotically, that the logic of events gives every evidence that the essential facts contained in the documents were not fabricated, and that the facts—the political facts, the international facts—are the things which are of vital importance to the American people and to the loyal representatives of the American people."

A week later, January 11, 1928, the Senate committee reported, quite without heat, that the Hearst documents were forgeries and fakes; that there was not the slightest evidence that any United States Senator or American clergyman or publicist had received or had even been offered Mexican gold.

There the matter rested. Hearst editors had paid $20,000 to men of tarnished repute for papers which imposed a mischievous hoax upon the public. U. S.–Mexican relations were strained to such an extent that a member of the firm of J. P. Morgan & Co. was called upon to cross the Rio Grande as ambassador and none other than Charles A. Lindbergh, the current national hero, gave over his holidays to serve as a missionary of good will to Mexico and other Latin-American countries.

A Tad cartoon in the Hearst papers in the Twenties.

Movies and a Touch
of Don Juanism

"The heart has reasons the mind can never know."

14

W. R. HEARST'S inimitable talent for reaching the mass mind and his insatiable urge to expand his audience inevitably led him, in March, 1913, into the field of motion picture production. Thereafter for more than twenty years he was a leading, if not a predominating, influence in America's astounding young Wonder Industry.

Hearst had long been interested in the new medium, as he was in everything new and exciting. As an expert photographer he kept eagerly abreast of scientific developments, scouring Europe and America for each new and improved camera as it became available. He was projecting crude, flickering pictures upon a screen in his home long before Charlie Chaplin came to America and pantomimed an intoxicated spectator in a vaudeville sketch called "A Night in an English Music Hall."

Early in 1913, Hearst enthusiastically endorsed a suggestion of Edgar B. Hatrick, head of his newspapers' photographic department, that an attempt be made to record on film Woodrow Wilson's first inauguration on March 4 of that year. The pictures created wide interest when shown at a Broadway theatre on March 5. Prints were rushed to leading cities throughout the country and soon America's first newsreel, Hearst-Selig Weekly, was an eagerly anticipated feature in hundreds of theatres. Hearst had added another arm to his enterprises.

Quickly he instilled some of his own seemingly inexhaustible energy and initiative into the new venture. When our imbroglio with Mexico flared into the seizure of Vera Cruz in 1914, several of Hearst's crack still photographers volunteered to serve the newsreel. One of these, Ansel Wallace, was rudely jailed for sneaking a candid shot of Mexico's cantankerous old Dictator-President, Victoriano Huerta, sipping brandy in his palace garden. Only a personal appeal from Mr. Hearst to William J. Bryan, Secretary of State in Mr. Wilson's Cabinet, obtained the newsreel man's release.

Similarly, when the writer, a roaming and callow young correspondent, "accidentally" managed to kick a bombastic Mexican commander in the eye during a swimming party, and was placed under arrest, the Chief opened the gates of the rusty hoosegow by bombarding Secretary of the Navy Josephus Daniels with phone calls and telegrams. As we trust this narrative has made plain, it was a part of Mr. Hearst's inner code to stand by his own.

Testing out various uses for his new medium, Hearst produced a succession of fast-moving melodramas in serial form, in association with Pathé. There was a fruitful idea involved. Simultaneous serialization of a story upon screens and in newspapers promoted patronage for two burgeoning mass media—movies and penny press. One of these pioneer "cliff-hangers," *The Perils of Pauline,* starring the immortal Pearl White, attained enormous popularity. Whistling, stamping crowds jammed movie houses to watch the beautiful Pearl's breath-taking adventures and daring escapes from death, her ultimate fate always left hanging in the balance until next week's instalment. *The Perils of Pauline* won rank as a cinema classic. Its genesis and Hearst's part in it were related to the writer by Charles W. Goddard, *Pauline's* creator, shortly before his death in 1951.

Charles Goddard, a promising playwright and younger brother of Morrill Goddard, editor of the *American Weekly,* was told by his brother at dinner one night: "Mr. Hearst is going into pictures in collaboration with Pathé Frères. He plans to start off with a racy adventure serial, preferably with a feminine heroine, to run about twenty weeks. He wants a background of wealth and power, melodrama with a suspense hangover carrying into the next instalment. Can you have a skeleton outline ready for him by tomorrow morning? If so, bring it to me at ten o'clock and I'll take you to Mr. Hearst's home and introduce you."

With the aid of many pots of coffee, the young dramatist prepared a condensed plot of about 500 words and presented it at his brother's house on time. The latter read the outline, fired questions and added touches. One Charles Goddard remembered vividly. It concerned the main theme of the plot which hung upon a deathbed will, written in faltering longhand by a millionaire. Morrill Goddard, with his quick picture sense, suggested that the holograph will be scrawled on the attending physician's prescription pad with its symbol ℞. The doctor could also testify that the dying man was in his right mind.

On the way to Mr. Hearst's residence, Charles Goddard confessed to his brother that his knees were limp at the prospect of his first meeting with the great publisher. "Don't worry," Morrill Goddard assured him. "Mr. Hearst is as easy to talk to as he is hard to get at and remember he hopes almost as much as we do that your plot is good."

Sure enough, Hearst's attitude put the young author at ease, listening with quiet attention and without interruption to a reading of the scenario. Upon reaching the incident of the prescription pad, which had not been written into the typed script, Charles caught a glint of approval which gave him confidence in answering the penetrating questions that followed. Each question illuminated a strong point or brought out a weakness. Once, when Mr. Hearst wondered how change of color and pace of plot could be varied with each instalment, the young author found himself explaining as to a collaborator that "sub-villains" could be introduced each week, aviators, society people, smugglers, phony Hindu princes, Mexicans, etc.

Mr. Hearst got the point instantly and passed on to others. In the skeleton outline not a single character had been given a name, merely appearing for brevity's sake as Hero, Heroine, Villain, Sub-Villain, Father, Doctor, etc. It took Mr. Hearst less than an hour to approve in its essential form the screen serial which was to become known to millions as *The Perils of Pauline,* a title which, by the way, Mr. Hearst invented upon the spur of the moment at that first morning story conference.

Outside the house, Charles Goddard remembered that a copy of the outline had not been left with Mr. Hearst. "Oh, he doesn't need a copy," commented Morrill Goddard confidently. "He has one in his memory." Weeks later, after the entire script had been completed, Mr. Hearst reminded the author that he had never done anything about the spirit of an Egyptian Princess which, in an early episode, had emerged from a mummy case. Although of minor importance, this was the only loose end the playwright had forgotten to tie up.

After the public's avid reception of *Pauline's* twenty-one instalments, Charles Goddard wrote *The Exploits of Elaine,* also starring the unforgettable Pearl White. Then came *The Seven Pearls, The Goddess,* written in collaboration with Gouveneur Morris and filmed by Vitagraph, and *The Mysteries of Myra. Elaine,* adapted from the late Arthur B. Reeve's *Cosmopolitan* magazine stories, ran for thirty-six episodes, consuming almost fourteen miles of film (73,000 feet), which gave it rank as the longest continued story ever exhibited.

All of these productions, as well as *Patria,* a serial of higher class starring Irene Castle, were directed and guided, titled, even partly written, by Mr. Hearst. The vogue for serials ended almost as suddenly as it had begun, except for a few Westerns, and Hearst's interest in movie making flowed into another channel. Judging that the American public would willingly turn from the pie-tossing, cop-chasing type of movie and support artistic productions at regular theatre prices, Hearst organized Cosmopolitan Productions, Inc., and embarked upon a stubborn and ambitious effort to become the country's premier producer of distinctive screenplays. Before retiring from this branch of the industry, he had sustained losses of many millions.

The Cosmopolitan productions were artistically successful, financially disastrous. "The whole trouble was that W. R. was ahead of the times," George d'Utassy explained. "He made 'super' pictures several years too soon. The public was not accustomed to paying two dollars to see a movie. It was the same with the movies as it always was with the newspapers— W. R. knew more about every job (I mean this literally) than any of his people. The pictures that were successful were the ones that he made himself. He chose the story, practically wrote the scenario, selected the cast, went over the 'rushes' day by day, directed the cutting and supervised the presentation. And all in his quiet, unassuming way. I ought to know, as I was the general manager of the company."

In its early years, Cosmopolitan Productions functioned in a huge, drab brick structure occupying an entire block front on Second Avenue between One Hundred and Twenty-sixth and One Hundred and Twenty-seventh Streets, New York. The property, with grounds extending toward the Harlem River in the rear, had once been a famous German picnic and athletic resort known as Sulzer's Harlem River Park Casino. Prohibition killed it.

Hearst transformed its tremendous spaces into motion picture studios and hired the best directors, scenic and costume artists and actors he could find. He enlisted Joseph Urban as his art director and astonished even this distinguished recruit by the prodigality of his expenditures. If the script called for the ladies of the ensemble to wear Irish lace, Belfast was asked to send entire bolts of its best and most costly hand-woven product. The result often was that preliminary schedules of expenses in every department at the studio were tossed out of the window; and screenplays that should have cost two or three hundred thousand dollars actually consumed two or three millions.

Although eventually compelled to suspend, becoming an independent unit of successive gigantic Hollywood studios, the Cosmopolitan Productions, Inc., of the pioneer days brought a definite measure of success to one of its stars. This was Marion Davies, née Douras, a slender, winsome blonde beauty.

A former fashion model and actress in the Ziegfeld Follies, Miss Davies was a sister-in-law of George W. Lederer, an old friend of Hearst. When Lederer learned that Hearst was to enter into the motion picture field as a producer, he asked Hearst to give the young woman a chance. Within two years, she had become the featured star of the Cosmopolitan company, and later attained rank as one of the half dozen most highly paid screen performers in the country.

227

Well along in her twenties when she met Hearst, Marion Davies was as much of a rebel as her employer himself. She was a born mimic, with a spontaneous sense of humor of a raffish sort. Behind an expression of angelic demureness lay a keen, quick, thoroughly aware brain.

Hearst, at fifty-six, and at the height of his powers, had thrown himself with all ardor into a new world of Make Believe where his imaginative and creative gifts could run riot. And into this world came a personable, stage-struck young woman eager and willing to be molded into a great actress. Small wonder that Hearst eagerly assumed the role of Pygmalion to Marion Davies' Galatea.

The young woman's first starring part under Hearst's direction was in *Cecilia of the Pink Roses.* She did not think the picture lived up to the enormous amount of publicity with which her mentor drenched it; and her press agent, Rose Shulsinger, asked Louella O. Parsons, motion picture critic of the *Morning Telegraph,* to lunch with Marion and assure her the picture wasn't entirely hopeless. In her chatty autobiography, *The Gay Illiterate,** Miss Parsons thus describes that first meeting which was to result in a lifelong friendship:—

"She had received so much publicity, I expected to find a haughty star, affected and sure of herself, waiting for me. But instead I found a golden-haired girl, little more than a child, who was dressed in a simple blue suit that a schoolgirl might have worn, and who spoke with a delightful and confused little stammer. It is impossible for anyone to meet Marion Davies and not like her. Even when she was very young she was never a gaga ingénue type. She didn't inherit that strong, determined chin for nothing. And while she looked like an angel, she had great wit and charm and poise. I liked her from the beginning. She had no false illusions about herself and kidded *Cecilia* with disarming frankness. And I was pleased that she seemed to like me, for she asked me to lunch with her soon again at the studio."

The strong-jawed angel won her first praise from impartial critics in a lavish production of *When Knighthood Was in Flower.* Louella Parsons, however, wrote an editorial in the *Morning Telegraph* rebuking Mr. Hearst for emphasizing the cost of the production. Addressing her remarks personally to Mr. Hearst, the brash critic of the *Telegraph* asked: "Why don't you give Marion Davies a chance? She is a good actress, a beauty and a comedy starring bet. Why talk about how much was spent on the lovely costumes and the production cost?"

A few days later Miss Davies telephoned to ask if she could accompany Miss Parsons to a dinner given by the Theatre Owners of America. It was arranged that Marion would pick Louella up at the critic's uptown apartment. Miss Parsons was still dressing when her guest announced herself on

* Doubleday & Co., New York.

the house phone. In response to an invitation to come up, Marion said: "I can't. I have a young man with me. We'll wait in the lobby."

The Gay Illiterate completes the anecdote:—

> Break my neck as I did getting dressed, it was still a good thirty minutes later when I dashed breathlessly down to the lobby to find to my horror that "the young man" in waiting was none other than William Randolph Hearst!
>
> Well, I was in for it now! Not only had I kept him waiting, but only the Sunday before my editorial panning him about "bragging" had appeared in the *Telegraph*. All right, let him be mad! I didn't feel any too kindly toward him anyway. Hadn't his friend and counselor, Arthur Brisbane, turned me down flat when I asked for a job in Chicago? So with my feathers ruffled a bit, the three of us got in the car and started for the banquet.
>
> What conversation there was was cheerfully carried on by Marion, and when we were almost to the hotel I happened to catch Mr. Hearst's eye. He was smiling. "I read your editorial," he said. "It was good. You should write more things like that!"
>
> You never know, as the saying goes, your luck!

Louella Parsons' luck, at that particular point of her extraordinary career, consisted of obtaining a lucrative contract from the Hearst newspapers at more than double her *Telegraph* salary, and an opportunity to become an American institution. The agreement, which *The Gay Illiterate* calls a "dream contract," was drawn up by a shrewd theatrical lawyer and contained so many tails and tassels and whereases and wherefores favoring the party of the second part that for weeks Mr. Hearst balked at signing it. Finally, he capitulated. The date was November 19, 1922; the place the Ritz Hotel in New York. By this time, Miss Parsons writes, "The contract looked like it had gone through the wars—all of them," adding:—

> It had lipstick stains on it, and across the back I had jotted notes about reviews or interviews.
>
> Mr. Hearst looked at it a minute—then picked up a pen and signed the dilapidated piece of paper. Suddenly, he glanced up, smiling:
>
> "I'm disappointed in you," he said.
>
> "Why?" I quaked.
>
> "Miss Parsons," he said, "you forgot to ask for *hairpins*."
>
> I was in no mood for comedy and I was halfway through the door when I heard Mr. Hearst speaking to me again. He was holding the contract toward me. "In making your escape," he drawled, "you have forgotten the guilty evidence!"

Something of the atmosphere of the sombre, barnlike old Cosmopolitan studios, circa 1921, was captured by M. R. Werner, one of its former publicity men, in a *New Yorker* magazine sketch of September 14, 1940:—

> Marion Davies was our star. Although pictures without her were also being manufactured at Sulzer's Harlem River Park Casino, the place was really a one-woman show and the other pictures were treated by Mr. Hearst and his satraps as comic relief from the chore of making America Davies-conscious. These films also kept the staff of expensive directors, actors and actresses, and scenario writers busy while waiting for a new Davies picture. . . . Mr. Hearst loved to see Miss Davies dressed in beautiful clothes, so most of her pictures used to have a fairy-tale interlude. We arbitrarily put "Sleeping Beauty" into one scenario of a Hearst magazine story that hadn't even mentioned "Sleeping Beauty," and several other nursery tales were interjected into otherwise routine nonsense. The scenario department was always busy with Hans Christian Andersen and the Brothers Grimm.

There were the usual temperamental didoes about the studio. Hearst was buying antiques with his customary prodigality at the Anderson Galleries and often trucks loaded with armor, bronzes and other rarities would back up to the unloading platform with instructions to Joseph Urban to "put them in the set." If the offerings did not meet Urban's artistic approval, his anguished wrath would resound throughout the building. On one occasion he clapped on his hat and, without bothering to resign, ran off on a ship to visit his old mother in Vienna. A mollifying radio message from Mr. Hearst, raising his salary, was required to lure him back. Such episodes pointed up a remark made by Hearst one day when someone asked him if there was any money in motion pictures. "There are several millions of my money in them," he retorted drily.

Mr. Werner further recalled:—

"In August, 1921, an artificial skating rink was constructed on our main stage floor, for a scene supposed to be St. Moritz in Marion Davies' *The Young Diana*. I remember the faces of the extras streaming with grease paint as they waited in heavy hired furs to take their parts as atmosphere. Then it was discovered that Miss Davies could not stand up on skates. Bobby McLean, a champion fancy skater, was hired to double for Miss Davies. The only trouble was that he had a very long nose. But they dressed him up in a duplicate of the white fur-trimmed costume Miss Davies wore, and he did superb fancy skating around the set. For the closeups Miss Davies was propped up by a couple of stagehands. Mr. Hearst didn't like the sequence and decided that a snow scene would be better, so at a cost of many more thousands of dollars another studio was hired in the Bronx, filled with artificial snow, and more extras pranced around in it."

230

At Christmas time Miss Davies would play Lady Bountiful to neighborhood tenement children, giving away mounds of fruit, candy and toys. Some of the beneficiaries, now middle-aged, remember and speak of her fondly.

After filming *Little Old New York* with Marion Davies, Mr. Hearst moved his production facilities to Hollywood, where Cosmopolitan operated successively as an autonomous unit of Metro-Goldwyn-Mayer, Warner Brothers, and Twentieth Century–Fox.

Perhaps the most successful pictures were those made in alliance with Metro-Goldwyn-Mayer. Among them were *The Floradora Girl, Blondie of the Follies* and *Peg o' My Heart,* all starring Miss Davies; *White Shadows in the South Seas, The Big House, Operator Thirteen,* and *Gabriel Over the White House.* Hearst also produced *Broadway Melody,* the first musical in sound.

In everything that he touched, during what might be termed his Hollywood phase, Hearst set a new standard for lavishness. "A job in a Marion Davies picture was considered a plum," observed Ilka Chase, who plucked a juicy one for herself in *The Floradora Girl.* The outspoken Miss Chase recalled: *

"Time meant nothing and your salary was apt to continue for weeks and weeks. It was rich in experience too, for if Marion liked you, you were for the duration of the shooting drawn into the orbit of that fabulous existence where the life of the Renaissance bloomed again. Almost all big stars have apartments or little cottages by way of dressing rooms, but Marion had a two-family Spanish *palacio* on the Metro lot with enough kitchen and bathroom paraphernalia to equip a hotel."

The while, Hearst was pouring millions into his barony at San Simeon in central California. The undertaking had assumed truly colossal proportions following the death of his mother in April, 1919, and Hearst's receipt of his rich patrimony. Perhaps if Phoebe Hearst's useful life had been prolonged, some of her beloved Will's more profligate extravagances might have been curbed. For this magnificent and indomitable old lady was the only individual on earth who could put a checkrein upon her obstinate son.

In Moviedom, where standards are more lax (despite anguished cries to the contrary by interested parties), knowledge of the relationship between Hearst and his blonde star was confined to a comparatively small circle. Then, in August, 1924, upon the record of proceedings in a New York court, the "scandal" was fed to the public in a garbled form designed to do the most harm. This is how it came about:—

For two years the Hearst papers in New York had been crusading against

---

* In an aptly titled autobiography, *Past Imperfect.*

phony investment firms known as bucket shops and their legal and political associates who were milking the public of untold millions. One of those caught in the net was William J. "Slippery Bill" Fallon, a notorious underworld lawyer and counsel for many leading bucket shop operators.

That August, 1924, Fallon went to trial in Federal Court on a charge of having bribed a juror named Charles W. Rendigs to hold out for acquittal in one of the bucket shop cases. Rendigs testified for the prosecution as did Fallon's former confidential man, one Ernest Eidlitz. Fallon's defense was that he had been framed by orders of Hearst because of his (Fallon's) knowledge of Hearst's private life.

Before the trial began, Fallon boasted that he would take the stand and bring into the open certain scandalous material bearing upon Mr. Hearst's purported "moral behavior." Victor Watson, editor of the New York *American,* telephoned to Mr. Hearst at San Simeon the day Fallon was due to testify and informed him of the coming storm.

"Well then, Mr. Watson," remarked the publisher with his usual calm, "you won't be in doubt as to what your headline will be for tomorrow's paper."

On the stand Fallon swore that his turncoat fixer, Eidlitz, had admitted to him that he had made perjurious charges against Fallon to editor Watson and other Hearst men. Then, speaking very deliberately and facing the jury, Fallon continued: "Eidlitz said to me that he had told Watson he was fearful he would be arrested, and that he (Eidlitz) knew I had the birth certificates of the children of a motion picture actress; and that I knew Mr. Hearst had sent a woman, who pretended to be a countess, to Florida to get evidence against his wife. He said he had told Watson that I intended to use that information to blackmail Mr. Hearst."

The courtroom was electric with tension as the witness continued:

"Eidlitz said he told Mr. Watson that I had the number of the car and the name of the man who went to Mexico with the same party, the same moving-picture actress. He said a few days later Hearst communicated with Watson and said to Watson: 'Fallon must be destroyed.' "

Summing up in his own defense, Fallon made the walls ring with dramatic and repeated allegations of a Hearst plot to ruin him. Calling upon all the forensic tricks of which he was an acknowledged master, he clapped his hand to his bulging breast, stalked to within inches of the jury box and exclaimed:

"Why, gentlemen, I have here in court the actual birth certificates of the illegitimate children of a certain motion picture actress!"

In their highly critical biography, *Hearst: Lord of San Simeon,* Carlson and Bates conclude:—

> Fallon did not produce the certificates; neither his word nor that of Eidlitz nor indeed that of anyone connected with the slimy case

was worthy of particular credence; and in any event, whether his statements were true or false, what had the private life of Hearst to do with Fallon's bribery of Rendigs? But the pure-minded jury reacted as pure-minded juries are wont to do and returned a verdict of acquittal. Thus the curious legal situation was created that Rendigs served his sentence for having been bribed by Fallon while Fallon went free because he had not bribed Rendigs. It was essentially similar to the legal fiasco of the Fall-Sinclair Teapot Dome trials. But at any rate, puritanic gossipmongers could lick their greasy chops anew at the expense of Hearst.

Not until after his death did Hearst let it be definitely known that he was fully aware of the whirlpool of rumor and conjecture which swirled constantly about his name and that of Marion Davies. Then he took occasion in his will to deny, categorically, that he had fathered any children save his sons George, William Jr., John, Randolph and David.

In all the intervening years, Millicent Hearst remained a steadfast and valued counselor of her husband. A bond was maintained, in person and by correspondence. Witness this sprightly telegram despatched by Hearst almost a year after the Fallon trial:—

Los Angeles, June 29, 1925

Mrs. W. R. Hearst, *Examiner,*
San Francisco, Calif.

Hope you had pleasant trip. It is cool today but has been quite hot. Dandy earthquake this morning. It did lot of damage at Santa Barbara. Railroad property damaged. Telegraph wires down, reservoir busted, some buildings fallen, etc. No harm at San Luis or the ranch so far as I can learn. Think I will go to ranch by auto. When do you leave for there? The boys insist on going to Tahoe. I suppose it's all right as they have been good boys studying hard, at least so they say. They will be back in a week and we will probably see enough of them. But they don't seem to have any more affection for their parents than a couple of bull calves. However I guess all young things are alike. We raise them and feed them until they can fly and then all we have got is a last year's nest. Telegraph me at the Ambassador. I will call you on the telephone.   W. R.

Their rare and mature attitude undoubtedly softened the shock of their separation for their sons. Then, too, the Hearsts by nature and training have always been a highly clannish family unit which no outside element could destroy. Although protean-mooded and distinctively individualistic, the Hearst sons all possess this clearly discernible trait. Unusual as it may appear to some, this quality enabled them to grow into manhood intensely loyal and affectionate toward both parents.

From their earliest adolescence, W. R. Hearst sought to embue his sons with his own devotion to journalism, its romance, its adventure, its sense of mission and dedication which led him once to assert with deep feeling that "the newspaper is the torch which Liberty holds aloft for the enlightenment of the world."

Hence, he was delighted when one by one his sons decided to make journalism their vocation. Painstakingly he tutored them from his own vast experience and lived to see each well launched in his career. Even in his personal letters, the master journalist mingled counsel and guidance. The following is a typical example. It was written to his second son and namesake who, at twenty-four, had been entrusted with a high post on the New York *American:*—

Los Angeles, July 18, 1932

Mr. W. R. Hearst, Jr.,
New York *American,*
New York, N. Y.
Dear Bill:

I am not dictating this on the Ediphone, which sounds like something to eat, and I have not any fancy typewriter, and I wish I had; it would be just the thing to print my radio talks on.

You seem to use the machine very well. Most people get rattled by it—I mean the Ediphone.

I have one which I will also give you if you want it but no automobile goes with it.

Come on out to the Coast. The weather is not warm here at all. It is almost too cool, but we expect to have some California weather before the month is out.

I am worried about your eyes. Send me a little telegram and let me know when everything is all right again.

Why do you have to set off that kind of firecrackers? The best kind are the strings of Chinese crackers. They make more noise than any other kind and are not a bit dangerous.

Hurry on out. The Olympic Games begin very soon. You can have my ticket for them if I have one. If there is anything I do not want to see it is a lot of ginks running around in their underdrawers.

However, we will go together to see the water sports, especially the swimming and diving. In fact I may enter in that competition myself. Getting pretty good on the spring boards.

I hope you got your mother something nice for her birthday. The Los Angeles shops do not as a rule have anything interesting and this year they seem to have less than ever.

I hope your percentage on the *American* amounts to something and it certainly will if you get in and make it amount to something.

Please put on a spurt this autumn not merely for increased advertising but for increased circulation. I do not like the way the *American* sticks at a certain circulation. It should increase regularly.

The trouble I believe is printing too many long articles. The paper needs more condensation, and then still more.

The most difficult thing to get editors to believe is that people have not the time to read long articles these days. The successful paper is the condensed paper.

I think we compare our paper too much with the other standard size papers, which are all miserably long-winded, and not enough with the tabloids, which are condensed and compact.

There is no reason why we should not have tabloid journalism in standard size sheets. Northcliffe did it with the London *Mail*. We could do it with the New York *American*. When you want your circulation spurt, try condensation. We have not tried it yet.

I suppose you have heard about George. He has had rather a hard time. He bumped into a drunken Mexican in an automobile, or the drunken Mexican bumped into him, or the Mexican bumped into—well anyhow, George got his shoulder broken and his knee badly cut.

His leg is in splints and so is his arm. He is out of the hospital but not out of the doctor's care.

I have more trouble worrying about you kids than a hen has with a lot of ducks.

You had to add to the excitement by getting your eye bunged up.

Now please take care of yourself and get in shape again, and as I say, send me a little telegram when everything is okey.

> *Affectionately,*
> *Pop*

The recipient of this letter is now editor of the Hearst newspapers and has developed into a writer of force and reflection,* with a realistic wit all his own. All his brothers have earned positions of influence and importance in the Hearst organization.

---

* Also an extraordinary reporter. Early in 1955, he accomplished the feat of interviewing the four highest figures in Russia (Khrushchev, Bulganin, Molotov and Zhukov), Prime Minister Churchill and President Eisenhower within a period of two weeks. The London *Daily Mail* called it "the most remarkable mission in postwar journalistic history. . . . No Western journalist—in fact, no Western minister or ambassador—has talked with so many top figures on both sides of the cold war front in so short a time."

French Dressing Down

15

IN THE YEARS 1928–30, William Randolph Hearst's restless activities as a journalist embroiled him, for the second time in as many decades, in a turbulent conflict with a European government.

On this occasion, in contrast with the coalition of nations which he took on single-handed during World War I, his sole opponent was the Government of the Republic of France. As a dramatic denouement Hearst, on September 1, 1930, was summarily expelled from French soil as an undesirable alien—for the alleged reason that two years previously he had surreptitiously obtained and published the text of a proposed secret Anglo-French naval treaty.

This disclosure created a world sensation and killed the agreement. Further, it demonstrated beyond doubt that secret diplomacy still ruled European chancelleries despite honeyed lip support for the disarmament efforts of such progressive statesmen as the American Secretary of State, Frank B. Kellogg, and of gallant old Aristide Briand of France.

At times the affair throbbed with all the excitement of a Hearst cinema melodrama. And there were farcical aspects, pure Molière, which brought out all the schizophrenic tendencies both in Hearst and in the French national character.

Neutral bystanders hugely enjoyed the lunges and thrusts and ripostes. When the whole business simmered down it was generally agreed that Hearst, with his quicksilver subtlety and instinct for probing an opponent's weak spots, had emerged the victor. However, the humiliation rankled and

Hearst subsequently coldly repulsed reconciliation overtures from prominent officials and citizens of France.

The chain of events preceding the theatrical climax of two years later began in the summer of 1928 when Hearst visited his favorite European spa, Bad Nauheim in Bavaria, to take the cure. The trip was partly occasioned by a desire to reduce the weight which had been creeping up on him for several years, handicapping his tennis and horseback riding and giving him a contour which resembled, as a waggish friend remarked, "an elephant with his pants on."

There is also some evidence that Hearst had learned before he sailed that England and France were negotiating a secret naval treaty to the detriment of the United States and other world powers and in contravention of the public utterances of their leading statesmen. Under the proposed pact, as later revealed, the two powers pledged themselves to act jointly (a) against any limitation of light cruisers for Britain and (b) in favor of "defensive submarines" and additional "trained defense forces" for France.

At the time, M. Briand was working mightily for a *rapprochement* between France and Germany, an idea warmly favored also by Hearst. According to a sensational and never denied series of articles in the royalist newspaper *L'Action Française,* August 14, 15, and 16, 1930, Briand was eager to have the terms of the proposed treaty published so that it might be discredited, and actually aided Hearst in obtaining an authentic copy.

The French Government's version, which remains "official" to this day, was that Hearst's principal correspondent in Paris, Harold J. T. Horan, procured the precious text through the "connivance or negligence" of two minor officials, M. de la Plante and M. de Noblet, both of whom were later exonerated by a French court. Horan himself was seized on the street, subjected to twelve hours of rigorous examination and given a choice of exile or imprisonment. He chose exile.

Mr. Hearst, the chief villain in the piece, simply asserted with the bland smile his colleagues knew so well that the document had been obtained not by any underhanded means but by "good, direct, 'Go-and-get-it' American methods."

The detailed account in *L'Action Française* cast a lurid, cloak-and-dagger atmosphere over the affair:—

> Mr. Hearst's visit to France at that time was a political venture that had been arranged a few months before by Madame de Jouvenel [a protégée of Briand] and Alain de Leche [an agent of the Prefecture of Police] in America during a lecture tour. As soon as he arrived in France, Hearst, a notorious enemy of France, received a scandalous welcome by the *Le Bienvenue* * [under Mad-

---

* Le Bienvenue Française, a Franco-American group in Paris which frequently staged welcomes or receptions for visiting Americans.

ame de Jouvenel]. . . . Leche established direct and personal relations between Hearst and Briand.

As to Mr. Hearst, what he wanted to get was the *very text* of the naval compromise that had been kept secret both in Paris and London. After much bargaining and numerous steps, on September 19 at 7 p.m. Hearst went to Quai d'Orsay where he had a long talk with Briand. The next day, September 20, Hearst was in possession of the pact and also of an authentic mimeographic copy of the circular letter. [Brief instructions to be sent to ambassadors.]

Having dropped this thrilling hint that two elderly gentlemen and a movie star from Hollywood were indulging in a dark game of international intrigue, *L'Action Française* said that Hearst left his priceless trophy with his correspondent Horan for transmission to New York and then took the first boat for England. On September 22, 1928, still quoting the newspaper account, Horan sent the following cablegram to the Hearst Universal Service in New York:—

Stansbury [Hearst man in London] on his way with authentic letter of Berthelot [the circular letter to all French ambassadors] and containing the real text of document in question. Am sending only four hundred now. Please inform if you want the whole approximately 4,000 or summary.

The genuineness of this message was later denied by Horan, who also denounced as spurious the following message allegedly sent by Hearst from London to Horan in Paris, also on September 22:—

I do not understand why French authorities dissatisfied with you. I got the naval agreement in the manner you know and have given it to you to be communicated in full to our papers. Besides the publication of the pact is a great advantage under circumstances as it was feared in America it might be far more serious than it is. If the French authorities want to expel me as completely undesirable I shall be quite pleased but I intended to expel myself from the country anyway.

The time and scene now shift to the summer of 1930, when Hearst suddenly decided to take another trip to Europe, principally to enjoy again the restful and soothing "cure" at his beloved Bad Nauheim. On the spur of the moment, he invited a sizable party of friends and business associates to accompany him.

The group spent a few days in London, then on July 26 crossed to Paris and passed four days at the Hotel Crillon. Quite unmolested, Hearst pottered around the stores and auction rooms, as he had since boyhood, buying art and antiques with his customary lavishness. Before the party left for the spa, rooms were reserved at the spacious, quiet Crillon for September 1, so that Hearst could begin the "after cure" of rest and mild recreation always advised by the Nauheim specialists.

In the closing days of his stay at Nauheim, Hearst granted an interview to the Frankfurt *Zeitung,* long sought by that paper, in which he discussed European and world problems freely. He pulled no punches in criticizing the Versailles Treaty, which he charged unjustly subjected the "now democratic" Teutonic peoples to the domination of Belgium, France, Italy, Yugoslavia, Czechoslovakia, Poland and Lithuania, adding:—

> I think if the nations of Europe actually desired permanent peace and mutual friendly relations, they would allow the peoples of the various ceded territories themselves to determine by plebiscites to which nation each one desired to belong, and to bestow its allegiance.
>
> The principle of self-determination which President Wilson enunciated was a good one and a sound one and a just one. It is a worthy policy for America to have had as its inspiration in the war. It is too bad that this noble principle was neglected in the Versailles Conference and forgotten by Mr. Wilson. It is, perhaps, not too late to have that splendid principle revived and eventually established as the firm basis of European peace. Until it is so established, there will be nothing but the continual menace of war. If that principle were firmly established in actual practice, then M. Briand's idea of a United States of Europe could probably be put into successful operation.

Emphasizing Germany's resentment over the territorial provisions of the Versailles Treaty, Hearst pictured an imaginary dismemberment of the United States by, say, Canada, Mexico and Spain after a defeat in war. Americans, he was certain, would not rest until the lost territory was regained, either through war or by any other means.

"Personally, I do not think there need be another war in Europe," he vouchsafed. "I believe that the moral sentiment, the intelligent opinion of the world could easily bring about a United States of Europe along M. Briand's ideas. By rectifying injustices here and there, a United States of Europe could be established and it would persist because it would be based upon mutual satisfaction and self-interest. A democratic United States of Europe is the peaceful and permanent solution of the European problem."

Having thus vigorously put himself on record against the treaty which

239

France had so large a share in shaping, Hearst and his party repaired to Stresa on Lake Maggiore for a brief stay; then entrained for Paris, arriving on the morning of September 1.

Just before luncheon Hearst was lounging in the lobby of the Crillon when he was approached by two suave, polite, mustachioed gentlemen in civilian attire who identified themselves as officials of the French Sûreté Générale, an agency of the Ministry of the Interior.

With many bows and expressions of personal esteem, the callers informed Mr. Hearst that the French Government "requested" him to leave the country within four days. It was their sad duty to further inform him that, if he did not leave within the time specified, he would be taken to the border under escort; and, should he return without authorization, would be subject to imprisonment.

Perhaps Mr. Hearst would be interested in receiving a copy of the official statement which would appear later in the press:—

> The President of the Council communicates the following:
>
> "William Randolph Hearst, proprietor of numerous papers in America, has been expelled from French territory. This measure, taken upon the order of the President of the Council, Minister of the Interior, had its origin in the role played last year [sic] by Mr. Hearst in obtaining and publishing a secret document pertaining to the Anglo-French naval negotiations."

Outwardly unperturbed, although obviously angered, Hearst broke the news to some of his companions: Colonel Joseph Willicombe, his secretary and confidant of many years; E. D. Coblentz, veteran editor of the New York *American;* and Harry Crocker. All agreed with him that the French were exacting reprisal, not for the Hearst exposure of the secret naval agreement, but because of his recent denunciation of the Versailles Treaty.

"I'll not wait four days," announced Hearst. "I'll catch the first boat train for England."

"I too," quoth valiant henchman Harry Crocker. "Chief, if France doesn't want you, I don't want France." The others spoke in similar vein.

Luggage was quickly packed and the party headed for the Gare du Nord. While waiting for the train to be made ready, Hearst strolled the platform munching peaches. While speeding through the countryside, Hearst sat in his compartment writing in longhand his version of the expulsion. His companions played cards.

In London, the affair was already a sensation. Journalists besieged Hearst's rooms in the Savoy. Smiling broadly and evidently enjoying the situation, Hearst gave out a précis of what had happened which was, perhaps, to gain wider circulation around the world than anything he had ever written. Light, good humored, in fact almost Gallic in flavor, Hearst's phrases contained an underlying bite which won him many adherents even in France. The statement:—

> I have no complaint to make. The officials were extremely polite. They said I was an enemy of France and a danger in their midst. They made me feel quite important.
>
> They said I could stay in France a little while longer if I desired, that they would take a chance on nothing disastrous happening to the republic.
>
> But I told them that I did not want to take the responsibility of endangering the great French nation; that America had saved it once during the war, and I would save it again by leaving.
>
> Furthermore, I was like the man who was told that he was going blind, and who said he did not mind, as he had seen everything, anyhow.
>
> Similarly, I had seen everything in France, including some very interesting governmental performances.
>
> Then I asked M. Tardieu's emissary to express to M. Tardieu my immense admiration at his amazing alertness in protecting France from the peril of invasion, and we parted with quite elaborate politeness.
>
> It was a little bit foolish but extremely French.
>
> The reason for the strained relations—to use a proper diplomatic term—was the publication of the secret Anglo-French treaty two years ago by the Hearst newspapers, which upset some international "applecarts" but informed the American people; and, of course, that being the reason, the French Government was entirely right in leveling its attack at me and quite wrong in its action toward Mr. Horan, who was only my agent.
>
> I think, however, that the general attitude of the Hearst press in opposing the entrance of the United States into the League of Nations, or any protective pacts to involve our country in the quarrels of European powers, is mainly responsible.
>
> Also, there might have been some slight irritation at the occasional intimations in our papers that France, now being the richest nation in the world, might use some of the German indemnity to pay her honest debts to America, especially because, if it had not been for America, she would now be paying indemnity instead of receiving it.
>
> If being a competent journalist and a loyal American makes a man *persona non grata* in France, I think I can endure the situation without loss of sleep.
>
> In fact, the whole affair reminds me of the story of the rather

241

effeminate young man who went to call on his best girl and found her in the arms of another young fellow.

The effeminate youth went into the hall, took up his successful rival's umbrella, broke it and said: "Now I hope it rains."

You see, for the French national policy of "revenge" to be completely successful, we will have to have rain.

Although the Hoover Administration raised not a finger in his behalf, expressions of support poured in upon Hearst.

Buoyantly he purchased the Elizabethan great chamber of Gilling Castle in Yorkshire and had it shipped to Wales to add to the attractions of St. Donat's. Then he and his party embarked for home on the North German Lloyd liner *Europa*.

In New York he was greeted as a distinguished patriot and told that demonstrations in his honor had been arranged in other large cities. On September 16 the *Europa* was met at quarantine by the excursion steamer *Hood Mountain* under the auspices of the American Legion, Disabled War Veterans and other patriotic bodies and with a congressional delegation aboard, including U. S. Senator Robert F. Wagner and Representatives Black, Bloom, Celler, Dickstein, La Guardia, Lindsay and Sirovich.

From New York, the publisher went to Boston to be the city's guest at its tercentennial; to Chicago for a parade of 5,000 automobiles and fifty bands; and to California for laudatory fetes in San Francisco, Los Angeles and Oakland. The only discordant note was struck in San Francisco where one bilious supervisor, opposing a resolution for a civic reception, remarked sourly: "Hearst is merely inviting himself to visit the city. Our reception would simply duplicate the one in New York where a few lame duck congressmen waddled down to the dock to welcome him." However, San Francisco turned out en masse to honor its returning native son.

In Los Angeles, Hearst made his first speech over the radio, President Merlin Aylesworth of the National Broadcasting Company introducing him as "a great editor who fearlessly thinks, writes and publishes what he believes to be for the best interests of our people and our country." Hearst said in part:—

Perhaps, fellow citizens, some of you will say to me, "Why did you not sue the French Government?" And I say, "First, because I did not want to magnify the incident; and second, because I had the simplicity to believe, fellow citizens, that somewhere among our paid servants at Washington there might be found some public official with backbone enough and American spirit enough to defend the right of law-abiding citizens sojourning abroad, and to

242

vindicate the validity of an American passport, and to maintain the liberty and dignity of American citizenship. . . ."

If Theodore Roosevelt had been alive, or if Grover Cleveland had been alive, you would have heard little of W. R. Hearst, for he was of no importance in this situation; but you would have heard much about the value and validity and inviolability of the American passport, and of due and necessary respect for the rights and liberties of the American citizen. Theodore Roosevelt and Grover Cleveland are dead. But let us hope that American spirit and American independence and American loyalty to the rights and liberties which we inherited from our fathers, and desire to hand down to our sons, did not die with these two great Americans.

Then the publisher spoke of the persistent efforts of France to seduce the American press and influential citizens of the United States. France's craftiest instrument of seduction, he asserted, was the "little red ribbon" of the Legion of Honor. This section of the broadcast contained one of his most brilliant epigrams (which we have italicized):—

The great Napoleon, who devised the Legion of Honor, knew human weaknesses and recognized the irrepressible inclination of the citizens of a republic to covet the titles and insignia their democ-

Secret Bride

NEW YORK JOURNAL

TRANSMITTED BY RADIOMARINE CORP. OF AMERICA

VOL. 1   NEW YORK, N. Y., OCT. 15, 1931.   No. 1

INVITE U.S. IN DISPUTE

SPAIN, VATICAN NEAR BREAK.

MADRID, Oct. 15 (INS). —Foreshadowing a complete break in relations between Spain and the Vatican, Monsignor Tedetchini, Papal Nuncio, has been recalled to Rome and will leave Madrid tonight, it was definitely learned this afternoon.

MADRID, Oct. 15 (INS).—A series of riots occurred in various parts of Spain today as public feeling over the government's anti-religious measures blazed into violence.

A. F. OF L. BACKS BEER.

VANCOUVER, B. C., Oct. 15 (INS).—The American Federation of Labor went on record today favoring return of 2.75 per cent beer. Reiterating the stand taken by previous conventions, the 51st convention passed favorably upon a resolution recommending the legalization of beer with that alcoholic content.

U. S. DEFICIT $512,666,000.

WASHINGTON, Oct. 15 (INS). — The government's deficit October 13 passed the half-billion dollar mark, amounting to $512,666,000, as compared with $28,333,000 the same date last year, Treasury figures revealed today. The present fiscal year started July 1.

LEAGUE OVERRIDES JAPAN.

NEW YORK, Oct. 15 (INS). —League determination to draw the United States into full participation and responsibility in attempted settlement of the Manchurian dispute was reported in Geneva dispatches this afternoon. The league is even ready to risk an affront to Japan by overriding Tokio's frankly stated objections, delivered to the "Big Five" of the League council today by Kenkichi Yoshisawa, Japanese delegate. Yoshisawa was quickly informed that the Japanese protest, based on the grounds that an unwise precedent would be set, was untenable.

DRYS WARN G. O. P.

WASHINGTON, Oct. 15 (INS)—Organized drys will demand an "all dry" Republican presidential ticket in 1932 and will not give President Hoover whole-hearted support if a wet candidate is named for the vice presidency, F. Scott McBride, superintendent of the Anti-Saloon League of America, said today.

EDISON NEAR DEATH.

WEST ORANGE, N. J., Oct. 15.—Thomas A. Edison today was on the threshold of the coma from which his physician does not expect he will ever awake.

MARY ASTOR

THE secret wedding of Mary Astor, lovely screen star, to Dr. Franklyn Thorpe, Hollywoow physician and surgeon, on June 29, in Yuma, Arizona, was revealed today.

FLYING PRIEST KILLED.

SEWARD, Alaska, Oct. 15 (INS).—A hunting accident today had cost the life of Father George H. Woodley, young "flying priest." According to meagre reports received here, his body was found at the base of a cliff from which he had plunged near Chickaloon. His neck had been broken by the fall, the report received here stated.

Hearst entered into radio in the 1930's as enthusiastically as into movies two decades earlier. His organization acquired stations in New York, Milwaukee, Pittsburgh, Baltimore. He financed development of a radio teletype for newspaper use. He encouraged experimentation with radio facsimile transmission of papers to ships (←——) and homes. Eventually, TV stations were brought into the organization.

racy teaches them to disdain. *All men are created equal in one respect, at least, and that is their desire to be unequal. . . .*

Many American newspaper men have been caught by this little red ribbon as guilelessly as bullfrogs are hooked by a bit of red flannel, but I have never allowed any member of my organization to accept civic decorations from any foreign nation, or to put themselves and my papers under obligations to any foreign government. Indeed, I think Congress should forbid the wearing of foreign decorations by American citizens, except military decorations honorably won in war.

At a civic banquet in Los Angeles, Hearst insisted that the episode of his expulsion was of no interest to him except as it revealed France's attitude toward America and Americans:—

France resents America for two very human reasons: first, because of the service we rendered her, which she does not like to acknowledge; and second, because of the money we loaned her which she does not like to repay. France has the largest gold supply per capita of any nation in the world, but she does not want to use any of it in paying her debts to America. In fact, she does not even like to have that obligation called to her attention. The situation reminds me of the gambler who came home to his wife in great indignation and said he had been accused of cheating at cards. His wife answered, "But you do cheat at cards, don't you, dear?" And the gambler replied, "Of course I do, but I don't like to have anyone speak about it."

The publisher closed a final talk in Oakland, Calif., on October 18, 1930, by remarking: "Now I am going to board a train and go down to my ranch and find my little hideaway on my little hilltop at San Simeon, and look down on the blue sea, and up at the blue sky, and bask in the glorious sunshine of the greatest state of the greatest nation in the whole world. You know, my friends, it is about time I finished my Nauheim cure."

Despite this touch of levity, the affair rankled deeply, as was evidenced in September, 1932, when Hearst spurned proposals from prominent private citizens and officials that he return to Paris and accept the hospitality of the French Government. He closed a long cablegram to his newspaper representative in Paris with these acidulous words:—

"I would be delighted to receive the French Government at my ranch at San Simeon and entertain them with amity and hospitality any time that they desire to enlarge their experience and broaden their minds. I can assure them, too, that they will not be ordered off the premises for being loyal to their own country."

244

As a sort of footnote to the whole business, Edmond D. Coblentz published after Hearst's death the contents of a message hastily scrawled to Hearst's valet:

Joseph—

Don't ever get me any socks or anything else made in FRANCE.

W. R. H.

From his college days, Hearst had taken keen interest in mankind's age-old struggle with the evils of alcohol.

His position, from which he never wavered, was that of an early hero, Thomas Jefferson, who advocated light wines and beer as the only remedy for "the poison of whiskey." When the great question of prohibition by law came forward in 1917, Hearst emphatically stated his belief that prohibition would "prohibit" only the milder and relatively harmless stimulants; and that the nation would again be placed on a whiskey basis as it was in the time of Jefferson. But when the Eighteenth Amendment was finally jammed through early in 1919, Hearst pleaded for a fair trial of prohibition; and, in a burst of wishful enthusiasm, wrote a signed editorial appearing in his newspapers January 17, 1919:—

> One hundred per cent efficiency has been added at one stroke to the people of America. . . . Half of the misery of half of the people has been abolished. Three hundred thousand saloons have been eliminated, three hundred thousand traps have been closed into which a considerable portion of the youth of the country fell every year; fell to degradation and to vice and to crime. . . . Strong drink has destroyed more each year than the World War destroyed. . . . The suppression of the drink traffic is an expression of the higher morality upon which we are entering.

Practically a teetotaler in his own person, enforcing only a rule against drinking in rooms for his numerous guests, Hearst stoutly defended the 18th Amendment despite a crime wave in California a year after enactment of the Volstead Act. "Prohibition has not failed as yet," he wrote Winifred Black of the San Francisco *Examiner,* adding: "I do not believe that crime and immorality . . . can be evaded by opening the saloons and dispensing vicious alcoholic drink. A crime wave occurred after most wars, and it was apparently due to the demoralization engendered by the hate and hysteria of war, and by the disturbed social and economic conditions which follow in the wake of war."

A year later he had begun to waver and by 1926 was asking sadly: "Has the younger generation profited by prohibition? Are they drinking less than formerly? Are they drinking more? Are other elements in the community drinking less or more, or drinking worse liquor than before prohibition?"

245

As the proliferating evils of prohibition became apparent to all save fanatics, Hearst's sadness turned to anger. He asserted flatly that "the noble experiment has become an ignoble failure":—

> Everybody knows that the law ought to be respected; just as everybody knows that women ought to be respected, and that women are respected by every decent man. But occasionally there is a woman who is not respected, who is not respectable, who does not respect herself, and whom no one in his heart can respect, no matter what outward observance of respect he may render. And so occasionally there are laws which cannot be respected, no matter how much they are respected by good citizens. And there are law-makers who cannot be respected—such, for instance, as gentlemen who impose dry laws upon the land and carry whiskey flasks in their hip pockets.

The Volstead Act had been on the books for ten years. Hearst enumerated some of its frightening failures: wholesale bribery of officials, increase in the use of deadly drugs, contempt for the Constitution and the law, organized wholesale crime, blindness and disease caused by poisonous alcohol, etc. In a vigorous signed editorial letter of January 9, 1929, Hearst asked, "What solution is possible?" and went on to offer four prizes for manuscripts outlining "the best plan of a temperance substitute for prohibition."

More than 71,000 papers were submitted. The winner of the first prize of $25,000 was Franklin Chase Hoyt, distinguished presiding justice of Children's Court, New York. Justice Hoyt's plan advocated outlawing "all alcoholic products of distillation," i. e., gins, whiskeys, brandies, etc.; and left to the states the manufacture and sale of "all malt, brewed and fermented beverages," i. e., wines and beer.

In concluding his proposal Justice Hoyt said: "It is inconceivable that any government can carry on a successful war against nature and force unwilling communities to obey sumptuary laws which they reject and despise. Such laws, as Blackstone has pointed out, are 'regulations destructive of liberty.' If our Federal Government persists in denying any latitude to the states in their regulation of fermented products, the states in their turn may refuse, one by one, to support the present illogical scheme of prohibition."

While the temperance contest was arousing feverish interest, Hearst made a radio address in which he tellingly quoted Lincoln's words: "The American people cannot be driven to do anything they do not want to do. The way to promote happiness is by moral suasion and not by force."

The editor advocated restricted manufacture of alcoholic beverages, preferably light wines and beer, under Federal license; and its sale in limited quantities to licensed restaurants and hotels for home consumption. Such a plan, he declared, had worked well in Canada and in Sweden and from it "the country could have the immediate benefit of genuine temperance, the re-establishment of law and order, an increased governmental income for greater works and needs, establishment of great industries, and greater sense of satisfaction and content in the nation, with less likelihood of serious political, social and economic disturbance."

In 1930, a young girl died in Gary, Indiana, during a drinking party, and five youths were held for murder. Hearst instantly rushed into print with an emotional demand that the 18th Amendment and the Volstead Act be swept away:—

> What is to be gained by a policy of prohibition which makes vicious drunkards of young innocent children and causes them to commit dreadful crimes? Is it not about time for the country to wake up and put an end to prohibition and prohibition parties? . . . Young people could not go into saloons, but they can go into speakeasies. . . . Prohibition has filled our jails with youth. Prohibition has corrupted our police until in many cases they are active allies of the law-breaking elements of the community. It has made our Federal enforcement officers sometimes murderers. It has made our President a dictator executing an unpopular law by force of arms.
>
> Is it not time that the calm, conservative portion of our people took stock of prohibition and determined whether this policy is worth all the trouble and all the evil that it costs? We have heard enough of fools and fanatics. Let us hear in the coming election from the sound and sane portion of the American people.

The sound and sane portion of the people spoke in no uncertain terms in the Presidential election of 1932; and almost in a matter of months "the great American tragedy" of prohibition, as Hearst had termed it, came to an end.

During the second and third decades of the century, Hearst's newspaper empire expanded in waves, sometimes with long intervals between.

In 1912, he invaded the South through purchase of the Atlanta *Daily Georgian*. The *Georgian* was one of the training schools of Jacob Dewey Gortatowsky, general manager of the Hearst newspapers from 1939 to 1955 and the continuing chairman of the board of the Hearst Corporation, president of King Features Syndicate and president of International News Service.

Born in Albany, Georgia, "Gorty" has served competently in every

247

branch of the newspaper business, from cub reporter and sports writer to business manager and director of feature services. He is probably the most popular veteran in the Hearst organization, scorning intrigue and intramural politics.

In 1913, Hearst acquired the conservative San Francisco *Morning Call* and transformed it into an evening paper. Characteristically, during the war years, when most publishers shied away from fresh commitments, Hearst bought the Washington *Times* and Boston *Daily Advertiser* in 1917, and the *Wisconsin News* of Milwaukee in 1918. During the business "readjustment" of 1921, he added to his string the Boston *Record,* the Detroit *Times,* and the Seattle *Post-Intelligencer.* Smoothing a knotty problem in Boston, the *Record* was merged with the ancient, conservative *Advertiser.* Some of the latter's features and departments were combined with Hearst's Sunday *American* and the meld issued as the Sunday *Advertiser.*

"I never plan extensions," remarked Hearst on his fifty-ninth birthday, "but newspapers just seem naturally to keep coming to me to be taken over. I am not as young as I once was, and the older we get the less likely we are to set out and conquer the world."

Whereupon, as though to mock this hint at possible retirement, he acquired no less than five newspapers in that year of 1922: the Washington *Herald,* the Rochester (N. Y.) *Journal,* the Oakland (Calif.) *Post-Enquirer,* the Los Angeles *Herald,* and the Syracuse (N. Y.) *Telegram.* The latter paper was merged three years later with Hearst's Syracuse *Journal.* Hearst also founded the tabloid *Daily Mirror* in New York, as indicated in a previous chapter.

A year after this burst of energy, the Californian bought the Baltimore *News;* and in 1924 the Albany (N. Y.) *Times-Union,* the San Antonio *Light,* and the Milwaukee *Sentinel.* Pausing for breath, he picked up the Pittsburgh *Sun-Telegraph* in 1927 and the Omaha *News-Bee* in 1928. That same year he moved his beloved pioneer New York papers, the *Journal* and the *American,* into a huge, barrack-like complex of buildings at 210–20 South Street on New York's East River waterfront—then the largest and most modern, if not the loveliest, structure in the world devoted exclusively to newspaper production.

The following year, 1929, Hearst purchased the San Francisco *Bulletin* and, by combining it with his *Call,* obtained a monopoly of the evening field. Similarly, in 1931, he bought the Los Angeles *Express* and merged it with the *Herald,* as the *Herald-Express.* Now, with his San Francisco *Call-Bulletin,* Hearst held a commanding position in the two largest cities of his native state. He spoke, weekdays and Sunday, to incomparably the greatest newspaper-reading audience on earth. His California papers alone earned a profit of five million dollars a year.

However, this extraordinary burst of acquisition marked the great journalist's apogee. Thereafter decline was to set in, followed by restriction and consolidation upon what eventually was to prove a more solid basis.

With the 1932 national election approaching, political leaders of both parties agreed that Hearst would be a figure of key importance. Also, since precedent seemed to dictate Herbert Hoover's renomination by the Republicans, the best guess was that the lord of San Simeon would support the Democratic ticket. There was no dearth of Presidential aspirants among the Democrats, the most eager and best financed being New York State's young Governor, Franklin D. Roosevelt.

In *William Randolph Hearst, A Portrait in His Own Words,** Edmond D. Coblentz reveals that Hearst first displayed more than casual interest in FDR as a Presidential possibility early in 1931, during Roosevelt's second term as Governor. Hearst, in California, sent this message to Coblentz in New York:—

> I like Governor Roosevelt's policies on power development, reforestation, elimination of duplicating taxing units and prison reform.
>
> We should have an editorial supporting Roosevelt's power plan, but warning him against contracts with private companies. It would seem that wherever the government has private corporations as partners the corporations swindle the government.
>
> However, I think we should print a vivid paragraphic summary of his message to the Legislature and send it to all our papers together with the editorial in which we support his policy.
>
> As Roosevelt is a probable Presidential nominee and the one whom we are most likely to support we should keep him and his policies before the nation. There has been no adequate promotion of him in our papers. We should begin now to see that there is.
>
> Please see him, and tell him of our desire to publicize him nationally.

Coblentz reported back to his chief under date of January 29, 1931:—

> As per your instructions, I had a session with Governor Roosevelt as to the best manner of promoting him in our papers. Here are some of the policies which he stresses, some of which, of course, are well known and have been widely publicized:
>
> 1—Public development and operation of water power sites.
>
> 2—A scientific reforestation program and a scientific survey of the farm lands of the state. He believes such a survey will facilitate a back-to-the-farms movement and reduce over-production and decrease unprofitable farming.

* Simon & Schuster, 1952.

3—A program for the reduction of costs of local or municipal governments. He states that most city governments are bankrupt, owing to uneconomical and unnecessary taxation. He proposes to reform the system of taxation, and claims to have the specific remedy, which will be outlined in a coming message. He contends that the waste in municipal governments applies to most of the small cities in the nation.

4—Prison reform program. This program contemplates scientific segregation of prisoners—boys in one prison, short-term offenders in an unwalled prison, incorrigibles in another, and so on. We will have an article on this program which I will send to all our papers.

Hearst's responding comment was succinct:—

The first two I imagine have been covered.

The second two are very interesting.

The fourth, the prison program, is very much in line with our ideas.

Of course we will handle all of Roosevelt's important utterances in a conspicuous way not only in New York but throughout the country.

I think you would better have the material for the papers outside of New York carefully prepared and sent out with instructions to print.

Make it paragraphic, and typographically easy to read.

An editorial should accompany each news article.

A year later, as editor Coblentz points out, Hearst's ardor for Roosevelt had cooled. He feared that the Governor was still tainted with Woodrow Wilson's hated "internationalism" and had quietly begun to groom John Nance Garner of Texas for the Democratic nomination.

Garner was newly elected Speaker of the 72nd Congress. He and Hearst had served together in the 58th and 59th Congresses, taking their seats the same day, but had had no personal contact since.

When Roosevelt's pre-convention managers, specifically Colonel Edward M. House, learned of Hearst's courtship of Garner, they got word to Hearst, through Coblentz, that their man was no longer an internationalist of the Wilson type. Colonel House said that Governor Roosevelt was eager to explain all this *privately* to Mr. Hearst.

Hearst's hackles rose at the idea of a meeting in camera and he returned a blistering refusal that must have burned the wires and reddened more than one pair of ears in FDR's camp. He told Coblentz:—

Please give my kind remembrances and sincere compliments to

250

Mr. House but tell him I beg leave to say that if Mr. Roosevelt has any statement to make about his not *now* being an internationalist he should make it to the public publicly and not to me privately.

He has made his numerous declarations publicly when he said that he *was* an internationalist and *was* in favor of our country joining the League of Nations even at the sacrifice of some portion of our nation's sovereignty.

He should make his declaration publicly that he has changed his mind and that he is NOW in favor of keeping the national independence which our forefathers won for us, that he is NOW in favor of NOT joining the League or the League Court.

I must say frankly that if Mr. Roosevelt is not willing to make public declaration of his change of heart and wants only to make his statement to me privately, I would not believe him.

My experience has proved that a man who is running for office and is not willing to make his honest opinions known to the public either has no honest opinions or is not honest about them. . . .

If he does not want to express his opinions publicly because he thinks they would hurt his candidacy, then he is cowardly; while if he is privately playing Peter to one and Paul to another—or rather Peter to one and Judas to another—then he is unworthy of public or private trust.

I do not see why politics cannot be open and honest and clean inside and out.

I am for Mr. Garner in this campaign, not because he is a friend of mine.

Not because he has persuaded me to support him. I have not talked to him or any representatives of his about politics in thirty years.

I am for him because he is plain and direct and sincere and honest—morally and mentally honest. . . . His record is consistent because Mr. Garner says and does what he honestly believes.

That is the kind of man who makes a good American citizen, and that is the kind of man who would make a good American President.

Having thus announced himself, Mr. Hearst took to the radio from Los Angeles on the evening of January 2, 1932, and formally nominated Speaker Garner for the Presidency, declaring that he was "a loyal American citizen, a plain man of the plain people, a sound and sincere Democrat; in fact, another Champ Clark."

"Making" and Breaking
with Franklin Roosevelt

16

ALTHOUGH NOT generally known, or even suspected, there was a warm bond of personal affection between Hearst and the kaleidoscopic Franklin D. Roosevelt.

So far as one individual may be said to have determined the destiny of another by giving him his opportunity at a time of crisis, William Randolph Hearst "made" Franklin Delano Roosevelt President of the United States. And our thirty-second President never concealed his gratitude.

In the dozen tremendous years of the Roosevelt era these strong, mettlesome men, so much alike yet so different, alternately belabored and placated each other. Each repeatedly outraged what the other held dear. Neither, though, for an instant doubted the other's patriotism and single-minded love of country. Even in the thunderous roar of battle, each permitted the other far more leeway than was reserved for any other adversary, to the puzzlement of partisan onlookers.

Finally, when the strange psychological tie was snapped with Roosevelt's premature death in April, 1945, there came a clue. Hearst, approaching his eighty-second birthday the same month, sorrowfully secluded himself in his study. He emerged with a moving tribute to the fallen leader in which it was declared:—

"The work and name of Franklin Delano Roosevelt will live on, not only today or tomorrow but in all the annals of recorded time. . . . He loved his country above all else and labored in its service with utter disregard of his own well-being, of his own comforts and conveniences, of life itself."

Tears dampened some of the pages scattered on the carpet about

Hearst's armchair. None saw them fall except the grieving man's constant companion, a dachshund, but others noted his red eyes.

Long after the manuscript had been sent on its way to the maws of his great presses, Hearst still sat musing in his study. What memories must have engulfed his mind of his long association with the man the world called FDR . . . 1932, 1936, 1940, 1944.

In 1932, Hearst's support of John Nance Garner changed the entire complexion of the contest for the Democratic Presidential nomination.

His strategy was to bring Speaker Garner to the Chicago convention with a sizable core of pledged delegates. Texas could be counted a certainty for its native son. Another populous state was needed.

In the California primaries the race had been considered a toss-up between Franklin Roosevelt and Al Smith—until Hearst entered an independent Garner slate headed by William G. McAdoo. In an explanatory memo for his confidential secretary, Joseph Willicombe, Hearst wrote: "I could get nothing but evasion from the Democratic Party leaders, and was finally compelled to run a separate Garner ticket. In doing this I had to make my combinations with Mr. McAdoo."

The primary result amply demonstrated the power of Hearst and his five newspapers in California. Garner drew 211,913 votes; Roosevelt 167,117; Smith 135,981. Garner and Hearst were off and running.

At all cost Hearst was determined to prevent the nomination either of his ancient enemy Al Smith or of an open disciple of Woodrow Wilson such as Newton D. Baker. He would put Garner over if he could, otherwise use his man as a fulcrum to force a nomination satisfactory to himself. His plans were carefully laid. Joe Willicombe was sent to Chicago with the California delegation with instructions to keep in constant touch with San Simeon by phone and wire. Another trusted employee, George Rothwell Brown, experienced political writer, was assigned to maintain close liaison with Speaker Garner in Washington.

Subsequent events are narrated in fascinating and authoritative detail by editor Edmond D. Coblentz in *William Randolph Hearst, A Portrait in His Own Words.*

Amid a background of tension and factionalism, the Democratic National Convention convened in the Chicago Stadium on Monday, June 27, 1932.

Governor Roosevelt entered the lists with a clear majority of the delegates but more than one hundred votes short of the two-thirds majority—768—necessary for a choice; and facing a formidable anti-Roosevelt bloc led by the fanatically loyal followers of Alfred E. Smith.

The Roosevelt camp suffered a serious blow at the outset, losing its effort to have the historic two-thirds rule abrogated. Roosevelt himself gave the order of retreat to his manager, James A. Farley.

The drama reached its climax at an all-night session June 30–July 1. The first ballot, recorded as a faint glimmer of false dawn showed in the East, disappointed the Roosevelt men who had hoped to smash their way to a quick nomination.

Roosevelt received 666¼ votes; Smith, 201¾; Garner, 90¼; Governor Harry F. Byrd of Virginia, 25; Melvin A. Taylor, Chicago banker, 42½; Governor Albert C. Ritchie of Maryland, 21; James A. Reed of Missouri, 24; Governor George White of Ohio, 52; "Alfalfa Bill" Murray, Governor of Oklahoma, 23. In addition, Newton D. Baker loomed as a possible dark horse by drawing eight votes from Indiana and one-half vote from Pennsylvania.

The second ballot gave Roosevelt only a dribble of added strength, 677¾ to 194¼ for Smith, with Garner firm at 90¼. Newton Baker's 8½ votes remained, pointing like an arrow to a possible compromise candidate.

A motion to adjourn was beaten down and the third ballot, taken in broad daylight, gave Roosevelt only another tiny advance to 682$^{79}/_{100}$. It was openly predicted that Mississippi, perhaps other wavering delegations, would quit him on the next ballot. Al Smith remained at 194¼; while Garner, with eleven new recruits from Oklahoma, advanced to 101¼. Newton Baker's mystifying 8½ votes remained with him. The anti-Roosevelt coalition confidently predicted that if Roosevelt began slipping on the fourth ballot he was through. At 9.15 a.m. on Friday, July 1, the weary, bleary-eyed delegates voted to adjourn until 8.30 p.m.

At this juncture W. R. Hearst, holding the strings like a puppeteer, acted dramatically and decisively.

George Rothwell Brown's telephone rang in Washington. Joe Willicombe was on the wire from Chicago. Mr. Brown, Mr. Hearst's intermediary with Speaker Garner, gives the conversation in a detailed account prepared for the Coblentz book: "Mr. Hearst has a request to make of you. I have been talking to him at San Simeon."

Willicombe continued: "He wants you to go to Speaker Garner and say to him that he is very fearful that on the next or some subsequent ballot delegations will desert Roosevelt, and that the nomination will then go to some candidate who will repeat the disasters to the party and the country of 1924 and 1928. Mr. Hearst is fearful that when Roosevelt's strength crumbles it will bring about either the nomination of Smith or Baker. Either would be disastrous. The Chief asks if you would mind saying these things to Speaker Garner, and say to him that nothing can now save the country from peril but for him to throw his delegates to Governor Roosevelt, who has proved that he commands a majority of the convention, though he cannot obtain a two-thirds majority."

"I knew it was perfectly true that Roosevelt was through if Garner did

254

not save him," remarks Mr. Brown. "There was no other way. But I thought that Garner might win out in the end, and I said as much to Colonel Willicombe. 'However,' I said, 'tell Mr. Hearst I shall do exactly as he requests.' "

The Rothwell Brown narrative continues:—

About eleven o'clock in the morning, an hour before the House was to convene, I went to the Capitol. Mr. Garner was alone in the Speaker's private room in the southeast corner, overlooking the Capitol grounds. Even his secretary was not there. I walked into the office. "Mr. Speaker," I said, "I have a message for you from Mr. Hearst."

He looked at me inquiringly from under his shaggy white eyebrows, and led the way into the embrasure of the south window. I think he knew what was coming. We stood in silence for a while, looking out on the beautiful green park.

I told the Speaker that Mr. Hearst had put through a call to me, and I gave him the message. "Mr. Hearst is fearful that the nomination will go either to Baker or Smith, unless you throw your strength to Roosevelt. He regards Baker as an internationalist and a reactionary. If Smith should be nominated we will have the fight of 1928 all over again, with the party torn asunder, and all hope of electing a Democrat gone."

I could tell from the expression in Garner's eyes that he felt the same way. I knew what the bitter campaign of 1928 had meant to him. Garner in 1920 had denounced the Ku Klux Klan, over which the Madison Square Garden Convention of 1924 was to be torn to shreds in a bitter struggle between Al Smith and William G. McAdoo. When some Texas members of Congress joined the Klan, Garner denounced it.

The Klan fought Garner, burned fiery crosses near his home in Uvalde. They carried some of the Garner counties against him, but he was re-elected.

I knew that Garner had supported Al Smith in 1928, when Herbert Hoover carried Texas, and that he had taken his political life in his hands to do it. Garner wanted no repetition of the 1928 campaign. I saw that Mr. Hearst's message had carried home. He turned to me and said substantially this:

"Say to Mr. Hearst that I fully agree with him. He is right. Tell him I will carry out his suggestion and release my delegates to Roosevelt."

I knew it was settled, and that William R. Hearst had made the next President of the United States, Franklin D. Roosevelt.

255

All afternoon rumors of the impending switch flew about hotel lobbies in Chicago. For hours Al Smith made frantic and futile efforts to contact Garner personally by phone. The wily Al had instantly recognized the hand of Hearst behind the maneuver which, if successful, would deprive Smith of his last chance at the prize he most coveted.

Garner, secluded in his rooms at the Washington Hotel, slipped up to the roof in the early evening for a brief meeting with Rothwell Brown and assured Mr. Hearst's emissary that he had formally instructed his manager, Sam Rayburn, to release the Garner delegates to Roosevelt.

"There was nothing more to be done in Washington," narrates Mr. Brown. "The die was cast. I made no use whatever of the inside news that I had. I had no instructions but I knew Mr. Hearst wanted it that way. There is not the slightest possible doubt that Mr. Hearst initiated the maneuver leading to the nomination and election of Franklin D. Roosevelt and that he did so within a few minutes after the convention had recessed at 9.15 o'clock Friday morning, July 1, 1932."

The shift of the Garner delegates touched off a landslide for Roosevelt. The vote on the fourth and final ballot gave Roosevelt 945 votes to a bitterly unyielding Al Smith's 190½. Smith later supported the ticket, grudgingly.

Next day Speaker Garner was unanimously chosen as the candidate for Vice-President. No gift of political divination is required to assume that Hearst was also the architect of this arrangement, either through a representative in Albany or by personal communication with the appreciative politician to whom he had thrown wide the doors of the White House.

As we have indicated, Hearst's manipulation of Roosevelt's nomination was from his point of view a choice of evils. He had early recognized the man's capacity for doing the country great good, or great harm. Yet he rose to Roosevelt's appealing, dynamic campaign—in itself a psychological lift to a nation wallowing in its worst depression—and on the eve of election sent him an enthusiastic personal message at Hyde Park:—

> Well, sir, you made a marvelous campaign, one that has stirred the mind and heart of the nation. I believe that you will be triumphantly elected, but in any case I shall retain an enduring admiration for yourself and your great work, and an abiding enthusiasm for your inspiring utterances. I think the country greatly needs you and the practical expression of your truly democratic ideas in the government, and I hope to learn Tuesday that the country has realized its need and made you our President.

While policies were in the making, the President-elect and Hearst were in close and cordial touch through Joseph P. Kennedy, editor Coblentz and others. Hearst solicited Roosevelt's opinion upon an eleven-point program which the publisher had formulated and was running at his editorial mast-head:—

1—Buy American and spend American.

2—Raise tariff duties on articles manufactured by foreign labor.

3—Encourage Pan-American reciprocity.

4—Develop our merchant marine to serve our trade in times of peace and supplement our navy in time of war.

5—Encourage American air fleets to cover our country and connect us more intimately with other countries.

6—Encourage our railroads to make transcontinental extensions and transcontinental combinations and to co-operate with steamship lines to connect our industry with world markets.

7—Complete east-and-west and also north-and-south transcontinental automobile highways sixty feet wide.

8—Complete Federal flood control of Mississippi River and Colorado River and other rivers whose overflow is a menace to the lives and property of adjoining communities.

9—Complete inland waterways projects.

10—Complete all necessary developments of rivers and harbors.

11—Complete all possible water conservation and power development projects.

Via Coblentz, Hearst sent Roosevelt a personal word: "Tell him his great glory will be the practical one of restoring prosperity, and he will be the idol of the country if he does this. I know that is his desire and it is our desire. Therefore we are going to work with him and support him, and if he will let us know from time to time what he wants newspaper help on, we will be glad to give it to him, when and in the way he wants. We do not want any jobs or favors."

To which, as an old campaigner, Hearst added a bit of wisdom for Roosevelt's ear: "If our friend can keep those Middle Western and Western states in the Democratic column, he will keep the Democratic Party in power for a generation. As long as he has those, he can be absolutely independent of New York and New England and any reactionary elements. That is why I am advising against too much Wall Street affiliation."

Roosevelt eagerly embraced most of Hearst's suggestions and sent word to Sam Simeon, through Coblentz, that there would be no one in his Cabinet "who knows his way to 23 Wall Street [the House of Morgan], no one who is linked in any way with the power trust or with the international bankers." He approved of Hearst's eleven-point program "for the present emergency" but disapproved of the "Buy American" agitation as a long-term policy, saying it would eventually result in retaliatory tariff barriers against us abroad.

Commenting upon Hearst's pet project for a five-billion-dollar "prosperity" bond issue, the President-elect said: "I approve of the program for the expenditure of Federal funds in flood control, inland waterways, harbor improvements, etc. An immediate issue of five billion dollars in bonds would seem too large at present. I do see, however, the necessity for the yearly bond issue of one billion dollars which would put men to work immediately."

Mr. Roosevelt wondered if Mr. Hearst could meet him in Warm Springs, Georgia, for a long talk later that month of January, 1933; then raising himself in his wheel chair in the library of his town house in East Sixty-fifth Street, New York, he remarked to Mr. Coblentz: "Here is an important point which I give you in confidence but which I wish Mr. Hearst to know of. If the fall in the price of commodities cannot be checked we may be forced to an inflation of our currency. This may take the form of using silver as a base, or decreasing the amount of gold in the dollar. I have not decided how this inflation can be best and most safely accomplished. I would not like this to get out lest people become unduly alarmed."

In conclusion Mr. Roosevelt expressed deep appreciation of Mr. Hearst's interest, saying: "We are working toward a common end. Tell him it won't make any difference to me if he disagrees with me on details as long as we are in agreement on the 'big methods.' "

Hearst was enormously pleased and no doubt a bit flattered at Roosevelt's response. He wrote Coblentz: "I find myself in enthusiastic accord with your friend about practically everything." However, he took occasion to plug for a manufacturers' sales tax, hit at "oppressive income taxes" and denounce the banks for their "conscienceless liquidation" of business enterprises and farm properties. "The banks," remarked Mr. Hearst, "are in the incongruous position of liquidating the United States with one hand while holding out the other hand to the United States Government for largesse for themselves. Reasonable reflation would be a patriotic service and an economic boon to the nation."

He added that he would gladly come East for a meeting with Roosevelt but that his doctor forbade the trip for the present. He had recently undergone a delicate though minor operation and had suffered a temporary setback.

Later, after the inauguration, Hearst visited the President at the White House. Coblentz asked him: "Chief, did you get anywhere with your suggestions?"

"I was greatly disappointed," replied Hearst. "The President didn't give me a chance to make suggestions. He did all the talking."

Part of the chat concerned some rare naval prints which Roosevelt, an avid collector, sought to acquire from the publisher. The latter, whose sense of possession had become almost a mania, made the casual excuse that he would be unable to locate the items among his hordes of art objects. Josh-

258

ingly, FDR remarked, with however an underlying note of seriousness: "Well, W. R., that's just the type of static wealth we are trying to put a stop to."

To Hearst, the idea was truly "crackpot Americana." Soon he began opening up on this and other phases of the New Deal; and there would be as much gall and wormwood as honey in his words for FDR's keen and receptive ears.

During the formative period of the New Deal, Roosevelt and Hearst played a game with each other like chess masters.

Hearst was in the family, yet not in it. He and FDR spat and fought, wrangled and reconciled, agreed and disagreed like spirited blood brothers. Each feared, respected, admired the other, and made concessions that would have been offered to no other individual. The only essential difference between them, so far as practical results were concerned, was that one was the legally crowned, the other the uncrowned King of Public Opinion. From his seat in the middle, editor Coblentz, the liaison man, watched the struggle in perplexity and enthrallment.

"Mr. Hearst disagreed with the philosophy of the NRA from the beginning," recalls Coblentz, "and when it was announced that the President intended to include in the draft of the measure a provision to license the press, he hit the ceiling. I believe that Mr. Hearst personally was largely responsible for dissuading the President from going through with his plan to fasten controls on the newspapers of the nation." Coblentz relates a crucial incident:—

Early in 1933, when the National Recovery Act was in its formative state, T. J. White, who was then general manager of the Hearst newspapers, phoned me from San Simeon: "Mr. Hearst wishes you to contact the President and inform him that he will fight him to the bitter end if he insists on his plan to license the press." "That's a serious and important message to deliver," I replied, "and I would prefer that the Chief dictate exactly what he wishes me to transmit to the White House." Mr. Hearst was on the phone in an instant. This is what he dictated:

"Please tell the President that I consider his proposal to license the press under NRA is in direct violation of the Bill of Rights; that it is an abridgement of the freedom of the press guaranteed by the Constitution; and that I will fight his proposal with every means at my command, even if it means taking it to the Supreme Court of the United States, and even if it costs me every nickel I possess."

I put through a call to the White House. Louis Howe came on the phone.

"I have a message, Louis, which Mr. Hearst has asked me to transmit to the President. Would you mind taking it?" I started to read.

He stopped me with: "Just a minute. I'll put Frank on the phone."

After the exchange of a few pleasant words of greeting, I slowly read the dictated words. There was a pause and the President said:

"My proposal is a regulatory measure and in no sense will it abridge the freedom of the press. It is similar, in a sense, to the fire department rules. When you violate the fire department regulations, the Chief steps in and compels you to conform, does he not?"

"Yes, Mr. President," I replied, "but he does not stop the presses."

The President laughed, and asked me to tell Mr. Hearst there was nothing to worry about. Mr. Roosevelt never went through with his plan.

When the Blue Eagle (NRA) was actually installed, with its cumbersome codes, endless red tape and onerous burdens upon business, Hearst fought it tooth and nail, to the covert applause of less courageous publishers. No one was more delighted when the Supreme Court branded NRA as unconstitutional.

"I do not actually look for any injury to the country if the NRA collapses," Hearst had written Coblentz in September, 1933. "I think its collapse may actually clear the way for better business conditions and greater business confidence. Business people everywhere are sullenly resentful of the needless and useless interference of the Administration in the details of business about which they know nothing." He continued, cuttingly:—

> Business is also worried about turning the whole country over to the labor unions, and will protest against that at the polls.
>
> The labor unions, moreover, are never very grateful. They take all they can get and then ask for more, and are mad if they do not get that.
>
> I think our experiment in Hitlerism is a failure, although the recovery program could have been a splendid success if they had left out the NRA phase of it.
>
> The economic recovery should have come first in the minds of the Administration; the social justice should have followed it, and would have followed it, with everybody satisfied and happy.
>
> However, they insisted upon putting the cart before the horse, and the result has made endless confusion and dissatisfaction and delay —probably nothing worse, because the genuine recovery measures of the Administration are sufficient to carry the country through.
>
> . . . This Administration has realized so many of the ideals of us American-minded folk that I would hate to see it lose in power or prestige or anything necessary for effective political leadership.

During 1934, Hearst's disagreements with the recovery program became

260

sharper. He thought public works should be centered upon a few greatly needed and permanently useful projects such as transcontinental highways. However, a wire to one of his editorial writers carried a strange note of softness: "When I am disposed to criticize the President for one thing or another, I consider the great contribution he is making to the safety and perhaps existence of the nation in the great navy he advocates and I feel that overshadows almost everything else. I cannot oppose him but I will try to help systematize the recovery program."

While abroad during the summer of 1934, Hearst kept in close touch with President Roosevelt's ceaseless activities via such messages as this:—

W. R. Hearst, London   August 9, 1934

Roosevelt after landing Portland spoke twice about nation's parks and drought relief. In Wisconsin this morning made first political speech, clearly a demagogic plea for voters' support. He spoke derisively of demand being heard that he must restore confidence as primary condition of recovery. Speech delivered with more apparent passion than heretofore shown. Ignored all signs of increasing unemployment, slackening business, declining markets. Wholly failed

This Fred Packer cartoon in Hearst's New York *Mirror* when Roosevelt began invading the realm of Congress was typical of the restrained criticism of the President at first.

in any reassuring note to business. Obviously class appeal rather unscrupulous and net effect of speech disappointing. Important you get full copy. Will await instructions.   E. D. COBLENTZ

Hearst responded by cable on August 10:—

Tell all papers morning evening keep free from violent political discussion or extreme political partisanship but to give moderate support to sound and judicious candidates of either party. Recovery is being retarded by visionary schemes of unsound radicals. Even American institutions are endangered. Patriotic conservatism regardless of party should be approved and supported.

Three weeks later, Hearst directly characterized the President as "visionary" but his tone was paternal: "Roosevelt should receive hearty editorial praise for his supporting merchant marine if it is genuine. I feared same attitude toward merchant marine as toward airways. He is so visionary, but we should encourage him sincerely to support navy and merchant marine."

Following the Democratic sweep in the Congressional mid-term elections of that autumn, Hearst wired Roosevelt that there had been no such rousing popular endorsement since the days of Thomas Jefferson and Andrew Jackson, adding a bon mot: "The forgotten man does not forget."

Nevertheless, inevitable disruption of the uneasy truce was not to be long in coming.

Early in April, 1935, Hearst wrote his man Coblentz: "I think we will have to settle down to a consistent policy of opposition to this Administration."

Hearst was particularly irked, even infuriated, by the continuous loose talk of the Roosevelt experimentalists of the necessity for redistributing wealth. FDR, accused Hearst angrily, had adopted the Huey Long share-the-wealth nostrum on the principle of robbing Peter to pay Paul. The publisher predicted, ultimately, a grand smashup "when Peter can no longer be robbed and Paul no longer be paid."

Repeating the age-old economic axiom that wealth cannot be distributed until created, the embattled journalistic critic relieved himself of some further pungent observations which would seem applicable today:—

"The whole spirit of America is being corrupted by this plan of getting something for nothing, and the conclusion will be a dependent class insisting on being supported, an exhausted industrial class, and a thoroughly corrupt political system. . . . By false representation the present Administration was elected, the American system was scrapped, and a political socialistic system under dictatorial direction installed in its place. . . . It is not the motley crowd of clowns and mountebanks with which Roosevelt has sur-

262

rounded himself that are responsible. It is the man who placed these mountebanks in positions of power and authority where they could exploit their ridiculous and disastrous policies."

Followed a spate of violent and provocative editorials in the Hearst papers. The President, Coblentz reports, was "nettled and disturbed," insisting the criticism was unjustified, and asked Mr. Hearst for "an opportunity personally to clear up these misunderstandings." Hearst designated Coblentz as his emissary:—

> On May 8, 1935 [writes Mr. Coblentz] I went to Washington in company with Raymond Moley, at that time Roosevelt's chief brain-truster, and Vincent Astor, one of his intimate friends. My memory is not clear as to why Moley and Astor were with me, although my impression is that Moley arranged the party.
>
> We arrived at the White House in the early evening, prepared to spend the night. The President was swimming in the White House pool specially built for him. We dressed for dinner and were ushered

This cartoon appeared in the same page with one of the editorials in the Hearst newspapers in 1935 referred to in the text above. The artist was Robert James Malone.

to the Oval Room, where cocktails were served. The hors d'oeuvres consisted of Beluga caviar—plenty of it—supplied by Mr. Bullitt, who was then Ambassador to Russia. At dinner we drank toasts in California wine. Mrs. Roosevelt was not present.

Over cordials and highballs the President, in a session that lasted nearly four hours, attempted to explain away the misunderstandings which he said had plagued both our papers and himself. Both Moley and Astor were present during the entire time.

I asked questions and made notes. On the following day I wrote Mr. Hearst a full report of what had transpired. Before sending this report to Mr. Hearst, I submitted it to both Moley and Astor to test its accuracy and to make sure that I was not indulging in further misunderstandings. They both agreed that the report was fair and honest, and asked if I was a shorthand reporter, which I am not.

The conversation covered almost a dozen subjects in great detail. Coblentz's summation report to Hearst comprised some 3,000 words. Its most startling passage was the following quotation from the President himself:—

I am fighting Communism, Huey Longism, Coughlinism, Townsendism. I want to save our system, the capitalistic system; to save it is to give some heed to world thought of today. I want to equalize the distribution of wealth. Huey Long says that ninety-two per cent of the wealth of this country is controlled by eight per cent of the population. He would change this situation by giving a five-thousand-dollar home to each head of a family, twenty-five hundred dollars a year, etc. To combat this and similar crackpot ideas it may be necessary to throw to the wolves the forty-six men who are reported to have incomes in excess of one million dollars a year. In other words, limit incomes through taxation to one million dollars a year. This can be accomplished through taxation.

Further, it may be necessary to see to it that vast estates bequeathed to one person are limited in size. This can be accomplished by inheritance taxes. Communists themselves are not the ones to be feared in this situation. The thinking men, the young men, who are disciples of this new world idea of fairer distribution of wealth, they are demanding that something be done to equalize this distribution.

The President spoke bitterly of the Robert McCormick (Chicago *Tribune*) press as persistently and dishonestly slanting the news against the New Deal, but did not include Mr. Hearst in this category.

In fact, FDR seemed eager to mollify Hearst. When Raymond Moley told him that many of his statements in the Coblentz report "would have been

264

best left unsaid," the President rushed a representative to San Simeon "to explain away his explanations," as Coblentz puts it. Coblentz, in turn, telephoned his Chief to assure him of the absolute accuracy of his written report. To his surprise, he received a new directive from Hearst under date of May 15. In part it read:—

> Please hold up articles critical of Administration for a while. We are getting into condition of chronic hostility. I think we would be fairer to Administration and also more effective in our criticism if we discriminated more and also if we had commendation for some measures; for instance, naval policy is very fine. . . . Again a securities act is necessary and a good securities act will be very beneficial to the country. In fact, our depressions are practically all caused by overspeculation and overcapitalization. Prevention of these speculative conditions and rigid restraint of capitalization are distinctly desirable. We can find some things to commend while finding other things to criticize, and I think an attitude of more or less obvious fairness and impartiality would be helpful.

The truce lasted just four days over a month. On June 19, in a message almost hysterical in its intensity, Hearst ordered open warfare upon Roosevelt's soak-the-rich and corporate surplus tax proposals:—

> President's taxation program is essentially Communism.
> It is, to be sure, a bastard product of Communism and demogogic democracy, a mongrel creation which might accurately be called demo-communism, evolved by a composite personality which might be labeled Stalin Delano Roosevelt.
> It contains the mistakes of both individuals, the evils of both systems, and is Russian in manner and utterly un-American in method and principle.
> It is a violation of the basic spirit of American institutions, a betrayal of the American ideals of equality and justice.
> It is primarily vindictive in purpose.
> It divides a harmonious and homogeneous nation into classes, and stimulates class distinction, class discrimination, class division, class resentment, and class antagonism.

Dislike of Roosevelt's policies and of the "crackpots" within his inner council gradually worked in upon Hearst like a zymosis.

Finally he whipped himself into a state where he actually became the spokesman and the idol of the fanatical, semi-psychotic Roosevelt haters who lived only to get That Man out of the White House. It was truly an Alice in Wonderland situation.

During this feverish period many wondered whether Hearst's judgments and ideas were not hardening with his arteries. Often the most effective master of the printed word on earth rushed impulsively into print with a chimerical attack or proposal which would obviously boomerang. Never had the autocrat of San Simeon so needed a strong, loyal adviser with the courage to stand up and cry "whoa."

This lack of a trusted "no" man may have led him into the most gargantuan political blunder of his entire career: personally selecting and promoting a colorless, undistinguished little Governor of a Midwestern state whose very name dripped with mediocrity, and sending him like a lamb to the slaughter against the leonine Roosevelt as Republican candidate for the Presidency in the campaign of 1936.

The result was a debacle such as this country has never witnessed before or since in a major political contest, with Landon carrying but two states, Maine and Vermont; and a loss of prestige and following from which Hearst was never to recover.

Incredible as it may seem, Hearst had never even heard the name Alfred M. Landon until a few months before he drove through his nomination at Cleveland. In a casual telephone talk, late in 1935, Hearst's political liaison man Coblentz mentioned that some Republicans were talking of Governor Landon as a possible candidate.

"Where is he from?" asked Hearst.

"He is from Kansas."

"Is he a good man?"

"I understand he is a good man," responded Coblentz, who completes the anecdote: "He couldn't resist a wisecrack. There came laughingly over the phone, 'How can he be good and come from Kansas?' But from that day on Mr. Hearst set every force at his command to support Landon, not only in the pre-convention days, but consistently and vigorously after his nomination. I have often wondered whether Mr. Hearst's earnest support of Landon was not due more to his disapproval of Roosevelt than his liking for the Governor of Kansas."

With his remarkable facility at rationalization, Hearst made himself believe, after a single meeting, that Governor Landon was a true man of destiny. We find him instructing Coblentz on May 4, 1936, a few weeks before the opening of the Republican convention, "to get the defeatist air and attitude out of our papers and out of our writers," further observing:—

> Everybody is assuming that it is going to be difficult, if not impossible, to beat Roosevelt.
>
> Everybody is giving the election to Roosevelt in advance.
>
> Six months ago they would have had a defeatist attitude toward Landon as regards the nomination.

266

Now they realize, however, that he is going to be nominated.

They are just a little slow in getting on the mental bandwagon.

It will not be long after Landon's nomination before they will all realize that the Republicans have nominated a man who can win.

I want them to try to realize it now.

After Landon's nomination Hearst continued to pull out all the stops in his support. The Executive Mansion in Topeka took on the complexion of a Hearst newspaper shop, aswarm with reporters, editors, publishers, special writers, financial experts. There was the same interfusing and confusing medley of reality and fantasy.

In the midst of the hubbub, Hearst posted off to Europe breathing confidence and leaving explicit instructions to keep whooping right through to Election Day.

Now Hearst became a hero in the very circles which he had long denounced as reactionary. His papers once again were welcomed in households whose pure portals had been barred to them for years. Well groomed commuters bound for Montclair, New Jersey; Greenwich, Connecticut; and Port Washington, Long Island, even forsook their bridge games in their eagerness to absorb and discuss the glaring anti-Roosevelt headlines, editorials and cartoons in the Hearst papers.

In the White House the imperturbable Roosevelt was quite undisturbed. One day he shouted gleefully to a Hearst correspondent: "What's old W. R. doing now to stir up the animals? Give him my regards." The President's words were a genuine expression of personal liking.

However, FDR was too astute a political strategist not to take advantage when Hearst intemperately accused him of allying himself with the Communists. The White House issued a formal statement attacking "the planned attempts of a certain notorious newspaper owner to make it appear that the President passively accepts the support of alien organizations hostile to the American form of government." Hearst's reply was cabled from Holland:—

I have not stated at any time whether the President willingly or unwillingly received the support of the Karl Marx Socialists, the Frankfurter radicals, Communists and anarchists, the Tugwell Bolsheviks and the Richberg revolutionists which constitute the bulk of his following.

I have simply said and shown that he does receive the support of these enemies of the American system of government, and that he has done his best to deserve the support of all such disturbing and destructive elements.

I do not find any pleasure as an American in saying this of an American President, but it is the truth.

267

Returning from Europe on the eve of Election Day, Hearst repeated his positive conviction in a radio broadcast that Landon would be elected. Editor Coblentz wryly comments: "As a political prophet, Mr. Hearst registered zero."

Election night, when it was already known that Landon had carried but two states, two of the Hearst sons, John and William, strolled into a New York night club. "Ah," sang out the quick-witted master of ceremonies, "here come Maine and Vermont!" The young men joined in the good-humored laughter.

The same spirit was shown by their versatile sire who, while admitting being stunned, allowed that FDR could be compared only with Andrew Jackson in popular appeal. He added, without turning a hair, "If Andrew Jackson's policies were essentially democratic, why is it not reasonable to concede that Mr. Roosevelt's policies may be equally so—dictatorial in manner and method but democratic in essence? When I was a great admirer of Mr. Roosevelt, I gave him a picture of Andrew Jackson and a letter of that great American. I thought then that Mr. Roosevelt resembled Jackson. Perhaps I was more nearly right then than later."

Thus the weird affair ended until it came time to take up the cudgels again.

"It's the Four R's Now" was the caption on this editorial cartoon by Enright in the Hearst newspapers in 1935.

Anti-Communism,
the Greatest Crusade

> And now you are face to face with that agony
> which has been suffered by all the great creators
> of the past; of which Tolstoy wrote to Rolland;
> that purgatory of the soul through which
> Shelley passed, and Rossetti, and Meredith, and
> Carlyle. Go ahead now and make your fight.
>
> *No Villain Need Be*
> VARDIS FISHER

17

"DEAR JOSEPHUS," Hearst wrote to his confidant and secretary, Joseph Willicombe, from Nauheim, Germany, September 17, 1934, "the cure is ended. The doctor says I am no worse than I was three years ago. The doctor further reassuringly said that I would last a few years yet if I got thin and took all strain off my heart. So when you see me I will be a slender sapling. No doubt about the *sap* anyhow."

Then he added, quite casually, that he had flown up to Berlin the previous day and had a long talk with Hitler whom he characterized as "certainly an extraordinary man. We estimate him too lightly in America. He has enormous energy, intense enthusiasm, a marvelous faculty for dramatic oratory, and great organizing ability. Of course these qualities can be misdirected."

The letter went on: "I only hope that he and the Germans may have sense enough to keep out of another war. Fascism seems to be spreading over here. We have got to keep crazy isms out of our country. If we can keep out Communism we can keep out Fascism. Fascism here and elsewhere has sprung up to prevent the control of countries by Communism. Both are despotisms and deprive people of the liberties which democracy assures."

Hearst had come to Europe that summer deeply apprehensive at the trend of events, particularly the foreboding racial and religious policies of Hitler, which were repugnant to the American in every fiber of his being.

The new dictator of Germany began pressing for a meeting the moment he learned that the influential publisher had arrived at Bad Nauheim. Hitler's intermediary was his altitudinal court jester, the ineffable Ernst "Putzie"

Hanfstaengl whose father, an internationally known art expert and dealer, had for many years enjoyed Hearst's patronage.*

Already, far in advance of many still bemused contemporaries, Hearst had seen and recognized the noxious, distorted thing into which Russian Communism had grown and dedicated himself to its destruction. Fascism he was beginning to regard as a twin evil, but his thought had not completely crystallized.

And so curiosity and his instincts as a journalist led to his one and only interview with the Führer. If he could have foreseen the consequences, there is little doubt that he would have shunned the meeting and his subsequent brief association with the Nazi regime. For this encounter set in motion a chain reaction of tempestuous, percussive events, engulfing governments and peoples and arraying against Hearst powerful, organized forces which all but accomplished his ruin. Indeed, only his courage, resourcefulness and transcendent ability as a journalist staved off actual bankruptcy.

As it was, he was compelled to recast his business structure, restrict his sybaritic living and spending habits, and for a term of years yield financial control of his publications to outside interests.

Although Hearst, throughout his career, had repeatedly demonstrated his lack of bias against any race, the most insidious campaign against him, based upon his contact with Hitler, was waged among the Jewish population of the United States and in other countries. Fed by the fact that the Hearst papers printed articles by Goering and other leading Nazis, and accepted the Nazi regime as a client of the Hearst news service, the agitation wreaked enormous damage in the form of boycotts, debilitating decline in circulation and advertising revenue, etc.

While the campaign was at its height, Hearst dictated a memorandum for his own men revealing in the third person details of his interview with Hitler. The document is reprinted in Edmond D. Coblentz's remarkable *William Randolph Hearst, A Portrait in His Own Words*. After explaining that he had conferred with Hitler only after consulting his friend Louis B. Mayer, who thought he might be able to accomplish some good in ameliorating the condition of the Jews in Germany, the Hearst memoir continues:—

> After the usual exchange of formal civilities, Hitler speedily came to the point of his inquiries. He asked: "Why am I so misrepresented, so misunderstood, in America? Why are the people of America so antagonistic to my regime?"
>
> Mr. Hearst replied: "One reason, of course, is that the people of the United States believe in democracy and are averse to dictator-

---

* But no more than Joseph Duveen. For an amusing account of Hearst's dealings with the London and New York supersalesman of art and antiques, see S. N. Behrman's biography, *Duveen* (1952).

ship. That idea has been inculcated in them from the foundation of the nation."

Hitler interrupted and said:

"But I am entirely a product of democracy. I, as a private citizen, appealed to the people of Germany. I was elected to my office by a majority vote of the people of Germany. I presented my proposals, my policies, to the people of Germany. They endorsed these policies by more than a two-thirds majority. We have a constitution, the Constitution of Weimar, and according to that instrument, the endorsement of a policy by the voters is a positive injunction to the government to put that policy into operation. Not to have done it would have been to deny the will of the people. That is democracy, is it not?"

"That might be democracy," said Mr. Hearst, "but it is also dictatorship in view of what those policies are. However, there is another reason," continued Mr. Hearst, "why the people of America are, as you phrase it, antagonistic to your regime. There is a very large and influential and respected element in the United States who are very resentful of the treatment of their fellows in Germany. And this element has the sincere sympathy of practically all other elements of the American public. It is not, therefore, merely the form of the German Government which creates antagonism in the United States. It is the drastic treatment by the German Government of these subject people."

"I understand perfectly what you mean," Hitler responded, "but I can assure you that those vigorous measures of the government are due to temporary circumstances, and that all discrimination is disappearing and will soon entirely disappear. That is the policy of my government and you will soon see ample evidence of it."

Mr. Hearst seemed gratified, and assured the Führer that tolerance would do much to dissipate any antagonism of the people of the United States. He left the interview convinced that he had been "able to accomplish some good."

After his talk with Hitler, Hearst lingered long in Munich, which had held a pervasive charm for him since his mother had first brought him there in his boyhood. He reveled in the theatres, shops, the museums, above all in the daily contact with the kindly, jolly Bavarians. As always, he passed delighted days in the National Museum, noticing, however, that sufficient care was not being taken of some of the priceless treasures and advising that certain tapestries be taken down at intervals and "rested" from the strain of hanging too long in one position. He was shocked at the decline of Munich's standards of art.

"What has become of Munich's art?" he asked a local interviewer. "It has gone Communist. The 'frightfulness' of the war seems to have persisted in modernistic art. I can see no other explanation for some of the pictures which disfigure the walls of modern art exhibits. The great artists are no longer here. The one thing which modern art does not require is an artist."

In the same interview, the noted visitor was asked his opinion of the German press. His reply clearly indicated that he was far from sold on Hitler & Company:—

> I think the German press has been among the best in the world, and for that matter, still is, considering the conditions under which it is published. But if I wrote what I think of those conditions I would be arrested and if you printed what I wrote you would be arrested.* So why discuss the subject at this time?
>
> I will only say that I think that any country without a free press— a press free to speak the truth fully and unreservedly—is without the fundamentals of liberty. However, I can see that attempts of Communists to seize control of the state and subject the people to a narrow and bigoted class government which would have destroyed all liberty, created conditions analogous to those of war, and we all realize that certain temporary restraints must be put upon publicity in time of war.

The American publisher observed further that "Communism is a contagion like a disease. It spreads not through reason but through hysteria. Logic and the lessons of history are impotent against it. Perhaps the only

* Following the death of William E. Dodd in 1940, *Liberty* magazine serialized portions of what was purported to have been a diary kept by Dodd while ambassador to Berlin. The diary included gossip that in the meeting with Hitler, Hearst negotiated with the German Chancellor for an International News Service contract. The inference was that German government money was paid over to the Hearst organization through the German government controlled news agency. Hearst immediately declared the statement a lie. "No such matters were discussed," he said. "My interview with Chancellor Hitler was purely a news interview such as I have had from time to time, and always endeavor to have, in the pursuit of my occupation as editor and correspondent, with leading public men everywhere." Hearst named Harry Crocker as a witness to the conversation. He added that "the question of whether I should see Mr. Hitler and what I should say to Mr. Hitler was discussed in general with Mr. Louis B. Mayer before the interview took place. All the evidence as to the accuracy of this statement of mine is at the disposal of your attorneys. Furthermore, the books of the International News Service are open to your investigation." Hearst demanded "an adequate retraction of an allegation which has no basis except in the vaporings of a lot of irresponsible Communists." After an investigation, *Liberty* devoted a full page to Hearst's letter and a statement that it was convinced that Dodd was misinformed. It concluded, *"Liberty* regrets the injustice which the publication of Mr. Dodd's erroneous statement has done you and is glad to publish this full retraction."

way to restrain anyone in an hysterical frenzy is in a strait jacket until he recovers his sanity."

While charges of anti-Semitism and pro-Fascism were gathering like a cloud about his head, Hearst's true sentiments are clearly shown through intimate communications presented by Edmond Coblentz. For example, a note to Karl von Wiegand, his correspondent in Central Europe:—

> The most dangerous thing to meddle with are people's religious beliefs. What Germany needs is political unity, and that can best be obtained with religious liberty. Religious conflicts can disrupt any nation. Jews, Catholics and Protestants can be united to make a political structure all the more powerful, because of the variety of its component parts.

To Joseph Willicombe:

> The situation here is very discouraging. I hope to heavens we keep out of it. Why we should want to join a lunatic asylum I don't see. If we do join it we are sure to be involved in the next war. The one thing which impresses everybody the most over here is how perfectly happy all these peoples could be if there were no political leaders. Perhaps we will have reason to have the same reflections about our own country.

To a friend in 1935 in response to a query:

> Will make another attempt to relieve races and religions of oppression. I discussed this matter in my interview with Hitler and received some little encouragement. I will try again by personal appeal. It is possible that he may now be more open to reason.

Hearst later sent a message to Putzie Hanfstaengl, obviously intended for Hitler's ear:—

> Now that all citizens, including Jews, are given political rights in Saar, why not give them representation in proportion to population? That is only one per cent and surely the mouse need not terrify the elephant.
>
> Such action would strengthen Germany immensely in United States, and I think everywhere. But if you do this, do it strikingly by manifesto in way to compel publication and attention everywhere.
>
> Do it so clearly and convincingly that professional agitators who make their living at present by stimulating class and sectarian hatreds will have no excuse for further agitation and misrepresentation.

273

As before, the results were nil and, as the situation steadily worsened in Germany, Hearst jotted down his final discouraging conclusion:—

"Hitler is following in the footsteps of Stalin.

"A tyrant is a tyrant, no matter whether he calls himself a Communist or a Socialist. The only protection against tyranny is democracy.

"A king is less of a tyrant than a dictator."

Uneasy as he was at the growth of Fascism and Nazism abroad, Hearst returned from Europe in the autumn of 1934 firmly convinced that Russian Bolshevism was an even greater menace.

Evidence had come to him on every hand that Stalin and his associates had thrown off their thin masque of humanitarianism and erected an atheistic despotism more ruthless, and far more efficient, than that of the Czars. Their aim, through subversion and infiltration, was world conquest. An example, he believed, of Communist penetration was the San Francisco general strike which had been suppressed that year only by a revival of vigilante tactics.

"We recognized Russia," Hearst wrote in a signed editorial on December 9, 1934. "Now it is just as well to recognize what we recognized. It is the same old Russia as under the Czars. It is the same old tyranny under a different name."

Whereupon the Great Dissenter launched a long and ceaseless battle, compared to which his preceding crusades were as zephyrs, against what he later labeled the Red Fascists and their American dupes and fellow travelers. As so often before, he swam against a tide of complacency and disbelief, but lived to see his course amply vindicated.

Hearst himself led the full-scale assault in a spectacular nation-wide radio address on January 5, 1935, presenting a documented and devastating picture of starvation, cruelty and human misery under the Stalin despotism. Quoting reports of the International Committee for the Relief of Soviet Russia, Hearst told of the starvation of millions of Russian peasants because their grain was seized for the Red Army; or to barter abroad for foreign exchange. He added:—

"Who is expected to see to it that Russia gets the 'much needed foreign exchange' to keep her hideous tyranny, her monstrous and monumental government failure going? Why, of course, we citizens of America; we despised American bourgeois. We are supposed to rescue this vile and vicious system of robbery and murder, so that these Communists can in return proselyte in our country to the end that we be robbed and murdered also."

This was a reference to the undercover activities of the Communist International.

"Does anybody," asked Hearst, "want the bloody despotism of Communism in our free America except a few incurable malcontents, a few sapheaded college boys and a few unbalanced college professors, who teach the young and inexperienced that the robbery and rapine of Communism is —God save the mark—ideology?

"The truth is that government by the proletariat, government by the least capable and the least conscientious element in the community—government by the mob, government by ignorance and avarice—government by tyranny and terrorism—despotism 'limited by nothing, by no kind of law and by absolutely no rule'—is the fearful failure that it needs must be and definitely deserves to be."

The publisher's forthright words stirred a hornet's nest. The Communists and their sympathizers, through their tightly organized network, launched a boycott against the Hearst newspapers.

Hearst himself, fighting fire with fire, unleashed a private witch hunt for Communists on the campuses and in the lecture rooms of American colleges and universities. There was plenty of grist for his mill, as has since been plenteously revealed. But the campaign tended to defeat itself. As was to happen so often afterwards, the zeal of Hearst's agents outran their judgment. They lashed out indiscriminately against honest liberals and progressives as well as the few actual Communists among the educators.

The result was that Hearst soon found practically the entire academic world arrayed against him. At the same time, men prominent in the Jewish communities of various cities were openly accusing him of anti-Semitism and pro-Nazism. His publications quickly felt the pinch—to such an extent that, on April 21, 1935, Hearst was moved to issue a Declaration of Principles, affirming his inflexible opposition to "Communism, Fascism or any other form of despotism, including governmental bureaucracy."

He summed up: "The Hearst papers are opposed to intolerance, as well as to fanaticism. They are opposed to race prejudice and class conflict. They believe in opportunity for all and equality before the law. They are opposed to government by any clique or class."

Whereupon, he continued ripping the sheep's clothing off the Russian bear.

Simultaneously, he kept up a constant, and for the most part unpopular, drumfire against President Roosevelt and the bulk of the latter's policies and appointments.

Hearst's travails came to a climax late in 1936.

Most of the late summer and early autumn he passed in England and at his castle in Wales, seeking to elect Alf Landon by remote control. With the German threat growing obviously more acute, a curious state of apathy, almost of self-hypnosis, seemed to grip most of the statesmen, press lords and other leading men with whom Hearst consorted. Among the few exceptions were the visitor's long-time friends Churchill and Beaverbrook.

Amid the atmosphere of tension, Hearst managed to score a thumping news beat by cabling to his papers that Edward VIII had definitely decided to give up his throne and marry Mrs. Simpson. Although the despatch was not signed, Hearst, pleased as Punch, acknowledged authorship and remarked with becoming modesty that the exploit did not indicate that he was a better reporter than his colleagues, "but sometimes I have contacts and opportunities which enable me to get news that other correspondents cannot secure."

The disastrous defeat of his candidate, Governor Landon, at the polls in November was followed in December by an even greater blow.

On Christmas Eve, Arthur Brisbane, who had been failing for several years, completed his last column—"Another Christmas has come, a birthday that means kindness and hope for so many millions of human beings" —and then, as gay revelers were streaming past his Fifth Avenue home, passed away at dawn. In attendance, among others, was a German specialist called in by Hearst.

A few hours before his death Brisbane had summoned Emil J. Steinheuser, for many years his secretary and dictaphone transcriber, and dictated this last communication to "My dear W. R.":—

> Your Doctor Groedel from Nauheim and my Doctor Stieglitz are feeding me hypodermics with morphine and other delicacies and they are rigging up an oxygen tent in my apartment "just in case." I don't think there is any real danger of anything but I send you these unfavorable Christmas details so you will understand, not that it makes any difference to you, any irregularity in my work for a short time.
>
> I hope you will have a good Christmas and a most prosperous New Year, starting a long series of them. No answer to this is necessary. It is just information.
>
> I like Dr. Groedel extremely. Perhaps he will tell you what he really thinks (doctors never tell their patients). If he does, I wish you would tell me, because on my family's account it is quite important for me to know.

One half of Brisbane's seventy-two years had been spent in the service of Hearst, who provided the medium which had made his chief editorial writer and columnist a national institution and enabled him to build up a fortune of millions. The two men had also been associated over the years in numerous business ventures, notably in New York City realty, hotels and office buildings.

Another disturbing factor about this time was that Hearst's affairs had become so tangled that, if he had passed away suddenly, death and inheritance taxes could have been met only through forced sales of many of his two-score newspapers and magazines.

It was then, in those melancholy months of 1937, that this amazing man of seventy-four, handicapped by a weakening heart, rallied his forces and saved himself by courageous effort.

Hearst had been in an embarrassing financial position since the mid-1920's. The glib phrases of the economists, "over expansion" and "lack of working capital," will suffice as an explanation.

In 1927, he was persuaded by a favored new adviser, an aggressive San Francisco lawyer of Irish-American stock, the remarkable John Francis Neylan, to fragmentize his sprawling empire and to permit the investing public to share some of his burdens. First, Neylan put together, as Hearst Magazines, Inc., five prosperous periodicals—*Good Housekeeping, Cosmopolitan, Harper's Bazaar, Motor,* and *Motor Boating*—and quickly sold an issue of $10,000,000 in six per cent debentures underwritten by a New York investment house.

Three years later the brilliant lawyer came up with another plan which brought no less than $50,000,000 into the till, although causing many a subsequent headache. Neylan combined Hearst's six West Coast newspapers with four papers in the East, the *American Weekly,* and the American Newsprint Corporation into Hearst Consolidated Publications, Inc.

By the simple exchange of a collateral note, all the voting common stock, 2,000,000 shares, was turned over to Hearst's personal holding corporation, Star Holding Company. Hearst Consolidated arranged to redeem the obligation by selling directly to the public 2,000,000 shares of seven per cent Class A preferred, non-voting stock at $25 a share. The deal was put over by pressure sales methods, including doorbell ringing, and a mighty ballyhoo in the Hearst papers.

To make the bait more enticing Hearst Con., as it soon became popularly known, inserted a clause in its incorporation papers and bills of sale stipulating that if four successive dividend payments were omitted by the company, the stockholders could step in and choose an entirely new board of directors. Although the new corporation paid its fat preferred dividend at least once a year from 1930 to 1937, this pledge came to hang like a Damoclean sword over Hearst and the management.

With the coming of the New Deal and the sharp rise in taxes on personal holding corporations, Star Holding Company, already weakened by its loss of clusters of prosperous properties, was converted into American Newspapers, Inc., with Hearst Consolidated directly under its control. One rung down the ladder, under direct ownership of American Newspapers, Inc., was an operating device called Hearst Enterprises. Through this private clearing house, ninety Hearst corporations cleared inter-company debts which, in 1935, totaled some $440,000 a day. Another subsidiary of American Newspapers, Inc. was a new semiholding company of 840,000 shares, Hearst Corporation, eventually destined to rise to the top of the heap.

The Crocker National Bank in San Francisco, the hub of the entire operation, bravely undertook the mammoth job of bookkeeping. How onerous this task was may be realized when one takes into account that practically all Hearst units owed each other and any bank that would lend them money. At one time there were twenty-eight straight commercial loans from banks, ranging in amount from $220,000 to $2,500,000. By 1930, some $60,000,000 in bonds, personally guaranteed by Hearst, were held by the banks, led by Chase National. Total debt was $126,000,000.

The cat was out of the bag for fair when, early in 1937, applications for bond issues totaling slightly more than $35,000,000 were made to the Securities & Exchange Commission on behalf of Hearst Publications and Hearst Magazines and had to be withdrawn under a gathering storm of protests.

Now the time had come for drastic action. Hearst entrained for New York and went into consultation with Clarence John Shearn, his friend of many years and one of his lawyers since 1900. Judge Shearn was also of counsel for the Chase National Bank. In June, after protracted negotiations, it was announced that Hearst had signed over to Shearn, as sole voting trustee for ten years, his controlling stock in his top holding company, American Newspapers, Inc. Hearst retained editorial direction and, with his family, beneficial interest in the stock. The news fell like a bombshell in publishing and financial circles.

It meant that Hearst, for the first time in his life, had yielded control of his finances to another, Shearn, and through the latter to the Chase Bank. His own salary as President of Hearst Consolidated was cut from $500,000 to $100,000.

Faced with one of the toughest retrenchment and reorganization jobs in economic history, Shearn moved swiftly and efficiently. Within little more than a year, he had effected a saving upwards of $5,000,000 annually. Six newspapers had been suspended or sold, including Hearst's beloved New York *American,* which was merged with the *Evening Journal.* Radio stations had been cut from ten to three. One magazine, *Pictorial Review,* had been scrapped; Universal [news] Service merged with International.

As a conservation committee, Shearn, with Hearst's advice, appointed seven executives, comprising T. J. White, chairman; H. M. Bitner, general manager Hearst newspapers; Richard E. Berlin, publisher Hearst magazines; J. V. Connolly, executive head of features, wire services and radio; Martin F. Huberth, in charge of real estate; F. E. Hagelberg, general auditor in charge of finances; and W. R. Hearst, Jr., publisher of the *Journal-American* and representative of the Hearst family. The council members were promptly dubbed the "Young Turks." Gradually they set about liquidating "collateral and unrelated investments," such as unprofitable realty holdings and culls from the immense art and antique collections.

The latter were disposed of at cleverly timed auctions and through sales at Gimbel department stores. It was like pulling teeth to gain Hearst's consent to the disposal of any given article. A bizarre item was a 12th century cloister, from one of two monasteries purchased by Hearst in Spain, dismantled stone by stone and shipped to America in crates at a cost of $500,000. The 10,751 numbered crates, containing the cloister, were bid in by Florida promoters and, in 1952, the edifice was reassembled in North Miami Beach and opened as a tourist attraction.

The principal element in what was to prove a resounding comeback for Hearst was the man himself. Accepting the new stringencies without complaint, he buckled down, with old-time enthusiasm, to making better, brighter newspapers.

Failing to find or develop a satisfactory successor to the great Arthur Brisbane, Hearst decided, at seventy-seven, to take on the burden of a daily column himself. His "In the News," unsigned but bearing his distinctive, unmistakable imprint, appeared in the Hearst press from March 10, 1940, through May 25, 1942, when it was discontinued due to wartime pressures.

Hearst wrote his columns in longhand, at any hour of the day or night, wherever he might be. Dealing with a wide variety of subjects, many of them sprightly autobiographical recollections, his output for "In the News" approached 2,000,000 words, an amazing achievement for a man nearing his eightieth milestone. Yet he seemed actually to thrive under the challenge. Some of his essays were truly classical, attracting wide attention and popularity.

When the bankers nominally took over the Hearst publications, they found that the man who had built them from scratch, by his own unique methods, was as hard to confine as quicksilver. On problems concerning merely profit and loss they found him co-operative, even docile. This attitude hardened abruptly at the threshold of his editorial sanctum. Upon matters of principle and conviction, Hearst was flint and steel. So, after a few significant clashes of will, the guardians of the moneybags left Hearst in sole control of his editorial policies.

With the coming of the second World War in 1939, strong pressures were placed upon Hearst to tone down his historic stand against intervention. John S. Brookes, Jr., representing the banking interests and Hearst's Canadian newsprint suppliers, had been installed as president of the top Hearst holding company, American Newspapers, Inc.

In September and October, 1939, the Hearst papers pressed vigorously for maintenance of our neutrality and continuance of our embargo against shipment of munitions to the belligerents, especially Great Britain. "There ensued a correspondence, both by letter and telephone, between Mr. Hearst on the one hand and Judge Shearn and Brookes on the other," writes editor Edmond D. Coblentz. "I was in the middle." In late September, Mr. Brookes wrote to Hearst at Wyntoon, McCloud, California:—

> I want to call your attention to the status of our relationship with the Canadian newsprint industry. This relationship is for many reasons so important to us that we must keep a watchful eye on the situation at all times.
>
> If any one of the suppliers dropped out, i.e., declined to continue to supply us under the present credit arrangement, the resultant situation would be extremely difficult. The impression which I wish to register with you is that the newsprint relationship is touch-and-go at the moment.
>
> With the outbreak of the war and the Canadian entrance therein, a new danger has developed. The Canadians are perfectly naturally thinking in this regard only from a partisan standpoint. They now find themselves vitally interested in our Federal government policy on the neutrality question. Naturally they are very anxious to see the present embargo lifted. They have been reading our papers and have discovered that we are violent objectors to this program.
>
> It would seem to be the part of wisdom in our own selfish interest to temper our position so that we do not stand out head and shoulders above the rest of the journalistic world in our partisanship.
>
> In order to safeguard against possibly disastrous repercussions, I very strongly urge that no further editorials or other policy moves be made effective involving this controversial question until they have been released by a committee here in the East which, through immediate contact with the newsprint situation, will be best able to judge the effect of any such step.
>
> I would suggest that this committee at the present time be composed of Coblentz, Bill Hearst, and either Gortatowsky or myself.

Three days later, Mr. Hearst sent this tart reply:—

> I always keep in touch with Mr. Coblentz, and as he and I both have a knowledge of the situation that seems to be quite all that is necessary.
>
> I have no desire for an advisory committee, and no need for one; in fact, there is nothing for such a committee to do.
>
> I do not want a lot of people meddling in something they do not know anything about.
>
> The slightest encouragement would have everybody sticking their

280

fingers, and their thumbs too, in the editorial broth; and too many cooks not only spoil the broth but drive away the clientele.

The pressure from the Canadians continuing, Hearst sent the following wire to his son, W. R. Hearst, Jr., with a copy to Coblentz:—

> I have been accustomed to consider these people as friends and very helpful associates, consequently what they might have to say as such would receive favorable consideration. But dictation regarding the American policies of American newspapers by alien interests would not be regarded as friendly or as favorable to good will, either personal or national.
>
> Furthermore our papers, while intensely American, are extremely well disposed toward England. Our policies are exactly those of the American Legion, who expressed their friendship for the Allies by fighting for them in the recent war but still do not want to see our country enmeshed in another European conflict.
>
> We intend to continue to entertain our American ideals of peace and neutrality and to exercise our American privilege of free speech.
>
> But if there is anything in the manner or method of expressing our views and presenting our policies which can be legitimately criticized, we will be glad to profit by such friendly criticism and to improve those methods for our own good, for international amity and for the effectiveness of our cause.
>
> Please approach the situation entirely on these lines, not submitting to undue interference but giving proper consideration to anything which is advanced in friendship and good faith.

Judge Shearn telephoned Mr. Hearst at Wyntoon and pleaded with him to drop his uncompromising stand for retention of the arms embargo. Hearst's reply was short and sharp:—

> Well, I have the choice of being a good American or a S. O. B.
> I am not taking an extreme position.
> I am going to run editorials in favor of maintaining the existing law.
> I will not do it in an offensive way, but I am not going to change the elemental policy.

After the swift conquest of the Low Countries, the occupation of Denmark and Norway by the Germans and the fall of France, the plight of Britain, standing alone, touched a chord in Hearst. On June 24, 1940, he printed in his personal column an imaginative allegory intended to hearten the British. It was called "The Lemmings" and many consider it his finest piece of writing. Some of its cadences were a psychological prose poem.

In ancient geologic times, Hearst recalled that the ratlike little lemmings, drawn by instinct, perished by the millions when they attempted to swim from Norway to the coast of Scotland. In a vein of mysticism most likely to impress Hitler, Hearst warned the power-mad Führer to "beware of the sea"—"the sea is a great conqueror. It can engulf armies, as it engulfed the hosts of Pharaoh. It can swallow up the invaders of its isles, as it swallows up the foolish little lemmings."

Reminding Hitler of alien fleets which had beaten themselves to pieces on "the wave-worn chalk cliffs of England," Hearst, with a touch of Old Testament grandeur, advised the dictator to "march no more across the land with brutal tread; turn back from further venturing; you have reached the sea." The allegory was widely reprinted and eagerly read in England and throughout the British Commonwealth.

Under the spur of the world ferment and his own adversities, Hearst's perceptive senses became sharper. Always a quick, retentive, eclectic reader, he now passed many of the quiet night hours with the Greek philosophers. Quoting Thucydides' brilliant phrase, "The abuse of democracy is the beginning of despotism," Hearst contended that practically everything occurring in New Deal America had occurred in Greece over two thousand years before "when democracy went to the extremes of demagogy and terminated in tyranny."

Early in 1940, Hearst became convinced that Franklin Roosevelt, impelled by social forces largely beyond his control, would seek a third term:—

> The understanding in American informed circles is that President Roosevelt will run for a third term if his European peace negotiations reach a successful conclusion.
>
> It may be stated with certainty—if not with authority—that if the President's peace negotiations succeed he will run; if they fail he will run; and if they result in a stalemate, he will run; in fact, whichever way the cat jumps, or if it does not jump at all, the President will still run.

Under date of February 27, 1940, the conductor of "In the News" announced:—

"Events of the past few days have made clear, first that Mr. Roosevelt is seeking the nomination for the Presidency—indirectly, but definitely. Second, that he is going to get the nomination, and third, that he has a very good chance of re-election."

Again, in one sweeping sentence, he summarized his opinion of FDR:

282

"The United States has never had in the Presidential chair an abler, keener, more resourceful or more relentlessly ambitious politician than Mr. Roosevelt."

When Roosevelt dropped John Garner and compelled the nomination of Henry A. Wallace for Vice-President, Hearst characterized Wallace as "a young gentleman who would not make a very creditable soda fountain clerk."

In the 1940 campaign Hearst supported Wendell Willkie, the Republican candidate, but with no particular enthusiasm. Once he remarked caustically: "Every time Mr. Willkie speaks he says something—but it is generally something which Mr. Roosevelt has said before and said better." By way of illustration, he offered the tale of the linguistic parrot who silently submitted to being thrown into the pot and boiled. When someone told the cook that the parrot spoke four languages, that unfeeling individual retorted: "Then why didn't he say sumthin' in one of them?"

As early as the summer of 1940, Hearst warned that the Roosevelt regime was contemplating the projection of the United States into the European war. Pleading for a speedup in preparedness, he forecast early conflict with Japan:—

> As Japan's navy gets stronger and the United States navy gets weaker, Japan's attitude toward the United States becomes more and more arrogant, truculent and impudent.
>
> There is little doubt that Japan would welcome war with the United States, and may take occasion any day to compel such a war.
>
> In the meantime, we are going fatuously forward in our Pacific Fools' Paradise, destroying our defenses and putting ourselves at the mercy of oriental invaders.

On July 24, 1940, when official quarters were scouting such ideas, Hearst flatly predicted that the United States would actively join the conflict:—

> The entry of the United States into the war may be considered more than a probability. In fact, it may be set down as a certainty.
>
> It is obvious to the most casual observer that the United States is preparing not merely for defense, but for war, and that the attitude of the United States towards England is entirely analogous to that of Italy towards Germany before Italy entered the war.
>
> At the present time the United States can give more effective aid to England by staying out of the war than by entering it. But within a year the United States will be in a position to join the British Em-

pire in effective warfare and will doubtless do so. England knows this and counts on it.

The Axis Powers know it and practically assert it. They declare with definiteness that peace would be obtainable today except for the confidence England possesses because of the positive commitment of the United States.

Therefore in estimating the forces on each side the accurate observer must consider the United States as an absolute ally of England.

The Hearst statement created a tremendous furor, especially in England, where it was hailed in great black headlines. Immeasurably lifted was the morale of the beleaguered people of Britain. For the first time in his life Hearst was toasted along Piccadilly.

With Pearl Harbor, Hearst threw himself wholeheartedly into supporting all-out war against both Germany and Japan.

The excitement and the action seemed to rejuvenate him. Once again Wyntoon and San Simeon throbbed with life. The master often joined his guests at his favorite pastime, croquet, and was again occasionally seen on horseback. As his financial reports assumed a rosier hue, he became more absorbed in the art catalogues which poured in from all over the world, and indulged in an occasional purchase.

Throughout the war years, Hearst's insight into Russian motivations and future moves was all but clairvoyant. On November 8, 1942, when America was sending enormous convoys of munitions and provisions to Russia, he spoke out against "Excessive Russianism":

"Let us not go overboard in our enthusiasm. Russia is not interested in democracy or the Four Freedoms. After the war she will be busy Communizing conquered Europe and trying to Communize us."

May 27, 1943, on "The Russian Objective":

"The main result that Russia hopes for after this war will be the permanent establishment of Russian Bolshevism over all Europe, despite Premier Stalin's modest disclaimer of such ambitious intent."

July 22, 1943, "Soviet Russia's Intentions":

"Russia intends to encroach in the Balkans. She intends to dominate Europe. Africa will be England's prize. Europe will be Russia's."

In January, 1944, the Russians loudly accused the British of seeking a separate peace with Hitler, and Hearst observed:—

> Russia is becoming—and indeed has become—the great dominating Power in Europe as well as in Asia. The dreams of Peter the Great are being realized.
>
> The "little window" which Peter opened at Petrograd from which to look upon Europe has become a vast corridor leading to the

heart of Europe from the now-called city of Leningrad. Through this ever widening corridor the Russian armies are marching under Stalin, not to look upon Europe with admiring and envious eyes, but to overrun Europe and make it a territorial possession or at least a political appanage of Russia's oriental despotism.

Ironically, it was the war which he strove so valiantly to prevent which restored prosperity to Hearst, as it did in lesser degree to many other harassed American publishers.

Not only did circulation boom as a result of stirring events, but the rationing of paper stocks limited space and brought keen competition from advertisers for every available inch.

Having redeemed the sixty-odd million in bonds, held by his client, Chase National, and other banks, Judge Shearn retired as trustee.

Shearn was succeeded in December, 1943, by a voting trust comprising: Richard Berlin, the magazine man; Martin Huberth, the New York realty expert; Edward H. Clark of San Francisco, a family cousin and long manager of the Hearst Estate; Henry S. MacKay, Jr., a Los Angeles lawyer; and John W. Hanes, former Under-Secretary of the Treasury. Subsequently, two of the Hearst sons, W. R., Jr. and John R. Hearst, and R. A. Carrington, Jr., publisher of the Los Angeles *Examiner,* became members of the voting trust.

Messrs. Berlin, Hanes and their associates completed the herculean task of conservation which had been initiated by Shearn. The pruning knife continued to cut deep. Two-thirds of the land surrounding San Simeon was sold for a forest preserve and other purposes, reducing its acreage to a mere 75,000. Eventually it was expected to become a state museum and park.

Many millions in personal debts were liquidated, as well as large sums owed suppliers and others. In one tremendous night, Berlin and Hanes sent out a master telegram to 43,000 holders of the troublesome seven per cent preferred stock of Hearst Consolidated; and were enabled to corral the bulk of the issue by offering $25 a share (par) against current market quotations of $17.

Following this coup, half a dozen newsprint paper mills in Maine and Canada were acquired outright. Hearst's personal salary was raised to $300,000. Hearst Corporation, the new top holding company, began setting aside fluid cash reserves sufficient for any foreseeable contingency.

Trimmed of its dead limbs, the Hearst Empire was again glowing with health, compact, efficient, and still by far the largest operation of its kind.

Truly, the King was back in the Countinghouse, counting out his money. The path ahead seemed serene.

Last Years

*"Now seems it more than ever rich to die
To come upon the midnight with no pain . . ."*

18

IN MANY RESPECTS, the final phases of William R. Hearst's life were the most remarkable of his panoramic career. His last years were shadowed by failing health and strength which he did not permit to interfere with his continued close personal control of his many affairs.

As early as 1930, experienced cardiovascular specialists both in Europe and in America had cautioned him that his heart must be watched and guarded against undue strain. Thereafter, for two decades, he lived under a constant cloud. Yet there was no perceptible change in his accustomed pattern of life, save for a certain tightening in the regimen of exercise and diet.

About this time, Hearst's intimate papers began to reflect a whimsical acceptance of the concessions exacted by advancing years. Observing on one occasion that every few days discoveries were being made "which enable us to tinker up the human chassis and live longer and probably better," he wondered whether there should not be "some reasonable limit to the desire to live," whether mankind would not be better off if we could "turn in the old corporeal car in the natural course of life and death and come back with a brand-new, up-to-date model with all the modern improvements."

For mere longevity as such, Hearst cared not a fig. His most cherished ambition was to die in harness, with intellectual acuity unimpaired, still directing with virtuosity and flexibility the great enterprises which he had created. Once he compared the task of supervising a number of newspapers to balancing a feather on the end of one's nose, remarking that the art

286

requires "consistent and concentrated attention. You cannot just put the feather there and expect it to stay."

At this time, the early 1930's, Hearst was gleefully engaged in planning and supervising the last and most unique of his private building operations in the sylvan fastnesses of northern California. His mother's summer residence, Wyntoon, on the banks of the McCloud River had burned down. The Norman chateau, which drew its name from a fast-vanishing tribe of Indians, held vivid early memories; and in its place Hearst erected a number of beautiful and picturesque Bavarian type buildings grouped about a green common. He called his creation "The Village."

There was the Cinderella House, the Sleeping Beauty House, the Brown Bear House, and the River House. The outer walls of each were decorated with dashing and dramatic murals done by Willy Pogany in his highly individualistic style. There, too, was Hearst's office and adjoining teletype room which kept him in constant touch with his newspapers and the outside world.

Further down the turbulent McCloud River was the Gables, housing the main assembly and dining halls; while a mile downstream was a rambling stone structure called "The Bend." Towering over all was majestic, snow-capped Mount Shasta.

As usual, Hearst did most of his work at night. Noon found him dawdling about the common in rough outing clothes; or rambling along the trails bordering the river. In time the new Wyntoon became Hearst's favorite seat. He seemed relaxed and carefree in the bracing, pine-laden air. Some of the seductive charm of this forest retreat and of his feeling for Wyntoon was put into verse by Hearst:—

> I am the Forest of Fir and Pine,
> Shadow and silence and peace are mine.
> Mine are the springs and the rills and brooks
> Which rising in quiet hidden nooks
> Join hands with the river and joyously flow
> To the wide-spread plains which lie below.

Guests lazying about the beautiful heated woodland pool or admiring rare examples of German mediaeval art, which were everywhere, gained no hint of the ceaseless activity going on behind the scenes in Hearst's private quarters.

Indeed, the whole life of Wyntoon's master, as for half a century, was concentrated in a quest for improvement and perfection of his beloved papers, typographically, editorially, above all in collecting and presenting the news. Fascinating glimpses of these pursuits and of Hearst's publishing techniques are presented in editor Edmond Coblentz's portrait of him.

Mr. Coblentz remarks that a voluminous volume could be compiled of Hearst's instructions over the years to his editors, publishers, mechanical superintendents, advertising directors and circulation managers. "All papers, yes, all of them, came under his daily scrutiny, and never a day passed that some one of his lieutenants did not receive a word of praise, criticism, or suggestion for change." *

Hearst was constantly exhorting his editors to get more interested in the news, more excited about it. After all, he thought, a newspaper stands or falls by its news interest. Once he advised Coblentz to recruit a lot of young people for the staff of the strangely static New York *American,* and to give them free rein:—

"Let them make a few mistakes. Maybe the public will like the mistakes. Maybe we are making the big mistake in not being vital enough. I am getting old—running down—going to sleep like a top before it keels over. We must not let the papers run down. They must not go to sleep."

Again he directed his editors:—

"Do not allow your features to encroach unduly on news space. The most important thing in a newspaper is the news. The features are something to be *added* to the news, not to be *substituted* for the news."

Expressing his distaste for mediocrity and conventional handling of the news, he observed: "News is like wool, or cotton, or raw material. How much you can sell it for is what you manufacture out of it."

In a letter to his mechanical superintendent, J. J. Shea, Hearst wrote:—

> Please remember that speed is not the first requisite.
> Fine printing is first and above all the desirable quality.
> I repeat, let us make our progress in the direction of fine printing and not fast printing.
> When I am told that a press will do 40,000 an hour, that statement leaves me cold.
> I would rather have a press that would do 25,000 an hour and print perfectly than a press that would do twice the number of pages and print in the sloppy manner that newspapers have never yet gotten out of.

Hearst was constantly searching out star engravers and inducing them to accept jobs as mechanical or art managers. When impressed by brilliant art work in one of his own papers or elsewhere, he would have the example circulated among his other publications. A note to secretary Joseph Willicombe:—

> Please show these to Los Angeles and San Francisco. These cities

* There is a 765-page volume, *Selections from the Writings and Speeches of William Randolph Hearst,* edited by E. F. Tompkins (Privately Printed, 1948).

print well but this shows what can be done with 85 screen, with careful and skillful engraving and good printing.

Good etching means good printing if the press room is at all efficient.

No progress in finer printing can be made without progress in engraving.

Hearst considered that the greatest improvement in the journalism of his time, in fact the only outstanding development, lay in the field of illustration. Responding to a query from the trade paper, *Editor & Publisher,* he wrote:—

> Fifty years ago we engaged star writers, sent the best correspondents to distant parts; did great public service feats in the papers and in the courts; used special trains to deliver special editions; sent up balloons instead of airplanes, did charity, saved lives, exposed graft, created reforms.
>
> The one thing we did not do was illustrate.
>
> When I took charge of the San Francisco *Examiner* we had the chalk process, which meant scratching pictures on a chalk-covered plate. Later we had line engraving, later half tones on zinc inserted in the stereotype plates.
>
> Now we have every mechanical means of perfect pictorial production, and we have an unprecedented public demand for pictures. The great development of the day is pictures. The success of the tabloids is largely pictures.

When tabloids, his own included, were springing up like mushrooms in various cities, Hearst impressed upon his editors that pictures must be primarily *news* photographs: "The *Daily News* in New York was a complete failure for two years. It was a picture paper but its pictures were not news pictures. When the editors woke up one day and began to print the NEWS in pictures, the paper began to be a success."

Hearst was an unremitting foe of the turgid, pontifical tone and content of most newspaper editorials. His point of view was best expressed in an intimate letter to his eldest son George whom he was grooming for an executive post on the San Francisco *Examiner.* Admonishing the young man to pay particular attention to improving his editorial page, Hearst observed that "very few of our papers have learned as yet that the public does not want to read the usual dull editorial" and continued:—

> These usual editorials are based on heavy topics and interest only the writer and the editor. You can go out to a hundred dinners or

289

any kind of collection of human beings of ordinary intelligence and never hear one of the subjects discussed that are discussed laboriously in the editorial columns. . . .

Now, George, an editorial writer firmly believes in his heart that the first essential of his business is to be dull, to be ponderous, to be imposing—and that generally means to impose on somebody, and to hand them a lot of dreary stuff that is supposed to be highbrow and that does not interest the average reader in the least.

I think I may say with reasonable accuracy that I would ten times rather have anything I wanted printed in the news columns; for I do not believe that more than ten per cent of the readers of the average newspaper read the editorials.

Now the fault is not with the readers. The fault is never with the readers. It is our business to give the readers what the readers will read. And the first thing to do is to stop being conventional in the editorial columns.

Stop writing about politics and economics, and write about subjects that human beings are interested in. . . .

Be human. Be interesting. And sometimes be amusing.

From the time of the first World War, when the unrestrained editorials of the fanatical pro-German Philip Francis ignited a blaze of hatred against his papers, Hearst insisted upon direct, personal supervision of all important national and international editorials. As soon as written, each editorial was telegraphed to Los Angeles, thence by direct wire to San Simeon or Wyntoon. It was placed in Hearst's hands as soon as taken from the teletype machines and sometimes stamped within a matter of minutes: "Following editorial is hereby released by Chief for publication in all morning papers, and afternoon papers where no mornings." At other times, editorials were rephrased or killed. Hearst himself wrote numberless editorials, the majority unsigned.

Despite the imperative speed of daily journalism, Hearst did not believe in helter-skelter editorial decisions. Once he advised editor Coblentz:—

I do not think it is necessary to commit ourselves immediately either for or against the appropriation veto.

The country is not eagerly demanding that we give it an immediate decision on this matter. Moreover, we do not decide anything, we merely advise.

It is important, however, that we give sound advice.

Furthermore, son, a good editorial is always more important than a hasty one.

Occasionally, Hearst would relieve his daily grind by indulging in a bit of pure whimsy, as when in 1942 he accidentally came across a request for an autograph from his son William's able secretary, Julia Ruman, who remarked in her memo that "your Pappy probably does not know me from Adam." The expression touched Hearst's sense of humor and he wrote Miss Ruman a gently kidding, friendly letter beginning, "I do know you and I DO know Adam." Adam, he recalled, was their mutual ancestor and he went on to roam through Biblical history, dwelling longest on Noah and his adventures. The letter has since been Julia Ruman's proudest possession.

Early in 1947 Hearst suffered several foreboding heart spasms, in one of which he lost consciousness. The same year his cherished friend and secretary, Joseph Willicombe, had been forced into retirement by ill health (he died in 1948). Now Willicombe came up to San Simeon from his home in Carmel Valley and added his authoritative voice to that of a consultation of physicians who diagnosed Hearst's condition as well-advanced auricular fibrillation, and advised immediate removal to a lower and milder climate.

Fortunately, a suitable dwelling was at hand in Beverly Hills, a large H-shaped mansion of cream-tinted stucco, in the prevailing Spanish style, with ample gardens, palm-ringed patios, guest house and the customary swimming pool, which Marion Davies had purchased some years before and lived in intermittently. A private elevator was installed and Hearst took possession of a suite of sunny and commodious rooms on the second floor.*

The details of running the establishment at Number 1007 Beverly Drive were handled by the housekeeper Ella ("Bill") Williams, an old friend of Miss Davies. Hearst's new secretary was E. O. ("Bill") Hunter, a former employee of the Los Angeles *Examiner,* who had been trained by Joe Willicombe and who was strikingly like him in temperament.

Soon Hearst was again conducting his affairs pretty much as usual, although at a necessarily reduced pace. He knew that he had suffered a mortal blow and that the end was only a matter of time; he faced the situation with courage and realism, and without a trace of morbidity. He placed himself unreservedly in the care of Dr. Myron Prinzmetal, a heart specialist chosen

---

* It was claimed in some irresponsible accounts published after his death that Hearst had moved in some of his prized paintings and other objects of art, including rugs and tapestries. The more interesting fact was that the main house was largely furnished from the stores of Barker Brothers and Sears, Roebuck and Co. The so-called "guest house," the completion of the furnishing of which occurred only shortly before Hearst's death, was wholly from Barker Brothers and Sears, Roebuck and Co. Other pieces of furniture in the main house were Miss Davies' own furniture and rugs, formerly used at the beach house. As a formality, Hearst bought the house from Miss Davies and later deeded it back to her, in lieu of a contemplated provision in his will, under an agreement giving him life tenure.

by his sons, and prepared to expend his remaining years as usefully as possible. Fortunately, there was no impairment of the intellectual powers which had already distinguished him far beyond the usual span.

Essentially Hearst was a fatalist and a believer in predestination.

"We like to think of ourselves as free agents," he once said, "but we are no more actually independent of our antecedents and our influences than a leaf which drops from a tree onto the surface of a flowing river. The character of the leaf is determined by the tree from which it drops. The course of the leaf is determined by the current of the river."

Those who knew the man best realized that Will Hearst could never settle into a life of complete inactivity. He had always reveled in change and variety. Tranquility and prolonged indolence he abhorred. Once he preached a little homily on the subject to a valued executive who wrote that he had retired to France, after a period of strain, to devote himself indefinitely to "quiet study and thought and the enjoyment of trees and flowers." Hearst approved such pursuits "as an occasional relaxation, yes; but as a constant and exclusive occupation, no," adding:—

> Who wants to hang like a sloth under the limb of a shady tree and blink all day at the beautiful green leaves, the fleecy clouds and the blue sky?
> . . . Beware of tranquility. It proclaims the toppling-over stage. It is the sleep which precedes dissolution. . . .
> There is no Utopia, and live people do not want Utopia. There is no Garden of Eden, and if there ever was one, I am sure that Adam and Eve were not driven out of it but left it and its boring idleness, its indolent contemplation of the "trees and flowers," for the keener enjoyment to be found in the active life of the world.

As Hearst passed the Biblical span, his family and circle of intimates took to marking his birthday in gala fashion. Sometimes there was a colorful costume party, with gay music and much hilarity; at other times a banquet with exciting favors and informal responses to toasts. Messages of felicitation poured in from every continent.

Such attentions pleased him and often evoked jocular or philosophic expressions. In the former mood, in 1941, he responded to a congratulatory message from the United Press:—

> Thank you but I am not having any more birthdays. Or if I do, I will have them in reverse, beginning at seventy-eight and going back to twenty-one. I appreciate your courteous congratulations, but please save them until I get back to twenty-one.

Congratulating a man on being seventy-eight is like felicitating him on being in an airplane accident. He may survive, but it is not exactly an enjoyment.

However, as my grandfather lived to ninety-four, I may have to endure a score or more accidents and receive pleasant salutations and give grateful acknowledgment to kind friends.

There was both pathos and grandeur about Hearst's last years.

The serious heart attack of 1947 left a residue of debilitating physical symptoms—a marked and continuing loss of weight, a palsy of the hands, a voice scarcely more audible than a whisper. These infirmities confined him for the most part to his rooms, broken only by an occasional motor drive or short walk in the gardens of the Beverly Hills house. His daily regimen was carefully supervised by Dr. Prinzmetal and nurses.

Yet the stricken man's mental acuity seemed little affected. Clear, concise, constructive directives still flowed to the desks of his principal lieutenants. Throughout his vast organization, no major move was made without the Chief's authorization. On his eighty-seventh birthday in 1950 the trade paper *Editor & Publisher,* always an admirer, proudly announced that "Mr. Hearst continues a vigilant and active publisher. He is still militant and alert after a career which developed lustily and mightily, and today is deeply encrusted in tradition and mystery."

A visitor one day was George E. Sokolsky, newspaper columnist and pioneer foe of Communism. They had not met since Sokolsky was a boy on New York's lower East Side and Hearst was a candidate for Mayor. Sokolsky recalled how Hearst had become the idol of the teeming neighborhood because of his efforts in behalf of newly arrived immigrants, and how he and such "visionary" associates as James G. Phelps Stokes, Robert Hunter, Rose Pastor Stokes and others had been denounced as radical Socialists. Hearst smiled in reminiscence and remarked:—

"Sokolsky, the reason you and I really understand the evils of Communism is that we were once familiar with the nature of Socialism."

"This is so true in the sense that he meant it," explained Sokolsky later. "For whereas Socialists whom he joined in the Independence League were seeking the betterment of mankind and the extension of liberty and opportunity, the so-called Marxists have perverted an ideal of human progress into the enslavement of man to the state."

On good days, the invalid was permitted to stroll in the open; and he and the old gardener exchanged horticultural lore as fellow experts. Flowers and growing things generally had always fascinated Hearst. He knew them both as a practical experimentalist and scientific student. Trees and flowers and plants he coupled with man's own growth and development as a part of Nature's master plan.

Although reared in the Episcopal Church, Hearst had never subscribed

293

to a formal religious creed. Yet with all his heart he believed in a living force, continuous and continuing. Once he wrote:—

> The acceptance of the doctrine of an immortal soul is not merely the result of religious teaching and blind faith; it is the factual and unavoidable recognition of an essential force or entity, dominating or different from the flesh, blood and bone which constitute the material elements of our body.
>
> It is the subconscious realization of a convincing truth revealed by the logic of our life and experience, our prevailing impulses and our habitual reactions.
>
> It is a spiritually acceptable explanation of the power that controls the substantial physical elements of our being, and which determines the action of the brain and mind, as well as the movements of the muscles.
>
> It is the illuminating interpretation of sense, sensibility, sensation, emotion, thought, intelligence, individuality, none of which can exist without some psychic reaction.

The same thought was expressed in the inspirational verse of the famous "Song of the River" which many think will outlive anything written by Hearst. This poem was first shown, timidly, to the author's friend Fremont Older and printed by the latter in the San Francisco *Call-Bulletin*. Some were surprised by Hearst's query:—

> So why prize life, or why fear death
> Or dread what is to be?

And by his bold admonition:—

> So don't ask why we live or die,
> Or whither or when we go,
> Or wonder about the mysteries
> Which only God may know.

With the passing of time the bond between Hearst and his family seemed to grow stronger. Even on his bad days he managed to summon strength for a chat by phone with his wife or one of their sons. It pleased him mightily to note the sons' growing grasp of executive responsibilities; also their deep feeling of camaraderie.

The remarkably clear old brain rallied itself magnificently in behalf of General Douglas MacArthur when, as Hearst and MacArthur viewed the situation, the latter was refused permission to "fight a victorious war" in

294

Korea. Hearst saw through the swirl of conflicting power politics and campaigned boldly and forcefully in behalf of MacArthur. The men had been friends and mutual admirers for two generations, often exchanging intimate views.

This was Hearst's last crusade. Like so many others, it was lost. Yet many Americans today hold with Hearst that MacArthur should have been permitted to fight an unfettered war in Korea.

With the coming of summer in 1951, Hearst's vitality waned visibly. It became evident to the trained and solicitous eyes of his doctors and nurses that the end was near.

During the second week-end in August members of the family were summoned. Transfusions were resorted to but were futile. Early on the morning of August 14, the patient lapsed into a coma and he died, painlessly and peacefully, at 9.50 a.m. Pacific Coast time. Hearst was in his eighty-ninth year.

In a matter of moments the electrifying news was flashing to the far corners of the earth.

Later that day William Randolph Hearst returned, finally, to the city of his birth, a city which he loved passionately and which knew and understood him. Everywhere in San Francisco flags were at half-mast and many faces registered shock, grief, even incredulity at the news conveyed in the great black headlines dominating the evening papers.

The heavy copper casket was placed in the Chapel of Grace in Grace Episcopal Cathedral on Nob Hill and for almost two days it lay in state while the public was permitted to file past and view California's most famous son for the last time. Great masses of roses, Hearst's favorite flower, covered the sides and the entire base of the casket. With all the lines of earthly care brushed away, there was little about the dark-clad, wasted frame to suggest the vital personality which had inhabited it in life.

Some recalled that Hearst had been born only a few squares from the great cathedral and that nearby was the first school he attended, as well as the office of the San Francisco *Examiner,* his first paper.

On the day of the funeral the cathedral was crowded with many hundreds standing and a great throng in California Street outside. Mrs. Hearst was accompanied by her five sons. The mourners included men and women of distinction in a dozen fields.

The honorary pallbearers were headed by California's Governor Earl Warren, who interrupted a vacation to be present, and Mayor Elmer E. Robinson, of San Francisco. Others included Herbert Hoover, B. M. Baruch, Roy Howard, Colonel Robert R. McCormick, Mrs. Ogden Reid, Arthur Hays Sulzberger, General Douglas MacArthur, John N. Garner.

The service, dignified and impressive, was from the Book of Common

Prayer, and lasted but half an hour. As prescribed by this form of liturgy, the name of the deceased was not mentioned; and there was neither eulogy nor sermon. The Right Reverend Karl Morgan Block, Episcopal Bishop of California, selected for his lesson the fifteenth chapter of the First Epistle of St. Paul to the Corinthians which dwells upon the resurrection of the dead and contains the immortal lines: "O death, where is thy sting? O grave, where is thy victory?" The organist played Bach and César Franck. Malotte's setting of the Lord's Prayer was sung by the men's chorus, and Dvořák's arrangement of the Twenty-third Psalm was sung by the full chorus.

When the brief ceremony was over, a cortege of twenty-two limousines, under motorcycle escort, set out upon the ten-mile journey to Cypress Lawn Cemetery in Colma. It halted at the Hearst mausoleum, of Grecian design, lying atop a grassy knoll amid a copse of trees—Australian silk oaks and Japanese plums—planted at Hearst's direction when the tomb was built in 1908. Here the committal ceremony was also brief, Bishop Block reading the church's service, then Hearst's own poem, "Song of the River."

Hearst's will reflected his deep concern and determination to insure the perpetuation of the brand of fearless, independent journalism with which his name had been identified for two-thirds of a century. A significant clause read:—

"I request my executors and trustees . . . not to part with the ownership or control of any newspaper, magazine, feature service, news service, photographic service or periodical, either directly or by sale, or by exchange of the capital stock . . . unless it shall, in their opinion, be necessary or prudent to do so."

The will set up three trusts, the first for the decedent's wife, comprising $6,000,000 worth of the parent Hearst Corporation preferred stock, with an additional outright bequest of $1,500,000 in cash to cover taxes which would be due on the stock.

The beneficiaries of the second trust were the Hearst sons. It contained enough Hearst Corporation preferred stock to insure each son an annual income of $30,000 to supplement his already comfortable income as a Hearst executive. Into this trust, also, went a hundred shares of Hearst Corporation voting common stock, a controlling interest.

The third trust, residuary, was for the benefit of the customary "charitable, scientific, educational and public purposes." The will directed that a memorial be built to the testator's "beloved mother," containing some of his remaining choice art treasures, "for the public enjoyment." Specifically named beneficiaries of this trust were the Los Angeles Museum, which had already received more than $3,000,000 in art objects from the Hearst collection; the University of California, to which the testator had made many gifts during his lifetime; and the California Foundation, a personal philanthropic organization set up some years before. This Foundation would receive the entire residuary estate, including the personal property at San Simeon, Wyntoon and New York, but not St. Donat's Castle.

Marion Davies was not named as a direct beneficiary in the will.

However, in 1930, Hearst had executed a trust fund under which she has a lifetime income from 30,000 shares of Hearst Corporation preferred stock, the principal to revert to his sons upon her death. On November 5, 1950, Hearst had signed, with Miss Davies, a voting trust agreement pooling his own 170,000 shares of preferred with her 30,000; and giving her sole voting power in the Hearst Corporation. If held valid, this document would have given her complete individual suzerainty over the entire Hearst publishing empire. It naturally stirred up a hornet's nest when presented to the executors.

When news of this astonishing apparent grant of power became public, extreme anti-Hearst elements in the daily and weekly press, whose venom extended beyond the grave, played up the story to the hilt in keen anticipation of a bitter and possibly scandalous legal battle. Fortunately cool heads prevailed on both sides and, after a few days of conferences, a joint statement was issued reading in part:—

> Miss Davies has relinquished all rights she may have to act as voting trustee for the stock of the Hearst Corporation for the reason, among others, that there is question as to when her right to act as voting trustee thereunder would commence. This question would have to be clarified by long court proceedings which all parties deemed unnecessary and undesirable.
>
> Miss Davies has every faith in the intentions and abilities of Mr. Hearst's sons and the other directors and executives of the Hearst enterprises to insure the continuity of Mr. Hearst's editorial policies, the furtherance of which would have been Miss Davies' only purpose in serving as a trustee.

Two months later, on October 31, 1951, at Las Vegas, Nevada, Marion Davies married Horace G. Brown, Jr., a skipper in the merchant marine. His second wife, Grace, had formerly been the wife of Lawrence Tibbett, the popular singer; and he had two sons by a still earlier marriage.

The passing of William Randolph Hearst demonstrated what a tremendous figure he had come to be in the world.

There was of course an avalanche of comment and appraisal in the press of the world and from individuals of prominence. Strange to say, words of charity, respect and appreciation far outnumbered critical strictures, although there were plenty of both, often in the same milieu. For instance, Lord Beaverbrook's *Daily Express* flatly asserted that Hearst's alleged anti-British bias had always been highly exaggerated and characterized him as "one of the great American figures of the age"; while the pontifical *Manchester Guardian* was equally positive that no man had ever done "so much to debase the standards of journalism."

The New York *Herald Tribune* concluded a thoughtful editorial with "one cannot assess the final influence of that long and spectacular career. One can only say that he was a man of extraordinary talents, energies and insights, and that it will be long before his mark fades from our times."

The New York *Times* wrote editorially: ". . . No history of American journalism can ever be written without reckoning with him, and however critically he is appraised it will have to be said of him that he brought the printed word to many who had previously come close to ignoring it."

Others, in profusion, chipped away at the titan, as in the case of noted men from time immemorial. Each comment was inevitably tinctured by the particular individual's point of view.

In May, 1955, the estate having been appraised and put in legal order, Superior Court in Los Angeles granted a petition placing full voting control of the Hearst Corporation, encompassing all of the enterprises of the far flung empire, in the hands of 13 trustees—the five sons and these employees: Richard E. Berlin, R. A. Carrington, Jr., William A. Curley, Ward Greene, Martin F. Huberth, Harold G. Kern, Gerald O. Markuson, Charles Mayer. Messrs. Greene, Markuson and Mayer were successors to three others designated in the will who had died: Walter Howey, William M. Baskerville, Henry S. MacKay, Jr.

Two months earlier, Mr. Kern, the publisher of the Boston Hearst newspapers, the *Record, American* and *Sunday Advertiser,* had succeeded J. D. Gortatowsky as general manager of all the Hearst newspapers. Mr. Gortatowsky, as stated in a previous chapter, remained as chairman of the board of Hearst Corporation and president of King Features Syndicate and International News Service. Mr. Kern came to the post with 30 years of experience in the Hearst organization, 15 of them with the Boston Hearst papers. Another who had come up through the ranks, Richard E. Deems, was elevated to the post of executive vice president in charge of all Hearst magazines. He started as an advertising salesman on *Harper's Bazaar.*

"Young Bill," the Chief's second son, is firmly in command of the editorial policies of the newspapers. In March, 1955, when directors of Hearst Corporation announced that the post of editor-in-chief, vacant since the Chief's death, would be filled by W. R., Jr., *Newsweek* commented, "To Hearst staffers this was recognition of what has long been apparent: The emergence of Bill Hearst, who looks strikingly like his father, as the organization's most powerful editorial figure."

Considered in the light of what happened in the following four years, the statement of Richard E. Berlin on Hearst's death was highly significant.

298

"He took great pride," Mr. Berlin commented then, "in training his top executives in a painstaking manner so that he could rely on them to carry on after his death with uninterrupted continuity."

In the spring of 1955, the trade publication *Advertising Age* assigned a team of reporters to get the answer to a question in the minds of men throughout the publishing industry since August, 1951: "What would happen to the immense Hearst communications empire, and who would administer it?" In its April 4, 1955, issue *Advertising Age* featured a three page report of its investigators' findings. The "revitalized Hearst organization," it summarized in its headlines, was "making money, adding properties." It quoted W. R. Hearst, Jr. as having said in 1952: "We don't sell newspapers, we buy them." The report went on to say: "And what has been going on in Hearst [enterprises] for the last three and a half years bears out the statement. For Hearst is not only a giant enterprise, it is also a wealthy and profitable one. Almost any time now, having paid the taxes and appraised the sprawling assets of the lord of San Simeon, the Hearst estate should be released from probate. The intervening years have been years of appraisal and discovery and pruning for the men who were trained by the Chief to take over for him." The report said the Hearst Corporation has assets "which can conservatively be pegged at more than $235,000,000 . . . Net profits after taxes, during the last ten years have averaged more than $11,000,000 annually. It was learned authoritatively that the Hearst Corporation has no funded debt and is extremely well insulated with cash and U.S. Government securities." The magazine concluded:

"The present crop of Hearst executives is, for the most part, Hearst-trained and Hearst-loyal. They've got the knowledge of the corporation, with its tremendous assets and properties, and they intend to make the big wheels roll."

In the last analysis, the Chief built and chose well.

Appendix

Practically from their start, the Hearst newspapers were identified in the public mind with distinctive comic art, the Hearst magazines with distinguished illustration. When *Puck* printed this significant drawing in 1904, a dozen or more Hearst newspaper cartoon characters were famous and immediately recognizable with a smile throughout the U.S.

Of the lasting influences of Hearst upon journalism, the most conspicuous is the predominance of comic strips amongst newspaper features. He is responsible for cartoons being the most popular form of entertainment and

300

the most potent newspaper circulation builder of them all. Any chosen day, each of a number of different serial strips or panels has an aggregate readership larger than that of any movie, or any radio or TV broadcast.

Practically all of the important names in the history of this most American of the graphic arts were employed by and owed their greatest successes to Hearst. His ideas permeate comic strips completely. Because he was a man of cosmopolitan tastes, with a profound sense of the tastes of others, there is high comedy as well as lowly slapstick—something for everybody— among the classic comic strips.

The Journal of Educational Sociology noted some years back, "The [newspaper] comics . . . have become an integral part of the progressive democratization of the country." Over 98% of daily newspapers feature comic strips, and over 80% of newspaper readers follow one or more comics day after day. Only front page headlines are read more regularly.

A group of the most famous of the strips with which Hearst newspapers built up this art, this social force, appears in the following pages.

Jimmy Swinnerton's "Little Bears" in the San Francisco *Examiner,* with which Hearst started his career as a publisher, were the first comic characters to appear regularly in a newspaper. They preceded the famous Teddy Bear stuffed toy. They were inspired by California's being the Bear State. When Hearst transferred Swinnerton to New York, Swinnerton switched to little tigers (see page 304), inspired by the Tammany tiger.

Outcault's first Sunday colored comic, in New York *World,* in November, 1894, featured a clown, a dog and a snake, and was entitled, "The Origin of a New Species." The artist and Sunday Editor Morrill Goddard fooled around with other ideas before the "Yellow Kid" (↓) emerged. To "get" this gag, it is necessary to remember Tammany Hall in 1897.

HOW THE GOAT GOT "KILT ENTIRELY!"

302

The Katzenjammer Kids started as close copies of *Max und Moritz,* a pantomime series by Wilhelm Busch that Hearst remembered from his childhood. As drawn by Rudolph Dirks, F. B. Opper and others according to Hearst's ideas, they soon took on a different character. This [↓] is the Katzenjammer family before Der Captain showed up as boarder and somehow became the man of the house.

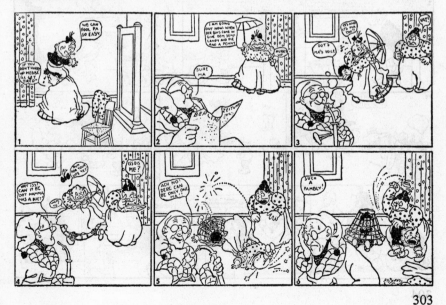

Jimmy Swinnerton transformed his "Little Tigers" pantomime panels (↑) into *Mr. Jack,* a strip with "balloons," and made another creation, *Mr. Batch,* a popular synonym for wedding-shy male, before he introduced his *Little Jimmy* (↓), a long time favorite, in 1905. He won note later as a painter and water colorist of desert scenes.

JIMMY—HE MINDS THE BABY

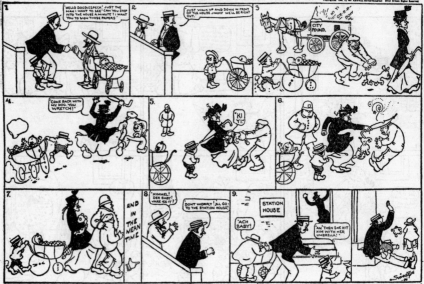

304

1. BOYS: "Now that we have Gran'pa pasted on the fence, we will go and find our dear grandparent."

2. GRANDPA: "While the boys are looking for me I will get busy with my little saw."

3. GRANDPA: "Here goes for the boys and a jolly good laugh."

4. BOYS: "Goodness! Look! Here comes our picture of Gran'pa."

GRANDPA: "Hello, boys. Here I am. Please unfasten me."

6. GRANDPA: "Dear me, what are you young mischiefs so frightened about? Can't you see it is only a little picture joke?"

Two generations of Americans acquired fond memories of "Foxy Grandpa," by Carl "Bunny" Schultze, who reversed the Katzenjammer Kid humor formula and let the grownup outwit the youthful pranksters. The strip was started in 1900.

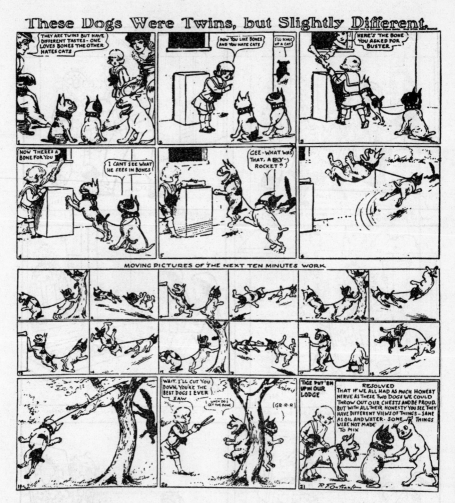

Bennett's New York *Herald,* which tried to ignore colored comics at first, finally tried to regain some of the Sunday circulation it had lost to its "yellow journalistic" rivals, the *Journal* and *World,* with a comic section. The *Herald* staged one coup by taking Outcault away from Hearst. Outcault started to draw another Hogan's Alley kid character, *Lil Mose,* for the *Herald.* The paper, mindful of its carriage trade, had him switch to a Fifth Avenue locale and poor little rich boy theme. The result was *Buster Brown,* who could have come from the pages of Frances Hodgson Burnett's *Little Lord Fauntleroy.* Hearst hired back Outcault and got *Buster Brown.* But Fred Opper remained the most popular comic section contributor and the one who influenced others the most.

306

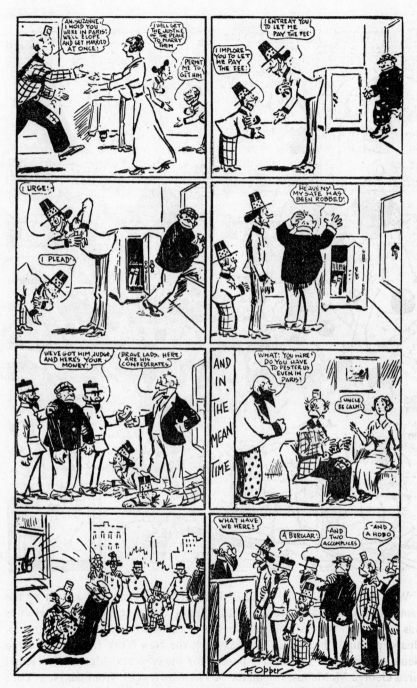

Opper's immortal *Alphonse and Gaston* with *Happy Hooligan*.

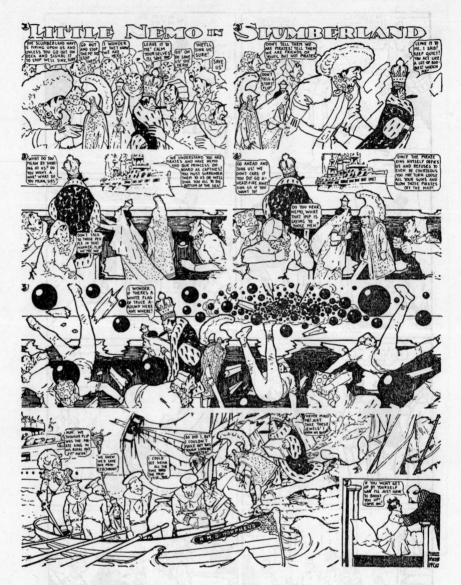

Winsor McCay's *In the Land of Wonderful Dreams,* best known by the name of its principal character, Little Nemo, was a new departure. Humor was secondary to an imaginative story and outstanding draftsmanship. Hearst promptly hired McCay away from the New York *Herald* and Little Nemo appeared in the Hearst papers for many years. Meanwhile Hearst hired George McManus, originator of *The Newlyweds,* from the New York *World* and started him drawing *Bringing Up Father.* The latter became a long-lived classic.

308

McManus' *Newlyweds* (↑) and an early *Bringing Up Father* (↓)

Comics were generally a Sunday feature until 1904, when Hearst's Chicago *American* started (↑) *A. Piker Clerk* by Clare Briggs. It gave readers a race tip a day and was followed by similar strips in other papers. One, which began in San Francisco *Chronicle* in 1907, became *Mutt and Jeff* (↓).

T. A. "Tad" Dorgan, who started as a sports writer and cartoonist on Hearst's San Francisco *Examiner,* evolved into a social satirist as penetrative as Daumier. While he attained his greatest fame with his panel, *Indoor Sports,* of which these are examples, he is memorable also for a series called *Judge Rumhauser* that was inspired by a headline divorce case.

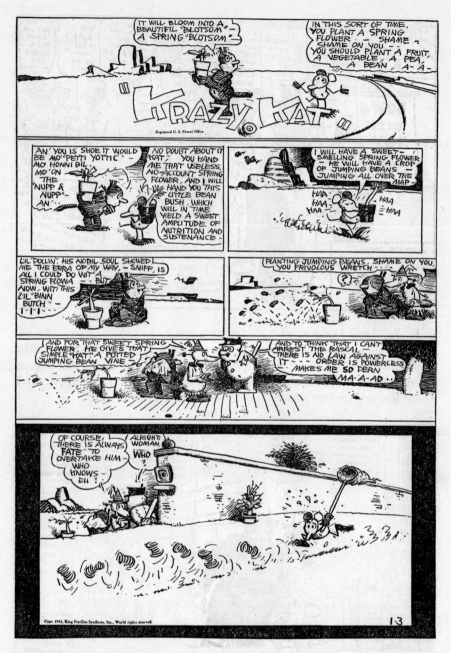

George Herriman's *Krazy Kat* was the comic strip most often hailed by contemporaries as a work of art. Ignatz Mouse, Krazy Kat's 'lil angel,' probably inspired Walt Disney's Mickey Mouse. Krazy Kat was the theme of a ballet and a symphony.

312

By far the most widely published and read newspaper feature in history is Murat "Chic" Young's *Blondie,* which started in the Hearst newspapers in 1930. This is one of the early strips, before the elopement of Dagwood Bumstead, son of a railroad tycoon, with Blondie Boopadoop, a stenog in his father's office. Soon after the marriage, for which Dagwood was disowned by his folks, his parents and Blondie's mother disappeared from the strip. Blondie and Dagwood settled down to being the gently humorous reflections of millions of parents in the United States—and humans of universal appeal. The fact of *Blondie's* being published regularly in a long list of countries, in a dozen languages, attests the extent to which the Hearst cartoon creations have gone around the world. Having pondered the fact that a few pictures painted upon cave walls remain our best means of visualizing life a hundred thousand years ago, Russel Crouse recently considered what pictures would be best to leave behind as a record of our time. He rejected photographs and paintings, in favor of cartoons, because "they more neatly reflect what goes on among the people who reflect our century than any other form of picture."

Barney Google and Snuffy Smith, which started in 1919, had the original popular hillbilly cartoon characters and made an imaginary race horse, "Spark Plug," more famous than Man O'War. The strip is the source of many vernacular phrases now in common use—"time's a wastin'," "Yard bird," "bodacious," "corn squeezins," "feather merchants." Tad's *Indoor Sports* coined a larger number of popular phrases: "hot dog," "baloney," "tank-town," "bunk," "23 skidoo," "crepe-hanger." The song "Yes, We Have No Bananas" was derived from one of Tad's catch lines.

314

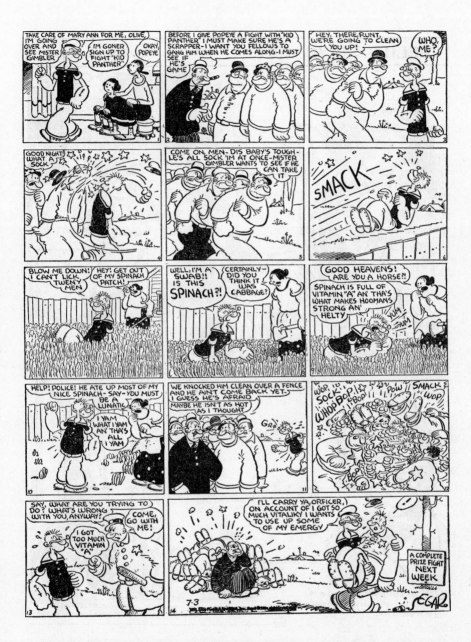

The first monument to a comic strip character was raised in Texas to Popeye. It was an act of gratitude for the prosperity that E. C. Segar's creation gave to the spinach growing and packing industry through such strips as this one. The word "jeep" was taken by the Army for its famous vehicle from a character in the Popeye strip.

315

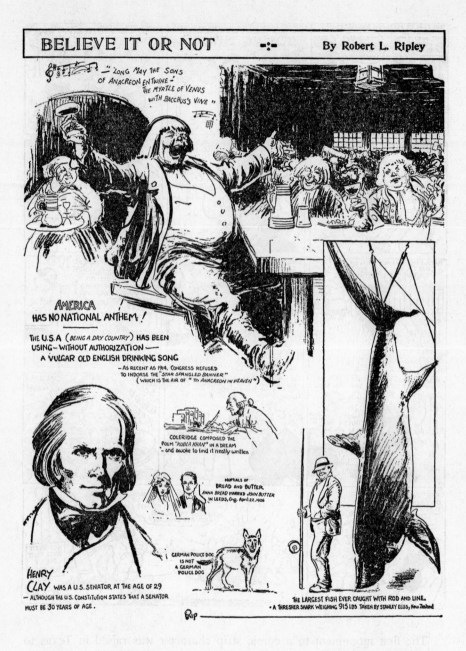

BELIEVE IT OR NOT -:- By Robert L. Ripley

"LONG MAY THE SONS OF ANACREON ENTWINE - THE MYRTLE OF VENUS WITH BACCHUS'S VINE"

AMERICA HAS NO NATIONAL ANTHEM !

THE U.S.A (BEING A DRY COUNTRY) HAS BEEN USING — WITHOUT AUTHORIZATION — A VULGAR OLD ENGLISH DRINKING SONG
— AS RECENT AS 1914, CONGRESS REFUSED TO INDORSE THE "STAR SPANGLED BANNER" (WHICH IS THE AIR OF "To ANACREON IN HEAVEN")

COLERIDGE COMPOSED THE POEM "KUBLA KHAN" IN A DREAM — and awoke to find it neatly written

NUPTIALS OF BREAD AND BUTTER. ANNA BREAD MARRIED JOHN BUTTER IN LEEDS, Eng. April 22, 1926

GERMAN POLICE DOG IS NOT A GERMAN POLICE DOG

HENRY CLAY WAS A U.S. SENATOR AT THE AGE OF 29 — ALTHOUGH THE U.S. CONSTITUTION STATES THAT A SENATOR MUST BE 30 YEARS OF AGE.

THE LARGEST FISH EVER CAUGHT WITH ROD AND LINE. — A THRESHER SHARK WEIGHING 915 LBS TAKEN BY STANLEY ELLIS, New Zealand

Rip

Hearst spotted the Ripley "Believe It or Not" drawings in a book and ordered Ripley being placed under a feature contract. The Ripley panels subsequently acquired an enormous readership. This Ripley cartoon was responsible for the *Star-Spangled Banner* being voted the national anthem.

316

Index

All mentions herein of 'Album' refer to the
Hearst Family Album insert between pages 166 and 167

323